Fodor's 3rd Edition

Belize & Guatemala

The complete guide, thoroughly up-to-date

Packed with details that will make your trip

The must-see sights, off and on the beaten path

What to see, what to skip

Mix-and-match vacation itineraries

City strolls, countryside adventures

Smart lodging and dining options

Essential local do's and taboos

Transportation tips, distances and directions

Key contacts, savvy travel tips

When to go, what to pack

Clear, accurate, easy-to-use maps

Fodor's Travel Publications • New York, Toronto, London, Sydney, Auckland
www.fodors.com

Fodor's Belize & Guatemala

EDITOR: Melisse Gelula

Editorial Contributors: Gary Chandler, Elbert Greer, Joanna Kosowsky, Lan Sluder

Editorial Production: Tom Holton

Maps: David Lindroth, *cartographer*; Rebecca Baer, Robert Blake, *map editors*

Design: Fabrizio La Rocca, *creative director*; Guido Caroti, *art director*; Jolie Novak, *photo editor*

Cover Design: Pentagram

Production/Manufacturing: Angela L. McLean

Cover Photo: Bo Zaunders/The Stock Market *(Coffee Canoe, Guatemala)*

Copyright

Third Edition

ISBN 0–679–00565–X

ISSN 1522–6123

Important Tip

Although all prices, opening times, and other details in this book are based on information supplied to us at press time, changes occur all the time in the travel world, and Fodor's cannot accept responsibility for facts that become outdated or for inadvertent errors or omissions. So **always confirm information when it matters,** especially if you're making a detour to visit a specific place.

Special Sales

Fodor's Travel Publications are available at special discounts for bulk purchases for sales promotions or premiums. Special editions, including personalized covers, excerpts of existing guides, and corporate imprints, can be created in large quantities for special needs. For more information, contact your local bookseller or write to Special Markets, Fodor's Travel Publications, 280 Park Avenue, New York, NY 10017. Inquiries from Canada should be directed to your local Canadian bookseller or sent to Random House of Canada, Ltd., Marketing Department, 2775 Matheson Boulevard East, Mississauga, Ontario L4W 4P7. Inquiries from the United Kingdom should be sent to Fodor's Travel Publications, 20 Vauxhall Bridge Road, London SW1V 2SA, England.

PRINTED IN THE UNITED STATES OF AMERICA

10 9 8 7 6 5 4 3 2 1

CONTENTS

Maps

ON THE ROAD WITH FODOR'S

VERY TRIP is a significant trip. Acutely aware of that fact, we've pulled out all stops in preparing *Fodor's Belize & Guatemala, 3rd ed.* To guide you in putting together your Belize and Guatemala experience, we've created multiday itineraries and neighborhood walks. And to direct you to the places that are truly worth your time and money, we've rallied the team of endearingly picky know-it-alls we're pleased to call our writers. Having seen all corners of Belize and Guatemala, they're real experts. If you knew them, you'd poll them for tips yourself.

About Our Writers

Guatemala contributor **Gary Chandler** has travelled extensively throughout Mexico, Central America, and the Caribbean. He has written for GORP.com, an online outdoor adventure magazine, on getting around Cambodia, and more recently for *Fodor's upClose Central America* on El Salvador. When not living out of a suitcase, he calls San Francisco home.

A former Peace Corps volunteer in the Central African Republic, **Joanna Kosowsky** updated the Guatemala chapter from her rustic abode on the north shore of Lago Izabal in eastern Guatemala, while volunteering for an environmental NGO.

Belize First magazine editor and publisher **Lan Sluder** has been banging around Belize for more than a decade. In addition to writing *The Belize Book of Lists 2000* and *Live Well in Belize*, he has written about Belize for *Caribbean Travel & Life*, the *Bangkok Post*, and Canada's *Globe & Mail*, among other publications.

We'd also like to thank our hosts and guides in Belize and Guatemala for their generosity and navigation. A special thanks to Yvette Batalla, Olivier Ordoñez with IN-GUAT, and Golda Tillet of the Belize Tourism Board for going the extra mile or two.

Don't Forget to Write

Keeping a travel guide fresh and up-to-date is a big job. So we love your feedback—positive and negative—and follow up on all suggestions. Contact the Belize and Guatemala editor at editors@fodors.com or c/o Fodor's, 280 Park Avenue, New York, New York 10017. And have a wonderful trip!

Karen Cure
Editorial Director

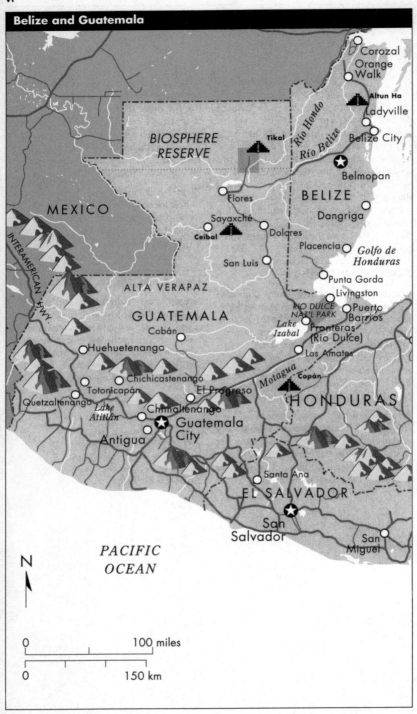

Belize and Guatemala

Corozal

Orange
Walk

Altun Ha

Ladyville

Belize City

BELIZE

Belmopan

Dangriga

Río Hondo

Tikal

Río Belize

Flores

Sayaxché

Ceibal

Dolores

San Luis

Placencia

*Golfo de
Honduras*

Punta Gorda

Livingston

*RIO DULCE
NAT'L PARK*

Puerto
Barrios

Fronteras
(Rio Dulce)

Los Amates

*Lake
Izabal*

BIOSPHERE
RESERVE

MEXICO

ALTA VERAPAZ

GUATEMALA

Cobán

Huehuetenango

Chichicastenango

El Progreso

Motagua

Copán

HONDURAS

Totonicapán

Quetzaltenango

*Lake
Atitlán*

Chimaltenango

Guatemala
City

Antigua

INTERAMERICAN HWY.

Santa Ana

EL SALVADOR

San
Salvador

San
Miguel

N

*PACIFIC
OCEAN*

0   100 miles

0   150 km

SMART TRAVEL TIPS A TO Z

Basic Information and Savvy Tips on Traveling in Belize and Guatemala

☞ For country specifics, *see* Belize A to Z *in* Chapter 2 *and* Guatemala A to Z *in* Chapter 3.

AIR TRAVEL

BOOKING

When you book **look for nonstop flights** and **remember that "direct" flights stop at least once.** Try to avoid connecting flights, which require a change of plane.

Ask your airline for an electronic ticket. Since it eliminates all paperwork, there's no ticket to pick up or misplace; you simply go directly to the gate and give the agent your confirmation number. There's no worry about waiting in line at the airport (unless you fly out of New York's JFK, where all customers must check in at the ticket counter) while precious minutes tick by.

CARRIERS

American Airlines, Continental, and TACA fly to Belize from the United States. The major departure gateways are Houston, with daily nonstop service to Belize City on TACA and Continental, which has two daily nonstops; Dallas, with daily nonstop service to Belize City on American; and Miami, with daily nonstop service on American and less frequent nonstop service on TACA. Some TACA flights to Belize City require a change of plane in San Pedro Sula, Honduras. TACA also flies to Belize City from San Francisco and Los Angeles with a stopover in San Salvador, El Salvador. Mexicana also has flights via Cancún.

Guatemala is served by American Airlines via Miami or Dallas, Continental via Houston, Iberia via Miami, Mexicana via Mexico City, TACA via Miami or Dallas, and United via Los Angeles. From New York, the only nonstop flights are on TACA. From London, Iberia flies direct to Guatemala City via Madrid.

Whereas Guatemala uses regular 727 airplanes for domestic travel between the capital and Flores, Puerto Barrios, Río Dulce, Huehuetenango, and Xela, domestic planes in Belize are twin-engine island-hoppers. The main carriers are Tropic Air and Maya Island Air, both of which fly to San Pedro on Ambergris Caye and Caye Caulker as well as Dangriga, Placencia, Punta Gorda, and Flores, Guatemala. Domestic flights from and to the municipal airport are between $45 to $90 round-trip, except for those flights arranged on Javier Flying Service, which will take you pretty much anywhere for $170 per hour and has regular flights to Chan Chich Lodge.

➤ MAJOR AIRLINES: **Aeroméxico** (☎ 800/237–6639). **American Airlines** (☎ 800/433–7300). **Continental** (☎ 800/525–0280). **Iberia** (☎ 800/772–4642). **Mexicana** (☎ 800/531–7921). **TACA** (☎ 800/535–8780 or 502/261–2144 in Guatemala).

➤ BELIZEAN CARRIERS: **Aerocaribe** (☎ 501/27–5213). **Javier Flying Service** (☎ 501/23–5360). **Maya Island Air** (☎ 501/24–4032, FAX 501/23–0585 or 501/23–0031). **Tropic Air** (☎ 501/24–5671; 713/521–9674 and 800/422–3435 in the United States).

➤ GUATEMALAN CARRIERS: **Aeroquetzal** (☎ 502/334–7689). **Aerovias** (☎ 502/332–7470). **Inter Airline** (☎ 502/360–1363). **Tikal Jets** (☎ 502/334–5631).

CHECK-IN & BOARDING

For international flights, except for those smaller flights between Belize and Guatemala, you should be at the airport at least two hours before your scheduled departure time; for domestic flights, about half an hour. Assuming that not everyone with a ticket will show up, airlines routinely overbook planes. The first to get bumped are passengers who checked in late and those flying on discounted tickets, so **get to the gate and check in as**

early as possible, especially during peak periods.

Always **bring a government-issued photo I.D. to the airport.** You may be asked to show it before you are allowed to check in.

CUTTING COSTS

The least expensive airfares to Belize and Guatemala must usually be purchased in advance and are nonrefundable. Airfares to Belize are often twice or more the cost of a ticket to Cancún or Cozumel Mexico, so, if you have the time, **it pays to fly into the Yucatán and take a bus to Belize.** From the Yucatán, a first-class or deluxe bus costs $15 or less, and takes a trip of five to six hours, to Chetumal, Mexico, a border town where you can transfer to a Belize bus. (If you fly into Cozumel you'll first have to take a ferry to Playa del Carmen.)

You'll save up to 50% on flights within Belize by flying to and from the Muncipal Airport near downtown Belize City, rather than to or from the International Airport north of the city in Ladyville. For example, a flight from Muncipal to San Pedro is $24 one-way, and about twice that from International.

It's best to **check the fares of several airlines or visit an Internet reservation service,** and when you are quoted a good price, book it on the spot—the same fare may not be available the next day. Always **check different routings** and look into using different airports. Travel agents, especially low-fare specialists (☞ Discounts & Deals, *below*), are helpful.

Consolidators are another good source. They buy tickets for scheduled international flights at reduced rates from the airlines, then sell them at prices that beat the best fare available directly from the airlines, usually without restrictions. Sometimes you can even get your money back if you need to return the ticket. Carefully read the fine print detailing penalties for changes and cancellations, and **confirm your consolidator reservation with the airline.**

➤ CONSOLIDATORS: **Cheap Tickets** (☎ 800/377–1000). **Discount Airline Ticket Service** (☎ 800/576–1600).

Tropical Travel (☎ 800/365–6232). **Unitravel** (☎ 800/325–2222). **Up & Away Travel** (☎ 212/889–2345). **World Travel Network** (☎ 800/409–6753).

ENJOYING THE FLIGHT

For more legroom, **request an emergency-aisle seat.** Don't sit in the row in front of the emergency aisle or in front of a bulkhead, where seats may not recline. If you have dietary concerns, **ask for special meals when booking,** and confirm your request 48 hours before your trip. These can be vegetarian, low-cholesterol, or kosher, for example. On long flights, try to maintain a normal routine to help fight jet lag. At night, **get some sleep.** By day, **eat light meals, drink water** (not alcohol), and **move around the cabin** to stretch your legs.

FLYING TIMES

To Belize City, it's roughly 2 hours from Miami and 2½ hours from Dallas and Houston.

To Guatemala City from Dallas or Houston the flying time is 2 hours; from Miami, 2½ hours; from Los Angeles, 7 hours; from New York or Chicago, 5½ hours; from Toronto via Miami or Mexico City, about 7 hours.

HOW TO COMPLAIN

If your baggage goes astray or your flight goes awry, complain right away. Most carriers require that you **file a claim immediately.**

➤ AIRLINE COMPLAINTS: U.S. Department of Transportation **Aviation Consumer Protection Division** (✉ C-75, Room 4107, Washington, DC 20590, ☎ 202/366–2220, airconsumer@ost.dot.gov, www.dot.gov/airconsumer). **Federal Aviation Administration Consumer Hotline** (☎ 800/322–7873).

AIRPORTS

International flights to Belize arrive at the Philip Goldson International Airport in Ladyville, just 19 km (12 mi) north of Belize City, probably the only airport in the world with a mahogany roof. Small domestic airports (which comprise landing strips with a one-room check-in building nearby) in Belize are in Belize

City, Dangriga, Placencia, Punta Gorda, and San Pedro.

The international airports in Guatemala are La Aurora in Guatemala City and Flores/Santa Elena Airport in El Petén near Tikal, which has service to Belize, Mexico, and Guatemala City.

➤ AIRPORT INFORMATION: **La Aurora International Airport** (✉ Guatemala City, Guatemala, ☎ 502/332–6084 or 502/332–6085). **Belize Municipal Airstrip** (✉ Belize City, ☎ no phone). **Flores/Santa Elena International Airport** (✉ Flores/Santa Elena, El Petén, Guatemala, ☎ 502/950–1289). **Philip Goldson International Airport** (✉ Ladyville, Belize, ☎ 501/25–2014).

DUTY-FREE SHOPPING

The international airports have several duty-free shops selling liquor, cigars, perfume, and other items.

BIKE TRAVEL

In Belize, the lightly traveled rural byways are good for biking, although the rough roads mean you should be prepared for a lot of flats. The Mountain Pine Ridge, with few cars and many miles of old logging roads, is an ideal spot for mountain biking. Bicycle racing has become an important sport in Belize, and you often see teams training.

Mountain biking is growing in popularity in Guatemala, particularly in highland towns like Antigua and Xela. Here the rolling hills, beautiful scenery, and decent (but not too crowded) roadways make for excellent two-wheel excursions. Road biking is less advisable and common, primarily because Guatemalan highways are narrow and largely insufficient for the growing number of cars and trucks on the road.

BIKE RENTALS

In Belize, you can rent mountain bikes in Cayo and road bikes in the Ambergris Caye and Placencia resort areas. In Guatemala, bike-rental shops are in all the good biking towns: Antigua, Panajachel, and Xela. Plenty of ecolodges and hotels throughout the country also rent bikes or lend them to guests free of

charge: mind you, these are not always in top shape.

BIKES IN FLIGHT

Most airlines accommodate bikes as luggage, provided they are dismantled and boxed. For bike boxes, often free at bike shops, you'll pay about $5 from airlines (at least $100 for bike bags). International travelers can sometimes substitute a bike for a piece of checked luggage at no charge; otherwise, the cost is about $100. Domestic and Canadian airlines charge $25–$50.

BOAT & FERRY TRAVEL

Since Belize has about 325 km (200 mi) of mainland coast and nearly 200 islands in the Caribbean, water taxis and small ferries are a primary form of transportation here. There is scheduled ferry service three or four times a day from Belize City to Ambergris Caye, Caye Caulker, and Caye Chapel, and also between those cayes. One-way fare from Belize City to Ambergris Caye is $12.50, and the trip takes 1¼ hours. To reach the more remote cayes, you're basically left to your own devices, unless you're staying at a hotel where such transfers are arranged for you. The resorts on the atolls run their own flights or boats, but these are not available to the general public.

Caye Caulker Water Taxis leave the Marine Terminal in Belize City for Placencia at 1 PM on Friday and Sunday, returning from Placencia at 7 AM on Saturday and Monday. The one-way fare is $25 and the trip takes about 2 hours. Ferries based in Belize City serve Dangriga, Placencia, and Puerto Cortes, Honduras ($50 one-way to Honduras). The Gulf Cruza ferry leaves the Southern Foreshore (just south of the swing bridge) at 6 AM Friday and stops at Placencia at 8:30 AM and Big Creek at 10 AM ($25 one-way) en route to Puerto Cortez, Honduras, where it arrives at 2 PM ($60).

For boat travel between Belize and Guatemala, scheduled water taxi service is available daily from Punta Gorda, Belize, to Puerto Barrios, Guatemala ($10 one-way), although there are some safety concerns on this route (☞ Safety, *below*). A boat leaves Puerto Barrios, Guatemala, for Punta Gorda, Belize, on Tuesday and Friday at 7 AM and takes 2½ hours. Smaller *lanchas* (motor boats, often with a retractable tarp) depart around 8–9 AM and 1–2 PM; the trip takes 50 minutes.For trips to Honduras, lanchas shuttle between Livingston, Guatemala, and Omoa, Honduras, every Tuesday and Friday. The boat leaves Livingston at 7:30 AM and leaves Omoa at noon. The trip takes 2–3 hours and costs $30.

Note that life jackets are typically not provided on boats and the seas can be rough. Postpone your trip if the weather looks bad, and don't be shy about waiting for another boat if the one offered looks unseaworthy or crowded.

➤ BOAT & FERRY INFORMATION: **Belize Marine Terminal** (N. Front St., at the swing bridge, Belize City, ☎ 501/23–1969). **Caye Caulker Water Taxis** (☎ 501/23–2969). **Gulf Cruza Ferries** (☎ 501/22–4506).

BUS TRAVEL

Belize has frequent and inexpensive bus service on the Northern and Western highways, and, also reasonable service to southern Belize via the Hummingbird, Manatee, and Southern highways. Elsewhere, bus service is spotty. There is no municipal bus service in Belize City, although most of Belize's franchised bus companies have their main terminals in Belize City.

In Guatemala, buses are the transportation of choice for locals and visitors. They can get you just about anywhere cheaply and quickly and are great for day trips, but they can get extremely crowded. Be prepared for tight squeezes—this means three to a two-person seat—and watch for pickpockets. Large bags are typically stowed on top, which may make you nervous, but theft from bus tops is rare. Drivers and *cobradors* or *ayudantes* (fare collectors, who call out the stops) are knowledgeable and helpful, if a bit gruff. They can direct you to the right bus, and tell you when and where to get off. To be sure they don't forget about you, **try to sit near the driver.** Incidents involving foreign travelers on public buses are rare. (☞ Safety, below.) In fact, the

most recent incidents have involved a large group of foreigners using chartered tour buses.

SHUTTLE TRAVEL

Shuttles in Guatemala are private minivans that hold up to eight passengers. They are faster and more comfortable than public buses, and they maintain a fairly reliable schedule. Advance reservations are usually required. Shuttles can be arranged at the airport, at travel agencies, and most hotels. Popular routes, like those to and from Guatemala City, Antigua, Chichicastenango, Panajachel, and Quetzaltenango, run 3–5 times daily; less common routes may have less frequent service. Prices run $7–$35, and as long as you deal with a legitimate travel agency or hotel, shuttles are reliable and safe. Atitrans and Servicios Turísticos Atitlán are two reputable companies that operate shuttles throughout the country.

➤ SHUTTLE CONTACTS: **Atitrans** (☎ 332–5788 or 832–0644). **Servicios Turísticos Atitlán** (☎ 832–1493 or 762–2075).

CLASSES

Expect to ride on old U.S. school buses or retired North American Greyhound buses. On some routes of Belize, there are a few express buses with air-conditioning and other comforts. These cost a few dollars more.

In Guatemala, inexpensive public buses, also of the converted school bus variety, crisscross the entire country, but they can be slow and extremely crowded, with a three-per-seat rule enforced. Popular destinations, such as Tikal or Santa Elena and Río Dulce, use Pullman buses, which are as well-equipped as American bus lines and are considerably more comfortable. Your hotel or INGUAT office can make bus travel recommendations and arrangements for you.

FARES & SCHEDULES

Belizean buses are extremely cheap (about $2.50–$15). Likewise in Guatemala, fares on public buses are a bargain at 25¢–$3.

In Belize, buses run according to reliable schedules; in Guatemala public buses follow loose schedules, sometimes waiting to leave until the bus fills up. Be aware that on some routes the day's very last bus isn't always a sure thing. Schedules for Pullman buses are usually observed.

PAYING

The main terminals in Belize City and some towns have ticket windows where you pay in advance and get a reserved seat. If you board at other points, you pay the driver's assistant and take any available seat.

In Guatemalan cities, you pay the bus driver as you board. On intercity buses, a fare collector will pass through the bus periodically to take your fare. They have an amazing ability to keep track of all the paid and unpaid fares in a bus jam-packed with riders. For shuttles, you may be asked to pay in advance, but only do so at legitimate agencies.

RESERVATIONS

Advance-purchase bus tickets and reservations are usually not needed or expected in Belize and Guatemala, even for Pullman departures. Arrive at bus terminals about one-half hour before your departure. Reservations are generally required for shuttle service in Guatemala.

BUSINESS HOURS

BANKS & OFFICES

Belize has two local banks, Belize Bank and Atlantic Bank, and two international banks, Barclays and Bank of Nova Scotia. Hours vary, but banks typically are open Monday–Thursday 8–1 and Friday 8–1 and 3–6. The Belize Bank branch at the international airport in Belize City is open 8:30–4 daily.

In Guatemala, most banks are open 9–4, but sometimes until 7 PM. Major banks, such as Bancafe, Banco Industrial, and Banco Occidente, change travelers checks.

GAS STATIONS

Modern, U.S.-style gas stations—Texaco, Esso, and Shell brands, some of them with convenience stores and 24-hour service—are in Belize City and in major towns. In remote areas, especially in southern Belize, gas up whenever you see a gas station. Pre-

mium unleaded gas costs about $3 a gallon. Attendants who pump gas for you do not expect a tip.

Guatemala's gas prices are similarly high. At most gas stations, an attendant will pump the gas and make change. Plan to **use cash**, as credit cards are rarely accepted.

SHOPS & SIGHTS

Belize is a very laid-back place that requires a certain amount of flexibility when shopping or seeing sights. Shops tend to open according to the whim of the owner, but are generally open 8–noon and 2–8. Larger stores and supermarkets in Belize City do not close at lunch. Some shops and businesses work a half day on Wednesday and Saturday. On Friday, many shops close early for the weekend, and on Sunday, Belize takes it very easy: few shops are open, flights are limited, and many restaurants are closed, except those in hotels. Organized sights, such as the Cahal Pech (closed Sun. and Mon.) and Xunantunich ruins close early at 4 and 4:30, respectively.

In Guatemala, most shops are open 10–7, with a lunch break 1–3. Museums are typically closed Monday. Tikal is open daily 8–6.

CAMERAS & PHOTOGRAPHY

In Guatemala's smaller towns, children may offer to pose for a picture, for which a small tip is expected. Likewise, if you snap a candid shot, they may ask afterward for a few *quetzales*. This is off-putting to some; but on the other hand, the children otherwise receive nothing for their participation, while the traveler gets a nice memento. An alternative is to bring a Polaroid camera, whose instant photos are treats for youngsters who very likely have never seen a picture of themselves.

It's best to **always ask permission before taking pictures of indigenous people,** particularly in market areas and rural villages. Although many are more than happy to comply, others may find it disrespectful, invasive, or possibly threatening. In April 2000, two visitors photographing children were killed in a market area of Todos Santos Cuchumatan, when villagers suspected the tourists of planning to abduct the children. Unless you are given permission or a child approaches you, limit your photographs and video taping to children accompanied by their parents or to adults who work in the tourism trade.

➤ PHOTO HELP: **Kodak Information Center** (☎ 800/242–2424). *Kodak Guide to Shooting Great Travel Pictures,* available in bookstores or from Fodor's Travel Publications (☎ 800/533–6478; $18.00 plus $5.50 shipping).

EQUIPMENT PRECAUTIONS

Always **keep your film and tape out of the sun.** Carry an extra supply of batteries, and **be prepared to turn on your camera or camcorder** to prove to security personnel that the device is real. Always **ask for hand inspection of film,** which becomes clouded after repeated exposure to airport X-ray machines, and **keep videotapes away from metal detectors.** In Belize, sand and high humidity are enemies of your camera equipment. To protect it, consider packing your gear in plastic ziplock bags.

FILM & DEVELOPING

In Belize, there are photo-finishing services in major towns and, in Belize City, one-hour photo labs. Guatemala has reliable and affordable photo-development shops, especially in big cities and tourist destinations. Many offer one-hour developing at no extra cost.

CAR RENTAL

Belize City and the international airport in Ladyville have most major car-rental agencies, as well as several local operators. Prices vary from company to company, but all are exorbitant by U.S. standards ($65–$130 per day). A four-wheel-drive Suzuki, with unlimited mileage from Budget, for instance, costs about $75 per day, though weekly rates are cheaper (about $450). Off-season, rates are lower. Most major hotels have all-terrain vehicles with guides for about $200 per day. Some hotels include transportation as part of your room rate. A few resorts have rental cars for about $95 per day.

For serious safaris, a **four-wheel-drive vehicle is invaluable,** particularly a Land Rover or an Isuzu Trooper. But since unpaved roads, mudslides in rainy season, and a general off-the-beaten-path landscape are status quo here, all drivers will be comforted with a four-wheel-drive vehicle, called (*doble-tracción*) in Spanish. Note that most Belize agencies do not permit their vehicles to be taken into Guatemala or Mexico.

Car rental has never really caught on in Guatemala, which, given the narrowness of the roads, is just as well. However, for obvious reasons, a car can be an asset to your trip. You don't have to worry about unreliable bus schedules, you have a lot more control over your itinerary and the pace of your trip, and you can head off to explore on a whim. If you do rent a car, **look for guarded parking lots or hotels with private parking,** to prevent theft or damage.

➤ MAJOR AGENCIES: **Alamo** (☎ 800/522–9696; 020/8759–6200 in the U.K.). **Avis** (☎ 800/331–1084; 800/879–2847 in Canada; 02/9353–9000 in Australia; 09/525–1982 in New Zealand). **Budget** (☎ 800/527–0700; 0144/227–6266 in the U.K.). **Hertz** (☎ 800/654–3001; 800/263–0600 in Canada; 020/8897–2072 in the U.K.; 02/9669–2444 in Australia; 03/358–6777 in New Zealand).

CUTTING COSTS

To get the best deal, **book through a travel agent who will shop around.**

INSURANCE

When driving a rented car you are generally responsible for any damage to or loss of the vehicle as well as for any property damage or personal injury that you may cause. Before you rent, see what coverage your personal auto-insurance policy and credit cards already provide. In Belize, unless covered by your credit card or personal insurance policy, Collision Damage Waiver insurance costs $10 to $15 a day, and you may still be liable for the first $500 to $1,500 in damages.

REQUIREMENTS & RESTRICTIONS

In Belize and Guatemala, rental-car companies routinely accept driver's licenses from the United States, Canada, and most other countries without question. Most car-rental agencies require a major credit card for a deposit, and some require you be over 25.

SURCHARGES

Before you pick up a car in one city and leave it in another, **ask about drop-off charges or one-way service fees,** which can be substantial. Car-rental agencies in Belize City will usually deliver vehicles to other areas for a one-time fee of $35 to $95. Note, too, that some rental agencies charge extra if you return the car before the time specified in your contract. To avoid a hefty refueling fee, **fill the tank just before you turn in the car,** but be aware that gas stations near the rental outlet may overcharge.

CAR TRAVEL

EMERGENCY SERVICES

When renting a car, ask the rental agency what they do if your car breaks down in a remote area. Most in Belize send a driver with a replacement vehicle or a mechanic to fix the car. For help in Guatemala, your best bet is to call the National or Tourist Police. In either country, **consider renting a cellular phone** (☞ Telephones, *below*).

➤ CONTACTS: **Guatemalan National Police** (☎ 110). **Guatemalan Tourist Police** (☎ 832–0532 ext. 35 or 832–0533 ext. 35).

ROAD CONDITIONS

Three of the four main roads in Belize, the Western Highway, Northern Highway, and Hummingbird Highway, are completely paved. These are two-lane roads that are generally in good condition. The Southern Highway, from Dangriga to Punta Gorda, has a 25-mile section near the southern terminus that is paved, and other sections are being prepared for surfacing. Aside from these main highways, expect fair to stupendously rough dirt, gravel, and limestone roads; a few unpaved roads may be impassable in the rainy seasons.

Immense improvements have been made to Guatemala's ravaged roads. A new highway from Río Dulce to

Tikal has cut travel time along this popular route significantly, although, there were no guard rails at press time. Roads in remote areas are frequently unpaved, rife with potholes, and can be treacherously muddy in the rainy season. Fourwheel-drive vehicles are recommended for travel off the beaten path. In cities, expect narrow and brick streets. Road signs are generally used to indicate large towns, although smaller towns may not be clearly marked. Look for intersections where people seem to be waiting for a bus—that's a good sign that there's an important turn-off nearby.

ROAD MAPS

The best available road map to Belize is the *Belize Traveller's Map* published by ITMB, Vancouver, Canada. **Buy this map before your trip** as it is not always readily available in Belize. *Emory King's Driver's Guide to Beautiful Belize,* updated annually and available in Belize, is a mile-by-mile guide to most roads in Belize. INGUAT and all major car rental companies have maps of Guatemala.

RULES OF THE ROAD

Driving in Belize and Guatemala is on the right. Seat belts are required, although the law is seldom if ever enforced. There are few speed limit signs, and speed limits are rarely enforced. However, as you approach villages and towns **watch out for "sleeping policemen",** a local name for raised speed bumps on the road. Belize has about a dozen traffic lights, and only Belize City has anything approaching congested traffic. Guatemala's narrow roads and highways mean you can be stuck motionless on the road for an hour while a construction crew stands around a hole in the ground. **Always allow extra travel time** for such unpredictable events, and **bring along snacks and water.** Otherwise, if you observe the rules you follow at home, you'll likely do just fine. Just don't expect everyone else to follow them.

CHILDREN IN BELIZE AND GUATEMALA

If you are renting a car, **plan to bring your own car seat,** although some of the international agencies may have them. Ask when you reserve.

FLYING

If your children are two or older, **ask about children's airfares.** As a general rule, infants under two not occupying a seat fly at greatly reduced fares or even for free. When booking, **confirm carry-on allowances** if you're traveling with infants. In general, for babies charged 10% of the adult fare you are allowed one carry-on bag and a collapsible stroller; if the flight is full, the stroller may have to be checked or you may be limited to less.

Experts agree that it's a good idea to use safety seats aloft for children weighing less than 40 pounds. Airlines set their own policies: U.S. carriers usually require that the child be ticketed, even if he or she is young enough to ride free, since the seats must be strapped into regular seats. Do **check your airline's policy about using safety seats during takeoff and landing.** And since safety seats are not allowed just anywhere in the plane, get your seat assignments early.

When reserving, **request children's meals or a freestanding bassinet** if you need them. But note that bulkhead seats, where you must sit to use the bassinet, may lack an overhead bin or storage space on the floor.

LODGING

Many hotels in Belize and Guatemala allow young children to stay in their parents' room at no extra charge, but many charge children age 11 or 12 or older for them as extra adults; be sure to **find out the cutoff age for children's discounts.**

Considering a kid-friendly hotel? Kids will see monkeys and parrots at Banana Bank Ranch, outside Belmopan, and Lamanai Outpost Lodge, in Lamanai, Belize. In Guatemala, the Posada de Don Rodrigo, in Panajachel, has a pool with a huge waterslide.

SIGHTS & ATTRACTIONS

Your kids will love Belize, especially if they like the beach and water activities. Among the top attractions are the Belize Zoo, Belize's six butterfly farms, and the many Maya sites where kids can clamber up and down ancient temples. Your children may enjoy taking a guided nature tour to see howler monkeys, crocodiles, snakes, and tarantulas in the wild. In Guatemala, consider taking the kids to the Reserva Natural Atitlán, in Panajachel, which has winding tree-lined paths, suspension footbridges, waterfalls, a spider monkey lookout, a butterfly terrarium, coffee production demos, and a beach. Climbing Pacaya, an active volcano near Antigua, is a thrilling and accessible hike for ages 10 and up, and the ruins of Tikal will inspire all ages, young and old. Places that are especially appealing to children are indicated by a rubber duckie icon in the margin.

SUPPLIES & EQUIPMENT

Baby formula and diapers are available in Belize and Guatemala, but prices are up to twice those in the United States. Pasteurized milk is available in some groceries, and canned or boxed milk is widely available.

COMPUTERS ON THE ROAD

If you're traveling in Belize with a laptop, be aware that the power supply may be uneven, and most hotels do not have built-in current stabilizers. At remote lodges, power is often from fluctuating generators. Electricity is a little more reliable in Guatemala, especially in the larger cities, however, most international hotels have computers and most cybercafés around the country have PCs and printers for reasonable prices. **Bring your own disks** if you want to save your work.

CONSUMER PROTECTION

Whenever shopping or buying travel services in Belize and Guatemala, **pay with a major credit card** so you can cancel payment or get reimbursed if there's a problem. **Make sure you're billed in the right currency** before signing your receipt. If you're doing business with a particular company for the first time, **contact your local Better Business Bureau and the attorney general's offices** in your own state and the company's home state, as well. Have any complaints been filed? Finally, if you're buying a package or tour, always **consider**

travel insurance that includes default coverage (☞ Insurance, *below*).

➤ BBBs: **Council of Better Business Bureaus** (⊠ 4200 Wilson Blvd., Suite 800, Arlington, VA 22203, ☎ 703/276–0100, FAX 703/525–8277 www.bbb.org).

CRUISE TRAVEL

Cruising is an increasingly popular way to see Belize. Ships calling on Belize are not the megaboats that cruise the main Caribbean but small ships usually carrying 200 or fewer passengers. Ports of call in Belize include Belize City, San Pedro (Ambergris Caye), Placencia, and several of Belize's remote cayes and atolls such as Turneffe Atoll, Goff Caye, Tobacco Caye, and West Snake Caye. Because these are not deep-water ports, passengers are taken ashore on tenders.

➤ CRUISE LINES: **American Canadian Caribbean Line** (☎ 800/556–7450). **Norwegian Cruise Line** (☎ 800/327–7030). **Premier Cruise Lines** (☎ 800/473–3262). **Royal Olympic Cruises** (☎ 800/872–6400). **Temptress Adventure Cruises** (☎ 800/336–8423). **Windstar Cruises** (☎ 800/258–7245).

CUSTOMS & DUTIES

When shopping, **keep receipts** for all purchases. Upon reentering the country, **be ready to show customs officials what you've bought.** If you feel a duty is incorrect or object to the way your clearance was handled, note the inspector's badge number and ask to see a supervisor. If the problem isn't resolved, write to the appropriate authorities, beginning with the port director at your point of entry.

IN AUSTRALIA

Australian residents who are 18 or older may bring home $A400 worth of souvenirs and gifts (including jewelry), 250 cigarettes or 250 grams of tobacco, and 1,125 ml of alcohol (including wine, beer, and spirits). Residents under 18 may bring back $A200 worth of goods. Prohibited items include meat products. Seeds, plants, and fruits need to be declared upon arrival.

➤ INFORMATION: **Australian Customs Service** (Regional Director, ⊠ Box 8, Sydney, NSW 2001, ☎ 02/9213–2000, FAX 02/9213–4000, www.customs.gov.au).

IN BELIZE AND GUATEMALA

Duty-free allowances for visitors entering Belize include 3 liters of liquor and one carton of cigarettes. All electronic and electrical appliances, cameras, jewelry, or other items of value must be declared at the point of entry. Visitors are allowed to bring in the equivalent of $250 in foreign currency per day of their stay. Any amount above that should be declared. You should have no trouble bringing a laptop computer into Belize. Firearms of any type and spear guns are prohibited.

Visitors may enter Guatemala duty-free with a camera, up to six rolls of film, any clothes and articles needed while traveling, 500 mg of tobacco, 3 liters of alcoholic beverages, 2 bottles of perfume, and 2 kg of candy. Unless you bring in a lot of merchandise, customs officers probably won't even check your luggage, although a laptop may be somewhat scrutinized.

ON DEPARTURE

To take home fresh seafood of any kind from Belize, you must first obtain a permit from the Fisheries Department. There is a 20-pound limit.

The U.S. State Department Web site has information on adopting a child from Guatemala and the customs process. It's illegal to export most Maya artifacts. If you buy any such goods, do so only at a well-established store, and keep the receipt. You may not take fruits or vegetables out of Guatemala.

➤ INFORMATION: **Belize Fisheries** (☎ 501/24–4552). **State Department** (www.travel.state.gov/adoption_guatemala.html).

IN CANADA

Canadian residents who have been out of Canada for at least 7 days may bring home C$500 worth of goods duty-free. If you've been away fewer than 7 days but more than 48 hours, the duty-free allowance drops to C$200; if your trip lasts 24–48 hours, the allowance is C$50. You may not pool allowances with family members. Goods claimed under the C$500 exemption may follow you by mail; those claimed under the lesser exemptions must accompany you. Alcohol and tobacco products may be included in the 7-day and 48-hour exemptions but not in the 24-hour exemption. If you meet the age requirements of the province or territory through which you reenter Canada, you may bring in, duty-free, 1.14 liters (40 imperial ounces) of wine or liquor or 24 12-ounce cans or bottles of beer or ale. If you are 16 or older you may bring in, duty-free, 200 cigarettes and 50 cigars. Check ahead of time with Revenue Canada or the Department of Agriculture for policies regarding meat products, seeds, plants, and fruits.

You may send an unlimited number of gifts worth up to C$60 each duty-free to Canada. Label the package UNSOLICITED GIFT—VALUE UNDER $60. Alcohol and tobacco are excluded.

➤ INFORMATION: **Revenue Canada** (✉ 2265 St. Laurent Blvd. S, Ottawa, Ontario K1G 4K3, ☎ 613/993–0534; 800/461–9999 in Canada, ℻ 613/991–4126, www.ccra-adrc.gc.ca).

IN NEW ZEALAND

Homeward-bound residents 17 or older may bring back $700 worth of souvenirs and gifts. Your duty-free allowance also includes 4.5 liters of wine or beer; one 1,125-ml bottle of spirits; and either 200 cigarettes, 250 grams of tobacco, 50 cigars, or a combination of the three up to 250 grams. Prohibited items include meat products, seeds, plants, and fruits.

➤ INFORMATION: **New Zealand Customs** (Custom House, ✉ 50 Anzac Ave., Box 29, Auckland, New Zealand, ☎ 09/359–6655, ℻ 09/359–6732).

IN THE U.K.

From countries outside the EU, you may bring home, duty-free, 200 cigarettes or 50 cigars; 1 liter of spirits or 2 liters of fortified or sparkling wine or liqueurs; 2 liters of still table wine; 60 ml of perfume; 250 ml of toilet water; plus £136 worth of other goods, including gifts and souvenirs. If returning from outside the EU, prohibited items

include meat products, seeds, plants, and fruits.

➤ INFORMATION: **HM Customs and Excise** (✉ Dorset House, Stamford St., Bromley, Kent BR1 1XX, ☎ 0207/202–4227, www.hmce.gov.uk).

IN THE U.S.

U.S. residents who have been out of the country for at least 48 hours (and who have not used the $400 allowance or any part of it in the past 30 days) may bring home $400 worth of foreign goods duty-free.U.S. residents 21 and older may bring back 1 liter of alcohol duty-free. In addition, regardless of your age, you are allowed 200 cigarettes and 100 non-Cuban cigars. Antiques, which the U.S. Customs Service defines as objects more than 100 years old, enter duty-free, as do original works of art done entirely by hand, including paintings, drawings, and sculptures.

You may also send packages home duty-free: up to $200 worth of goods for personal use, with a limit of one parcel per addressee per day (except alcohol or tobacco products or perfume worth more than $5); label the package PERSONAL USE and attach a list of its contents and their retail value. Do not label the package UNSOLICITED GIFT or your duty-free exemption will drop to $100. Mailed items do not affect your duty-free allowance on your return.

➤ INFORMATION: **U.S. Customs Service** (✉ 1300 Pennsylvania Ave. NW, Washington, DC 20229, www.customs.gov; inquiries ☎ 202/354–1000; complaints c/o ✉ 1300 Pennsylvania Ave. NW, Room 5.4D, Washington, DC 20229; registration of equipment c/o ✉ Resource Management, ☎ 202/354–1000).

DINING

The restaurants we list are the cream of the crop in each price category.

MEALS & SPECIALTIES

You can eat well in Belize. The country has no unique cuisine, but a gastronomic gumbo of Mexican, Caribbean, Maya, Garifuna, English, and American dishes provides a tasty variety of dining choices. Belize has restaurants serving French, Thai, Indian, Chinese, and even Sri Lankan food. On the coast and cayes, seafood—especially lobster, conch, and locally caught fish such as snapper and grouper—is fresh, inexpensive, and delicious. Try Creole specialties such as cow-foot soup (yes, made with real cow's feet), "boil up" (a stew of fish, potatoes, plantains, cassava and other vegetables, and eggs), and the ubiquitous "stew chicken" with rice and beans. Many Creole dishes are seasoned with red or black *recado,* a paste made from annatto seeds and other spices. In border areas, enjoy mestizo favorites such as *escabeche* (onion soup), *salbutes* (fried corn tortillas with chicken and a topping of tomatoes, onions, and peppers), or *garnaches* (fried tortillas with refried beans, cabbage, and cheese. In Dangriga and Punta Gorda or other Garifuna areas, try dishes such as *sere lasus* (fish soup with plantain balls) or cassava dumplings. In most areas of Belize, you can chow down on American classics like fried chicken, pork chops, and T-bone steaks.

In general, Guatemala does not have a distinguished national cuisine; most of the top restaurants serve Continental fare. The classic Guatemalan dish is tasty but unremarkable: eggs, refried black beans, meat (either sliced beef or chorizo), cheese, and Guatemala's thick corn tortillas. There a few standouts though, including róbalo, a common and delicious native whitefish called snook elsewhere; ceviche, chilled marinated seafood flavored with lime or a tomato broth; and few dishes not seen on North American menus, such as *tepisquintle,* (the world's largest rodent) and *sopa de tortuga* (turtle soup). Note that while such animals may be exotic fare, in Central America they're often hunted to extinction. Street vendors typically sell fried chicken and french fries, or *churrosquitos* (sliced beef or chorizo served with pickled cabbage and tortillas). *Huevos motuleños* (layers of fried eggs served on a crispy tortilla with cheese, beans, hot sauce, and sometimes ham) make an amazing breakfast. Vegetarians in both Belize and Guatemala may be "bean-ed out"

after a week or so, although *ensalada aguacate* (avocado salad), *pan de banana* (banana bread), and *flan* (a crème caramel dessert) never get dull. Warning: while eating on the street is as Guatemalan as it gets, many travelers have gotten sick doing so.

MEALTIMES

In Belize, breakfast is usually served from around 7 to 9, lunch from 11 to 2, and dinner from 6 to 9. Few restaurants are open late. Unless otherwise noted, the restaurants listed in this guide are open daily for lunch and dinner. Remember, though, that small restaurants in Belize may open or close at the whim of the owner. Off-season, restaurants may close early if it looks as if there are no more guests coming, and some restaurants close completely for a month or two, usually in the late summer.

In Guatemala, lunch is the biggest meal, or at least the longest, running from noon to 2 or 3. Breakfast starts at 7, and dinner not long after sundown. Restaurants in major tourist areas may stay open later, but most towns are all but deserted by 9 PM.

Unless otherwise noted, the restaurants listed in this guide are open daily for lunch and dinner.

PAYING

Only the most expensive restaurants accept credit cards and traveler's checks.

RESERVATIONS & DRESS

Reservations are always a good idea: we mention them only when they're essential or not accepted. We mention dress only when men are required to wear a jacket or a jacket and tie. In Belize, reservations don't so much confirm that you'll have a table but rather alert the cook that you are coming so that he or she can get the necessary ingredients. For this reason, let them know if you must cancel.

WINE, BEER, & SPIRITS

Many restaurants in Belize serve beer and terrific, tropical mixed drinks; few offer wine. About the only beer you'll see in Belize is Belikin. The lager is available in regular and premium versions (the premium is sold mostly in more expensive bars and restaurants). Belikin Stout is also available, and the brewery that makes Belikin, Bowen & Bownen, also brews Guiness Stout locally, under license. American and other imported beers are available in some groceries, but prices are high. Several Belize companies manufacture liquors, primarily rum but also gin and vodka. Traveller's Rum is a particularly good choice, with a slight vanilla flavor. The drinking age in Belize is 18.

Guatemala has no real wine market to speak of, but top restaurants often have excellent imported bottles. The national beers Gallo and Cabro are decent, while imported liquor and local spirits distilled from sugar cane can be found most everywhere. The official drinking age in Guatemala is 20.

DISABILITIES & ACCESSIBILITY

Wheelchair accessibility in Central America is extremely limited. Outside major cities, roads are unpaved, making wheelchair travel difficult. Exploring Central America's attractions usually involves walking down steep trails, muddy paths, or cobblestone streets. In Belize, boats and small planes are used to get to the cayes and to remote areas. Airplanes often lack jetways, and passengers must walk down rollaway steps to the pavement. Buses are not equipped to carry wheelchairs, so wheelchair users should hire a van to get around. However, there is a growing awareness of the needs of people with disabilities, and the friendly, helpful attitude of the people goes some way toward making up for the lack of provisions.

➤ LOCAL RESOURCES: In Belize, **Central American Information Center** (✉ Box 50211, San Diego, CA 92105, ☎ 619/262–6489). In Guatemala, **IN-GUAT** (✉ 7 Avenida 1–17, Zona 4, ☎ 331–1339 or 331–1333).

LODGING

When discussing accessibility with an operator or reservations agent, **ask hard questions.** Are there any stairs, inside *or* out? Are there grab bars next to the toilet *and* in the shower/tub? How wide is the doorway to the room? To the bathroom?

For the most extensive facilities meeting the latest legal specifications, **opt for newer accommodations.**

SIGHTS & ATTRACTIONS

Few sights in Guatemala were designed with travelers in wheelchairs in mind, and fewer still have been renovated to meet that need. Newer destinations may have the necessary facilities and accommodations, but don't count on it—it's best to call ahead or get a recommendation from someone who has visited the property.

➤ COMPLAINTS: **Disability Rights Section** (✉ U.S. Department of Justice, Civil Rights Division, Box 66738, Washington, DC 20035-6738, ☎ 202/514–0301 or 800/514–0301; TTY 202/514–0383 or 800/514–0383, FAX 202/307–1198, www.usdoj.gov/crt/ada/adahom1.htm) for general complaints. **Aviation Consumer Protection Division** (☞ Air Travel, *above*) for airline-related problems. **Civil Rights Office** (✉ U.S. Department of Transportation, Departmental Office of Civil Rights, S-30, 400 7th St. SW, Room 10215, Washington, DC 20590, ☎ 202/366–4648, FAX 202/366–9371) for problems with surface transportation.

TRAVEL AGENCIES

In the United States, the Americans with Disabilities Act requires that travel firms serve the needs of all travelers. Some agencies specialize in working with people with disabilities.

➤ TRAVELERS WITH MOBILITY PROBLEMS: **Access Adventures** (✉ 206 Chestnut Ridge Rd., Scottsville, NY 14624, ☎ 716/889–9096, dltravel@prodigy.net), run by a former physical-rehabilitation counselor. **Flying Wheels Travel** (✉ 143 W. Bridge St., Box 382, Owatonna, MN 55060, ☎ 507/451–5005 or 800/535–6790, FAX 507/451–1685, thq@ll.net, www.flyingwheels.com).

DISCOUNTS & DEALS

To save money, **look into discount reservations services** with toll-free numbers, which use their buying power to get a better price on hotels, airline tickets, even car rentals. When booking a room, always **call the hotel's local toll-free number** (if one is available) rather than the central reservations number—you'll often get a better price. Always ask about off-season prices, special packages, or corporate rates.

When shopping for the best deal on hotels and car rentals, **look for guaranteed exchange rates,** which protect you against a falling dollar. With your rate locked in, you won't pay more, even if the price goes up in the local currency.

PACKAGE DEALS

Don't confuse packages and guided tours. When you buy a package, you travel on your own, just as though you had planned the trip yourself. Fly/drive packages, which combine airfare and car rental, are often a good deal.

ECOTOURISM

Central America is the original eco-tourism destination, and, as a result, you'll see the term used liberally everywhere. With respect to lodging, it can be used to describe deluxe, private cabanas on a tidy beach, or a hut in the middle of nowhere with pit toilets. It may also point to environmental conservation efforts by parks or tour companies who are conscious of natural resources and their role in not depleting them. Or it may mean just the opposite. Wildlife parks, butterfly farms, cloud forests, and trips to Maya ruins are some of the incredible eco-destinations in this area. And mountain biking, bird-watching, jungle hiking, scuba diving, cave tubing, fishing, and white-water rafting are just some of the eco-activities.

ELECTRICITY

There is **no need to bring a converter or adapter** as electrical current in Belize and Guatemala is 110 volts, the same as in the United States, and outlets in both countries take U.S.-style plugs. In a few remote areas, lodges and hotels may generate their own electricity, and after the generators are turned off at night, power, if there is any, comes only from kerosene lanterns or your flashlight.

EMBASSIES

Citizens of Australia and New Zealand may contact the British High Commission.

➤ CANADA: **Honorary Consul of Canada,** 83 N. Front St., Belize City, ☎ 23/1060, FAX 23/0060.

➤ GUATEMALA: **Embassy of Guatemala,** 8 A St., Belize City, ☎ 23/3150, FAX 23/5140.

➤ MEXICO: **Embassy of Mexico,** 20 N. Park St., Belize City, ☎ 23/0194, FAX 27/8742.

➤ UNITED KINGDOM: **British High Commission,** Belmopan, ☎ 82/2146, FAX 82/2761.

➤ UNITED STATES: **Embassy of the United States,** 29 Gabourel Ln., Belize City, ☎ 27/7161, FAX 23/0802.

ENGLISH-LANGUAGE MEDIA

BOOKS

Due to import taxes, books are more expensive in Belize than in North America or Europe. Almost every major tourist destination in Guatemala has one or two stores with used paperbacks in English. Some are willing to trade books or lend books, too. Guatemala City is the only place in the country where you will find a significant selection of new books.

NEWSPAPERS & MAGAZINES

Belize has no daily newspapers, but it has a number of brash weeklies. As in most countries, crime and politics make the front pages, often in sensational headlines. *The Reporter,* published in Belize City, is the best independent newspaper. For visitors, the chatty *San Pedro Sun,* one of two weeklies on Ambergris Caye, is a good source of information, as are the weekly *Cayo Trader* in San Ignacio, and the monthly *Placencia Breeze* in Placencia.

The U.S. travel magazine *Belize First* also has a Web site (www.turq.com/belizefirst), and is a good resource for cultural, dining, lodging, and service information.

The monthly Guatemalan journal *Revue* (4 Calle 0riente 23, Antigua, Guatemala, ☎ 832–4619) is more of an advertisement with a few articles on local trends than a guidebook. *Lugares y Destinos* is a free bilingual guide produced by INGUAT, the Guatemalan Tourist Commission. *Destination Guatemala* and *Central America Guide* are detailed visitor and business guides, and are available in most upscale hotels.

The better or international chain hotels usually have fairly current editions of a few major U.S. and European newspapers, typically *USA Today, The Economist,* and *Newsweek*.

RADIO & TELEVISION

Belize's most informative television news is on Channel 5, which also offers its daily news summaries on the Web at www.channel5belize.com. Love-FM Radio (95.1 Mhz) is the nation's leading radio station, playing standards and soft rock.

Cable TV is a popular amenity in Guatemalan hotels. You can expect HBO, Showtime, ESPN, TNT, the Discover Channel, MTV (a Spanish variety), and one or two feeds from regional stations in the United States (usually from Denver, curiously). Radio stations generally play a mix of American pop, rock, and Latin favorites.

ETIQUETTE & BEHAVIOR

Belizeans and *Chapins* (the nickname for a Guatemalan) are incredibly kind and friendly. Let them know you are, too, and always greet someone with a "Good morning" or "Buenos dias" before asking for directions, for a table in a restaurant, or when entering a store or museum, for example. It will set a positive tone and you'll be received much more warmly for having done it.

Don't take pictures inside churches. Do not take pictures of indigenous people without first asking their permission. Offering them a few pesos as thanks is customary.

Since the civil war ended, Guatemala has become a popular country for North Americans looking to adopt children. Although most adoptive parents go through perfectly legal channels, it is also believed by some Guatemalans that many children may be adopted illegally or even stolen from birth mothers, since it is often a lucrative process. Guatemalans, particularly those in rural areas who may interact less with travelers on the whole, may be sensitive to foreigners approaching their children, no matter how amiable one's intentions. For this reason, **always be respectful when interacting with children,** and never pick them up or attempt to unless you are invited to do so by the child's parents. In April 2000, two visitors were killed in a market area of Todos Santos Cuchumatan when villagers feared that their children were in danger of abduction.

With the exception of Pullman buses and shuttles, the seats on Guatemalan buses are expected to fit three abreast. Though tourists are often larger than the average local, you should respect the rule, and make room for others. It's perfectly fine to step into the aisle to let someone take a middle or window seat. Also in Guatemala, as rude as it may seem, a quick hiss or whistle is an acceptable way to get someone's attention—you may even take up the habit yourself, particularly with waiters. Unfortunately men may catcall women in this way as well, which unfortunately is not considered terribly rude either.

BUSINESS ETIQUETTE

Business dress in Belize is casual. Men rarely wear suits and ties, and even the prime minister appears at functions in a white shirt open at the neck. The business environment is more formal in Guatemala, where suits are more the norm.

GAY & LESBIAN TRAVEL

Most Belizeans have a very conservative view of sexual orientation. There are no openly gay or lesbian clubs or bars, and the only publicly gay resort, on Ambergris Caye, has closed. Likewise, Guatemala is conservative, although there are gay nights at clubs (mostly male) in Guatemala City, like Pandora's Box, which has been around forever.

➤ GAY- & LESBIAN-FRIENDLY TRAVEL
AGENCIES: **Different Roads Travel** (✉
8383 Wilshire Blvd., Suite 902, Beverly Hills, CA 90211, ☎ 323/651–
5557 or 800/429–8747, FAX 323/651–
3678, leigh@west.tzell.com). **Kennedy
Travel** (✉ 314 Jericho Turnpike,
Floral Park, NY 11001, ☎ 516/352–
4888 or 800/237–7433, FAX 516/354–
8849, main@kennedytravel.com,
www.kennedytravel.com). **Now
Voyager** (✉ 4406 18th St., San Francisco, CA 94114, ☎ 415/626–1169
or 800/255–6951, FAX 415/626–8626,
www.nowvoyager.com). **Skylink
Travel and Tour** (✉ 1006 Mendocino
Ave., Santa Rosa, CA 95401, ☎ 707/
546–9888 or 800/225–5759, FAX 707/
546–9891, skylinktvl@aol.com,
www.skylinktravel.com), serving
lesbian travelers.

HEALTH

Belize has a high standard of health
and hygiene. You can drink the water
in Belize City, on Ambergris Caye,
and in most other areas you are likely
to visit. In remote villages, however,
water may come from shallow wells
or cisterns and may not be safe to
drink. Assume, while in Guatemala,
that the water is not safe to drink
except the best hotels. Bottled water,
agua mineral or *agua pura* in Spanish,
is available even at the smallest *tiendas* (stores) and is cheaper than in
North America.

DIVERS' ALERT

**Do not fly within 24 hours of scuba
diving.** For emergencies, San Pedro
has a hyperbaric chamber (financed
by a $1 "tax" on tank rentals) just
north of the airstrip.

FOOD & DRINK

The major health risk in Belize and
Guatemala is Montezuma's Revenge,
or traveler's diarrhea, caused by
eating contaminated fruit or vegetables or drinking contaminated water.
So **watch what you eat.** Avoid ice: in
Guatemala, ask for your drinks *sin
hielo,* without ice. Also skip
uncooked food and unpasteurized
milk and milk products, and **drink
only bottled water** or water that has
been boiled for at least 20 minutes,
even when brushing your teeth. Mild
cases may respond to Imodium
(known generically as loperamide) or

Pepto-Bismol (not as strong), both of
which can be purchased over the
counter, although you should bring
along your own stash. Also, drink
plenty of purified water or tea—
chamomile is a good folk remedy. In
severe cases, rehydrate yourself with a
salt-sugar solution: ½ teaspoon salt
(*sal*) and 4 tablespoons sugar (*azucar*)
per quart of water.

MEDICAL PLANS

No one plans to get sick while traveling, but it happens, so **consider signing up with a medical-assistance
company.** Members get doctor referrals, emergency evacuation or repatriation, hot lines for medical
consultation, cash for emergencies,
and other assistance.

➤ MEDICAL-ASSISTANCE COMPANIES:
International SOS Assistance (✉ 8
Neshaminy Interplex, Suite 207,
Trevose, PA 19053, ☎ 215/245–4707
or 800/523–6586, FAX 215/244–9617,
www.internationalsos.com; ✉ 12
Chemin Riantbosson, 1217 Meyrin 1,
Geneva, Switzerland, ☎ 4122/785–
6464, FAX 4122/785–6424; ✉ 331 N.
Bridge Rd., 17-00, Odeon Towers,
Singapore 188720, ☎ 65/338–7800,
FAX 65/338–7611).

OVER-THE-COUNTER
REMEDIES

Most medicines requiring a doctor's
prescription at home also require one
in Belize. Pharmacies in Guatemala sell
a wide range of medications, including
U.S. prescription-only drugs. Ask for
what you want with the generic name.
Some pharmacies are open 24 hours,
and deliver directly to hotel rooms.
Most hotel proprietors will direct you
to such services.

PESTS & OTHER HAZARDS

In Belize and Caribbean Guatemala,
sand flies (also known as sand fleas
or no-see-ums), which are common
on many beaches, cayes, and in
swampy areas, can infect their victims
with leishmaniasis, a disease which in
its cutaneous form may cause the skin
to develop sores that can leave scars.
In rare cases, the visceral form of
leishmaniasis, if untreated, can be
fatal. Using repellent containing a
high concentration of DEET, or, some
say, lathering on Avon's Skin So Soft

THE GOLD GUIDE / SMART TRAVEL TIPS

or a citronella product called Natu-rapel, can help deter sand flies.

If you're a light sleeper, you might want to pack ear plugs. Monkeys howling through the night and birds chirping at the crack of dawn are only charming on the first night of your nature excursion.

SHOTS & MEDICATIONS

According to the National Centers for Disease Control (CDC) there is a limited risk of malaria, hepatitis A and B, dengue fever, typhoid fever, and rabies in Central America. In most urban or easily accessible areas, you need not worry. However, if you plan to spend a lot of time in the jungles, rain forests, remote regions, or stay for more than six weeks, **check with the CDC's International Travelers Hotline.** In areas where malaria and dengue, both of which are carried by mosquitoes, are preva-lent, use mosquito nets (pack your own—it's the only way to be sure there are no tears), wear clothing that covers the body (not shorts), apply repellent containing DEET, and use spray for flying insects in living and sleeping areas. Also **consider taking antimalarial pills**; Chloroquine is sold as Aralen™ in Central America, and Mefloquine as Lariam. There is no vaccine for dengue. Rabies is always a concern when you get bitten by a stray dog or other wild animal; scrub the wound under clean, running water with soap or iodine—or, failing those, some local rum—and get an antirabies shot immediately.

Children traveling to Central America should have current inoculations against measles, mumps, rubella, and polio.

➤ HEALTH WARNINGS: **National Centers for Disease Control** (CDC; National Center for Infectious Dis-eases, Division of Quarantine, Trav-eler's Health Section, ✉ 1600 Clifton Rd. NE, M/S E-03, Atlanta, GA 30333, ☎ 888/232–3228 or 800/311–3435, FAX 888/232–3299, www.cdc.gov).

INSURANCE

The most useful travel-insurance plan is a comprehensive policy that in-cludes coverage for trip cancellation and interruption, default, trip delay,

and medical expenses (with a waiver for preexisting conditions).

Without insurance you will lose all or most of your money if you cancel your trip, regardless of the reason. Default insurance covers you if your tour operator, airline, or cruise line goes out of business. Trip delay covers expenses that arise because of bad weather or mechanical delays. Study the fine print when comparing policies.

If you're traveling internationally, a key component of travel insurance is coverage for medical bills incurred if you get sick on the road. Such ex-penses are not generally covered by Medicare or private policies. U.K. residents can buy a travel-insurance policy valid for most vacations taken during the year in which it's pur-chased (but check preexisting-condi-tion coverage). British and Australian citizens need extra medical coverage when traveling overseas.

Always **buy travel policies directly from the insurance company**; if you buy them from a cruise line, airline, or tour operator that goes out of business you probably will not be covered for the agency or operator's default, a major risk. Before making any pur-chase, **review your existing health and home-owner's policies** to find what they cover away from home.

➤ TRAVEL INSURERS: In the United States: **Access America** (✉ 6600 W. Broad St., Richmond, VA 23230, ☎ 804/285–3300 or 800/284–8300, FAX 804/673–1583, www.previewtravel.com), **Travel Guard International** (✉ 1145 Clark St., Stevens Point, WI 54481, ☎ 715/345–0505 or 800/826–1300, FAX 800/955–8785, www.noelgroup.com).

➤ INSURANCE INFORMATION: In the United Kingdom: **Association of British Insurers** (✉ 51–55 Gresham St., London EC2V 7HQ, ☎ 0207/600–3333, FAX 0207/696–8999, info@abi.org.uk, www.abi.org.uk). In Australia: **Insurance Council of Aus-tralia** (☎ 03/9614–1077, FAX 03/9614–7924).

LANGUAGE

English is Belize's official language. Spanish also is widely spoken especially in northern and western Belize. Several Maya dialects and the Garifuna language are also spoken. Creole, which uses versions of English words and a West-African–influenced grammar and syntax, is spoken by many Belizeans, especially around Belize City, Hopkins, and Dangriga.

In Guatemala, wherever tourist traffic is heavy, you'll find English speakers; you'll have considerably less luck in places off the beaten path. In addition, many Guatemalans will answer "yes" even if they don't understand your question, so as not to appear unkind or unhelpful. To minimize such confusion, try posing questions as "Where is so-and-so?" rather than asking "Is so-and-so this way?"

LANGUAGES FOR TRAVELERS

A phrase book and language-tape set can help get you started.

➤ PHRASE BOOKS & LANGUAGE-TAPE SETS: *Fodor's Spanish for Travelers* (☎ 800/733–3000 in the United States; 800/668–4247 in Canada; $7 for phrasebook, $16.95 for audio set).

LODGING

In Belize, you'll likely stay in one of four types of lodging: a traditional hotel, a jungle lodge, a beach hotel, or a lodge on a remote caye. Traditional hotels, usually found in Belize City and in larger towns, run the gamut from basic budget places to international-style hotels such as the Radisson Fort George in Belize City. Jungle lodges are concentrated in the Cayo and Orange Walk districts, but they can be found most anywhere. Jungle lodges need not be spartan; most have electricity (though the generator may shut down at 10 PM), a number have swimming pools, and a few even have air-conditioning. The typical jungle lodge has a roof of bay thatch and may remind you of a Maya house gone upscale. Beach hotels also come in various levels of luxury, from a basic seaside cabin on Caye Caulker to a small, deluxe resort such as the Inn at Robert's Grove or Rum Point Inn in Placencia. On Ambergris Caye, many resorts are "condotels"—small, low-rise condominium complexes with individually owned units but managed like a hotel. Lodging choices

on remote cayes appeal to the diving and fishing crowd. Amenity levels vary greatly, from cabins with outdoor bathrooms to simple cottages with composting toilets to comfortable villas with air-conditioning. Regardless of the kind of lodging, you'll almost invariably stay at a small place of 2 to 25 rooms where the owners actively manage the property. Thus, Belize accommodations usually reflect the personalities of their owners, for better or worse.

Although hotels in Belize have published rates, in the off-season at least you may be able to negotiate a better rate, especially if you are staying more than one or two nights. Walk-in rates are usually lower than pre-booked rates, and rooms booked direct on the Internet may be lower than those booked through agents.

Unlike 10 years ago, Guatemala now has lodging options that go well beyond the needs of the backpacker, in the form of reliable international hotels, classy colonial charmers, and rustic retreats with local flair. International chain hotels like the Radisson, Marriott, and Camino Real, have rooms and facilities equal to those at home. The only thing lacking in this type of lodging is a sense of place, of something uniquely Guatemalan. Fortunately, you don't have to sacrifice hot water or room service for a touch of culture—Antigua has colonial class (plus modern amenities and service) down to an art at the Hotel Santo Domingo, Casa del Angel, Mesón Panza Verde, and others. Add to the list the Hotel Atitlán in Panajachel, the Mayan Inn in Chichicastenango, and the Mansión San Carlos in Guatemala City, and you'll experience modern comforts surrounded by the art and architecture of Guatemala's rich colonial past. For something a little cheaper and out of the way, the Posada Santiago and the Casa del Mundo, both overlooking Lake Atitlán, offer comfort and culture in utter isolation. Hammocks and views in this class of lodgings substitute for TVs and telephones common in modern hotels.

The lodgings we list are the cream of the crop in each price category. We always list the facilities that are available—but we don't specify whether they cost extra: when pricing accommodations, always ask what's included and what costs extra.

Assume that hotels operate on the **European Plan** (EP, with no meals) unless we specify that they use either the **Continental Plan** (CP, with a Continental breakfast), **Breakfast Plan** (BP, with a full breakfast), or the **Modified American Plan** (MAP, with breakfast and dinner) or are **all-inclusive** (including all meals and most activities).

APARTMENT & HOUSE RENTALS

If you want a home base that's roomy enough for a family and comes with cooking facilities, **consider a furnished rental.** These can save you money, especially if you're traveling with a group. Home-exchange directories sometimes list rentals as well as exchanges. In Belize, you can most easily find vacation rentals on Ambergris Caye. The Ambergris Caye Web site (www.ambergriscaye.com) has a good selection of rental houses and condos.

➤ INTERNATIONAL AGENTS: **Hideaways International** (✉ 767 Islington St., Portsmouth, NH 03801, ☎ 603/430–4433 or 800/843–4433, FAX 603/430–4444 info@hideaways.com www.hideaways.com; membership $99). **Vacation Home Rentals Worldwide** (✉ 235 Kensington Ave., Norwood, NJ 07648, ☎ 201/767–9393 or 800/633–3284, FAX 201/767–5510, vhrww@juno.com, www.vhrww.com). **Villas and Apartments Abroad** (✉ 1270 6th Ave., 15th floor, New York, NY 10020, ☎ 212/897–5045 or 800/433–3020, FAX 212/897–5039, vaa@altour.com, www.vaanyc.com).

CAMPING

If you don't mind a few mosquito bites, you can camp in Belize. It's generally prohibited in the national parks and preserves but is allowed at Cockscomb Preserve, at Half Moon Caye National Monument, and in the Mountain Pine Ridge Reserve at Augustine Village. A number of hotels and lodges in Cayo district, including Clarissa Falls, Trek Stop, and Ian Anderson's Caves Branch Adventure

Camp permit camping. Two lodges, Chaa Creek and Mountain Equestrian Trails, have safari camps, which are permanent camp sites on platforms. There are only a few RV campgrounds with hook-ups in Belize—two are in Corozal District in northern Belize, the Lagoon Campground and Caribbean Village—but some hotels in rural areas allow those with RVs or trailers to park (no hook-ups) on their property.

Camping is very popular among the backpacker crowd in Guatemala, and there are campgrounds on the outskirts of Antigua, Quetzaltenango, Santiago Atitlán, and San Pedro Atitlán. Very large cities and very small towns are less likely have such sites. Travel agencies that arrange outdoor adventures from climbing volcanoes to mountain biking and white-water rafting are usually the most informed about camping options in the area, either independently or as part of a trek. In some cases, they can rent equipment as well.

HOTELS

All hotels listed have private bath unless otherwise noted.

RESERVING A ROOM

Most hotels in Belize, and many in Guatemala, are now on the Internet, and 80% or more of bookings are made by e-mail. Use www.fodors.com to find the Web address of hotels in mentioned in this book.

➤ TOLL-FREE NUMBERS: **Best Western** (☎ 800/528–1234, www.bestwestern.com). **Choice** (☎ 800/221–2222, www.hotelchoice.com). **Clarion** (☎ 800/252–7466, www.choicehotels.com). **Holiday Inn** (☎ 800/465–4329, www.basshotels.com). **Radisson** (☎ 800/333–3333, www.radisson.com). **Ramada** (☎ 800/228–2828 www.ramada.com).

MAIL & SHIPPING

When sending mail to Central America, be sure to include the district in the address. Belizean mail service is excellent, and the stamps, mostly of wildlife, are beautiful. An airmail letter takes about a week to the United States.

From Guatemala, letters to the United States take one to two weeks, and slightly longer to Canada and the United Kingdom.

OVERNIGHT SERVICES

If you have to send something fast, use DHL, which is expensive but does the job right.

➤ MAJOR SERVICES: **DHL** (Belize: ✉ 38 New Rd., Belize City, ☎ 501/23–1070; Guatemala: ✉ 7 Avenida 2–42, Zona 9, Guatemala City, ☎ 502/332–3023).

POSTAL RATES

In Belize, an airmail letter to the United States is 30¢, a postcard, 15 cents; to Europe, 37½¢ for a letter, 20 cents for a postcard.

A letter or postcard from Guatemala to anywhere in the Americas costs 40¢; to Europe, Asia, and the Pacific it's 80¢.

RECEIVING MAIL

In Belize you can receive mail sent Poste Restante at the **main post office** (✉ Front St., at northern edge of swing bridge, Belize City, Belize, ☎ 27/2201), where it will be kept for at least a month (bring a passport or other I.D. to pick it up). The post office is open Monday–Thursday 8–5 and Friday 8–4:30. **American Express** (✉ Belize Global Travel, 41 Albert St., Belize City, Belize, ☎ 27/7363) handles mail for cardholders free of charge.

In Guatemala, travelers can receive mail addressed to Poste Restante Guatemala at the **main post office** (✉ Correos Central, 12 Calle between 7 and 8 avenidas, Zona 1, Guatemala City, Guatemala, ☎ no phone). American Express cardholders or traveler's check holders can use the **American Express office** (✉ Avenida La Reforma 9–00, Zona 9, Guatemala City, Guatemala, ☎ 331–1311); you must show your card or check when you pick up your mail.

SHIPPING PARCELS

In Belize, parcels have to be standard, wrapped in brown paper, and, if you are in Belize City, sent from a special post office.

In Guatemala, it's safer to use a major shipping service like UPS, or a smaller service like Quick Shopping.

➤ SHIPPING CONTACTS: **Belize City parcel post office** (Church St., next to BTL offices, ⊙ Mon.–Thurs. 8–noon, 1–4:30, Fri. 8–noon, 1–4). **Quick Shopping** (✉ 6 Calle Poniente 27, Antigua, Guatemala, ☎ 332–0697). **UPS** (✉ 4 Calle 6–56, Zona 9, Guatemala City, ☎ 331–2421).

MONEY MATTERS

There are two ways of looking at the prices in Belize: either it's one of the cheapest countries in the Caribbean or it's one of the most expensive countries in Central America. A good hotel room for two will cost you upward of $100; a budget one, as little as $10. A meal in one of the more expensive restaurants will cost $25–$35 for one, but you can eat lobster and salad in a small seafood restaurant for as little as $10–$15 or the classic Creole dish of stew chicken and rice and beans for $5. Prices are highest in Belize City and Ambergris Caye. Taxi service between towns may start at $30.

Guatemala can be remarkably inexpensive, especially in the highlands, but prices for first-class hotels approach those in developed countries. Trips into remote parts of the jungle or specialty travel like river rafting and deep-sea fishing are also relatively expensive. Sample costs: a cup of coffee, 4 quetzals; bottle of beer, 8 quetzals; ½-km taxi ride, 25 quetzals. Prices throughout this guide are given for adults. Substantially reduced fees are almost always available for children, students, and senior citizens. For information on taxes, *see* Taxes, *below.*

ATMS

Most Belizean banks have ATMs, but except for Barclays Bank ATMs, the machines generally don't accept foreign cards.

In Guatemala, banks with a "Credomatic" symbol accept most ATM cards, including those in the Cirrus/MasterCard and PLUS/Visa networks. Ask your home bank to recommend a bank in Guatemala for you to use, as it may have a particular "sister bank." Also, your PIN should

THE GOLD GUIDE / SMART TRAVEL TIPS

have no more than four digits; you can change your PIN at your local branch.

CREDIT CARDS

Throughout this guide, the following abbreviations are used: **AE,** American Express; **DC,** Diner's Club; **D,** Discover; **MC,** MasterCard; and **V,** Visa.

CURRENCY

The Belizean dollar (BZ$) has for many years been fixed to the U.S. dollar at a rate of BZ$2 per dollar. Most tourist prices are quoted in U.S. dollars, but smaller restaurants and hotels tend to work in BZ$. Because misunderstandings can happen, if it's not clear, **always ask which currency is being used.** When leaving Belize, you can exchange Belizean currency back to U.S. dollars (up to $100 U.S.) at Belize Bank at the international airport, or use whatever you have left to pay the airport exit tax of BZ$25.

The quetzal, named after Guatemala's national bird, is divided into 100 centavos. There are 1-, 5-, 10-, and 25-centavo coins, and a 1 queztal coin. Bills come in denominations of ½, 1, 5, 10, 20, 50, and 100 quetzals. In January 2000, the quetzal was worth about 13¢; or 7.75 quetzals to the U.S. dollar. Unless otherwise stated, prices are quoted in U.S. dollar amounts.

CURRENCY EXCHANGE

If you're not from the United States, it's best to convert your money to U.S. currency before arriving in Belize. Other currencies, including Canadian dollars, are not widely accepted in Belize, and you'll have a hard time finding a place that will exchange your money. Since the U.S. dollar is accepted almost everywhere, you'll just need a little Belizean currency to walk around with, so don't change much. When paying in U.S. dollars, though, you may get change in Belize or U.S. currency, or in both. For those who put it off at home, money changers at the border usually give 2:1 rate for U.S. dollars, though at times they offer $2.10 or higher. Banks generally exchange at $1.98 or less. The best place to get Mexican pesos is in Corozal, where the exchange rate is quite good. At the

Guatemala border near Benque Viejo del Carmen, you can exchange Belizean or U.S. dollars for quetzales—money changers will approach you on the Belize side.

In Guatemala, it seems, U.S. currency is never turned away in shops and restaurants. You can exchange cash on the street in the area around the central post office for slightly more than the official rate, but it's illegal, and you run the risk of being short-changed.

For the most favorable rates, **change money through banks in Guatemala.** Although ATM transaction fees may be higher abroad than at home, ATM rates are excellent because they are based on wholesale rates offered only by major banks. You won't do as well at exchange booths in airports, in hotels, in restaurants, or in stores.

➤ EXCHANGE SERVICES: **International Currency Express** (☎ 888/278–6628 for orders, www.foreignmoney.com). **Thomas Cook Currency Services** (☎ 800/287–7362 for telephone orders and retail locations, www.us.thomascook.com).

TRAVELER'S CHECKS

Do you need traveler's checks? It depends on where you're headed. If you're going to rural areas and small towns, go with cash; traveler's checks are best used in cities. Lost or stolen checks can usually be replaced within 24 hours. To ensure a speedy refund, buy your own traveler's checks—don't let someone else pay for them: irregularities like this can cause delays. The person who bought the checks should make the call to request a refund.

OUTDOORS & SPORTS

Nearly everything worth doing in Belize involves the outdoors. Diving and snorkeling are the number-one reasons why visitors come to the cayes and coast of Belize. Fishing for tarpon, bonefish, and sailfish is another good reason to visit. Birding, wildlife spotting and photography, and hiking are world-class attractions of Belize's mainland rain forests, lagoons, and landscapes. Canoeing and sea kayaking are growing sports in Belize. A mountains-to-the-sea canoe race is held each year in March. With miles of limestone caves, Belize has some of the best caving in the region, and mountain biking is popular in the Mountain Pine Ridge and elsewhere. Until recently, you couldn't play golf in Belize, but in late 1999 a championship 18-hole course opened in a spectacular setting on Caye Chapel. Tennis is not big in Belize, but you can play on courts on Ambergris Caye, on Caye Chapel, and in Placencia. Among Belizeans, soccer and basketball are the most popular sports, and bicycle racing has many fans. The British colonial legacy didn't succeed in leaving many cricket fans, but the game is played here and there in Belize.

Hiking is surely Guatemala's greatest outdoor attraction. Whether its up the steaming black shoulder of an active volcano or amid Maya ruins and dense rain forest, a pair of sturdy shoes and a sense of adventure are well-rewarded in Guatemala. More specialized eco-tourism is expanding, with a few tour operators offering bird-watching, white-water rafting, caving, and mountain-biking trips. The Pacific coast has what many consider to be the best billfishing in the world, and world records have been set here. Soccer and basketball are popular sports among Guatemalans.

PACKING

Pack light—baggage carts are scarce at Central American airports and international luggage limits are increasingly tight—and bring casual, comfortable, hand-washable clothing. T-shirts and shorts are acceptable near the beach and in tourist areas; modest attire is appropriate in smaller towns and the same long sleeves, pants, or mid-calf skirt will protect your skin from the ferocious sun and mosquitoes. Bring a hat to block the sun from your face and neck. If you're heading into the Cayo, the mountains, or the highlands, bring a light sweater, a jacket, and something warm to sleep in, as nights and early mornings can be chilly. Sturdy sneakers or hiking shoes or boots with rubber soles for rocky underwater surfaces are essential. A pair of san-

dals (preferably ones that can be worn in the water) are good, too.

Be sure to bring insect repellent, sunscreen, sunglasses, and an umbrella. Other handy items include tissues, a plastic water bottle, and a flashlight (for occasional power outages or use in areas without street lights). A mosquito net for those roughing it is essential. Snorkelers should consider bringing their own equipment if there's room in the suitcase. Sand and high humidity are enemies of your camera equipment. To protect it, consider packing your gear in plastic ziplock bags. Also bring your own condoms and tampons. You won't find either easily or in familiar brands.

In your carry-on luggage, **pack an extra pair of eyeglasses or contact lenses** and **enough of any medication you take** to last the entire trip. You may also ask your doctor to write a spare prescription using the drug's generic name, since brand names may vary from country to country. In luggage to be checked, **never pack prescription drugs or valuables.** To avoid customs delays, carry medications in their original packaging. And don't forget to carry with you the addresses of offices that handle refunds of lost traveler's checks.

CHECKING LUGGAGE

How many carry-on bags you can bring with you is up to the airline. Most allow two, but not always, so make sure that everything you carry aboard will fit under your seat or in the overhead bin, and get to the gate early. Note that if you have a seat at the back of the plane, you'll probably board first, while the overhead bins are still empty. Two smaller bags are better than one big suitcase when traveling to the Belizean cayes, as they fit better in the smaller planes and boats.

If you are flying internationally, note that baggage allowances may be determined not by piece but by weight—generally 88 pounds (40 kg) in first class, 66 pounds (30 kg) in business class, and 44 pounds (20 kg) in economy.

Airline liability for baggage is limited to $1,250 per person on flights within the United States. On international flights it amounts to $9.07 per pound or $20 per kilogram for checked baggage (roughly $640 per 70-pound bag) and $400 per passenger for unchecked baggage. You can buy additional coverage at check-in for about $10 per $1,000 of coverage, but it excludes a rather extensive list of items, shown on your airline ticket.

Before departure, **itemize your bags' contents** and their worth, and label the bags with your name, address, and phone number. (If you use your home address, cover it so potential thieves can't see it readily.) Inside each bag, **pack a copy of your itinerary**. At check-in, **make sure that each bag is correctly tagged** with the destination airport's three-letter code. If your bags arrive damaged or fail to arrive at all, file a written report with the airline before leaving the airport.

PASSPORTS & VISAS

When traveling internationally, **carry your passport** even if you don't need one (it's always the best form of I.D.) and **make two photocopies of the data page** (one for someone at home and another for you, carried separately from your passport). If you lose your passport, promptly call the nearest embassy or consulate and the local police.

ENTERING BELIZE AND GUATEMALA

To enter Belize and Guatemala, only a valid passport is necessary for citizens of Australia, Canada, the EU, New Zealand, and the United States—no visa is required. If, upon arrival, the customs official asks how long you expect to stay, give the longest period you might stay—you may legally stay in each country for up to 30 days—otherwise the official may endorse your passport with a shorter period. You can renew your entry permits for up to six months for a fee of $12.50 per month. If you're young and entering Belize by land from Mexico, you may be asked to prove you have enough money to cover your stay. If you enter Guatemala by land, you may need a multiple-entry visa, available at the Guatemalan consulate in your home country.

PASSPORT OFFICES

The best time to apply for a passport or to renew one is in fall and winter. Before any trip, check your passport's expiration date, and, if necessary, renew it as soon as possible. Consider renewing by mail or check out express renewal services near you or on the Internet that might reduce the time and hassle. Officially, Belize and some airlines flying here require that your passport be valid for six months past your arrival date, though this rule may not be enforced.

➤ AUSTRALIAN CITIZENS: **Australian Passport Office** (☎ 131–232, www.dfat.gov.au/passports).

➤ CANADIAN CITIZENS: **Passport Office** (☎ 819/994–3500 or 800/567–6868, www.dfait-maeci.gc.ca/passport).

➤ NEW ZEALAND CITIZENS: **New Zealand Passport Office** (☎ 04/494–0700, www.passports.govt.nz).

➤ U.K. CITIZENS: **London Passport Office** (☎ 0990/210–410) for fees and documentation requirements and to request an emergency passport.

➤ U.S. CITIZENS: **National Passport Information Center** (☎ 900/225–5674; calls are 35¢ per minute for automated service, $1.05 per minute for operator service).

REST ROOMS

You won't find many public rest rooms in Belize, but hotels and restaurants usually have clean, modern rest rooms with American-style—indeed American-made—toilets. Hot-water showers in Belize often are the on-demand type, powered by butane gas.

Rest rooms in Guatemala use Western-style toilets, although bathroom tissue generally should not be flushed but discarded in a basket beside the toilet.

SAFETY

There is crime in Belize City, but it rarely involves visitors. When it does, Belize has a particularly rapid justice system for such crimes, meaning that the offender often gets a trial within hours and, if convicted, can be sent to prison ("the Hattieville Ramada") the same day. Tourist police patrol Fort

George and other areas where visitors convene. If you avoid walking around at night (except in well-lit parts of the Fort George area), you should have no problems. Outside of Belize City, and possibly the rougher parts of Dangriga and Orange Walk Town, you'll find Belize to perfectly safe and friendly.

Pickpockets are probably the most common threat in Guatemala—but by using common sense and taking certain precautions, crime shouldn't interfere with your trip. Pickpockets and other thieves typically work in pairs or threes; one will distract or disrupt you in some way, while another slips a hand into your pocket or backpack during the commotion. This typically happens in a crowded market or street corner, especially if your hands are full with your luggage or purchases. They are so skilled, you often you won't realize you've been robbed until quite some time later. If you know you'll be passing through a crowded area (entering or leaving the bus terminal, for example) carry only the money you'll need for the bus or taxi to your hotel, and stow the rest in your money belt, and carry your backpack in front of you. If you have a homebase, just bring a day pack along—you'll be significantly less vulnerable without a lot of stuff. There have been a few ugly incidents of robbery and rape of foreign tourists on buses (1998), so it's best to avoid traveling at night, particularly in remote areas. If you're returning late to your hotel, avoid going alone, and use a taxi—if you have to ring the bell to enter the hotel, ask the driver to wait until you are safely inside.

In May 2000, passengers aboard a water taxi traveling from Puerto Barrios, Guatemala, en route to Punta Gorda, Belize, were shot at. Six were killed, and one American aboard was injured. It's suspected that increased tensions, due to the border crossings of Guatemalans into Belize, are the cause, since no one boarded the boat, nor was anyone robbed. Consider flying between the two countries instead.

LOCAL SCAMS

Most Central Americans are extremely honest and trustworthy. It's not uncommon for a vendor to chase you down if you accidentally leave without your change. That said, most organized scams arise with tours and packages, in which you're sold a ticket that turns out to be bogus. **Arrange all travel through a legitimate agency,** and always get a receipt. If a problem does arise, the Belize Tourism Board or INGUAT may be able to help mediate the conflict.

WOMEN IN BELIZE AND GUATEMALA

Many women travel alone or in small groups in Belize without any problems. Machismo is not as much a factor in the former British Honduras as it is in Latin countries in the region. Unfortunately, in the past, Guatemala has been the site of some disturbing assaults on women. These have occurred on buses, usually late at night in remote areas. Women should avoid making such trips, especially alone. More common is catcalling, which is typically more of an annoyance than a legitimate threat, and most women, locals and foreigners alike, try to brush it off. That said, however, women make up a large percentage of the travelers in Guatemala, and the vast majority have positive experiences.

SENIOR-CITIZEN TRAVEL

Discounts for seniors in Belize and Guatemala are pretty rare, unless you travel with a North American tour company or educational program that offers them. Of course, it doesn't hurt to ask, following the protocol used at home: to qualify for age-related discounts, **mention your senior-citizen status up front** when booking hotel reservations (not when checking out) and before you're seated in restaurants (not when paying the bill). When renting a car, ask about promotional car-rental discounts, which can be cheaper than senior-citizen rates.

➤ EDUCATIONAL PROGRAMS: **Elderhostel** (⊠ 75 Federal St., 3rd floor, Boston, MA 02110, ☎ 877/426–8056, FAX 877/426–2166, www.elderhostel.org). **Interhostel** (⊠ University of New Hampshire, 6 Garrison Ave., Durham, NH 03824, ☎ 603/862–1147 or 800/733–9753, FAX 603/862–1113, learn.dce@unh.edu, www.learn.unh.edu).

SHOPPING

If you're a shop-till-you-drop type, you won't be happy in Belize or Guatemala. Stores at their best offer mundane merchandise at prices higher than at home. Belize imports most of what it consumes, and import duties and shipping charges add to the cost. Guatemala, on the other hand, has a strong arts and handicraft tradition, and most shops focus on these goods. But there's nothing in the way of fashionable stores with the exception of one or two shops in Guatemala City and Antigua.

KEY DESTINATIONS

Ambergris Caye, an island that harks back to the way the Caribbean used to be, is Belize's most popular destination, with good hotels, restaurants, and water sports, plus streets still made of sand. The Cayo District, Belize's "Wild West," with jungle lodges, Maya ruins, butterfly farms, and all types of activities including river tubing and caving, is the second-most-visited. The Placencia peninsula, the third-hottest spot, is a little bit of the South Pacific on the southern mainland, with a growing number of excellent small hotels and restaurants on a 16-mi stretch of sandy beach. Stirring things up is the somewhat remote Caye Caulker and the rural Orange Walk District, two up-and-coming destinations to consider before everyone else does.

Guatemala's main draws are the Maya ruins of Tikal. Interest in the country's unspoiled natural beauty, present-day indigenous people, markets, and culture often figure in as well. Thus, most head to Flores, Tikal, via Río Dulce to the north, and Antigua, Lake Atitlán, and Quetzaltenango (Xela) to the south. Guatemala City is typically used as a business and transportation hub.

SMART SOUVENIRS

Belize does not have the rich crafts tradition of its neighbors Guatemala and Mexico. Gift shops offer the usual collection of off-color T-shirts and bad-taste gewgaws, but there are handicrafts, furniture, Belize music (punta rock), local foods and drinks, and other items that make good souvenirs or gifts from Belize. Don't buy items that contribute to the destruction of endangered wildlife or the reef, such as items made from coral, including black coral and turtle or tortoise shells. Some gift shops in Belize also carry high-quality textiles and other items from Guatemala. Rum, Belikin beer, Marie Sharp's hot sauces and jams, and hammocks make good buys.

For souvenir seekers, Guatemala's handicrafts, called *artesanía* or *típica* always draw the most attention, particularly the handwoven tapestries, carved wooden masks, handblown glass, and traditional indigenous clothing, such as women's *huipiles*. Such goods are beautiful and inexpensive, and they're sold throughout the country. Miniature wooden or ceramic frames make great little keepsakes, as do small hand-painted wooden jewelry boxes or masks. More exclusive items include jade carvings and jewelry, antiques, and particularly complex weavings, especially those made of silk instead of cotton, and are best purchased in Guatemala City, Antigua, and to a lesser extent Quetzaltenango.

WATCH OUT

Be wary of purchasing items that may have been pilfered from archeological sites, particularly stone carvings. They may be confiscated when you leave the country, and perhaps worse, your souvenir shopping aids in the destruction of irreplaceable historical and cultural relics. The export of Maya artifacts is strictly prohibited.

SIGHTSEEING GUIDES

In Belize, all tourist guides are required to take a series of training courses and must be licensed by the government. If in doubt about the credibility of a guide, ask to see the guide's license.

A guide's license in Guatemala means little. Here, nothing beats a personal recommendation. Ask other travelers first, and your hotel second. Otherwise, stick to the established agencies to avoid getting cheated. Tikal is an exception: official guides wear a "Carnet de Guía de Turismo" (Tourist Guide I.D.), and can be hired at the visitors center. Many hotels also arrange guided tours to the ruins and surrounding sights.

STUDENTS IN BELIZE AND GUATEMALA

Central America is a fantastic place for students and those on a budget. You can live well on $15 a day in Guatemala. Belize is more expensive; expect to shell out $35–$45 a day. There are no youth hostels as such, but Guatemala and Belize are packed with cheap lodging possibilities. Any option near the bus station is usually affordable. One of the cheapest ways to spend the night, of course, is camping, and as long as you have your own tent it's easy to set up camp just about anywhere. To get good tips and advice on traveling within a budget, look for informational bulletin boards and talk to other backpackers.

➤ I.D.s & Services: **Council Travel** (CIEE; ✉ 205 E. 42nd St., 14th floor, New York, NY 10017, ☎ 212/822–2700 or 888/268–6245, FAX 212/822–2699, info@councilexchanges.org, www.councilexchanges.org) for mail orders only, in the United States. **Travel Cuts** (✉ 187 College St., Toronto, Ontario M5T 1P7, ☎ 416/979–2406 or 800/667–2887 in Canada, www.travelcuts.com).

TAXES

The Belizean government levies a hotel tax of 7% and an airport-departure tax of US$18.75, which must be paid in cash (in either U.S. or Belize dollars) when you leave the country. An on-land border fee is US$10, and is charged at the Guatemalan and Mexican borders, even for day trips. In this case, you can **ask that your border-crossing fee be applied toward your airport-departure tax** as credit. For most consumer goods and services, including restaurant meals, tours, rental cars, and diving, there is an 8% sales tax.

Most Guatemalan hotels and some tourist restaurants charge an additional 10% tourist tax. The airport-departure tax is US$20.

VALUE-ADDED TAX

The unpopular Belize Value Added Tax has been repealed. Guatemalan stores, restaurants, and hotels charge a 10% V.A.T.

TELEPHONES

AREA & COUNTRY CODES

The country code for Belize is **501**; for Guatemala, **502**. The country code is 1 for the United States, 61 for Australia, 64 for New Zealand, and 44 for the United Kingdom.

DIRECTORY & OPERATOR ASSISTANCE

To obtain directory information for Belize from the United States, dial ☎ 412/555–1515. For Guatemalan operator assistance (Spanish) dial 121; for information (Spanish) dial 124.

INTERNATIONAL CALLS

When dialing a Belize number from abroad, drop the initial 0 from the Belize area code. Belize telephone numbers shown in this guide do not include the initial 0, so when calling from the United States, dial 011-501-XX/XXXX. Calls to Guatemala don't require this.

In Belize you can place international calls from a Belize Telecommunications Limited (BTL) office, located in most towns including Belize City. Offices are open Monday–Saturday 8 AM–9 PM, Sunday 8–6.

In Guatemala, there are direct phones to AT&T U.S. operators in the airport and at Telgua, the telephone company of Guatemala, located in most towns. They generally close for a few hours at lunch. You can make phone calls and send faxes inexpensively in Antigua at the Villa San Francisco, in Panajachel at the Grapevine, and in Quezaltenango at the Tecun Saloon.

➤ International Calling Contacts: **Belize Telecommunications Limited (BTL)** (✉ 1 Church St., ☎ 23/2868). **Grapevine** (✉ Calle Santander, Panajachel, Guatemala). **Tecun Saloon** (✉ Pasaje Enriquez, off the central park, Quetzaltenango, Guatemala). **Telgua** (7 Avenida, between Calles 12 and 13, Zona 1, Guatemala City). **Villa San Francisco** (✉ 1 Avenida Sur 15, Antigua, Guatemala).

➤ Resources: **BTL** (☎ 27/7960, www.belizeweb.com, sales@btl.net). **Telgua** (www.telgua.com.gt).

THE GOLD GUIDE / SMART TRAVEL TIPS

CELLULAR PHONES

You can rent a cell phone in Belize starting at $2 a day. Check at the BTL booth just outside the arrival lounge at the international airport, or contact BTL (☞ *above*). In Guatemala, you can rent a phone, not to mention a car, from Avis (☞ *above*).

E-MAIL AND INTERNET ACCESS

Belize is wired: most hotels now have e-mail and Web access, and some will permit guests to send or receive e-mail for a small fee. Internet cafés can be found in San Pedro, Belize City, San Ignacio, Placencia, Punta Gorda, and other areas. Rates are usually around $10 an hour. By law BTL is the only Internet Service Provider in Belize. Service is usually good, but rates are much higher than in the United States. Contact BTL to arrange short-term Internet access.

Business-friendly hotels in Guatemala have Internet access in their rooms and in computer rooms where they charge guest by the hour for access. Cybercafés are everywhere, too, and are best for checking e-mail and for surfing.

LONG-DISTANCE SERVICES

AT&T, MCI, and Sprint access codes make calling long distance relatively convenient, but you may find the local access number blocked in many hotel rooms. First ask the hotel operator to connect you. If the hotel operator balks, ask for an international operator, or dial the international operator yourself. One-way to improve your odds of getting connected to your long-distance carrier is to travel with more than one company's calling card (a hotel may block Sprint, for example, but not MCI). If all else fails, call from a pay phone. MCI WorldPhone is not available in Belize.

➤ BELIZE ACCESS CODES: **AT&T** (☎ 811 from pay phones or 555 from hotels). **MCI** (☎ 815 from pay phones or 557 from hotels). **Sprint International Access** (☎ 812 from pay phones or 556 from hotels).

➤ GUATEMALA ACCESS CODES: **AT&T** (☎ 190). **MCI** (☎ 189). **Sprint International Access** (☎ 195).

PHONE CARDS

In Belize you can buy phone cards from any BTL office for amounts from BZ$5–BZ$50. Guatemala's public pay phones use prepaid calling cards, which you can purchase at small grocery markets, pharmacies, and Telgua offices. Ask for a *tarjeta telephónica*. They come in denominations of 20, 30, and 100 quetzales; calls within Guatemala cost 15 to 50 centavos per minute.

PUBLIC PHONES

Belize has a good nationwide phone system. There are pay phones on the street in the main towns. Local calls cost BZ25¢; calls to other districts, BZ$1. Drop the area code for calls within the same one.

In Guatemala, it's easier to make local calls from your hotel. Telgua is the national phone company, and every decent-size town has a Telgua office, most of which are open daily 7 AM–midnight. You usually have to wait to submit your number to the cashier, and then wait again to be called to use a phone. Do not use the black, red, or blue wall-mounted phones with signs that read "Free Collect Call." They charge a whopping $10 per minute and have a five-minute minimum.

TIME

Belize and Guatemala time is the same as U.S. Central Standard Time. Daylight Savings Time is not observed.

TIPPING

Belize restaurants rarely add a service charge, so in better restaurants, tip 10–15% of the total bill. At inexpensive restaurants, leave small change or tip 10%. Many hotels and resorts add a service charge, usually 10%, to bills, so at these places additional tipping is not necessary. In general, Belizeans tend not to look for tips. It's not customary to tip taxi drivers.

In Guatemala, restaurant bills do not typically include gratuities; 10% is customary. Bellhops and maids expect tips only in the expensive hotels. Guards who show you around ruins and locals who help you find hotels or give you little tours should also be tipped. Children will often charge a quetzal to let you take their photo (☞ Cameras & Photography, *above*.)

TOURS & PACKAGES

Because everything is prearranged on a prepackaged tour or independent vacation, you'll spend less time planning—and often get it all at a good price.

BOOKING WITH AN AGENT

Travel agents are excellent resources. But it's a good idea to collect brochures from several agencies as some agents' suggestions may be influenced by relationships with tour and package firms that reward them for volume sales. If you have a special interest, **find an agent with expertise in that area**; ASTA (☞ Travel Agencies, *below*) has a database of specialists worldwide.

Make sure your travel agent knows the accommodations and other services of the place they're recommending. Ask about the hotel's location, room size, beds, and whether it has a pool, room service, or programs for children, if you care about these. Has your agent been there in person or sent others whom you can contact?

Do some homework on your own, too: local tourism boards can provide information about lesser known and small-niche operators, some of which may sell only direct.

BUYER BEWARE

Each year consumers are stranded or lose their money when tour operators—even large ones with excellent reputations—go out of business. So **check out the operator.** Ask several travel agents about its reputation, and try to **book with a company that has a consumer-protection program.** (Look for information in the company's brochure.) In the United States, members of the National Tour Association and the United States Tour Operators Association are required to set aside funds to cover your payments and travel arrangements in the event that the company defaults. It's also a good idea to choose a company that participates in the American Society of Travel Agents' Tour Operator Program

(TOP); ASTA will act as mediator in any disputes between you and your tour operator.

Remember that the more your package or tour includes the better you can predict the ultimate cost of your vacation. Make sure you know exactly what is covered, and **beware of hidden costs.** Are taxes, tips, and transfers included? Entertainment and excursions? These can add up.

➤ TOUR-OPERATOR RECOMMENDATIONS: **American Society of Travel Agents** (☞ Travel Agencies, *below*). **National Tour Association** (NTA; ⊠ 546 E. Main St., Lexington, KY 40508, ☎ 606/226–4444 or 800/682–8886, www.ntaonline.com). **United States Tour Operators Association** (USTOA; ⊠ 342 Madison Ave., Suite 1522, New York, NY 10173, ☎ 212/599–6599 or 800/468–7862, FAX 212/599–6744, ustoa@aol.com, www.ustoa.com).

GROUP TOURS

Among companies that sell tours to Belize and Guatemala, the following are nationally known, have a proven reputation, and offer plenty of options. The classifications used below represent different price categories, and you'll probably encounter these terms when talking to a travel agent or tour operator. The key difference is usually in accommodations, which run from budget to better, and better-yet to best.

➤ SUPER-DELUXE: **Abercrombie & Kent** (⊠ 1520 Kensington Rd., Oak Brook, IL 60521-2141, ☎ 630/954–2944 or 800/323–7308, FAX 630/954–3324). **Travcoa** (⊠ Box 2630, 2350 S.E. Bristol St., Newport Beach, CA 92660, ☎ 714/476–2800 or 800/992–2003, FAX 714/476–2538, www.travcoa.com).

➤ FIRST-CLASS: **Brendan Tours** (⊠ 15137 Califa St., Van Nuys, CA 91411, ☎ 818/785–9696 or 800/421–8446, FAX 818/902–9876). **Caravan Tours** (⊠ 401 N. Michigan Ave., Chicago, IL 60611, ☎ 312/321–9800 or 800/227–2826, FAX 312/321–9845).

PACKAGES

Like group tours, independent vacation packages are available from major tour operators and airlines. The companies listed below offer vacation packages in a broad price range.

➤ AIR/HOTEL: **Tropical Travel** (☎ 800/365–6232).

➤ FROM THE U.K.: **Journey Latin America** (☎ 0208/747–8315, FAX 0208/742–1312). **South American Experience** (☎ 0207/976–5511, FAX 0207/976–6908).

THEME TRIPS

➤ ADVENTURE: **Adventure Center** (✉ 1311 63rd St., #200, Emeryville, CA 94608, ☎ 510/654–1879 or 800/227–8747, FAX 510/654–4200, trip-info@adventurecenter.com, www.ad-venturecenter.com). **American Wilderness Experience** (✉ Box 1486, Boulder, CO 80306, ☎ 800/444–0099, FAX 303/444–3999, www.gorp-travel.com). **Himalayan Travel** (✉ 110 Prospect St., Stamford, CT 06901, ☎ 203/359–3711 or 800/225–2380, FAX 203/359–3669, www.gorp.com/himtravel/htm). **International Expeditions** (✉ One Environs Park., Helena, AL 35080, ☎ 205/428–1714 or 800/633–4734, FAX 205/428–1714). **International Zoological Expeditions** (✉ 210 Washington St., Sherborn, MA 01770, ☎ 503/655–1461 or 800/543–5343, FAX 503/655–4445). **Mountain Travel-Sobek** (✉ 6420 Fairmount Ave., El Cerrito, CA 94530, ☎ 510/527–8100 or 888/687–6235, FAX 510/525–7710, info@mtsobek.com, www.mtsobek.com). **Slickrock Adventures** (✉ Box 1400, Moab, UT 84532, ☎ 800/390–5715, FAX 435/259–6996). **Wilderness Travel** (✉ 1102 Ninth St., Berkeley, CA 94710, ☎ 510/558–2488 or 800/368–2794, info@wildernesstravel.com, www.wildernesstravel.com).

➤ ART AND ARCHAEOLOGY: **Archaeological Conservancy** (✉ 5301 Central Ave. NE, #1218, Albuquerque, NM 87108, ☎ 505/266–1540, FAX 505/266–0311, www.gorp.com/archcons). **Far Horizons Archaeological & Cultural Trips** (✉ Box 91900, Albuquerque, NM 87199, ☎ 505/343–9400 or 800/552–4575, FAX 505/343–8076, journey@farhorizon.com, www.farhorizon.com). **Meetings and Incentives in LatinAmerica (MILA)**

(✉ 100 S. Greenleaf Ave., Gurnee, IL 60031, ☎ 847/249–2111 or 800/367–7378, FAX 847/249–2772, mi-lalatin@aol.com, www.milatours.com or www.mayapath.com). **Sanborn's Viva Tours** (✉ 2015 S. 10th St., Box 519, McAllen, TX 78505, ☎ 956/682–9872 or 800/395–8482, FAX 210/682–0016, santours@hiline.net, www.sanborns.com).

➤ BIRD-WATCHING: **Victor Emanuel Nature Tours** (✉ Box 33008, Austin, TX 78764, ☎ 512/328–5221 or 800/328–8368, FAX 512/328–2919, info@ventbird.com, www.ventbird.com).

➤ FISHING: **Artmarina** (1390 S. Dixie Hwy, Suite 2221, Miami, FL 33146, ☎ 305/663–3553, FAX 305/666–6445, fish@artmarina.com, www.artmarina.com). **Fishing International** (✉ Box 2132, Santa Rosa, CA 95405, ☎ 707/542–4242 or 800/950–4242, FAX 707/546–3474, fishint@wco.com, www.fishinginternational.com). **Rod & Reel Adventures** (✉ 566 Thomson La., Copperopolis, CA 95228, ☎ 209/785–0444 or 800/356–6982, FAX 209/785–0447, info@rodreeladventures.com, www.rodreeladventures.com).

➤ SCUBA DIVING AND SNORKELING: **Go Diving** (✉ 5610 Rowland Rd. #100, USA, MN 55343, ☎ 612/931–9101 or 800/328–5285, FAX 612/931–0209). **Rothschild Dive Safaris** (✉ 900 West End Ave., #1B, New York, NY 10025, ☎ 212/662–4858 or 800/359–0747, FAX 212/749–6172). **Scuba Diving & Snorkeling Worldwide** (✉ Box 471899, San Francisco, CA 94147, ☎ 415/922–5807, FAX 415/922–5662). **Tropical Adventures** (✉ 111 2nd Ave. N, Seattle, WA 98109, ☎ 206/441–3483 or 800/247–3483, FAX 206/441–5431).

➤ HIKING/TREKKING/WALKING: **Backroads** (✉ 801 Cedar St., Berkeley, CA 94710, ☎ 510/527–1555 or 800/462–2848, FAX 510/527–1444. **Country Walkers** (✉ Box 180, Waterbury, VT 05676-0180, ☎ 802/244–1387 or 800/464–9255, FAX 802/244–5661). **Quetzalventures** (✉ 4 Calle Poniente 38, Antigua, Guatemala, ☎ 502/406–8709 or 502/406–8710, www.quetza-lventures.com).

➤ YACHT CHARTERS: **Ocean Voyages** (✉ 1709 Bridgeway, Sausalito, CA

94965, ☎ 415/332–4681, ☒ 415/
332–7460). **TMM (Belize) Ltd.** (☒
Coconut Dr., San Pedro, Belize, ☎
501/26–3016, ☒ 501/26–3072).
Windsong Charters (☒ 926 West 6th
Ave., Denver, CO 80204, ☎ 303/983-
3739, ☒ 303/623–7352).

TRAIN TRAVEL

There is no train service in Belize or
Guatemala.

TRAVEL AGENCIES

A good travel agent puts your needs
first. Look for an agency that has
been in business at least five years,
emphasizes customer service, and has
someone on staff who specializes in
your destination. In addition, **make
sure the agency belongs to a profes-
sional trade organization.** The American Society of Travel Agents (ASTA),
with 27,000 agents in some 170 countries, is the largest and most influential
in the field. Operating under the motto
"Integrity in Travel," it maintains and
enforces a strict code of ethics and will
step in to help mediate any agent-client
disputes if necessary. ASTA also maintains a Web site that includes a directory of agents. (If a travel agency is
also acting as your tour operator, *see*
Buyer Beware *in* Tours & Packages,
above.)

➤ LOCAL AGENT REFERRALS: **American Society of Travel Agents** (ASTA;
☎ 800/965–2782 24-hr hot line, ☒
703/684–8319, www.astanet.com).
Association of British Travel Agents
(☒ 68–71 Newman St., London W1P
4AH, ☎ 0207/637–2444, ☒ 0207/
637–0713, information@abta.co.uk,
www.abtanet.com). **Association of
Canadian Travel Agents** (☒ 1729
Bank St., Suite 201, Ottawa, Ontario
K1V 7Z5, ☎ 613/237–3657, ☒ 613/
521–0805, acta.ntl@sympatico.ca).
**Australian Federation of Travel
Agents** (☒ Level 3, 309 Pitt St.,
Sydney 2000, ☎ 02/9264–3299, ☒
02/9264–1085, www.afta.com.au).
**Travel Agents' Association of New
Zealand** (☒ Box 1888, Wellington
10033, ☎ 04/499–0104, ☒ 04/499–
0827, taanz@tiasnet.co.nz).

VISITOR INFORMATION

➤ TOURIST INFORMATION: **Belize
Tourist Board (BTB)** (☒ 421 7th
Ave., Suite 701, New York, NY

10001, ☎ 212/563–6011, ☒ 212/
563–6033). For information on
Guatemala, contact the **Guatemalan
Embassy** (☒ 2220 R Street NW,
Washington, DC 20008, ☎ 800/464–
8281, ☒ 561/241–7687). To contact
INGUAT, the tourism board in
Guatemala, call toll-free ☎ 801/464–
8281.

➤ IN THE UNITED KINGDOM: For
information on Belize, contact the
Belize High Commission (☒ 10
Harcourt House, 19A Cavendish Sq.,
London W1M 9AD, ☎ 0207/499–
9725). For information on
Guatemala, contact the **Guatemalan
Embassy** (☒ 13 Fawcett St., London
SW10 9HN, ☎ 0207/351–3042).

➤ U.S. GOVERNMENT ADVISORIES: **U.S.
Department of State** (☒ Overseas
Citizens Services Office, Room 4811
N.S., 2201 C St. NW, Washington,
DC 20520, ☎ 202/647–5225 for
interactive hot line, 301/946–4400
for computer bulletin board, ☒ 202/
647–3000 for interactive hot line);
enclose a self-addressed, stamped,
business-size envelope.

WEB SITES

Do check out the World Wide Web
when you're planning your trip.
You'll find everything from current
weather forecasts to virtual tours of
famous cities. Fodor's Web site,
www.fodors.com, is a great place to
start your online travels. When you
see a 🐚 in this book, go to
www.fodors.com/urls for an up-to-
date link to that destination's site.

For information on Belize, visit:
www.travelbelize.org,
www.turq.com/belizefirst/, or
www.belizenet.com. For destination-
specific information, check out
www.ambergriscaye.com, www.
belizex.com for the Cayo district;
www.placencia.com for Placencia;
and www.corozal.com for northern
Belize.

For general information on
Guatemala, go to
www.guatemala.travel.com.gt or
www.travel-guatemala.org.gt. For
information on Lake Atitlan destinations, also see www.atitlan.com or for
Río Dulce www.mayaparadise.com.

WHEN TO GO

The Central American climate has two basic seasons. The rainy season, in Spanish-speaking areas called *invierno* (winter), lasts from April through November; the dry season, called *verano* (summer), runs from November through April. However, by "dry season" Belizeans usually mean the months in late spring, before seasonal rains begin in June, when temperatures inland may reach 100 °F.

If you want to escape crowds and prices and don't mind getting very wet, visit in the rainy season. Though some restaurants may close and hotels may offer limited facilities, reservations are easy to get, even at top establishments, and you'll have the Maya ruins and beaches to yourself. Note that Guatemala's busiest time of the year is around Holy Week, from Palm Sunday to Easter Sunday, and that hotels in Antigua, Panajachel, and Chichicastenango fill up months ahead of time.

CLIMATE

Guatemala's Caribbean coast, for example, gets sweltering, humid weather with soaring temperatures, while the mountains in the northern Western Highlands (as in Belize's peaks) can have downright chilly evenings. Central America's rainy season is marked by sporadic downpours that occur without warning; rainfall is generally heavier in the afternoon than in the morning, so you may want to do the majority of your sightseeing and shopping in the morning, leaving the afternoon flexible. In Belize, only in the far south is the rainy season really wet; the Toledo district gets 160 inches or more of rain annually. However, northern Belize gets about the same amount of rain annually as Atlanta, Georgia, and on the cayes rain usually comes in brief squalls, after which the sun comes back out. The wet season on the cayes is often accompanied by lashing northerly winds known in Creole as Joe North. In a bad year, Joe North can turn into Hurricane Hattie. Hurricane season in the western Caribbean is June through November, but historically storms usually hit September through early November.

Central America's tropical temperatures generally hover between 70°F and 85°F. It's the high humidity that'll make you sweat. Remember to drink plenty of bottled water to avoid dehydration.

The following are average daily maximum and minimum temperatures for cities in Belize and Guatemala.

BELMOPAN, BELIZE

Jan.	81F	27C	May	87F	31C	Sept.	87F	31C
	67	19		75	24		74	23
Feb.	82F	28C	June	87F	31C	Oct.	86F	30C
	69	21		75	24		72	22
Mar.	84F	29C	July	87F	31C	Nov.	83F	28C
	71	22		75	24		68	20
Apr.	86F	30C	Aug.	88F	31C	Dec.	81F	27C
	74	23		75	24		73	23

GUATEMALA CITY, GUATEMALA

Jan.	73F	23C	May	84F	29C	Sept.	79F	26C
	52	11		60	16		60	16
Feb.	77F	25C	June	81F	27C	Oct.	76F	24C
	54	12		61	16		60	16
Mar.	81F	27C	July	78F	26C	Nov.	74F	24C
	57	14		60	16		57	14
Apr.	82F	28C	Aug.	79F	26C	Dec.	72F	22C
	58	14		60	16		55	13

➤ FORECASTS: **Weather Channel Connection** (☎ 900/932–8437), 95¢ per minute from a Touch-Tone phone.

1 DESTINATION: BELIZE AND GUATEMALA

A CENTRAL AMERICAN RENAISSANCE

N THIS PARTICULAR HISTORICAL MO-MENT, in a swiftly transforming part of the world, Belize and Guatemala emanate a kind of innocence inspiring thoughts of how life should always be. Many head for Belize in particular and never make the return trip, lulled by the serenity, the possibility, and the simple way of life. And yet, in Guatemala's case, there's a knowing sense of just how wrong things can go: unspeakably beautiful natural landscapes and a rich cultural heritage are paired with an unstable political past and unpredictable natural disasters. The most recent disaster starred Hurricane Mitch, which, in 1999, rubbed up against Belize and Guatemala, giving them a good scare, but then went on to devastate Honduras and Nicaragua to the south, leaving over 2 million homeless and 10,000 dead. It is this type of provocative contradiction that exemplifies Central America's allure, although, as in Costa Rica, the pendulum swings less between these poles in Belize and Guatemala than elsewhere on the Central American isthmus.

Belize has long been a world-class diving destination, second only to Australia's Great Barrier Reef, and was always more Caribbean in character than Central American, escaping Spanish domination and much of the exploitation endured by its neighbors largely because it lacked the gold and silver found in the rest of the continent. And Guatemala, while a popular destination for backpackers and Spanish-language students for decades, now teems with sophisticated travelers lured by a stable political climate, value for the dollar—particularly in the colorful markets—and, above all, the mystery of the incomparable Maya ruins. In this era of sociopolitical calm, visitors to these slow-paced and friendly countries are left stunned by the blue perfection of the Caribbean Sea around the cayes; the archeological remnants of a 2,000-year-old civilization that have not been carted off to museums but rather stand (or crumble) where the Maya left them; the seemingly untrodden sights of mind-blowing natural beauty; and the resilience of politically impassioned, ethnically diverse peoples who have survived colonization and, in Guatemala, civil war up through the late 20th century.

The history of Central America is one of oppression. The statues of Spanish conquistadors that adorn plazas throughout the continent serve as constant reminders of the roots of Central America's "civilization." An abundance of silver, gold, indigo, and trusting natives was Central America's constitutional curse. Spanish fortune seekers began colonization in the early 1500s, and Catholic priests followed in their footsteps, seeking to convert native souls. A central cathedral—constructed by the indigenous people themselves—was always the first building erected in a newly founded community. Only little Belize was spared Spanish colonization, although it was claimed by the Spanish in the 1520s, and, in the 20th century, folded into Guatemala as its "13th province." For years Guatemala claimed Belize as its own Alsace or Lorraine, and it's not so unusual to find maps that delineate Guatemala's boundaries all the way to the Atlantic. In 1991, Guatemalan president Serano recognized Belize's autonomy, but a small military British presence in Belize remains, perhaps just in case Guatemala changes its mind.

As for Guatemala, textbooks will tell you that independence was reinstated some 300 years after the Spanish, but U.S. intervention soon became its functional equivalent. In the early 1960s, Central America was thrust into a grisly descent of apocalyptic revolutionary violence. Caught up in a complex web of poverty, rapid urbanization, Uncle Sam's fatherly love, and wicked dictatorships for the next 20 years, Central America grabbed headlines throughout the world. By the late 1970s and throughout the 1980s, the situation was dangerous in Nicaragua, El Salvador, and Guatemala, and incipiently volatile in Honduras and Panama. During the Guatemalan government's "scorched-earth" counterinsurgency campaign in the early '80s, some 100,000 people—

mostly indigents—were tortured and mutilated and denied land ownership.

But a new, gentler wind has blown across the region in recent years. The transformation from AK-47s to ballots and from guerrilla warfare to political dialogue has given Central America a desperately needed break from the violence. What remains is still widespread poverty, a lack of employment opportunities, and nations struggling to reconstruct themselves and their democracies, *de cabo a rabo* (from head to toe). Even as some countries, such as Costa Rica, Belize, and Guatemala, are leading the race to recovery, it's likely that most of Central America will continue to feel the crippling effects of economic instability well into the new millennium. And yet the visitor will not find a defeated people. Life does not only go on in this troubled isthmus, it positively vibrates with humor and vitality. The tourist is usually welcomed with open arms; well, the local thinking goes, things must be getting better if the gringos are coming here to visit.

Historically, Central America has been somewhat of an oversight for the traveler sans backpack, although this is changing. As Belize and Guatemala follow Costa Rica's suit, dismissing corrupt political leaders, resolving the economic disparities that generated unrest, and uniformly implementing running water and electricity, more and more nature lovers and adventure seekers are waking up to the countries' redeeming qualities that have been here all along. Well-to-do travelers tired of the European tour are part of a growing visitor class, along with a new breed of excursion seekers whom we might call the what-to-do travelers, looking for unpretentious destinations in less-obvious lands.

At the top of the seven-country isthmus fusing North and South America, Guatemala, like Mexico, has both an Atlantic and Pacific coast, only the distance between them is just five hours by car. The sun beats down over lowland fields of sugarcane and orange groves that seem to expand, then melt away in the wavy, dreamlike heat. In the Guatemalan highlands, the invigorating mountain air provides a respite from the taxing tropical climate. The fertile volcanic soils of these looming cones yield most of the region's material wealth. In the cloud forests, evanescent vapors hover over the agricultural patchwork, lending an opaque, mystical twist. A mere sliver on the Caribbean just south of the Yucatán, Belize diffuses beyond the boundaries of land, incorporating cayes, atolls, and reefs into its surreal landscape. On a clear day, climb Tikal's Pyramid IV or on a clear night on the Belizean coast look up at the zodiac for a view so stimulating it leaves your knees weak.

The Caribbean or Mosquito coast hums its own tune. Here lives a polychromatic mix of indigenous, Ladino, and Afro-Caribbean folk called Garifuna, who proceed at their own, relaxed pace. The fate of this region has historically been linked to a yellow, oblong fruit—this is the original banana republic. Along the Central American coasts, foreign interests such as the United Fruit Company planted their flag on vast tracts of unused land, settling towns and enlisting locals for labor. Much of Guatemala's political instability can be traced to the actions of United Fruit, which in the 1940s was the nation's largest landholder, when they grossly underreported the value of usurped lands to avoid taxation. In 1954, then-president Jacobo Arbenz Guzmán expropriated the land, redistributing it to peasants, and compensating United Fruit according to the value the company itself had declared on its tax forms (touché!). United Fruit complained to Washington, and the U.S. staged a military invasion, forcing Arbenz from office and inaugurating a string of military dictators that would last until 1996. Agrarian and suffrage reforms instituted by Arbenz (and his predecessor Juan José Arévalo) were immediately rolled back, police and military repression grew, and by 1960 guerrilla opposition groups began to coalesce. Thus, in no small way, the United Fruit Company, responding to land reforms, helped precipitate the civil war that claimed 140,000 lives and wracked Guatemala for 36 years.

The peace accord signed in December 1996 provided for the reduction of the army and secret police and grants a long-overdue increase in rights for the nation's majority indigenous population. The accord has, however, disappointed human rights advocates with a vaguely worded, practically blanket amnesty for the participants in what Amnesty International has called the most extreme example of state-sponsored violence in the Western Hemisphere. Most of this violence and upheaval has thankfully come to an end—the only uniforms you now see are those of the Belizean Defense Force and the crisp white shirts of the Belizean bobby. The Peace Accords have allowed for two consecutive free presidential elections in Guatemala, and signs of recovery are everywhere in the form of new roads, new farms, a steadily modernizing infrastructure, and a growing cosmopolitanism in the cities—and, of course, a greater focus on tourism. For all its turmoil, this region more and more assumes the shape of an ideal vacation place.

For the most part, Central American countries have reaped the benefits of the growing tourism industry, drawing in much-needed foreign capital to bolster national coffers. The costs of tourism are less obvious, however. Among other effects, traditional indigenous communities and lifestyles are somewhat exoticized and undermined by increasingly tourist-oriented economies: cultivating a plot of land no longer supports a family, but selling knickknacks in the streets does. There is no easy solution to this dilemma, and balancing the advantages of tourism against its drawbacks is, and will remain, a constant struggle for Central American nations. The long-term effects are as much dependent on the attitudes and behavior of visitors as they are on prudent national policies.

Unlike Europe, where a visit to the capital cities is a must, distinctions between urban and rural environs here are more fluid. Skipping the capital cities for the smaller market villages, coastal towns or cayes, or the Maya ruins is the way to go, especially since today's capitals are locales chosen in the 20th century for their safety from natural disasters. Guatemala City was essentially founded in 1976 as refugee camp, albeit with permanent dwellings, when Antigua, the former colonial capital, with its gorgeous valley setting and quaint cobbled streets, was rocked by earthquakes again and again. When Belize City was trounced by Hurricane Hattie in 1961, the capital was relocated inland to Belmopan, a dreary loop of concrete buildings in the middle of nothing special. With avoiding natural disasters as an impetus for their creation, these cities lack the culture and history found outside of them. In fact, most *ciudadanos* (city dwellers) retain ties to the agricultural

sector, routinely migrating in search of seasonal labor. The nation's affluent reign as the distributors of all things agricultural—in Belize landowners are still largely non-Belizeans. They can be spotted speeding through the better neighborhoods in their BMWs on their way to top-notch restaurants or exclusive hilltop homes that accentuate the extreme dichotomies between affluence and indigence.

In addition to class, the cultural composition of Belize and Guatemala is shaped by religion and gender politics. Catholicism is still the largest social institution, and the Church has long held sway over the daily lives of the Central American faithful. In a world where your father can suddenly "disappear" into the clutches of a clandestine military faction and where you must improvise daily to feed your family, the church is a necessary source of stability and spiritual sustenance. The regimen, the rules, and the guarantee of a better life after death bring structure to a region that has long lacked just that. Plenty of pre-Colonial religious practices have endured. Creoles and Garifunas observe spiritual practices derived from African traditions, and some of Belize's and Guatemala's indigenous people incorporate Maya or pagan beliefs alongside Catholic ones. A point of convergence centers on the belief in various Catholic patron saints and an array of Maya gods and deities.

Although the Christian model of family dictates that men are the breadwinners, the ones in charge, superior to "their women," economic necessity has effectively played a role in dissolving gendered work roles. As men leave villages for agricultural work, an increasing number of women are taking part in the current economic evolution, traipsing to markets to sell wares before the sun is up and returning after dark. But women are also part of a detectable entrepreneurial class, establishing crafts or weaving workshops, and training other women to produce and sell traditional fabrics; they are also owners of small businesses and restaurants. If the majority of men still uphold an old-line custom of machismo, women aren't just hanging the clothes on it.

Social privilege in Central America follows—and has for centuries—the troubling and predictable pattern of light-skinned entitlement. The Spanish who settled here soon subdivided into various social strata founded on degrees of ethnic purity and even place of birth. The Spanish crown dictated that only the *peninsulares* (those born in Spain) could serve as governors, judges, and administrators, so these Spaniards came to monopolize wealth and power. The Creoles (those born in the colonies) were relegated to inferior positions, but eventually had their day when independence destroyed the aristocracy. Further down the social ladder of colonial Central America were Ladino, who fell in where the "pure" bloods left off—in small business and small-scale plantation farming. For the most part, they spoke Spanish and embraced European culture, though they were never fully entitled to its perks. At the bottom were full-blooded Indians and blacks, who were oppressed as serfs and slaves and suppressed by every religious, political, and economic institution that colonialism created.

Roads and communications in Central America are still underdeveloped, due in no small part to the mountains running through each of the countries. It was only under President Kennedy's Alliance for Progress that a highway linking Guatemala and Panama was built, although Belize remains somewhat cut off, with unevenly paved mountain roads into Guatemala and irregular water transportation down the coast to Honduras. Even within nations, the mountains and jungles have kept populations separate: in Guatemala there are no fewer than 23 distinct ethnic groups, and an equal number of languages—to be sure, Spanish is *not* the most widely spoken among them. Likewise, many of the peoples on the Caribbean coasts of Belize have more relatives in New Orleans, New York, or Miami than in Belmopan.

A popular conception of Central America is one of jungle, dense with color and resounding with a cacophony of insects, reptiles, and birds. The Caribbean and Pacific coasts, the cloud forests, and the supernatural desolation of the volcanoes add to transcendent visions. Though this romantic view is not wholly false, the hand of man is everywhere apparent. Beyond the agro-industrial tracts of bananas, cotton, and coffee, most agriculture is rudimentary: land is cleared, trees are cut down, and the biomass is burned. The soil,

often deceptively meager under the canopy of natural growth, rapidly loses nutrients as minerals are leached away, and the patch of land is then abandoned for another. Scrub weeds take over, and underfed cattle graze where forests once stood. The damage is extended by the need to cultivate wild and even extremely steep tracts of land to keep up with the demands of a rapidly growing population, particularly in northern Guatemala and southern Mexico. This slash-and-burn technique produces alarming erosion and generalized destruction from which there is little hope of recovery.

For nearly 200 years, Belize was a logging colony, harvesting fine hardwoods such as mahogany, and much of the area was left with a meager scrub of gnarled trees and undergrowth. The destruction of natural habitats, including the rain forests that once characterized the region, is driving many species, notably exotic birds and wildcats, to the brink of extinction. Fortunately, preservationist efforts in Central America are picking up steam, and both local and global organizations are looking for ways to ensure that economic stability in the region doesn't come at the cost of the environment. The land is now starting to recover, and forests cover some 60% of the country.

What does the future hold for Belize and Guatemala? In a region characterized by the extremes of the political pendulum, the future is difficult to predict. While the Belizean economy draws more and more foreign investment, more ex-pats setting up hotels, and continues to vie with Costa Rica for tourism dollars, the 1999 Guatemalan presidential election has reawakened demons of the not-so-distant past, with the election of Alfons Portillo of the right-wing Guatemalan Republican Front. Portillo is a protégé (some would say puppet) of former-dictator and current legislative president Efrain Rios Montt. Widely regarded as the most vicious of Guatemala's rulers, Rios Montt presided over the "scorched earth" campaigns of 1982–83, in which hundreds of indigenous villages were razed and tens of thousands of civilians were murdered. His landslide victory, so soon after the Truth Commission's Report, and with the support of peasants and middle-class Guatemalans alike, is truly mind-boggling, and casts a troublesome pallor over Guatemala's future.

Though he has made no effort to distance himself from Rios Montt (quite the contrary), Portillo claims to be independent and has included a number of liberals on his cabinet. His true intentions remain to be seen, and, in the meantime, Guatemala is holding its breath.

Central America is and will remain a place of spectacular natural beauty and rich cultural history, and travelers should keep in mind its troubled history when appreciating the enduring colonial cities and the Maya ruins, and particularly when interacting with people who lived through these terrible times. It seems almost impossible to fathom that these people and their cultures and buildings could live through so much and yet be continually welcoming and trusting. And yet it is home to some of the friendliest people a traveler can ever hope to meet, whose openness belies the horrors they have suffered. An informed understanding of Central America's past and present enriches a visit, and such understanding helps make tourism a positive influence in a region due for a change of luck.

PLEASURES AND PASTIMES

Archaeological Ruins
The ancient Maya empire, which once occupied much of present-day Guatemala and stretched north into Mexico, east into Belize, and south into Honduras and El Salvador, disintegrated in the middle of the 16th century, leaving one of the richest cultural and archaeological legacies in the world. Only a fraction of the thousands of Maya ruins have been excavated from the jungle that has swallowed the once-splendid cities over the centuries. Of the many sites in the northern Guatemalan department of El Petén, Tikal is the most majestic, its spectacular temples towering above pristine rain forest; a visit to the top of Temple IV is an unforgettable experience. Although the ruins here are somewhat more excavated than elsewhere in Guatemala, evidence of the Maya are everywhere in the area, from the harder-to-reach Aguateca ruins to the crumbling pottery in Belizean caves. In Be-

lize, Maya ruins are clustered in the north and west; the most impressive sites include Altun Ha, 45 km (28 mi) north of Belize City; Lamanai, the oldest Maya site in the country, about 2½ hours west of Belize City; and Caracol, a few miles from the Guatemalan border.

Bird-Watching
Belize and Guatemala will make a birdwatcher out of anyone. Those who make it their business to memorize their field guide will have to share their binoculars with one and all when toucans at Tikal, flying one at a time, from tree to tree, capture the attention and interest of groups that turn away from the ruins to watch. If you're a skilled birder in search of the hard-to-find motmot, you can go off the beaten path to Guatemala's Lake Izabal or stay on it, and make a beeline for Belize's Cayo. Of course, Guatemala's Quetzal Reserve is the place to see the elusive long-feathered quetzal. Come here between April and June when your chances are greatest. Tour operators and plenty of Belizean resorts offer bird-watching tours.

Nature's Bounty
Nearly two-thirds of the estimated 4.5 million species of animals and plants on earth live in the tropics—making moist tropical forests the most species-rich ecosystems on the planet. Belize and Guatemala thus have between them a nearly unfathomable natural wealth. To preserve this natural heritage, the Guatemalan government has set up protected areas known as *biotopos* and a national park system, both of which, despite chronic underfunding, aim to preserve both the country's natural resources and wildlife, and its immense archaeological heritage. In Belize, the promotion of ecotourism has resulted in well-run national parks, nature reserves, and wildlife sanctuaries. Many of the protected areas in both countries are in remote locations and are often difficult to reach; some are accessible only by all-terrain vehicles and even boat trips through the jungle. As long as you're prepared for the long journey ahead, getting there will indeed be half the fun.

Scuba Diving and Snorkeling
It's no secret that the Barrier Reef, a coral necklace stretching the length of Belize, offers some of the world's best diving. The reef is not only the longest in the West-

ern Hemisphere, but also the most spectacular: clear, unpolluted water and a smorgasbord of marine and coral life make diving here an exhilarating experience. Although the diving is excellent almost anywhere along the reef, the very best is around the many coral atolls farther out to sea, where you can take some of the most spectacular wall dives in the world—the water falls away, within sight of the shore, to as much as 3,000 feet. Particularly spectacular is the diving around Turneffe Island and Lighthouse Reef, site of the famous Blue Hole; first dived by Jacques Cousteau in 1970, this has become something of a pilgrimage for divers from all over the world. Snorkelers will want to head to Hol Chan Marine Reserve and Shark-Ray Alley—you'll be amazed at what you can see without a tank.

Sportfishing

Some of the most exciting sportfishing in the world lies off the coast of Belize. Fly-fishing is excellent on the shallow flats between the reef and the coast, giving anglers one of their few opportunities to achieve the "triple crown"—tarpon, bonefish, and permit—in one day. Out to sea, pelagics like sailfish, wahoo, and marlin abound. Several specialty resorts and fishing camps, such as Turneffe Flats, El Pescador, and the Setee River Lodge, cater to the angler, but most hotels can help you organize excellent fishing trips.

WHAT'S WHERE

Belize

Look for a mere geographical sliver wedged between Mexico and Guatemala and you'll find Belize. Along its coast are 175 cayes, some no larger than a tennis court. In the Maya Mountains—the central highlands that form the watershed for Belize's thousands of streams and rivers—there is dense rain forest; in the north, savanna and sugarcane. Because it has the lowest population density of any Central American nation—El Salvador, the only smaller country, has 10 times the population—and because Belizeans are by temperament and tradition town dwellers, most of this green interior is still the province of scarlet macaws, tapir, kinkajous, mountain

lions, and howler monkeys. Even reduced to vapid statistics—300 species of birds, 250 varieties of orchids, dozens of species of butterflies—the sheer variety of Belize's wildlife is breathtaking. The same goes for its nearly 600 Maya ruins, which range from the metropolitan splendor of Caracol to the humble burial mounds sprinkled throughout the country.

Guatemala

Guatemala, roughly the size of Ohio, packs cloud forests, mountains, caves, and volcanoes, white-water rivers, extraordinary Maya ruins, and rain forests full of monkeys, toucans, iguanas, and massive mahogany trees draped with mosses, ferns, vines, bromeliads, and rare orchids. The land is also home to 10 million people of varying ethnic origins—Maya, but at least 22 different ethnicities; Ladinos, the descendants of Indians and Spaniards; Garifunas, the handful of Guatemalans of Afro-Caribbean descent; and the European minority, predominantly Hispanic, which has maintained its imported bloodline and colonial lease on power. In the Lake Atitlán and highland areas are humble lakeside dwellings and gorgeous village markets. Take a white-water rafting trip to the Pacific coast. Colonial Antigua has crumbling monasteries, quaint cobblestone streets, and perhaps the country's top restaurants and hotels, all with volcano views. Boating around the Atlantic Lowlands and birding on pristine Lago Izabal are newer adventures. Río Dulce and Livingston on the Atlantic coast spice things up with water sports and a Caribbean flavor. And everywhere are traces of the Maya, particularly in El Petén to the north, where the stately Tikal pyramids stand.

NEW AND NOTEWORTHY

Belize is going upmarket. Even jungle lodges and resorts on remote cayes are building swimming pools, adding air-conditioning, and installing 24-hour electricity. While you can still find a clean, pleasant place to stay for under $50, you can also spend hundreds of dollars a night at luxurious new resorts such as Cayo Espanto and Caye Chapel Golf Course &

Marina. The condotel (condo-meets-hotel) is the hot trend on Ambergris Caye, offering more space for guests and a pied-á-mer for investors. The Placencia and Hopkins are booming—at least by Belize standards—driven by real estate and the growing number of North Americans who dream of owning a home on the Caribbean. Reef, ruins, rum, and rain forests still are the main lures, but, with the opening of casinos in Belize City, San Pedro, and elsewhere, with spas popping up at jungle lodges like Chaa Creek, and with fancy beach resorts vying for the Coppertone-and-Cosmo set, Belize is suddenly a lot more than an eco-travel and adventure destination.

In Guatemala, new lodgings, including hotels in renovated colonial buildings, are going up in Chichicastenango, Antigua, Guatemala City, and in the increasingly charming city of Flores in El Petén. A paved road now connects Tikal with the capital, which has cut travel time along this route in half. More in-country flights are now available between major towns, including Flores and the capital. With the new democracy in Guatemala has come a newly trained National Civil Police force, which is subtly present throughout Guatemala. In Antigua, specially appointed tourist police circulate about in uniforms of white shirts and green pants. They are friendly and offer information and help to anyone. Ecological and adventure tour companies are opening Guatemala's wilderness to more travelers every year. Jungle treks, white-water rafting, cave exploration, volcano climbs, river trips, and deep-sea fishing can all be combined with trips to striking Indian villages or ancient ruins.

FODOR'S CHOICE

Archaeological Sites

★ **Altun Ha, Belize.** The best-excavated and most accessible Maya ruin in the country is over 2,000 years old. At its peak it was home to 10,000 people.

★ **Caracol, Belize.** The most spectacular Maya site in Belize, Caracol had five plazas and 32 large structures over nearly a square mile. As many as 200,000 people lived here.

★ **Lamanai, Belize.** Nearly 60 Maya structures are spread over this 950-acre reserve, including a massive temple that is the largest pre-Classic building in the country.

★ **Quiriguá Guatemala.** This important erstwhile trading center is renowned for its massive stelae, the largest in the Maya world.

★ **Tikal, Guatemala.** Guatemala's most famous ruin is the best embodiment of the extraordinary accomplishments of the Maya. This vast array of awesome temples and intricate acropoli was once a teeming metropolis.

Dining

Note that dining and lodging costs are much higher in Belize than in Guatemala. What's considered expensive in Guatemala might very well be inexpensive or moderate for Belize.

BELIZE

★ **Elvi's Kitchen, Ambergris Caye.** The banner on the letterhead at this Belizean restaurant states that this is "DI PLACE FOR SEAFOOD," and we cannot but agree. $$

★ **Capricorn, Ambergris Caye.** This stylish new restaurant can only be reached by water taxi, but the trip is well worth it. $$$

★ **Fort Street Guesthouse, Belize City.** Enjoy British Honduras atmosphere, sea breezes on the veranda, and a moderately priced menu of seafood and Continental choices that never fails to please. $$

★ **Rendezvous, Ambergris Caye.** Recommended, even if it weren't Belize's first and only Thai–French restaurant to date, for its inventive sweet-and-hot dishes and wine bottled at the restaurant. $$–$$$

GUATEMALA

★ **El Bistro, Panajachel.** Come here for the romantic lakeside setting and the delicious, homemade Italian food. $$

★ **Jake's, Guatemala City.** Twenty-five daily specials augment the excellent international menu in this restored farmhouse. $$$

★ **Las Puertas, Flores.** Six sets of swinging doors give Las Puertas its name, and its concern for fresh and natural ingredients, like sandwiches on fresh homemade bread and just-picked fruit smoothies, give this popular spot its top honors. $

★ **Welten, Antigua.** The handmade pasta, with inspired sauces and organic vegetables, and the plant-filled patio setting, with hammocks and cascading orchids, couldn't be more pleasing. $$$

Lodging
BELIZE

★ **Chaa Creek, Cayo district.** The mixture of jungle seclusion and candlelit conviviality, combined with impeccable service and top-quality food and amenities—not to mention a new perfectly placed hilltop spa—make Chaa Creek the queen of the jungle resorts. $$$

★ **Chan Chich Lodge, Gallon Jug, Orange Walk district.** Built atop the plaza of a Maya temple, so close to nature that your neighbors are howler monkeys and toucans, and so safe that there are no locks on your cabaña door, this is one of the most scenic and sensory lodges in all of Central America. $$$

★ **Inn at Robert's Grove, Seine Bight Area.** Breathing high standards into mainland resorts with personal attention and terrific food—mostly tropical takes on Continental dishes—these haciendas on the Caribbean near Placencia won't be a secret for long. $$$–$$$$

GUATEMALA

★ **Hotel La Posada, Cobán.** This simple, refurbished colonial inn off Cobán's main square offers the peaceful respite essential to any vacation, with a lovely porch café, hammocks for napping, and tastefully decorated rooms with exposed hardwood beams and fireplaces. $$

★ **Mesón Panza Verde, Antigua.** In a colonial building with an interior courtyard, this enchanting hotel with a terrific European restaurant captures the past without omitting any modern luxuries. $$$$

★ **Ni'tun Ecolodge, San Andrés.** Hidden in the forest on the shores of Lake Petén

Itzá are the thatched-roof wood-and-rock cabins that comprise this gorgeous ecolodge, which brings culinary considerations to the forefront and leads the way in customized eco-adventures. $$$$

★ **Posada de Santiago, Santiago Atitlán.** Sandwiched between two volcanoes on the shores of a lagoon, this hotel offers American-style comfort in a traditional Indian-village environment. $$

Special Moments

★ **Night diving at Hol Chan Marine Reserve, Belize.** If you're a strong swimmer, this is a special treat: nocturnal animals, including the octopus and the spider crab, casually go about their business in water lighted by bioluminescence.

★ **Sunrise over the New River Lagoon at Lamanai, Belize.** Take a secluded jungle paradise and add exotic wildlife, Maya ruins, and a romantic lagoon, and all you need to complete the fantasy is a sunrise.

★ **Good Friday in Antigua, Guatemala.** This religious feast is Guatemala at its most festive and mystical: processions of costumed disciples weave their way through flower-carpeted streets, leaving a trail of incense.

★ **Sunrise on Temple IV, Tikal, Guatemala.** Imagine that you're Maya royalty—or an intrepid archaeologist—as the emerging rays wake the jungle into its noisy daily activity.

★ **Spotting dolphins in the Río Dulce River Canyon, Guatemala.** You will probably only get to see these magical mammals from a canoe, but the paddling will be well worth it as you float quietly between banks of jungle foliage, with egrets and iguanas perched overhead.

★ **Soaking in the clear water pools of Semuc Champey, Guatemala.** Here the beautiful white water of the Cahabón River momentarily comes to a pause at a land bridge: the universe's intention it seems, is serene soaking for the weary traveler.

2   BELIZE

Belize has got it right. This tiny country's diverse landscapes and people; spectacular diving at the Barrier Reef; and, of course, some 2,000 Maya ruins, ranging from the metropolitan splendor of Caracol to the humble living mounds throughout the country, make it a magical place. Here aquatic athletes can travel in harmony with archaeology buffs.

By Simon
Worrall

Updated by
Lan Sluder

A **SLIVER OF LAND** wedged between Mexico and Guatemala, Belize is no larger than the state of Massachusetts—280 km (174 mi) long, and 109 km (68 mi) wide at its broadest point—but don't let its diminutive size fool you. Within its borders, Belize probably has the greatest variety of landscapes, peoples, flora, and fauna of any country of its size in the world.

In the Maya Mountains, the central highlands that form the watershed for thousands of streams and rivers, there is dense rain forest; in the north, there is savanna and sugarcane. Because Belize has the lowest population density of any country in Central America—El Salvador, the only smaller country, has 10 times as many people—and because Belizeans are by temperament and tradition town dwellers, most of the green interior remains uninhabited. Less than an hour's flight from the green heartland is the Barrier Reef, a great wall of coral stretching the length of the coast. Dotting the reef like punctuation marks are 175 cayes, and farther out to sea, three coral atolls—all superb for diving and snorkeling. Some of the cayes are no more than Robinson Crusoe islets of white coral sand and mangroves, inhabited by frigate birds, pelicans, and the occasional fisherman, who will spend a few days diving for conch and lobster, sleeping under a sheet of canvas strung between trees. Others, like Ambergris Caye, are becoming increasingly lively, with an ample supply of bars, restaurants, and small hotels.

The name Belize is a conundrum. According to *Encyclopaedia Britannica,* it derives from *belix,* an ancient Maya word meaning "muddy water," and anyone who has seen the Belize River swollen by heavy rains will vouch for its aptness. Others trace the origin to the French word *balise* (beacon), though no one ventures to explain why a French word would have caught on in this Spanish-dominated region. Another theory is that it's named for the Maya word *belikin,* but as this is the name of the national beer, this may be a drinker's tale. Some say that Belize is a corruption of Wallace, the name of a Scottish buccaneer who founded a colony in 1620; still others say the pirate wasn't Wallace but Willis, wasn't Scottish but English, and founded a colony not in 1620, but in 1638. We'll never know if Wallace and Willis were one and the same, or how "w" could become "b" and "a" slip to "e"; perhaps it was too much Belikin. But what's in a name, anyway? For centuries, Belize did fine as British Honduras.

There was indeed a pirate named Wallace, a onetime lieutenant of Sir Walter Raleigh who later served as British governor of Tortuga. Perhaps it was liquor or lucre that turned Governor Wallace into pirate Wallace. Sometime between 1638 and 1662 he and 80 fellow renegades washed up on the Viego River (now known as the Belize River), behind St. George's Caye, and proceeded to live for years off the booty from cloak-and-dagger raids on passing ships. The two men on Belize's flag are not pirates, however, but two stout woodcutters, standing in the shade of a logwood tree. Under them is a Latin inscription, *sub umbra floreat:* "In the shade of this tree we flourish." What's most remarkable about the men is that one is black, the other white—a celebration of Belize's historic and emblematic racial mixture.

Belize's whites are descendants of the English buccaneers and subsequent settlers of what was first known as the Honduran Bay Settlement. They worked under grueling conditions in the jungles and forests to export logwood to England, where it was prized as a valuable textile dye. As the craftsmen of Europe learned the value of mahogany, the loggers were joined by many more.

Many of today's blacks descended from slaves who were brought from Jamaica to work in the logging industry, but in Belize the vicious divisions of slave society were loosened and humanized thanks to its geographical isolation and the residents' innate dislike of authority in any form. Surrounded by hostile terrain and subject to attacks by Maya Indians in the interior and Spanish warships on the coast, white and black had only one choice. Domination gave way to mutual dependence, cooperation, and, very often, love and marriage.

Not all blacks came as slaves; some came as free men, others as escapees, and still others were shipwrecked on the Mosquito Coast. By the early 18th century, the number of people of African descent in Belize outnumbered those of British origin, and they probably enjoyed greater human rights than much of Central America does today. Slaves were routinely armed, but instead of training their guns on their white masters, they eventually united with them to defeat a common enemy.

That enemy appeared off the coast of Belize early on September 10, 1798, in the form of 31 Spanish naval vessels manned by 500 seamen, carrying 2,000 well-armed troops, and commanded by the Captain-General of the Yucatán. After more than a century of trying to uproot this upstart colony from its backyard, the Spanish had finally come to exterminate it.

The Baymen (as the settlers were known), their slaves, and a few British troops totaled 350, and they had a total of one sloop, some fishing boats, and seven rafts. The battle was over in two hours, with the Baymen—thanks to their knowledge of the turf and their sheer tenacity—triumphant. Many patriotic poems have been written to celebrate the victory; they revel in the gore as well as the glory, piling images of hideous carnage one on top of the other like so much pastrami. In truth, there were only two casualties, both Spanish, and the history of the battle became a fable. That was the last time the Spanish attempted forcibly to dislodge the settlement, though bitter wrangles over British Honduras's right to exist continued for nearly a century.

In the 19th century, Belize's early settlers and its original inhabitants, the Maya, were joined by mestizos fleeing the Yucatán during the War of the Castes and by a group of Black Caribs, known as the Garifuna, who, after numerous insurrections on the island of St. Vincent, settled in the Stann Creek area. Later came Mennonites fleeing persecution in Europe. All of these peoples, like Belize's most recent refugees—the thousands of Salvadorans and Guatemalans who fled their countries' death squads in the 1970s—found in this tiny country a tolerant and amiable home. In a country where almost everyone is a foreigner, no one is.

Belize's most recent wave of immigrants, the Chinese, has been arriving since the communists regained Hong Kong in 1997. Construction sites with signs in Chinese characters have sprung up all over. Many Belizeans are questioning the passports-for-cash deal struck by the government in the mid-1990s and wondering whether this influx of people with very different business customs will upset Belize's complex ethnic balance. Odds are, it won't.

The dominant social and ethnic group is mestizo—people of mixed Indian and European heritage who typically speak Spanish as a first language—now representing 44% of the population. Half African, half Anglo-Saxon, Creoles consider themselves the heirs of the colonial era and hold most university, police, and government positions. In Belize City, they form approximately 70% of the population. Happily, the races associate harmoniously, and you're likely to see people with facial structures and skin colors you haven't seen before—blacks with blue eyes; half-Maya, half-Creole people with green eyes. Belize is a breath of fresh air in a world so often plagued by ethnic strife.

Belize has always belonged more to the British Caribbean than to Central America, and it still has more in common with Trinidad or St. Kitts than with Mexico or El Salvador. The most obvious difference is English, the official language, which is closely allied to the English of the British Caribbean ("tea" refers to just about any meal, for example, as it does in the West Indies and cockney London). Among themselves, many Belizeans also speak Creole patois, a language spun from English with its own vocabulary and intonations. Only in a few aspects is Belize like its neighbors: Spanish is widely spoken in the north, west–central regions, and south, while Maya is heard mainly in the Toledo District, in the south. Moreover, the population is 62% Roman Catholic and only 12% Anglican.

The British, who at the request of the Belizean government had maintained a small military presence since independence in 1981, finally pulled out in 1994, but relations between the two countries remain close. Belize's defense force is still trained by the Brits; and Harrier jump-jets, which used to inspire gasps of amazement from arriving tourists by flying backwards over the airport, are still on call in case Guatemala should try to reassert its claim to what it has called its 13th province. At the same time, initiatives like Mundo Maya—an effort by Central American states to coordinate tourism to Maya sites—are paving the way for greater regional cooperation.

Meanwhile, more and more travelers are making the journey to this small country of huge contrasts. Fortunately, the government has an enlightened attitude toward conservation and the environment; there is little industry—not by default but by choice—and tourism remains small-scale. Some of the resorts can be a bit funky, but the best offer a charm and attention to visitors' needs unmatched elsewhere in the Caribbean. Ecotourism—getting travelers into nature without destroying it—is very big in Belize, and although there are signs that increased traffic is causing minor degradation of the Barrier Reef, people are acutely aware of nature's fragility. Everyone from fishermen to schoolchildren discusses the need to protect the environment.

So if you're looking for Daytona Beach or a golfer's paradise, look elsewhere. If, on the other hand, you want to take a night dive through a tunnel of living coral, ride a horse through a jungle resounding with the call of howler monkeys, clamber on ancient Maya ruins, or canoe through the rain forest, the "adventure coast"—as Belize is rightly called—will not disappoint. Experiencing the rich diversity of colorful birds and animals that still survive here, and perhaps showing them to your children, is another of this friendly, easygoing country's richest gifts. Clever Belize will probably remain a nature lovers' haven for decades to come.

Pleasures and Pastimes

Beaches

Much of the mainland coast is fringed with mangrove swamps and therefore has few beaches. The few that do exist are not spectacular. This changes dramatically on the cayes, particularly Ambergris. The beaches are not expansive—generally a small strip of sand at the water's edge—but their white-coral sand, palm trees, and mint-green water assure you that you're in the Caribbean. The best beach on the mainland is in Placencia, in the south. The Hopkins/Sittee Point area also has a good beach.

Boating

Hitting the water is rightly popular on the mainland, cayes, and atolls alike. Many resorts rent Windsurfers, small sailing dinghies, catamarans, and sea kayaks. Bareboat and captained charters of sail or motorboats are available in San Pedro, Punta Gorda, and Belize City.

Caving

Belize is riddled with hundreds of caves, many of them unexplored in modern times. The most easily visited are those in Cayo, in Western Belize. Near San Ignacio are the caves at Barton Creek, best visited on a guided trip, and Che Chem Ha, on private land. Che Chem Ha, like many caves in Belize, contains Maya pottery and other artifacts. In the Pine Ridge is the popular Rio Frio cavern. Near Belmopan, is Caves Branch Jungle Lodge with their tours of Footprint Cave, and other cave systems. Also in the area are St. Herman's, Actun Tunichil Muknal (with its wealth of Maya artifacts), and others. The remote Chiquibul system along the Guatemala border contains Cebeda, thought to be the country's largest cave. Toledo District has least two cave systems: you don't need a guide to visit an open cavern such as Rio Frio, but, as some caves are in remote areas and are subject to sudden flooding, or are off-limits to individual visitors due to the Maya relics they contain, you'll need an experienced guide.

Dining

Belizean cuisine is not one of the world's greatest, but it might be the best Central America has to offer. Tasty treats—like the johnnycake, a sconelike cornmeal roll fried to a golden crisp and served at breakfast—rice and beans, fried chicken, and tasty Creole "stew" chicken are the staple entrées. Added to these are such acquired tastes as iguana (known as "bush" or "bamboo chicken") and gibnut, a small rodent christened "the royal rat" after Her Majesty dined on it during a state visit, and oddities of the British culinary heritage, like bread-and-butter pudding and cow-foot soup. But with the world's second-largest coral reef running the length of the coast, Belize whips up seafood as tasty as any in the Caribbean. Belizean chefs have learned how to prepare fish for a lighter northern palate (no deep frying), and at their best, dishes like grilled grouper or red snapper in a citron sauce, shrimp and coconut, or blackened shark steak squirted with fresh lime can be sublime. Just be aware that there is no fresh lobster during spawning season (February 15–June 14), and no conch July through September. Of late, the growth of shrimp farming here has meant more restaurants serve it and at moderate prices. Throughout the country, meals are washed down with delicious fresh-squeezed juices, such as lime, watermelon, and orange. However, you may decide that the national drink of Belize is Orange Fanta or Belikin beer.

The best restaurants are mostly in hotels and resorts, and bear comparison with good, though not first-class, eateries in North America or Europe. Ambergris Caye has established itself as Belize's epicenter of fine dining with the opening of several excellent restaurants, such as Capricorn, Rendezvous, and Mata Chica. More and more restaurants now carry substantial wine lists, although the import taxes are high, so you may pay more than you'd like. Be careful not to judge a restaurant by the way it looks; some of the best cooking comes from the humblest-looking cabanas. So follow your nose.

Belize is a casual place and demands little in the way of a dress code. A few expensive restaurants and clubs in Belize City prefer, but do not require, a jacket and tie for men; otherwise, you'll probably get served if you're wearing shoes and a shirt. On the cayes, you won't even need shoes at most restaurants. Reservations are advisable at high-end places.

Prices vary considerably between the interior, Belize City, and the cayes. Because it's the most developed, Ambergris Caye is the most expensive; here, a meal for two at one of the best restaurants costs $50–$70. You can, however, eat well for much less. Lobster runs $10–$20, depending on the restaurant. A fish like grilled grouper usually costs about $10; a substantial American-style breakfast, $5; and a hamburger, $3.

CATEGORY	COST*
$$$$	over $40
$$$	$25–$40
$$	$10–$25
$	under $10

*per person for a three-course meal, excluding drinks, service, and 8% tax

Fishing

Some of the most exciting sportfishing in the world lies off Belize's coast and cayes. Fly-fishing is excellent on the shallow flats between the reef and the coast, giving anglers a rare opportunity to achieve the "triple crown"—tarpon, bonefish, and permit—in one day. Out to sea, pelagics like sailfish, wahoo, and marlin abound. Several specialty resorts and fishing camps, such as Turneffe Flats, El Pescador, and the Lillpat Sittee River Lodge, cater to the angler, but most hotels can help you organize excellent fishing trips. Note well: Belize's attention to ecology means that catch-and-release fishing is usually the rule.

Gambling

With the election of the People's United Party in late 1998 came new laws permitting gambling in Belize. Two casinos have opened, and others are planned. Belize City has the largest so far, with about 500 electronic machines plus live tables for poker, blackjack, and other games at the Princess Hotel and Casino. A much smaller casino, The Palace, is in San Pedro. Others are in the works, including one near Corozal Town in Northern Belize and another in Placencia.

Horseback Riding

In Belize's interior, particularly in Cayo, horseback riding is one of the best ways to see the mountainous landscape. You can also ride through the jungle or to a Maya ruin. The horses tend to be small, tough local breeds; quarter horses often suffer in the climate.

Lodging

Belize has little in the way of standardized, Holiday Inn–style accommodations, as large hotels are the exception rather than the rule. The best lodgings are small, highly individual resorts with personalized service; these are very much shaped by the tastes and interests of their owners, who are mostly American or British. Most have traveled widely themselves and are excellent hosts, but the quality of facilities among resorts varies greatly. The best resorts are run by professionals, people with some previous training and experience in hotel-keeping; the worst are those opened on a whim by people who vacationed in Belize, fell in love with the place, and opened a resort to finance their escape to paradise. Because of the salt and humidity, operating a hotel in the tropics is an art in itself, the closest thing to keeping house on the deck of a ship. Without constant maintenance, things start to rust, the thatch (a frequently used natural building material) leaks, and the charms of paradise quickly fade.

Except for budget properties, most accommodations provide private bathrooms with showers. Unless otherwise stated in the listings below, you can assume that rooms have private baths.

Hardest to find are good accommodations at moderate prices. Lodgings tend to leap from tropical spartan to luxury Caribbean, and the middle ground is often occupied by either grand hotels that have fallen on hard times or small ones that are overcharging. Budget travelers have a wide selection, ranging from $8–$10 dorm-style digs to $15–$20 double rooms.

Generally, rooms are more expensive than elsewhere in Central America. A moderately priced room in Belize buys you only the amenities you had in a cheap room in Guatemala. Rooms are priciest in Belize City and Ambergris Caye, where prices are usually quoted in U.S. dollars, but they're also the best values for your money, because the infrastructure is more developed and there is more competition.

CATEGORY	COST*
$$$$	over $165
$$$	$100–$165
$$	$50–$100
$	under $50

*All prices are for a standard double room, including 7% tax but excluding the 10% service charge and 3%–5% credit-card fee charged by some hotels. Off-season (May–October), reductions of 15%–40% are common.

✎ following the text of a review is your signal that the property has a Web site, where you will find details and, usually, images; for a link, visit www.fodors.com/urls.

Scuba Diving and Snorkeling

The Barrier Reef, a coral necklace of 320 km (198 mi) stretching south from the Yucatán Peninsula to the Guatemalan border, is the longest in the Western Hemisphere. If you add to this the three coral atolls farther out to sea—Lighthouse Reef, Glover's Reef, and the Turneffe Islands—Belize has more than 560 km (347 mi) of reef just waiting to be dived, more than in Bonaire, Cozumel, and all the Caymans put together.

Belize has some of the best scuba diving and snorkeling in the world. The cast of aquatic characters is enormous. One moment you can go around an outcrop of coral in 70 ft of virgin water and come upon an 8-ft, 40-pound, spotted eagle ray, its great wings flapping and its needlelike tail streaming out behind; the next minute you may find the feisty little damselfish, a bolt of blue no bigger than your little finger, with sides as smooth as black marble and iridescent blue markings that glitter like rhinestones. There are bloated blowfish hovering in their holes like nightclub bouncers; lean, mean barracuda patrolling the depths; and queen angelfish that shimmy through the water with the puckered lips and haughty self-assurance of a model. In all, several hundred species of Caribbean tropicals frequent the reef, including 40 kinds of grouper, numerous types of cardinal fish, damselfish and wrasses, squirrel fish, butterfly fish, parrot fish, snappers, jacks, pompanos, and basslets.

Shopping

Belize is a good place to kick the consumer habit. There simply isn't much to buy, and most of the crafts are from Guatemala. Hotel shops sell a few carvings, mostly of wildlife (jaguars and dolphins) or Maya themes, made of zericote wood, a hardwood native to Belize. The best of these are quite good, though nothing compared to African carvings. Other worthy souvenirs are Marie Sharp's famous hot sauces, jams, and jellies, rare Belizean coffee from Gallon Jug Estates, a Creole "brukdown" or raunchy Punta rock tape, and fine mahogany furniture from Cayo, and herbal medicinal products like Belly Be Good and Flu Away from Ix Chel Tropical Research Foundation.

Tours

The number and variety of guided tours has grown hugely in recent years. Standard activities, like visits to Altun Ha and snorkeling trips on the reef, have been joined by more exotic outings, such as swimming with manatees or floating through subterranean caves in an inner tube. Tour operators used to stay close to their own area (for example, outfits in Belize City offered day trips to nearby Maya ruins and nature reserves, while those in San Pedro focused on diving and snorkeling), but as Belize's transportation network improves, many are running trips far and wide.

Wildlife

Belize's natural world is almost peerless. Within this patch of land are scarlet macaws, tapir, jaguars, kinkajous, mountain lions, and howler monkeys, making Belize one of the best places on earth to get close to the color and variety of tropical wildlife. Most hotels can book you a wildlife tour, and many jungle lodges, in Cayo, in particular, have their own guides and vehicles.

Windsurfing

Belize offers no surfing, save for possibly right before a hurricane, but windsurfing is becoming an important sport on the cayes and coast. Ambergris and Caulker cayes are the most popular spots, and January through March, when skies are clear and tradewinds blow a consistent 15 to 20 mph, is the best time for it.

Exploring Belize

Although it's not the capital, Belize City is still very much the country's hub. From here you can access the Maya ruins and nature reserves of the north; the beaches and Barrier Reef of the cayes and atolls; the rugged, mountainous, Spanish-accented Cayo district; or the relaxed Afro-Caribbean villages along the coast to the south. However, the majority of travelers, having heard rumors of crime and mayhem (greatly exaggerated) in Belize City, choose to move on quickly. You may want to base near San Ignacio or Belmopan to explore the western part of the country, in Placencia to explore the country's southern coast and mid-section, in Corozal Town to check out the north, or even on Ambergris Caye or Caye Caulker, from which you can make day trips to the mainland while enjoying the Caribbean.

Great Itineraries

Numbers in the text correspond to numbers in the margin and on the maps.

IF YOU HAVE 2–4 DAYS

It's said that Belize is the only country where you can scuba dive before breakfast and hike in the rain forest after lunch, but to do this you have to move fast. Spend your first night in **Belize City** ① and, after a good dinner nearby and a night at a hotel in the Fort George area, take a morning flight to **Ambergris Caye** ⑫. Spend a few days in San Pedro, the main town, and on the nearby Barrier Reef; or, if you fancy a laid-back tropical paradise with fewer tourists and less development, fly to **Placencia** ㉜, in the south, where you can also dive and snorkel. For the jungle experience, head to the Cayo for adventure excursions at Caves Branch or relaxation at Chaa Creek Lodge and Spa. If you drive here, stop at the **Belize Zoo** ②, drop in for lunch at the Jaguar Paw resort, and continue via **Belmopan** ⑳ to **San Ignacio** ㉒. From your jungle lodge there you can explore the Maya ruins at **Xunantunich** ㉓

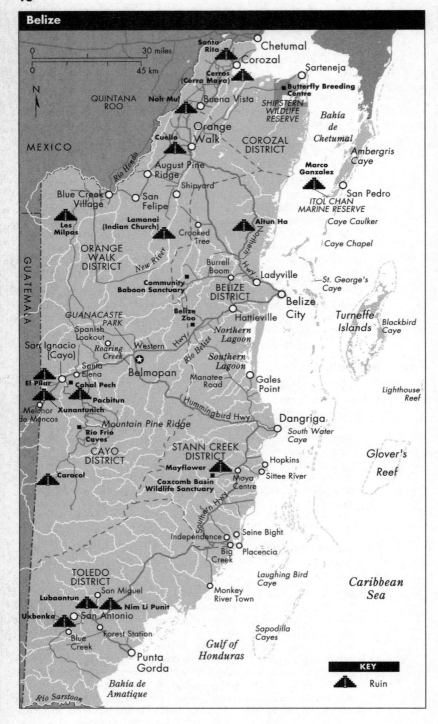

Belize

30 miles
45 km

N

QUINTANA
ROO

MEXICO

GUATEMALA

Chetumal

**Santa
Rita**

Corozal

Sarteneja

**Cerros
(Cerra Maya)**

**Butterfly Breeding
Centre**

Noh Mul

Buena Vista

*SHIPSTERN
WILDLIFE
RESERVE*

*Bahía
de
Chetumal*

Orange
Walk

Cuello

COROZAL
DISTRICT

*Ambergris
Caye*

August Pine
Ridge

Shipyard

**Marco
Gonzalez**

San Pedro

*ITOL CHAN
MARINE RESERVE*

Blue Creek
Village

San
Felipe

Caye Caulker

**Les
Milpas**

**Lamanai
(Indian Church)**

Crooked
Tree

Altun Ha

Caye Chapel

ORANGE
WALK
DISTRICT

New River

Burrell
Boom

Ladyville

*St. George's
Caye*

**Community
Baboon Sanctuary**

BELIZE
DISTRICT

Belize
City

*Turneffe
Islands*

*Blackbird
Caye*

**Belize
Zoo**

Hattieville

*Northern
Lagoon*

*GUANACASTE
PARK*

Spanish
Lookout

*Roaring
Creek*

Western

Río Belize

*Southern
Lagoon*

San Ignacio
(Cayo)

Santa
Elena

Cahal Pech

Belmopan

Manatee
Road

Gales
Point

*Lighthouse
Reef*

El Pilar

Pacbitun

Melchor
de Mencos

Xunantunich

Mountain Pine Ridge

Hummingbird Hwy

Dangriga

*South Water
Caye*

*Glover's
Reef*

**Rio Frio
Caves**

CAYO
DISTRICT

STANN CREEK
DISTRICT

Hopkins

Sittee River

Caracol

Mayflower

**Coxcomb Basin
Wildlife Sanctuary**

Maya
Centre

Southern Hwy

Independence

Seine Bight

Big
Creek

Placencia

TOLEDO
DISTRICT

San Miguel

*Laughing Bird
Caye*

*Caribbean
Sea*

Lubaantun

Nim Li Punit

Uxbenka

San Antonio

Monkey
River Town

Blue
Creek

Forest Station

*Sapodilla
Cayes*

*Gulf of
Honduras*

Punta
Gorda

*Bahía de
Amatique*

KEY

Río Sarstoon

Ruin

or cross the Guatemalan border to Tikal, canoe down the Macal River, or hike through the rain forest.

IF YOU HAVE 5 DAYS

With a bit more time, you can combine caye and jungle (as outlined above) for a surf-and-turf sort of trip. If you would rather expand your underwater horizons than come inland, move on to one of the remote coral atolls, such as **Turneffe Atoll** ⑯ or **Lighthouse Reef Atoll** ⑰.

IF YOU HAVE 7-10 DAYS

If you have more than a week, it's worth spending a bit more time around **Belize City** ①. For Maya ruins, put **Altun Ha** ⑤ or **Lamanai** ⑦ on your list. If it's nature you want, visit the **Crooked Tree Wildlife Sanctuary** ⑥ and **Community Baboon Sanctuary** ③. Fly to San Pedro, on **Ambergris Caye** ⑫, for two or three days of diving and sunbathing; then fly back to Belize City and head for the Cayo resorts around **San Ignacio** ㉒, in the Cayo, to see the rain-forest wildlife that makes Belize a naturalist's paradise. Finally, head south to **Placencia** ㉜ or Hopkins/Sittee Point for a luscious last few days of snorkeling and relaxing under palm trees. Or, if you've had enough beach time, explore Belize's least-visited spots, **Punta Gorda** ㉝ in the far south or **Corozal** ⑧ in the north.

When to Tour Belize

Despite popular opinion, Belize is a year-round destination, but some seasons are better than others. The dry season, from March to May, can be the least attractive time for inland trips, with dust and wilting vegetation. The rest of the year, from May to late February, Belize is at its best. Rainy season is in June and July, extending in some areas through October. The wet season varies dramatically between the north and south—in the far south, as much as 160 inches of rain falls annually, but in the rest of the country (where you're likely to travel), there's much less. Moreover, the rain is not continuous; it falls Florida-style, in sudden thunderstorms, and then stops. On the cayes, the wet season can be accompanied by lashing winds, known in Creole as Joe North. Hurricane season in the western Caribbean is June through November. Belize's relatively rare hurricanes—they've hit on average about once every 10 years—come in September, October, and early November. In Halloween week 1998, Hurricane Mitch scared the bejeebers out of Belize, but ended up veering away and causing virtually no damage. It did devastate parts of Honduras and Nicaragua, however.

Scuba enthusiasts can dive all year, but the water is at its glasslike clearest from April to June. Between November and February, cold fronts from North America can push southward, producing blustery winds known as "northers," which bring rain and rough weather and tend to churn up the sea, reducing visibility. (Normal visibility is 100–150 ft.) Water temperatures rarely stray from 80°F, so many people dive without a wet suit; if you're making several dives a day, you may prefer to use a short suit in winter and a Lycra skin in summer.

Some festivals and seasonal events worth noting are:

March 19: **Baron Bliss Day** hears three cheers for Baron Henry Edward Ernest Victor Bliss, a wealthy English sportsman who gave Belize an immense estate in return for a holiday devoted to the traditional pursuits of the warm-weather gentleman: sailing and fishing.

Mid-August: The **San Pedro Costa Maya Festival** is a four-day multicultural bash held on Ambergris Caye. The entertainment comes from Belize and other Central American and Caribbean countries.

September 10: The **Battle of St. George's Caye** celebrates the David-and-Goliath defeat of the Spanish navy by a motley crew of British settlers, buccaneers, and liberated slaves. A week of carnivals and general partying keeps the memory alive. In 1998, the country celebrated the 200th anniversary of the rout with a grand display of pageantry.

September 21: **National Independence Day,** during the already festive Carnival month, honors Belize's achievement of independence from Great Britain in 1981.

November 19: **Garifuna Settlement Day** marks the arrival of Black Carib settlers, known as Garifuna, from the West Indies in 1823. Processions and traditional dancing abound, mainly in Dangriga.

BELIZE CITY AND ENVIRONS

"Dump" used to be the word that sprang to many visitors' minds when they saw Belize City. With its open drains, rusting swing bridge, and dilapidated buildings, it seemed to symbolize everything that anthropologist Claude Lévi-Strauss implied in the title of his book *Tristes Tropiques*. From the air, you realize how small it is—more town than city, with a population of about 80,000 and few buildings taller than the palm trees. After a few miles, the city simply stops and gives way to a largely uninhabited country where animals still outnumber people. Belize City is generally a staging post from which to see the natural wonders outside its limits.

Perhaps because of its strange, renegade history, Belize was one of the most neglected colonies of the Pax Britannia. The British, who were generally generous in such matters, left little of either great beauty or interest in the capital of their former colony—no parks or gardens, no university, no museums. Indeed, one of the clichés about Belize City is that the most exciting thing that happens here is the opening of the swing bridge on Haulover Creek twice a day.

In 1961, the city was almost annihilated by Hurricane Hattie, and authorities decided to move Belize's capital to Belmopan, thereby robbing Belize City of its middle class. Thus began a long, dark night here, culminating in the arrival in the late 1980s of crack cocaine, which in sweeping through the city caused even more damage than Hurricane Hattie. So bad was Belize City's rap that press accounts of street crime made the place sound like south-central Los Angeles. It never was quite that bad, but in the mid-1990s both the government and private sector began a concerted effort to stop the hemorrhage of travelers, and thus money, away from the capital.

In 1995, $45 million was set aside to make Belize City more attractive. A new waterfront walkway was built along Eve Street. Open drains are gradually being replaced with septic tanks. Main roads have been resurfaced, traffic lights and signage added, and a series of new roundabouts have been built on the Northern Highway. As more and more fine old colonial buildings are restored, the Fort George area is an increasingly pleasant place to stay. Most importantly, the government has cracked down heavily on crime. In 1995, a Tourism Police Unit was created, and their foot patrols are now a familiar sight. More and more travelers are basing themselves at one of the city's fine hotels—which can arrange everything from scuba diving to rain-forest hikes, house most of the city's best restaurants, and often offer very competitive packages—and exploring the rest of the country from there. There's still a lot of work to be done, but Belize City *is* slowly re-creating itself.

Numbers in the margin correspond to points of interest on the Belize City and Northern and Central Belize map.

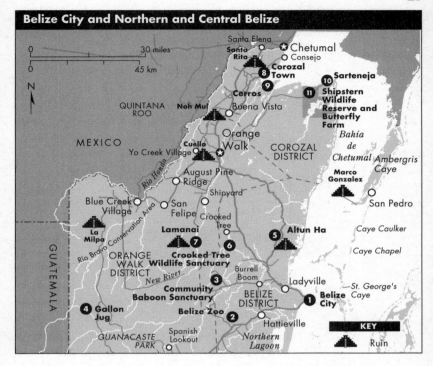

Belize City and Northern and Central Belize

0 —— 30 miles
0 —— 45 km

N

Santa Elena
Santa Rita ● **Chetumal**
○ Consejo
8 ▲ **Corozal Town**
9 ○ **Cerros**
Noh Mul ○ **Buena Vista**
QUINTANA ROO
10 **Sarteneja**
11 ● **Shipstern Wildlife Reserve and Butterfly Farm**
MEXICO
▲ ○ **Orange Walk**
Yo Creek Village ○ Cuello
Bahía de Chetumal
COROZAL DISTRICT
Ambergris Caye
Marco Gonzalez ▲
○ **San Pedro**
August Pine Ridge ○
Shipyard ○
Blue Creek Village ○
San Felipe ○
Crooked Tree ○
Caye Caulker
La Milpa ▲
Río Bravo Conservation Area
Lamanai ▲ **7**
6 ● **Crooked Tree Wildlife Sanctuary**
5 ▲ **Altun Ha**
Caye Chapel
GUATEMALA
ORANGE WALK DISTRICT
New River
Burrell Boom
Ladyville
St. George's Caye
3 ● **Community Baboon Sanctuary**
BELIZE DISTRICT
1 ● **Belize City**
4 ● **Gallon Jug**
Belize Zoo **2** ●
Hattieville
GUANACASTE PARK
Spanish Lookout ○
Northern Lagoon

KEY
▲ Ruin

Belize City

❶ If you're prepared to take the time and trouble, Belize City will repay your curiosity. Belizeans are natural city dwellers, and there is an infectious sociability on streets like Albert and Queen, the main shopping areas. The finest British colonial houses—graceful white buildings with wraparound verandas, painted shutters, and fussy Victorian woodwork—are on the North Shore, near the Radisson Fort George, the most pleasant part of the city to stroll. Overlooking the harbor from the south bank of Haulover Creek is the **Bliss Institute** (2 Southern Foreshore, between Church and Bishop Sts., ☎ 27/2110, ☉ weekdays 8:30–noon and 1–5), which houses the National Arts Council and hosts cultural events throughout the year. At the south end of Albert Street, is **St. John's Cathedral** (☎ 27/2137), the oldest Anglican church in Central America and the only one outside of England where kings were crowned. From 1815 to 1845 four kings of the Mosquito Coast (a British protectorate along the coast of Honduras and Nicaragua) were crowned here.

Government House. The finest colonial structure in the city, is said to have been designed by the illustrious British architect Sir Christopher Wren. Built in 1812, it was once the residence of the Governor General, the Queen's representative in Belize. After he and the rest of government moved to Belmopan in the wake of Hurricane Hattie, the house became a venue for social functions and a guest house for visiting VIPs. (The Queen stayed here in 1985, Prince Philip in 1988.) It is now open to the public, and you can peruse its archival records, silver, glassware, and furniture, and mingle with the tropical birds that frequent the gardens. ⊠ *Regent St., at Southern Foreshore,* ☎ *27/3050.* ⊡ *$2.50.* ☉ *Mon.–Fri. 8:30–4:30.*

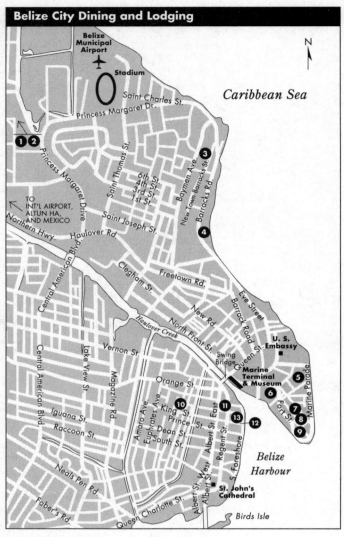

Belize City Dining and Lodging

Dining and Lodging

$–$$ ✕ **Sea Rock.** Sea Rock has the best Indian food in Belize. Period. The spicy tandoori fare is cooked in a clay oven and served in a comfortable, if unprepossessing, dining room enlivened by a few trinkets from India. It's a good first stop for vegetarians, as many meat-free dishes are served. ⊠ *190 New Town Barrack Rd., near the Princess Hotel,* ☎ *23/4105. AE, MC, V. Closed Sun.*

$–$$ ✕ **Three Amigos.** Three Amigos occupies the old GG's location, serving well-prepared versions of what might constitute Belizean comfort food: fish fingers, beans and rice, burgers, grilled T-bone steak with croquette potatoes and garlic bread. Daily lunch specials such as stewed chicken and rice are a real value at around $4. ⊠ *2B King St.,* ☎ *27/9936. No credit cards. Closed Sun.*

$ ✕ **Dit's Saloon.** Dit's is a Belize City institution. More pastry café–cum-saloon than restaurant, it's a real local place, with cheery striped tablecloths and a homey feel. (Like many other older Belizean restaurants, it has a sink right in the dining room.) The cakes—try the three-milks cake or the coconut tarts—are sticky and sweet, and breakfasts—toast, eggs, and beans, washed down with ample mugs of tea—are an excellent value. The fresh-squeezed juices are delicious, and nobody does beans and rice better. ⊠ *50 King St.,* ☎ *27/3330. No credit cards.*

$ ✕ **Macy's Café.** The wall of this cozy restaurant holds a letter from the bishop of Belize, congratulating the staff on its catering feats, and a photo of Harrison Ford during the making of *The Mosquito Coast* (his was the table by the door). If you're an eco-freak or a vegetarian, you may shudder at Macy's: You've seen the wildlife? Now you can eat it. Wrap your mouth around stewed armadillo, brocket deer, "royal" gibnut, and, by request, stewed iguana, known locally as bamboo chicken. Macy, the Jamaican-born proprietor, says it's tough to prepare—it has to be scalded, then washed in lime juice and vinegar—but delicious to eat. Bring your own booze. ⊠ *18 Bishop St.,* ☎ *27/3419. No credit cards.*

$$$ ✕⊡ **Princess Hotel & Casino.** Big-time gambling arrived in Belize in January 2000 when the country's first Las Vegas–style casino opened in the former Fiesta Inn, which was formerly the Ramada Inn. Maybe the third time's a charm? The hotel, with 118 rooms and suites, the largest in Belize, was expanded extensively to house the casino. It's not quite the MGM Grand, but it's as serious. As you enter the casino, slot machines, video poker, and other electronic gaming machines, nearly 500 altogether, fill the central part of the room. Live tables—black jack, roulette, craps, and poker—are toward the back. As of yet the guest rooms have not been upgraded, but hotel management says that's to happen "soon." Until this takes place, the rooms here are a definite step down from those at the Radisson (☞ *below*). As in Vegas, players get free drinks and a free buffet. To cut down on walk-in moochers, the casino gatekeeper may require you to ante up $50 for chips, although you don't have to use them and can cash them in when you leave. Perhaps owing to the Las Vegas showgirl precedent, dancing girls put on two shows in the evening. Belize's first **movie theater** is also here. The casino is open from noon until 4 AM. ⊠ *Newtown Barracks, Box 1758,* ☎ *23/2670; 800/228–9898 in the U.S.,* 𝖥𝖠𝖷 *23/2660. princessbz@btl.net. 113 rooms, 5 suites. Restaurant, bar, air-conditioning, exercise room, dive shop, fishing, casino, dance club, business services, convention center, travel services. AE, MC, V.*

$$$ ✕⊡ **Radisson Fort George.** Porters in pith helmets and a bright-red Royal
★ Mail pillar box on the steps keep British colonialism in the air at Belize City's finest hotel. The 102 air-conditioned rooms are distributed over three areas. Rooms in the main building have private verandas overlooking the pool and gardens; the six-story tower has panoramic views of the ocean through tinted glass; and the 37 rooms in the Executive Wing across the road overlook the river and one of the hotel's two pools. All have phones with direct access for U.S. calling cards, cable TV, coffeemakers, hair dryers, irons and ironing boards, and the best minibars in Belize. Lush red and ochre fabrics, faux-leopard carpets, and reproduction rattan and hardwood antiques re-create the British Raj of the 1880s. Service is always sprightly, and hotel staffers are relentlessly efficient and friendly. The Bayman's Tavern is one of the city's premier watering holes, and although the hotel's dining room is not held in quite as high local regard, it can serve up a tasty snapper fillet or grilled chop. Emory King, who was shipwrecked in Belize in 1954 and stayed on to become one of country's most popular authors, composing (*Hey, Dad, This Is Belize* and *The Driver's Guide to Beautiful Belize*) often holds court over breakfast. ⊠ *2 Marine Parade,* ☎ *27/7400; 800/333–3333 in the U.S.,* 𝖥𝖠𝖷 *27/3820. 102 rooms. Restaurant,*

bar, air-conditioning, room service, 2 pools, exercise room, laundry service, business services, convention center, travel services. AE, MC, V.

$$ ✕▦ **Bellevue Hotel.** Overlooking the harbor and the bay beyond, this fine old colonial house, built in 1900, has a tradition of excellent hospitality. Personally Speaking, the ground-floor restaurant, serves terrific fresh-baked bread with its Continental fare, and the wine list—an extensive one for Belize—is European, too. The second-floor Harbor Room, which has white wicker chairs and blue-and-pink decor, is a favorite meeting place for the city's expatriate crowd and hosts live music on weekends. Rooms are large, but a little timeworn, although most have air-conditioning and cable TV. Ask for one with a sea view. ⊠ *5 Southern Foreshore, Box 428,* ☎ *27/7052,* ℻ *27/3253. 35 rooms. Restaurant, bar, pool. AE, D, MC, V.*

$$ ✕▦ **Chateau Caribbean.** The rooms in this handsome, white colonial-style building overlooking the water are furnished in the bright colors of the Caribbean, with rattan chairs and writing desks of Belizean hardwoods. The suites have balconies overlooking the harbor, and all rooms have cable TV. But as this is Belize, don't expect everything to work perfectly—the louvered windows in your room may not close, defeating the air-conditioning. Fortunately, all rooms have phones, so you can call the desk. Chateau Caribbean is best known for its second-floor restaurant. With white tablecloths, gleaming cutlery, abstract art, and great ocean views, it's a charming place to eat, and less expensive than most other hotel dining rooms. The menu is an unusual combination of Chinese and Caribbean dishes, so you can have grilled snapper with rice and beans, your dining companion sweet and sour pork. ⊠ *6 Marine Parade,* ☎ *23/0800,* ℻ *23/0900. 25 rooms. Restaurant, bar, air-conditioning, room service. AE, MC, V.*

$$ ✕▦ **Fort Street Guest House.** Formerly the private residence of a leading Belizean doctor and his family, this 1920s-vintage house, with white trim and green-and-white-striped awnings, has an authentic British Honduras ambiance, enhanced by the warm hospitality of owners Hugh and Teresa Parkey. As a key member of the Hotel Association, Teresa has been instrumental in getting Belize City's hotels upgraded. In 1999 and early 2000, Teresa did some upgrading herself, adding private bathrooms and air-conditioning to several of the hotel's atmospheric rooms. Beds are exotically draped with baldachin-style mosquito nets, and you order breakfast by placing your selections in a bottle outside your door. Hemingway would have felt right at home here, and indeed one of the rooms (alas, not with private bath) is named for him. The second-floor restaurant with a wraparound porch that catches the sea breezes is one of the city's best. A chalkboard menu tells you the specials, which might be fresh seafood or a creatively prepared brace of pork chops. The restaurant also serves excellent breakfasts. (For hotel guests, the Continental option is complimentary.) Hugh Parkey can arrange just about any tour you want, especially if it's underwater; his reputable company Belize Dive Connection operates out of the Radisson (☞ *above*). ⊠ *4 Fort St.,* ☎ *23/0116,* ℻ *27/ 8808. 6 rooms, 3 with bath. Restaurant, bar, laundry service, travel services. AE, D, MC, V.*

$$ ✕▦ **The Great House.** The white, floodlit exterior of this grand colonial house, with its beautiful butterfly staircase, is one of the most-pleasing sights in the Fort George area. Steve Maestre, the owner, has been an influential figure on Belize City's tourist scene for many years (he managed the Radisson at one time), and he has now turned his house into a fine little inn. The 12 guest rooms are furnished with squishy decorative bed pillows, quilts in bright colors, and cable TV. The large bathrooms have both bath and shower. The wraparound verandas are pleasant places to sit and read. On the ground floor, a tiny gallery of

shops leads to The Smoky Mermaid, a much-needed addition to Belize City: a restaurant where you can dine under the stars. In a large courtyard shaded by breadfruit and sapadilla trees, with tables arranged on elevated hardwood decks, the amiable foodservers bring Caribbean-influenced seafood dishes, inventive pasta, and savory barbecues. The best table? The little elevated deck on the roof of the bar. ⊠ *13 Cork St.,* ☎ *23/3400,* FAX *23/3444. 12 rooms. Restaurant, bar, air-conditioning, fans, refrigerators, beauty salon. AE, DC, MC, V.*

$$ ⊞ **Colton House.** Good mid-priced accommodations are rare in Belize,
★ so this beautiful 1920s West Indian–style house across the street from the Radisson is a real find. The wraparound veranda is furnished with hammocks and white rattan furniture; the interior is decorated with antiques and cool, polished wooden floors. All rooms have private baths, and the garden room has air-conditioning, a microwave, TV, and refrigerator. The proprietors, Alan and Ondina Colton, have added all the charms you'd find in a bed-and-breakfast, albeit without the breakfast. Alan, who came here with the British armed forces and decided to stay, becoming a Belize citizen, has accumulated an enormous collection of ecology books and videotapes, which he's happy to share with guests. Reservations are essential. ⊠ *9 Cork St.,* ☎ *24/4666,* FAX *23/0451. 4 rooms, 1 suite. No credit cards.*

$$ ⊞ **Embassy Hotel.** If you just want a place to overnight en route to somewhere else, this hotel is only 250 ft from the international airport. Charm it has little, and, though it was built in 1998, some of the rooms already look down at the heels, but it's convenient, safe, and clean. Besides single and double rooms with private baths and air-conditioning, the hotel has seven suites, a restaurant, and a fourth-floor rooftop deck with hammocks and table tennis. ⊠ *Belize International Airport,* ☎ *25/3333,* FAX *25/2267. 40 rooms, 7 suites. Restaurant, bar, travel services. MC, V.* ✎

$$ ⊞ **Villa Boscardi.** If you're edgy about overnighting in Belize City, this new B&B in Belize's northern 'burbs just might be your cup of herbal tea. Franco and Françoise Boscardi (he's Italian, she's Belgian) opened their home, in a quiet residential area between the Northern Highway and the Caribbean, to guests in 1999. The three large rooms, each with cable TV, are bright, sunny, and stylishly decorated, with a hint of Europe here, a taste of Belize there. A full breakfast is included, as is free airport transportation Monday to Saturday. ⊠ *6043 Manatee Dr. (turn toward sea off Northern Hwy. at Golding Ave., then left on second lane to fifth house on right),* ☎ *23/1691,* FAX *23/1691. 3 rooms. Air-conditioning. AE, MC, V.* ✎

Scuba Diving

If you're interested in a dive trip to the reef or the atolls, *see* the Scuba Diving sections *in* Cayes and Atolls, *below.* Operated for years by Hugh Parkey, co-owner of the Fort Street Guesthouse, **Belize Dive Connection** (⊠ 2 Marine Parade, Belize City, ☎ 23/4526, FAX 27/8808) runs trips to suit your every whim from the Radisson Fort George dock.

Shopping

Try the **National Handicraft Center** (⊠ Fort St., just past Fort Street Guest House, ☎ 23/3636) for Belizean products of all kinds. The **Fort Street Guest House** (⊠ 4 Fort St., ☎ 23/0116), the **Radisson Fort George** (⊠ 2 Marine Parade ☎ 33/3333), and **Princess Hotel & Casino** (⊠ Newtown Barracks, ☎ 23/2670) all have good gift shops. Belize's beautiful stamps are available from the **Philatelic Society** (⊠ Queen St., behind post office). **Go Tees** (⊠ 23 Regent St., ☎ 27/4082 or 27/5512) has T-shirts for adults and children and a good selection of crafts.

Brodies supermarket (Mile 2½, Northern Hwy., ☎ 23/5587) and **Save-U** supermarket (✉ Belikin Area Plaza, ☎ 23/1291) are Belize's largest groceries and good places to buy picnic supplies, beer and liquor, and snacks.

The Book Centre (✉ 4 Church St., ☎ 27/7457) sells magazines and the classics. **The Belize Bookshop** (✉ Regent St., ☎ 27/2054) has magazines, books, and local and U.S. newspapers; it's open weekdays except Wednesday afternoon.

Belize Zoo

☞ ➋ *48 km (30 mi) west of Belize City; buses from Belize City to San Ignacio stop at the zoo; by car from Belize City, take the Western Highway to Mile 30.*

You turn a sharp corner on the jungle trail, and suddenly you're face to face with a black jaguar, the largest cat in the Western Hemisphere. What is there to do when you're 2 ft from 250 pounds of untamed muscle power? The big cat's teeth look as big as Michael Jordan's shoes as it growls a deep rumbling threat. Involuntarily, you jump back, thankful a strong but inconspicuous fence separates you and the jaguar.

The Belize Zoo is one of the world's smallest, but arguably one of the best, with only animals native to Belize, all in settings as natural and wildlife-friendly as the little zoo's budget allows. As you stroll the trails on a self-guided tour, you visit several Belizean ecosystems—rain forest, lagoons, pine ridge, and riverine forest—and spot more than 125 species of wild things native to Belize, including the jaguar: the zoo has both the spotted and the rare black jaguar. You'll also see the four other wild cats of Belize: the puma, margay, ocelot, and jaguarundi. Probably the most famous resident of the zoo is April. She's a Baird's tapir—the largest of tapirs, which are a relative of the horse and rhino—and the national animal of Belize, known locally as the mountain cow.

The Belize Zoo comprises just 29 acres, but it packs a lot of nature in a small space. Walk the wild trails of the zoo, with charmingly hand-lettered signs to point the way, and soon you'll find other denizens of the bush: howler monkeys (Belizeans call them baboons), kinkajous, crocodiles, fer-de-lance snakes, toucans, scarlet macaws, and two jabiru storks, the Western Hemisphere's largest flying birds, standing almost as tall as a human with a wingspan of up to 9 ft.

The zoo exists because of the vision and drive of one gutsy, dedicated woman, Sharon Matola. Matola is an American who came to Belize as part of a wildlife film production and who stayed on to care for some of the semi-tame animals used in the film. She opened the zoo in 1983 in a small facility, and in 1991 it moved to its present location not far from the original site. In addition to running the zoo, Matola is an active conservationist.

You also can tour the Belize Zoo's 84-acre Tropical Education Center adjacent to the zoo for bird-watching from a bird deck, hiking a boardwalk trail through the savanna, canoeing, and educational programs. The center is involved in a green iguana breeding project. Dormitory accommodations, with outdoor toilets, are available at the center. Overnighters can take a nocturnal zoo tour ($10). In late 1999, it was learned the zoo itself could become an endangered species if a proposed landfill, announced by the government, is in fact located next door. The zoo has launched a petition drive to have the landfill site changed. ☎ 81/3004. ✉ *$7.50 adults, $3.75 children 13 and under.* ☉ *Daily 9–4:30.*

Community Baboon Sanctuary

❸ *50 km (31 mi) west of Belize City; take Northern Highway and turn left on road to Burrell Boom.*

This baboon sanctuary (the "baboon" is actually the black howler monkey) is one of the most interesting wildlife conservation projects in Belize. It was established in 1985 by a zoologist from the University of Wisconsin and a group of local farmers, with help from the World Wildlife Fund. Protection of the howler monkey—an agile bundle of black fur with a derriere like a baboon's and a roar that sounds like a cross between a jaguar and a stuck pig—began after it had already been zealously hunted throughout Central America and was facing extinction. In Belize, it found a refuge. An all-embracing plan, coordinating eight villages, more than 100 landowners, and a 32-km (20-mi) stretch of the Belize River, was drawn up to protect its habitat. Today there are nearly 1,000 black howler monkeys in the sanctuary, as well as numerous other species of birds and mammals. Exploring is made easy by about 5 km (3 mi) of trails starting at the small museum. The visitor center has a few rooms for rent, but you need to reserve well in advance. ☎ 27/7369. ⌨ $5. ☉ Dawn to dusk.

Belize City and Environs A to Z

Arriving and Departing
BY AIRPLANE
Philip Goldson International Airport (⌨ Ladyville) is 14 km (9 mi) north of the city. Cabs to town cost $15. The **municipal airstrip** in Belize City has flights to San Pedro and down the coast to Dangriga, Placencia, and Punta Gorda.

BY BUS
Belize City is the hub of the country's fairly extensive bus network, so you can catch regular service to various regions of Belize and connections to the Guatemalan and Mexican borders (☞ Getting Around By Bus *in* Belize A to Z, *below*).

BY CAR
There are only two highways to Belize City—the Northern Highway, which leads from the Mexican border, 165 km (102 mi) away, and the Western Highway, which runs 131 km (81 mi) from Guatemala. Both roads are paved.

Getting Around
BY TAXI
There is no bus service within Belize City, so if you don't have a car, you'll get around by taxi or on foot. Do not walk around after dark, however, except in the Fort George area. Cabs cost $3 for one person between any two points in the city, plus $1 for each additional person. Outside the city, you're charged by distance, but there are no meters, so be sure to set a price before you leave. Pick up a taxi at Market Square, by the swing bridge, or call **Cinderella Taxi** (☎ 24/5240) or **Caribbean Taxi** (☎ 27/2888).

Contacts and Resources
EMERGENCIES
Hospital. Belize Medical Associates (⌨ 5791 St. Thomas St., ☎ 23/0303) and **Karl Heusner Memorial** (⌨ Princess Margaret Dr., ☎ 23/1548) have 24-hour emergency rooms.

Dentist. Dr. Osbert Usher (16 Magazine Rd., ☎ 27/3415) has a dental clinic across from the Venus bus station, and one of the dentists can usually see you on short notice.

Brodie's Pharmacy (⊠ Regent St. at Market Sq.) is open Monday, Tuesday, Thursday, and Saturday 8:30 AM–7 PM; Wednesday 8:30 AM–12:30 PM; Friday 8:30 AM–9 PM; and Sunday 9 AM–12:30 PM. **Community Drug Stores** (⊠ 5 locations in Belize City, including Farmer's Market) are open daily including holidays from 8 AM–8 PM.

VISITOR INFORMATION

The **Belize Tourist Board** (⊠ New Central Bank Building, Level 2, Gabourel Lane, Box 325, Belize City, ☎ 23/1913 or 800/624-0686, FAX 23/1943, ✆) is open weekdays 8–noon and 1–5.

NORTHERN AND CENTRAL BELIZE

Because Belize is so small, much of the country is accessible from Belize City. This is especially true of the north, whose Northern Highway is much better for travelers than many of the circuitous routes and bad roads of the south. The landscape is mostly flat—this is sugarcane country—and although the north sees fewer travelers than the Cayo, it holds some of Belize's most interesting Maya sites as well as several first-class resorts.

Numbers in the margin correspond to points of interest on the Belize City and Northern and Central Belize map.

Gallon Jug

❹ *3½ hrs west of Belize City.*

What's notable about this village in western Belize, besides its curious name, is Chan Chich Lodge and the adjoining 250,000-acre Río Bravo Conservation Area, which was created with the help of the Massachusetts Audubon Society and the distinguished British naturalist Gerald Durrell. The extensive nature trails at Chan Chich veritably teem with wildlife and, above all, birds. A night walk here might be one of the most exciting things you do in Belize.

Dining and Lodging

$$$ ✕📶 **Chan Chich Lodge.** It remains to be seen whether the spirit of Smoking Shell or another fierce Maya ruler will one day take revenge on Barry Bowen, Chan Chich Lodge's owner, for erecting a group of cabanas slap in the middle of a Classic Period (AD 250–900) Maya plaza. But since it opened in 1988, Chan Chich has established itself as one of the best jungle lodges in all of Central America. President Jimmy Carter is among the many illustrious guests who have stayed here. You can fly in on a charter flight from Belize City, although the trip by car is an incredible experience. The four-hour drive takes you through deep bush, including the 240,000 acres of the Rio Bravo Conservation Area. You might encounter deer, wildcats, a flock of oscellated turkeys, a dense shower of butterflies—anything but another vehicle. Bowen is one of the wealthiest men in Belize (he owns everything from Belikin beer to shrimp farms), and in the late 1980s, having seen which way the wind was blowing, he decided to join the boom in ecotourism. The result is a magnificent property near Bowen's 2,500 Gallon Jug farm (the only place in Belize that grows coffee in commercial quantities), with excellent tour guides for wildlife excursions into the several hundred thousand acres of surrounding bush. You are more likely to see the elusive jaguar here than anywhere else outside the Belize Zoo: the lodge averages about one sighting a week. The 12 thatch-roof cabanas, each with two queen beds, have 24-hour electricity, bath with hot- and cold-water shower, and a wraparound veranda. The cabins farthest from the restaurant kitchen and on the edge of the lodge grounds, such as

Nos. 2 and 9, are most desirable. A gorgeous pool is screened to keep out bugs. Tours include canoe trips on the river; bird-watching (some 350 species have been identified here); and horseback tours to Maya ruins that have *not* yet been built upon, which in a country such as Belize, would be hard to do. ⊠ *Box 37, Belize City,* ☎ *027/5634; 800/ 451–8017 in the U.S.,* FAX *27/6961. 12 cabanas. Restaurant, bar, pool, horseback riding, travel services. AE, MC, V.*

Altun Ha

❺ *45 km (28 mi) north of Belize City; take Northern Highway to Old Northern Highway to turnoff for ruins.*

If you've never visited an ancient Maya city or want to see one without too much exertion, make a trip to Altun Ha. It's not the most dramatic site in Belize—Caracol takes that award—but it is the most thoroughly excavated and the most accessible. Human residence here spanned 2,000 years: the first inhabitants settled shortly before the crowning of the ancient Egyptian king Sheshonk I, in 945 BC, and their descendants finally abandoned Altun Ha the year after King Alfred of England died, in AD 900. At its height, the city was home to 10,000 people.

The team from the Royal Ontario Museum that first excavated the site in the mid-1960s found 250 structures spread over more than 1,000 square yards. At Plaza B, in the Temple of the Masonry Altars, the archaeologists also found the grandest and most valuable piece of Maya art ever discovered—the head of the sun god Kinich Ahau. Weighing 9¾ pounds, it was carved from a solid block of green jade. In the absence of a national museum, the head is kept in a solid steel vault in the central branch of the Bank of Belize. ☎ *No phone.* ⌨ *$2.50.* ☺ *Daily 9–5.*

Crooked Tree Wildlife Sanctuary

❻ *53 km (33 mi) northwest of Belize City.*

Founded by the Belize Audubon Society in 1984, this sanctuary encompasses a chain of swamps, lagoons, and inland waterways covering 3,000 acres. At its center is **Crooked Tree**, one of the oldest inland villages in Belize, with a population of about 800, mostly Creoles; the community has a church, a school, and one of the surest signs of a former British territory—a cricket pitch.

Crooked Tree is paradise for bird-watchers. Snowy egrets, snail kites, ospreys, and black-collared hawks, as well as two types of duck—Muscovy and black-bellied whistling—and all five species of kingfisher native to Belize can be spotted. The sanctuary's most prestigious visitor, however, is the jabiru stork, a kind of freshwater albatross with a wingspan of up to 9 ft. It's the largest flying bird in the Americas.

The best way to tour the sanctuary is by canoe, and there are a number of excellent guides in the village, including **Sam Tillet**. Your adventurousness will be rewarded: by boat, you're likely to see iguanas, crocodiles, coatis, and turtles. For birders, the best time to come is in the dry season, roughly February to early June, because lowered water levels mean that birds tend to group together to find water and food, making them easy to spot. ⊠ *Turn west off Northern Hwy. at mile 30.8, then drive 3 km (2 mi),* ☎ *27/7745.* ⌨ *$4.*

Dining and Lodging

$–$$ ✕▥ **Bird's Eye View Lodge.** Though you may think the two-story concrete hotel, lately covered with climbing vines and flowers, looks a little out of place at the edge of the lagoon, inside this Belizean-owned spot you'll find spic 'n span rooms and someone with a smile to make you feel welcome. Choose from a private room or one of eight beds in a dorm-style room. The hotel's appealing little dining room serves no-frills but filling Creole fare. ⊠ *Box 1976, Crooked Tree,* ☎ *23/2040,* ⅩX *22/4869. 10 rooms with bath, 8 bunks. Restaurant, canoeing, horseback riding. AE, MC, V. www.belizenet.com/birdseye.*

$–$$ ✕▥ **Paradise Inn.** This is the kind of place where you want to stay for a week, and regret having to leave when you do. It's operated by Rudy Crawford, who helped get the Crooked Tree sanctuary started, with help from several of his nine children. Simply furnished, well-maintained thatched cabanas sit right on the lagoon, with sweeping views. You can have all your meals here for under $15 a day. A bonus: Rudy brews some mean cohune palm wine. ⊠ *At north end of Crooked Tree village area, on lagoon,* ☎ *27/7745. 5 cabanas. MC, V.*

Lamanai

★ ❼   *2½ hrs northwest of Belize City via Orange Walk Town, which is 106 km (66 mi) northwest of Belize City. About 18 mi (30 km) by boat from New River Park Hotel area south of Orange Walk Town.*

Lamanai ("submerged insect" in Maya, often mistranslated as "submerged crocodile") was the longest-occupied Maya site in Belize, inhabited until well after 1492. In fact, archaeologists have found signs of continuous occupation from 1500 BC until the 16th century.

The people of Lamanai carried on a way of life that was passed down for millennia, until the Spanish missionaries arrived. You can still see the ruins of the church the missionaries built in the nearby village of **Indian Church.** The same village also has an abandoned 19th-century sugar mill. With its immense drive-wheel and steam engine—on which you can still read the name of the manufacturer, Leeds Foundry in New Orleans—swathed in strangler vines and creepers, it's a haunting sight.

In all, 50 or 60 Maya structures were spread over what is now the 950-acre Archaeological Reserve here. The most impressive of these is the largest Pre-Classic structure in Belize: a massive, stepped temple built into the hillside overlooking the river. A ball court, numerous dwellings, and several other fine temples remain. One of Belize's finest stelae is here, an elaborately carved depiction of the ruler Smoking Shell, as well as Belize's only archaeological museum, where caretakers will be glad to show you a 2,500-year progression of pottery, carvings, and small statues.

Many structures at Lamanai have been only superficially excavated. Trees and vines grow from the tops of the temples, the sides of one pyramid are covered with vegetation, and another pyramid rises abruptly from the forest floor. There are no tour buses or cold-drink stands here—just ruins, forest, and wildlife, including howler monkeys.

There are several ways to get here. One option is to drive, on a good all-weather unpaved road from Orange Walk Town. From here head west to Yo Creek, then southwest to San Felipe village, a total of 39 km (24 mi). In San Felipe, go straight (the road to Chan Chich turns to the right) for another 19 km (12 mi) to Indian Church Village near the Lamanai ruins. It's about a 1½-hour drive. The best way to approach the ruins, however, is by boat, which takes just a little longer. Boats leave from the New River Park Hotel area near the toll bridge, about

10 km (6 mi) south of Orange Walk. You can also take a charter plane from Belize City, for a 15-minute trip. 🖃 *$2.50.* ☉ *Daily 9–5.*

Various Belize City and Orange Walk Town tour operators (☞ Guided Tours *in* Belize A to Z, *below*) and a few local tour guides, including **Mr. Godoy** (Orange Walk, 32/2969), run day trips up the New River. Several boats leave from **New River Park Hotel** (☎ 32/3987) on the Northern Highway, near the toll bridge just south of Orange Walk Town.

Dining and Lodging

$$$ ✕🖼 **Lamanai Outpost Lodge.** Built by the late Colin Howells, a legend in Belizean hospitality circles, and now run by his son and daughter-in-law Mark and Monique Howells, Lamanai Outpost perches on a low hillside with a view of the beautiful New River Lagoon. The lodge is closely involved with archeological and nature study programs through the Lamanai Field Research Center, which is home to resident naturalists, archaeologists, and ornithologists. But this is a popular spot for anyone with a Nature Channel kind of curiosity, and guests typically include those on Elderhostel programs and kids who love Lamanai for the monkeys, parrots, and other creatures that always seem to be around. This is owing in part to Monique, who takes in injured or abandoned animals and cares for them until they can be safely returned to the wild. Even when you sneak off to the bar lounge, The Digger's Roost, you'll find archaeological memorabilia and a full-size reproduction of a Lamanai stela showing Lord Smoking Shell. A dock extends 130 ft into the lagoon and is a good place for star-gazing and swimming— just keep an eye out for Ol' Mister Croc. Bird-watching is superb in this area, with at least 370 species identified within a 3-km (2-mi) radius of the lodge. The thatch cabanas with 24-hour electricity are set among hillside gardens. All have porches with lagoon views, and lots of screened windows, designed so you can see out and those outside can't peek in. Beds, cabinets, and other furnishings were custom-made from local hardwoods. The Lamanai ruins are within walking distance, as is a small community butterfly education center, Xochil Ku. Don't miss taking a night-spotting tour ($36 per person)—the New River Lagoon and New River are fascinating at night. ✉ *Box 63, Indian Church,* ☎ *23/3578,* 𝔽𝔸𝕏 *21/2061. 17 cabins. Restaurant, bar, fans, boating. AE, MC, V. Closed Sept.* 🐾

Corozal Town

❽ *153 km (95 mi) north of Belize City.*

The last town before the Río Hondo, the border separating Belize from Mexico, Corozal, like Ambergris Caye, was originally settled by refugees from the Yucatán during the 19th-century caste wars. Though thoroughly ignored by today's visitors, Corozal is one of the friendliest, safest, and least expensive areas in the country. It's a place to slow down, relax, and enjoy at least a few days of easy living by the turquoise waters of Corozal Bay. There's not a whole lot to see here, and no real beaches (but good swimming in the bays and lagoons), with just a few memorable hotels and restaurants. Yet the climate is unequivocally appealing, with less rain than almost anywhere else in Belize, the fishing is excellent, and the sunny disposition of residents—mestizos, Creoles, Mayans, and even North Americans—is compelling.

That said, the slow pace of Corozal may be set to change. The Corozal Free Zone, just south of the Santa Elena border crossing, is starting to make a name for itself as a place where businesses are free from many of the restrictions and high import duties of the rest of Belize. Mexicans cross the border for the cheaper gas, and at least one casino is being built in the Zone.

Though English is still the official language here, Spanish is just as common. The town has been largely rebuilt since Hurricane Janet nearly destroyed it in 1955, so it's neat and modern. Many houses are clapboard, built on wooden piles, though a growing clan of expats, especially in the Consejo Shores area north of town, are putting up new houses that would not look out of place in Florida. One of the few remaining historic buildings is a portion of the old fort in the center of town, and the town hall, which has a colorful mural by Manuel Villamar Reyes depicting local history.

In a landmark 100-year-old building near the market, **Corozal Cultural Center,** now a museum and tourist information center, was once a lighthouse. The museum has hand-blown rum bottles, a traditional Maya thatch hut, and a spiral staircase, and parts of the original lighthouse beacon remain on display. *Off First Ave., at the edge of Corozal Bay,* ☎ *42/3176.* ▣ *$1.50.* ◷ *Tues.–Sat. 9–noon, 1–4:30.*

Not far from Corozal are several Maya sites. The closest, **Santa Rita,** is a short walk from the center of the town. Only a few of its structures have been excavated, so it takes some imagination to picture this settlement, founded in 1500 BC, as one of the major trading centers in the district. ☎ *No phone.* ▣ *$2.50.* ◷ *Daily 8–4.*

❾ **Cerros,** a late Pre-Classic center, is south of Corozal on the coast. As at Santa Rita, little has been excavated, but the site, which dates from about 2000 BC, includes a ball court, several tombs, and a large temple. The best way to get here is by boat from Corozal, around $60 to $75 for up to four people. ☎ *No phone.* ▣ *$5.* ◷ *Daily 8–4.*

Dining and Lodging

$ ✕ **Café Kela.** The last place you'd expect to find a French café is in Corozal Town, but this tiny restaurant with just five tables in a cozy round bayside palapa is proof that in Belize you never know what will turn up. Everything is delicious, from the French crepes to fresh grouper sautéed with herbs. And the prices? *Mais oui,* it's hard to spend more than a few dollars a person here. No alcohol served, but you can BYOB, and the fresh-squeezed fruit juices are heavenly. ✉ *First Ave., across the street from the bay, about 2 blocks north of Corozal Cultural Center,* ☎ *no phone. No credit cards.*

$$ ✕▦ **Casablanca by the Sea.** It's worth a short trip to Consejo, about 18 km (8 mi) northeast of Corozal Town, just to see the inn's hand-carved mahogany doors gracing the entrances of each room. Once here, though, you'll want to stay awhile. Consejo, a tiny village on the water across the bay from Chetumal, is one of those quiet, off-the-beaten-path places in Belize that could easily steal your heart and make packing to leave near impossible. Beverly Tempte, an expat from New England, and her husband, a medical doctor, bought an unfinished building next to the Consejo customs office and created this charming small hotel. The best room in the house is the bayside suite with queen bed, air-conditioning, cable TV, and minibar. The other rooms, all on the small side, have white-plaster walls with native hardwood trim, tile floors, and ceiling fans. The first-floor, 50-seat restaurant serves tasty Belizean and American food and often caters to groups. ✉ *Box 212, Consejo, next to the customs shed in the village, 8 mi northeast of Corozal Town,* ☎ *43/8018,* ℻ *43/8003. 7 rooms, 1 suite. Restaurant, bar, air-conditioning, travel services. AE, MC, V. www.cbbythesea.com.*

$$ ✕▣ **Hok'ol K'in Guesthouse.** Run by a former Peace Corps volunteer and her Belizean business partner, Hok'ol K'in (a Yuacatec Maya phrase for welcoming the rising sun) is a nine-room motel just across the street from Corozal Bay. Thanks to the stiff breezes from the bay, guest rooms are naturally cooled. They're a bit crowded by two queen beds, but verandas with a hammock give you a little more space. All rooms overlook the bay, but the best views are from the second-floor rooms. One room is wheelchair accessible. The guest lounge has TV, VCR, and a small library. The restaurant serves inexpensive breakfasts, snacks, and the best burgers in town. Inexpensive and interesting tours, including one that visits local schools, are available. ⊠ *Box 145, Corozal Town, 1 block south of the market,* ☎ *42/3329,* 𝔽𝔸𝕏 *42/3569. maya@btl.net 9 rooms. Restaurant, bar, travel services. AE, MC, V.*

$$ ✕▣ **Tony's Inn.** For almost 30 years, Tony and Donna Castillo's little motel has been a popular stopping place for those passing through from Mexico. The restaurant, where locals go for a splurge, specializes in steak, shrimp, and fried lobster. A new bar and grill, replacing the venerable bayside palapa bar (somebody ought to have put up a historic landmark sign in memory of that Belikin-soaked spot), opened in early 2000. Tony's has a marina and can arrange fishing trips. The hotel claims a beach, although it's really more of a patch of ground with imported sand. The more expensive digs on the second floor are the way go to here—they're big, with cable TV, king or two double beds, tile floors, and some of the coldest air-conditioning in Belize. ⊠ *Box 12, Corozal Town; at south end of town, on the Northern Hwy., south of 10th St.,* ☎ *42/2055,* 𝔽𝔸𝕏 *42/2829. 24 rooms. Restaurant, bar, beach, marina, fishing, laundry services, travel services. AE, MC, V.*

$–$$ ✕▣ **Hotel Maya.** This small, friendly, family-run hotel with a Mexican and Belizean restaurant is at the southern end of Corozal. The rooms are clean and cheerful, with brightly colored Mexican rugs and bedspreads, and light-colored walls with sunny yellow curtains on the windows. The more expensive rooms are air-conditioned. ⊠ *c/o Rosita Mai Mendzies, Box 112, Corozal Town,* ☎ *42/2082,* 𝔽𝔸𝕏 *42/2827. 20 rooms. Restaurant, bar, travel services. MC, V.*

Sarteneja

❿ *32 km (20 mi) by boat from Corozal, 97 km (60 mi) by car via Northern Highway south to Orange Walk and northeast on road to Sarteneja; this drive usually takes an hour and a half, but the rough road makes it seem a lot longer*

This village is a small community of mestizo fishermen and farmers who make a living from lobster fishing and pineapple farming. Traditionally, their links were north, across the Bay of Chetumal to Mexico, rather than south to the rest of Belize, but this is changing with the construction of the road to Orange Walk, which is now served by several daily buses.

The 81 square km (31 square mi) of tropical forest that now form the **⓫ Shipstern Wildlife Reserve** are, like the Crooked Tree Wildlife Sanctuary, a paradise for bird-watchers. Look for egrets (there are 13 species here), American coot, keel-billed toucans, flycatchers, warblers, and several species of parrots. Mammals are in healthy supply as well, including deer, peccaries, pumas, jaguars, and raccoons, as well as a dizzying variety of insects and butterflies. The butterfly farm next to the visitor center used to export pupae but is now only a small education area with a few flitting butterflies. For overnight stays, cabins on the reserve may be available, for $10 a night, and Sarteneja village has a couple of guest houses—ask in the village what's open. ⊠

Sarteneja village, Belize Audubon Society: ☎ *23/4533,* ℻ *23/4985.* *www.belizeaudubon.org* ✉ *$5.*

Northern and Central Belize A to Z

Arriving and Departing

BY AIRPLANE

Tropic Air (☎ 24/5671; 800/422–3435 in the U.S., ℻ 26/2338) has flights to Corozal from both San Pedro, on Ambergris Caye, and Belize City. The journey takes 20 minutes and costs $84 round-trip from Belize City, $64 from San Pedro.

BY BUS

Novelo's (Batty Bros.) (✉ 15 Mosul St., Belize City, ☎ 27/2025) and **Venus Bus Service** (✉ Magazine Rd., Belize City, ☎ 27/7390 or 27/3354) make the three-hour journey from Belize City to Corozal ($4 one-way) several times a day. Buses also continue from there to Chetumal, Mexico.

BY BOAT

An old, renovated sugar barge ferries passengers and cars across the New River between Cerros (just south of Corozal Town) and the Shipstern peninsula. It operates from 6 AM to 9 PM daily. To get to the ferry from Corozal Town, take the Northern Highway toward Orange Walk Town to just south of Jal's Travel and Paula's Gift Shop. Turn left, and follow the road (and the power lines) for 4 km (2½ mi) to the ferry landing. When you get off the ferry, you're about 4 km (2½ mi) from Copper Bank Village, and about 9 km (5½ mi) from Progresso. This saves 66 km (40 mi) over roads via Orange Walk Town. You may be able to hail down a Venus bus from Orange Walk.

BY CAR

From Belize City, Corozal is the last stop on the Northern Highway before you hit Mexico. The 153-km (95-mi) journey will probably take you a good two to three hours, longer if you stop off at Altun Ha or the Crooked Tree sanctuary on the way.

Getting Around

If you don't have your own wheels, you'll have a hard time exploring the north, as there are few cross-country bus services and too little traffic to count on hitchhiking. You can find taxis in Corozal, but they're costly. The town has a large expatriate community, so if you're stuck, try hooking up with them.

THE CAYES AND ATOLLS

Imagine bouncing over sea-green water after a day's snorkeling, the white prow of your boat pointing up into the billowing clouds, the base of the sky darkening to a deep lilac, the spray pouring over you like warm rain. To the left, San Pedro's pastel buildings huddle among the palm trees like a detail from a Paul Klee canvas. To the right, the surf breaks in a white seam along the reef. Over the surface of the water, flying fish scamper away like winged aquatic hares.

This and many other delicious experiences lie off the coast of Belize, where 175 cayes (the word comes from the Spanish *cayo*, "low island or reef," but is pronounced "key," as in Key Largo) dot the Caribbean like punctuation marks in a long, liquid sentence. Most cayes lie inside the Barrier Reef, and over the centuries it has acted as a breakwater, allowing them to form and develop undisturbed by the tides and winds that would otherwise sweep them away. Their names are evocative, and often funny: there is a Deadman's Caye, a Laughing Bird Caye, and—why ask why?—a Bread and Butter Caye. Some names suggest the kind of company you should expect: Mosquito Caye, Sandfly Caye, and even Crawl Caye, which is supposedly infested with boa constrictors. Many, like Cockney Range or Baker's Rendezvous, simply express the whimsy or nostalgia of the early British settlers. The vast majority are uninhabited except by possum, frigate birds, pelicans, brown- and red-footed boobies, and some lewd-sounding creatures called wish-willies (which are actually a kind of iguana).

Farther out to sea, between 48 and 96 km (30 and 60 mi) off the coast, are the atolls, which from the air look impossibly beautiful. At their center, the water is mint green: the white sandy bottom reflects the light upwards and is flecked with patches of mangrove and rust-colored sediments. Around the fringe of the atoll, the surf breaks in a white circle before the color changes abruptly to ultramarine as the water plunges to 3,000 ft.

The origin of Belize's atolls is still something of a mystery, but evidence suggests that unlike the Pacific atolls, which formed by accretion around the rims of submerged volcanoes, these grew from the bottom up, as vast pagodas of coral accumulated over millions of years on top of limestone fault blocks. The Maya were probably the first humans to discover and use the atolls, as stopovers on their trading routes. Piles of seashells and rocks, known as "shell maidens" and thought to have been placed there as markers, have been found on the Turneffe Islands.

The battle fought by the Spanish and English for control of the high seas spilled over into nomenclature. With the rout of the Spanish at the Battle of St. George's Caye, in 1798, English names took precedence: Turneffe, for Terre Nef; Lighthouse Reef for Quattro Cayos; Glover's Reef, for Longorif.

Until recently the atolls were sparsely inhabited. Lobster fishing, sponge gathering, and coconut plantations provided a small permanent population with a difficult living. For the most part, small dive resorts have begun to open on the atolls, and on more of the cayes, bringing economic rejuvenation. For logistical reasons—power, water supply, transportation (several can be reached only by charter boat)—some are very basic, with no electricity and spartan accommodations. Others cater increasingly to an exclusive clientele.

Though they're designed mainly for divers, these resorts are also marvelous hangouts for those who simply want to swing in a hammock, snorkel, and read. If you want a real castaway experience, this is the place to find it. If, on the other hand, you like a bit of nightlife and sociability, you might go stir-crazy. Most of the resorts lie in the upper price range. (The five resorts on the atolls, for example, cost $1,200 per person and up.) Because of their isolation, many offer only eight-day, seven-night packages, and because all have only limited space, you must reserve well in advance, particularly for the high season (November–April).

Scuba Diving

Dive destinations are often divided into two broad categories—the reef and the atolls. Most reef diving is done on the northern section, particularly off Ambergris Caye. Here the reef is just a few hundred yards from shore, making access to your dive site extremely easy: the journey by boat usually takes 10–30 minutes. The farther south you go, the farther apart are coast and coral, and longer boat trips make for greater dependence on weather. On Ambergris, in contrast, you might be stuck inside for a morning storm, but you still have a good chance of getting out in the afternoon. Most of the cayes' dive shops are attached to hotels, and the quality of dive masters, equipment, and facilities varies considerably.

Many resorts offer diving courses. A one-day basic familiarization course costs between $125 and $175. A four-day PADI certification course costs $350 to $400. A popular variant is a referral course, in which you do the academic and pool training at home, then complete the diving section here; the cost, for two days, is $250.

If you want to experience something truly dramatic, head to the atolls, which make for some of the world's greatest diving. The only problem with the atolls is that they're awfully far from where you're likely to stay. If you're based on Ambergris Caye, Glover's Reef is out of the question for a day trip by boat, and you don't want to be too optimistic about getting to Lighthouse Reef's Blue Hole—even when the weather is perfect, which it often isn't in winter, it's a two- to three-hour boat trip. Turneffe is more accessible, but even that is a long and comparatively costly day trip, and you're unlikely to reach the atoll's southern tip, which has the best diving.

If you're determined to dive the atolls, you basically have three choices: stay at one of the atoll resorts, go on a live-aboard dive boat, or do a fly-and-dive trip. Live-aboards can be great fun if the weather is good.

The **Belize Aggressor III** (✉ Aggressor Fleet, Drawer K, Morgan City, LA 70381; ☎ 504/385–2628 U.S.; 800/348–2628; FAX 504/384–0817, 🐟) runs a shipshape, navy-style operation with a khaki-outfitted crew of four. It uses a purpose-built, 120-ft luxury cruiser powered by twin 500-horsepower Detroit Diesels and equipped with the latest communication systems. Weather reports come by fax from Norfolk, Virginia. The schedule—five single-tank dives a day, including one night dive—will leave you begging for mercy. Staterooms are, well, almost stately. The spacious double-berth cabins are brightened with sky-blue fabrics, light-wood trim, and multiple windows instead of small port-holes. All have private baths, TVs and VCRs, and individual climate controls. Weeklong tours depart from the dock at the Radisson Fort George. The boat makes scheduled stops at all three atolls, but most dives are on the southeast corner of Lighthouse Reef.

Similar to *Belize Aggressor III,* the 120-ft cruiser **Wave Dancer** (✉ Waterway II, Suite 2213, 1390 S. Dixie Hwy., Coral Gables, FL 33146; ☎ 305/669–9391 U.S.; 800/932–6237, 🐟) has berths with toast-color walls, bright floral-print bedspreads, TV/VCR, and private bath. Little extras include bathrobes and hairdryers. Some cabins have queen-size beds. Trips are led by well-known diver Peter Hughes.

Because all of the above operations run about the same price as a week in one of the atoll's resorts ($1,200–$1,700), they're not for everyone. An alternative is the *Offshore Express,* a 50-ft live-aboard dive boat based in San Pedro and operated by Alan Forman of the **Coral Beach Hotel &Dive Club** (☎ 26/2817, FAX 26/2864, 🐟). This is no yacht, but it's an affordable way to spend time diving the Blue Hole and other areas around the atolls and to see Half Moon Caye. The boat has no private rooms, just 14 bunks. Depending on the weather, you can spend the night on a hammock or cot on a dock, rather than on the boat. Two full days of diving, meals, and drinks costs $250, three full days of diving, $350.

An excellent budget alternative is a day trip with the **Blue Hole Dive Center** (✉ Barrier Reef Dr., San Pedro, Ambergris Caye, ☎ 26/2982, FAX 026/2810), run by Chris Allnatt, on his powerful and fully equipped

The Cayes, Atolls, and Barrier Reef

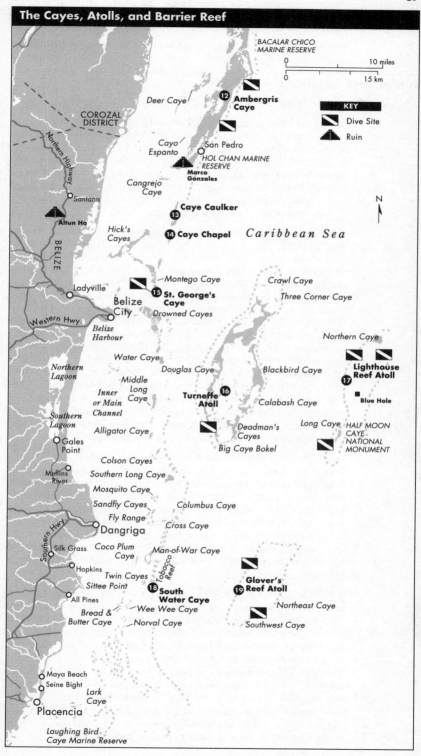

BACALAR CHICO
MARINE RESERVE

0 _____ 10 miles
0 _____ 15 km

KEY

◨ Dive Site

▲ Ruin

Deer Caye

⑫ **Ambergris Caye**

COROZAL
DISTRICT

Cayo
Espanto

San Pedro

HOL CHAN MARINE
RESERVE

Marco
Gonzales

Cangrejo
Caye

⑬ **Caye Caulker**

Santana

Altun Ha

BELIZE

Hick's
Cayes

⑭ **Caye Chapel**

Caribbean Sea

Ladyville

Montego Caye

⑮ **St. George's Caye**

Crawl Caye

Three Corner Caye

Belize
City

Drowned Cayes

Western Hwy.

Belize
Harbour

Northern Caye

Water Caye

Douglas Caye

Blackbird Caye

◨◨ **Lighthouse Reef Atoll**

Northern
Lagoon

Middle
Long
Caye

⑯ **Turneffe Atoll**

⑰

Inner
or Main
Channel

Calabash Caye

Blue Hole

Southern
Lagoon

Alligator Caye

Deadman's
Cayes

Long Caye

HALF MOON
CAYE
NATIONAL
MONUMENT

Gales
Point

Big Caye Bokel

Mullins
River

Colson Cayes

Southern Long Caye

Mosquito Caye

Columbus Caye

Sandfly Cayes

Fly Range

Cross Caye

Dangriga

Coco Plum
Caye

Man-of-War Caye

Silk Grass

Hopkins

Twin Cayes

Tobacco Reef

⑱ **South Water Caye**

Glover's Reef Atoll ⑲

Sittee Point

All Pines

Bread &
Butter Caye

Wee Wee Caye

Norval Caye

Northeast Caye

Southwest Caye

Maya Beach

Seine Bight

Lark
Caye

Placencia

Laughing Bird
Caye Marine Reserve

N

boat. A one-day trip from San Pedro to the Blue Hole, Lighthouse Reef, and Turneffe Atoll is $165 ($125 for snorkeling).

Numbers in the margin correspond to points of interest on the Cayes, Atolls, and Barrier Reef map.

Ambergris Caye and San Pedro

⑫ *56 km (35 mi) northeast of Belize City.*

At 40 km (25 mi) long and 7 km (4½ mi) wide at its widest, its northern tip nuzzled up against the Yucatán Peninsula, Ambergris is the queen of the cayes. On early maps it was often referred to as Costa de Ambar, or the Amber Coast, a name supposedly derived from the blackish, marbled substance secreted by the sperm whale and often washed up on beaches. For centuries it was used in perfumery and medicine. No proof exists, however, that ambergris was ever found here, although there's also an Ambergris Caye in the Bahamas.

A few years ago, when you flew into the caye's main town, San Pedro, the tips of the plane's wings almost touched the laundry hanging in people's backyards. Once landed, you could walk from one end of town to the other in 10 minutes. Now, you need a bike or a golf cart just to get from one end of the airstrip to the other. The heart of the town is still the same: a couple of streets of brightly painted, mostly two-story wooden houses with the ocean on one side and the lagoon on the other. Old men still lean over their balconies in the evenings to watch the world go by, and many people still go barefoot. The stores and restaurants still have names like Lily's, Alice's, or Martha's. But every year there are more cars, more souvenir shops, and a bit less innocence. In 1999, for the first time, Sanpedranos paved one of the island's sandy streets, a short section of Coconut Drive next to the airstrip. Ambergris will never be like Cancún, but it is the most developed—some would say too developed—of the cayes. For this reason, it also has Belize's greatest range of accommodations and restaurants. And, thanks to resorts like Mata Chica and Capricorn, the culinary standard has really shot up.

San Pedro's main street—officially Barrier Reef Drive, but known colloquially as Front Street—is a sandy lane running parallel to the sea. It is San Pedro's commercial center, with two banks, numerous gift shops, and most of the town's hotels and restaurants. With a population of fewer than 3,000, San Pedro remains a small, friendly, and prosperous village. It has one of the highest literacy rates in the country and an admirable level of ecological awareness about the fragility of the reef from which it now makes its living. The large number of substantial private houses being built on the edges of town is proof of how much tourism has enriched San Pedro.

If you like some action at night and don't want to spend too much, a hotel in town is ideal. Accommodations are generally simple and cheap ($15–$100), and though rooms on the main street can be noisy, it's not so much with cars as with late-night revelers. There are also numerous small bistros. Don't expect The Ritz. Often as not, you'll be eating with your feet in the sand. But the fish arrives at the table with the taste of the ocean still clinging to it. At night, a fleet of water taxis plies different parts of the caye, and the fast, often bumpy, ride is as thrilling as a ride in a New York cab. If you want silence and sand, blue water and palm trees, you have to go out of town, for the larger, resort-style accommodations. Generally, whether in town or out, hotels run snorkeling and fishing tours, and many have their own dive shops.

Whether you arrive in San Pedro by air or by ferry from Belize City, you'll be met by a small crowd of cab drivers, friendly but a little pushy, offering cheap deals on lodging. Keep in mind that hotels pay a commission to these drivers, and the commission is reflected in the hotel rate. For the best rate, call the hotel directly when you arrive. During the off-season (March–Oct.), Ambergris Caye hotels discount aggressively, and walk-in rates are often a third less than advertised rates. Island hotels are rarely full, although late January through March, Christmas/New Years, and Easter are the busiest times, and the best hotels likely will be 100% booked then.

Although development on Ambergris continues relentlessly, the far north of the island remains pristine, or close to it. At the top of the caye, butting up against Mexico, Bacalar Chico National Park encompasses 105 square km (41 square mi) of land, reef, and sea. Here you can still find whitetail deer, ocelots, saltwater crocodiles, and, according to some reports, pumas and jaguars. Diving, snorkeling, and fishing are excellent, especially off Rocky Point. You'll need a boat and a guide to take you to Bacalar Chico, and you must pay a $2.50 entrance fee.

The Ambergris Museum & Cultural Center. Ambergris was settled by an eclectic bunch of Maya, pirates, missionaries, and fishermen. In less than half an hour in this little air-conditioned building, you can see just how their collaboration formed Ambergris Caye. Local grannies have emptied their trunks and families have researched their histories to create this simple and pretty little museum. Among other things, you'll see a few Maya pots, a 17th-century ebony cross, and deer-horn tools that were used here up until the deer hunting stopped in the 1960s. ⊠ *Island Plaza on Barrier Reef Dr., at Pelican St.,* ☎ *26/2298.* ▣ *$2.50.* ☻ *Mon.–Sat. 2–8, Sun. 1–6.*

Next door to the Ambergris Museum is **CyberCoffee** (Barrier Reef Dr., ☎ 26/3015), one of several places on the island where you can snack and check your e-mail while from paradise—$10 buys you all-day Internet access plus free coffee, tea, and cookies.

Dining
Besides the restaurants in town, lots of resorts, like Capricorn and Mata Chica, also have terrific restaurants that are open to the public.

$$–$$$ ✕ **Rendezvous Restaurant & Bar.** Next to Journey's End (☞ *below*) is Belize's first and only Thai restaurant. The *Som Tum,* shredded unripe papaya and *cho cho* (a local squash) in a tangy sauce with peanuts, coriander, and dried, ground shrimp make a great starter. Then hit the hot Thai chicken curry, smoothing it out with chocolate truffle cake with Belizean *wongla* (sesame) seed candy. The owners, who have lived and worked in Thailand and Singapore, also make and bottle their own wines, using imported grape concentrate. A honeymoon suite above the restaurant can be rented if you can't bear the water-taxi ride back to your hotel. ⊠ *9.6 km (6 mi) north of San Pedro by water taxi,* ☎ FAX *26/3426. AE, MC, V.*

$$ ✕ **El Patio.** This may be the only place where you can eat and watch people shop for groceries at the same time. An annex of Rocks Grocery store, this indoor-outdoor restaurant serves particularly good grilled seafood, like the grouper marinated in lime and served with a cilanto butter sauce. In the evening, amidst Mexican decor and romantic lighting, two Mexican guitarists and a bubbling fountain serenade you at your white wrought-iron table. ⊠ *¼ mi south of San Pedro, Coconut Dr.,* ☎ *26/3063. AE, MC, V. No lunch Tues.*

40

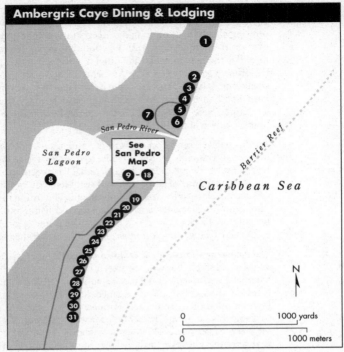

Ambergris Caye Dining & Lodging

$$ ★ **Elvi's Kitchen.** When Elvi, a savvy Creole from San Pedro, started her restaurant in 1964, she had but a few tables on the dirt sidewalk under a flamboyant tree. Over 30 years later, the tree is still here (albeit pollarded to fit inside the roof) and the floor is still sand, but Elvi's has come a long, long way from being a street café. It now has massive, carved-mahogany doors, a staff of a couple of dozen in snappy black-and-white outfits, and a fancy bar; it remains immensely popular with tourists for its local color. Wednesday night is Maya Buffet Night, which includes *pibil* (pork and chicken wrapped in banana leaves), cooked on hot stones in the sand. An excellent Maya flutist provides musical accompaniment. ⊠ *Pescador Dr.,,* ☎ *26/2176. AE, MC, V. Closed Sun.*

$$ ✕ **Jade Garden.** Classic Cantonese dishes have a Caribbean twist at Jade, as in fish chow mein and conch kebabs, but you can find the more banal beef foo yung here, too. This attractive restaurant fills the top two floors of a white colonial-style building just outside town. It's outfitted with handsome rattan furniture, pastel tablecloths, and a well-stocked bar, making it one of the caye's more elegant restaurants as well the source of the best Chinese food around. ⊠ *¼ mi south of airstrip,* ⊠ *Coconut Dr.,* ☎ *26/2126. AE, MC, V.*

$–$$ ✕ **Estel's.** Estel's father-in-law was a World War II flier with a squadron called "Di Nah Might." (His flying jacket and an old photo are up on the wall.) Not surprisingly, then, this is one of the best places in town to get an American-style breakfast, as well as burgers, sandwiches, and excellent seafood. The little white-and-aqua building is right on the beach, and reflects this with a sand floor and porthole-shape windows. There's a terrace outside, where you can sit under an umbrella of palapa leaves and watch pelicans hit the water. ⊠ *Front St.,* ☎ *26/2019. No credit cards.*

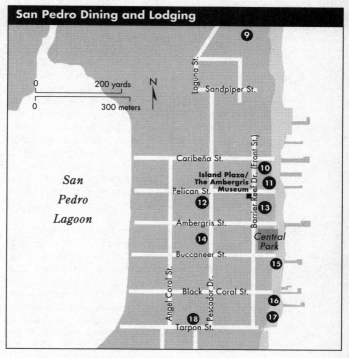

San Pedro Dining and Lodging

$–$$ ✕ **Fido's Courtyard.** Sooner or later, you'll end up at Fido's, sipping something cold and having a burger, fish-and-chips, or a slice of pizza. This casual, seaside restaurant and bar is one of the most popular venues in San Pedro. It's open every day for lunch and dinner, and some nights, depending on the season, there's live music. ✉ *Barrier Reef Dr., just north of the Catholic Church,* ☎ *26/3176.*

$–$$ ✕ **Sweet Basil.** In a quiet residential area 1 mi north of San Pedro, Sweet Basil is the place to get fixins' for an epicurean picnic. Since it's on a stretch of deserted North Ambergris beach, you'll have to take your bike or golf cart up Pescador Drive and across the "cut," a cross-caye channel where a hand-pulled ferry will take you and the cart across the 60 ft of water for $1.50. Look for the deli-cum-bistro's two-story pink-and-green house a quarter of a mile on, where you can relax on the upstairs veranda eating some of Belize's scarcer commodities, like lox, prosciutto, and imported cheese. Salade niçoise or tapenade is served here 10–5 daily except Monday. ✉ *Tres Cocos area, North Ambergris,* ☎ *26/3870. No credit cards.*

$ ✕ **Micky's.** Just across the street from Tropic Air, this is the place for a hearty, inexpensive Belizean breakfast before you board your plane. ✉ *San Pedro Airport,* ☎ *no phone. No credit cards.*

$ ✕ **The Reef.** Looking for authentic local cooking at low prices? This is your place. There's no sea view here, no atmosphere, just big portions of fresh fish, chicken, and beans and rice. The lunch menu has Mexican dishes at rock-bottom prices. Avoid the specials at dinner, which are overpriced. ✉ *Pescador Dr., just north of Elvi's,* ☎ *26/3212. No credit cards..*

Lodging

$$$$ ✕⛾ **Cayo Espanto.** If you arrive at this private island west of Ambergris Caye intending to fill your days with diving and trips to ruins, you may find, if you're like most guests, you'll rarely leave the pint-size caye,

except, perhaps, to scuba dive. And why should you? Your own luxurious villa, with splash pool, cable TV, music system, and personal butler means you'll never have to. The villa walls literally fold back to let in the Caribbean sun via your personal verandah, and rooms have king-size beds with Egyptian linens. Meals, prepared by chefs who took home awards from the 1999 Caribbean Culinary Federation competition, are brought to you at your villa, to enjoy at your own waterside table. You can expect a range of fare from local rock crab to grilled breast of duck. When owner Jeff Gramm opened Cayo Espanto in 1999, he raised the bar on luxury accommodations in Belize, with a staff-to-guest ratio of one-to-one and amenities once available only on islands like St. Bart's. For all this personal care, you'll pay a small fortune, around $600 to $1,500 per night, so why not enjoy it? Is Belize ready for this kind of place? Stay tuned. ⊠ *4.8 km (3 mi) west of Ambergris Caye by boat, Box 90, San Pedro,* ☎ *800/666–4282 in U.S.,* ☎ FAX *21/ 3001. 4 villas. Restaurant, bar, fans, room service, spa, fishing, travel services. AP. AE, M, V.* ✎

$$$$ ✕🏨 **Mata Chica.** Mata *Chic* would be an equally appropriate name
★   for this stylish resort, which opened in 1998 at the caye's northern end. The landscape of variegated stucco casitas in mango, banana, and blueberry accentuated by the brilliance of the white sand look like something out of a Gauguin painting. Fabrics inside each casita echo the colors of the exterior, as do the original murals by a French artist in each room and Mexican tiles in the uniquely styled bathrooms. For larger groups, two new two-bedroom, two-bath villas with kitchenettes were recently added. Not that you'll want to cook for yourself: "Food and love are the most important things in the world," says the warm, exuberant Italian co-owner, Nadia Torcelli. The variety and delectability of the meals served at the resort's restaurant, **Mambo Cuisine,** reflects this dictum, particularly with respect to the seafood and pasta dishes—the tortellini is made fresh every day. The soaring palapa dining room has charming decorative touches, like the seashells used as salt and pepper shakers. Nadia and her French husband, Philippe, worked in the fashion business in L.A. for 10 years and have brought with them a guest list of stars that includes Mick Jagger; but you'll feel special and well-looked-after by this charming couple, even if your 15 minutes haven't arrived. If you crave the water, Philippe is an expert boatman and can take you on day or overnight cruises on his 40-ft catamaran. ⊠ *8 km (5 mi) north of San Pedro by water taxi,* ☎ *21/3010,* FAX *21/3012. 13 casitas. Restaurant, bar, massage, beach, snorkeling, boating, fishing, travel services. AE, MC, V.* ✎

$$$–$$$$ ✕🏨 **Ramon's Village Resort.** One of the first resorts to open on the cayes, Ramon's keeps on growing, adding new cabanas, suites, and, in 1999, a beautiful new meandering pool. Despite the slightly jammed-up feeling with 60 units at the tidy little beach, the resort has kept a good deal of its sand and thatch atmosphere to which it has added manicured grounds with hibiscus plants creeping up and around porches for privacy. The cabanas, many of them two-story, are close together and somewhat dark (and consequently a wee bit damp), but with their mahogany floors and fittings, modern baths and amenities, and views of the ocean, they're certainly comfortable. The newer rooms closest to the water are the best. Whereas other resorts may be too laissez-faire, Ramon's has got it together. Lots of people may be milling about (plenty of whom are repeat guests), but you'll have the sense here that your needs are being met. Evening brings margaritas or Belikin Premium at the poolside bar (regular Belikin isn't served here), or, on Tuesday and Friday, a beach cookout with live music until 10 PM. After a tasty breakfast—try the Mayan eggs, with surprisingly nongreasy deep-fried tortillas, cheese, and beans, with your fresh-squeezed O.J., arrange for a diving excursion or spend the day zooming about San Pedro on your rented golf cart. ⊠ *Coconut Dr. (Box 4407, Laurel, MS 39441),* ☏ *26/2071; 800/624–4315 in the U.S.,* FAX *26/2214. 60 rooms. Restaurant, bar, air-conditioning, pool, dive shop, dock, travel services. AE, MC, V.* ☙

$$$–$$$$ ✕▥ **Victoria House.** With its bougainvillea-filled gardens, palm trees,
★ and white-coral sand, this beautiful property, 3 km (2 mi) south of San Pedro, has the style and seclusion of a diplomatic residence. In the white colonial-style house with airy verandas and tiled walkways are three ample suites, with tiled floors, sea-chest-style mahogany furnishings, and large bathrooms. They share a wraparound veranda that looks through the treetops to the turquoise sea. All rooms have verandas facing the sea, but the best views are from the second-floor units. Ten more rooms are in stone-and-thatch casitas arranged in a half moon around a lawn shaded by palm trees; all of these have screened windows, mahogany fittings, and private porches overlooking the sea. A luxury suite on the beach has a king-size bed with silver headboard, colorful murals on the walls, and an ocean-view terrace. Eight "plantation rooms" in two motel-like buildings also have tile floors, and lovely dark wood trim and doors. The staff of 30 are charming and attentive, and managers Brent and Janet, from Vancouver, inspire gracious and efficient service. The restaurant serves excellent buffet meals, and a seaside bar pours some of the best local drinks. Sea kayaks, catamarans, Windsurfers, and a full array of diving and sightseeing tours are also available. ⊠ *Coconut Dr., 3¾ km (2¼ mi) south of San Pedro (Box 1549, Decatur, GA 30030),* ☏ *26/2067; 800/247–5159 in the U.S.,* FAX *404/ 373–3885. 23 rooms, 8 suites. Restaurant, bar, beach, dive shop, snorkeling, boating, windsurfing, travel services. AE, MC, V.* ☙

$$$ ✕▥ **Capricorn Resort.** Clarence and Annabel Burdes (he's French-Canadian; she's British) are part of the second wave of entrepreneurs who have come to Belize to live their dream. Unlike their earlier colleagues, who had to struggle for years and were thrilled with any recognition, the Burdeses packed a good bit of attitude along with their style and panache. They don't give a fig about publicity and want to keep their operation small. They call it a resort, but in truth it's a restaurant with three stylish cabanas in the garden. The cabanas are roomy, with two double beds each, generous bathrooms, and sea views, and the main building has a luxury suite. But what people really come here for is Clarence's food—rosemary foccacia; medallion of filet maison with sautéed shrimp; French crepes with seafood—and the Burdeses' distinctive brand of hospitality. Reservations are essential for dinner. ⊠ *6.4 km (4 mi) north of San Pedro by water taxi,* ☏ *26/2809,* FAX *26/2091. 3 cabanas, 1 suite. Restaurant, bar, beach. AE, MC, V.* ☙

$$$ ✕▥ **El Pescador.** Everyone on Ambergris says they offer fishing trips, but if you're *seriously* into fishing—for bonefish, tarpon, or other gamefish—and rank having the best guides, boats, and gear in Belize over the need for fancy lodging, this is the place for you. Although occasionally described as a "fishing camp," El Pescador is in fact a handsome colonial house on a beautiful stretch of beach 5 km (3 mi) north of San Pedro. Operators Logan and Ali Gentry and their guides know all about reef and flats fishing, and they speak your language, whether you do fly or spin fishing. Accommodations here are homey but comfortable. Rooms have fans; if you want air-conditioning you'll have to pay an extra $15 a night. The best arrangement here is the weeklong fishing package, which includes round-trip airfare from Belize City, three meals a day (served family style), taxes, and the use of a boat and guide for six eight-hour days of fishing, all for under $2,000 per person. ⊠ *Box 793, Belize City,* ☏ *26/2398,* FAX *26/2977. 13 rooms. Restaurant, pool, beach, dock, fishing. MC, V.* ☙

$$$ ✕⌂ **Journey's End.** Once touted as a destination for the rich and fa-
mous, this resort at the north end of Ambergris became a victim of its
own hype in the early 90s and went belly up. Under the energetic di-
rection of Jim Scott, a capable young manager formerly at Chaa Creek
(☞ San Ignacio *in* The Cayo, *below*), it has repositioned itself as an
all-around, family-oriented resort. With 70 rooms on 47 acres, it's the
caye's largest resort, and for those who like to keep busy, there are ac-
tivities day and night. You can spend the day windsurfing or sea kayak-
ing, playing volleyball and tennis (the only two courts on Ambergris, but
don't expect Wimbledon), or snorkeling and diving on the reef. Come
back for dinner, followed by live music. A renovation program has spiffed
up the public areas—the landscaped grounds with coconut palms and cedar
trees are well maintained—and some of the rooms, especially in the cir-
cle of ocean-front cottages, have been restyled, with newly painted walls
in bright hues, Mexican-tile bathrooms, and air-conditioning. The lagoon
rooms, in two-story concrete blocks, are rather lugubrious, but comfortably
sleep groups of 10. And if you're lucky you might see a crocodile from
your patio. ✉ *9.6 km (6 mi) north of San Pedro by water taxi (5847
San Felipe St., Suite 2195, Houston, TX 77057),* ☎ *26/2173; 800/460–
5665 in the U.S.,* ℻ *713/780–1726. 70 rooms. Restaurant, bar, snack
bar, refrigerators, pool, hot tub, dive shop, snorkeling, boating, fish-
ing, travel services. AE, MC, V.* ☜

$$$ ✕⌂ **SunBreeze Beach Hotel.** This mid-size resort at the south edge of
town always enjoyed an unbeatable location, and now, under the no-
nonsense hand of manager Julia Edwards, the place has truly blossomed.
Rooms, albeit motel-like, are grouped around a plant-filled central courtyard and are quite large, with tile floors and dark-wood furnishings;
all have cable TV and telephones. Five deluxe rooms have whirlpool
baths. All units are equipped for guests with disabilities. The SunBreeze
also has a small beach area (but there's a seawall here, separating the
water from the beach), a well-shaded pool, and a dive shop. The on-
site restaurant, **Caruso,** specializes in Italian and seafood. The first paved
street on the island is just outside SunBreeze's door, a short strip of
cobblestone by the airstrip, put down in 1999. ✉ *Coconut Dr., across
from airstrip,* ☎ *26/2191,* ℻ *26/2346. 36 rooms. Restaurant, bar, air-
conditioning, pool, beach, boating, travel services. AE, MC, V.* ☜

$$$ ✕⌂ **Tropica.** If a good beach is your top priority, you couldn't do bet-
ter than Mar de Tumbo, where this fast-expanding resort is located,
about 3 km (2 mi) south of town. Opened in 1997 with eight rooms,
the resort was qickly enlarged by owner Gary Sogorka to 16 rooms,
with the total expected to reach 32 in late 2000. Along the way he added
a pool, bar, and the **Seagrill** restaurant, in which hundreds of crab spec-
imens from around the world are mounted on the walls. All the guest
rooms are in two-story four-plexes; they're smallish but nicely furnished,
with two full-size beds and rattan headboards. Dressers and other furni-
ture are made of Belizean hardwoods, and the windows have slatted-wood
louvers instead of curtains. You won't always be overwhelmed by super-
friendly service here, but it's adequate, and the top-notch beach and pool
may compensate for any shortcomings in other areas. ✉ *Coconut Dr., 3
km (1¼ mi) south of San Pedro (721 Rte. 23, Pompton Plains, NJ 07444),*
☎ *26/2701 or 888/778–9776 in the U.S.,* ℻ *26/2699 or 973/835–5955
in the U.S. 32 rooms. Restaurant, bar, air-conditioning, pool, beach,
dive shop, bicycles, travel services. AE, MC, V.* ☜

$$ ✕⌂ **San Pedro Holiday Hotel.** This group of four colonial-style houses,
with cheery pink-and-white trim and seaside ambience, is the closest
you'll get to a resort in the center of town. It's owned by Celi McCorkle,
a pioneer in San Pedro tourism and one of the first Belizeans to open
a hotel here. Her guest rooms are spic-and-span, with white walls and
Clorox-white bedspreads. No gunky carpets here, as the floors are pol-

ished hardwood. The larger, pricier rooms have air-conditioning, refrigerators, and views of the hotel's small in-town beach and, beyond it, a busy pier and the sea. **Celi's** is one of the Caye's better restaurants, with salads, sandwiches, and other light fare served beachside. ⊠ *Barrier Reef Dr.,* ☎ *26/2014,* FAX *26/2295. 16 rooms, 1 suite. Restaurant, bar, beach, dive shop. AE, MC, V.* ✑

$ ✕ ⊞ **Ruby's.** If you're a tightwad or near broke, you'll like this clean, inexpensive hotel in town and on the sea, about a block from the airstrip. A new group of air-conditioned rooms on the seaside, added in 1999, all have private baths and balconies facing the water, yet they're under $50. Try the breakfast burritos at the hotel's little restaurant, which opens early at 6 AM for the fish-and-dive crowd. ⊠ *South end of Barrier Reef Dr., at Tarpon St. (Box 56, San Pedro),* ☎ *26/2063,* FAX *26/ 2434. 17 rooms, 6 with shared bath. Restaurant, air-conditioning. AE, MC, V.* ✑

$$$$ ⊞ **Villas at Banyan Bay.** If you like plenty of space, little luxuries like a whirlpool bath in your room and a first-class beach, this upscale condo development a little less than 3 km (2 mi) south of town will suit you splendidly. Each two-bedroom condo, in red tile–roofed, two-story buildings, has a veranda with sea views, kitchen, hot tub, cable TV, phones, and stylish furnishings. At around 1,000 square ft, these are indeed the largest and most luxe apartments on the island. Furnishing and fixtures, such as the custom-made mahogany cabinets, Mexican-tile floors, and original art are of high quality, and clearly the work of a competent interior decorator. A large pool on the grounds has a swim-up bar, and Mar de Tumbo nearby is at the top of a short list of good swimming beaches. ⊠ *Coconut Dr., 3.2 km (2 mi) south of San Pedro (Box 91, San Pedro),* ☎ *26/3739,* FAX *26/2766. 42 two-bedroom apartments. Air-conditioning, kitchens, pool, dive shop, dock. AE, MC, V.* ✑

$$$–$$$$ ⊞ **Captain Morgan's Retreat.** Getting here in a speedboat that zips you ☾ up the Ambergris coast over impossibly beautiful water is a pleasure. What you'll find when you arrive is a long, quiet stretch of sand with palms trees, hammocks, and, behind them, private thatched cabanas (some with two queen beds) and upstart two-story condos with whirlpools—also with thatch roofs. Each cabana has its own porch— and all have unobstructed views of the Caribbean; front windows let in light, although the furnishings are somewhat dated and can make an otherwise decent cabana feel a tad shabby. Good-size tile showers in the otherwise narrow bathrooms are an intelligent use of space. The new condos are brighter and have a sitting room, kitchen, and new wicker furnishings. Although it's possible to hang in the hammocks all day, Captain Morgan's has a youthful kind of energy about it, no doubt imparted by the young staff and the renovations still in progress at press time. A new restaurant is in the works, but until the food situation gets ironed out, you're better off taking your meals elsewhere. The swimming pool surrounded by a hardwood deck offers an alternative to sea bathing, which is not at its best here (with the possible exception of off the hotel's dock). Be sure to arrange a top-notch snorkeling trip to Hol Chan and Shark Ray Alley with the dive shop. ⊠ *5.6 km (3½ mi) north of San Pedro by water taxi,* ☎ *26/2567 or 888/653–9090 in the U.S.,* FAX *307/587–8914. 15 cabanas, 12 suites in condo villas. Restaurant, bar, air-conditioning, pool, beach, dive shop. AE, DC, MC, V.* ✑

$$$ ⊞ **Banana Beach Resort.** Tim Jeffers, a transplant from Montana, took everything he learned from building and operating the popular Coconuts (☞ *below*) and put it to good use when he opened this new condo-tel in late 1998. The building is a three-story rectangle, influenced, says Tim, by the architecture of Mérida, Mexico, and plunked directly on the sandy beach, which also happens to be one of the is-

land's nicest. The expansive apartments (about 600 square ft) enclose a courtyard with swimming pool and an open breezeway to the sea. All have full kitchen, a large, airy bedroom with king or queen beds, and cable TV. Fourteen suites face the ocean, with balconies just feet from the sea, and another 12 have ocean views. The choicest digs are the four corner seafront apartments on the second and third floors. There's no restaurant here, but several are within walking distance. The staff, surely among the friendliest on the island, is glad to arrange diving and snorkeling trips, fishing, boat charters, and other activities. ✉ *Coconut Dr., 3 ¼ km (2 mi) south of San Pedro,* ☎ *26/3890,* FAX *26/3891. 36 suites. Air-conditioning, kitchen, beach, pool, dock, bicycles, travel services. AE, MC, V.* ✦

$$$ 🏨 **Belize Yacht Club.** Is this an upscale condo-tel, a time-share, or a full-service convention hotel? These days, it seems to be a bit of all three. The attractive, Spanish-style villas of the Yacht Club (although it's not a private club at all) are arranged around a central area with a swimming pool. All condos have phones, kitchenettes, and verandas angled to face the ocean. Tile floors, rattan furniture, and fabrics in tropical pastels give the rooms a summery you're-away-from-home kind of feeling. The choice seaside second-floor condos have covered verandas with views of the barrier reef. The dock has fueling facilities for sea dogs; the gym is one of the better-equipped in Belize; and, of course, there's a requisite dive shop. New management has added a convention and meeting center, bar, and restaurant. A seawall runs along the beachfront. ✉ *Coconut Dr., ½ km (¼ mi) south of San Pedro,* ☎ *26/2777; 800/396–1153 in the U.S.,* FAX *26/2768. 44 apartments. Restaurant, bar, air-conditioning, kitchenettes, room service, pool, exercise room, beach, dive shop, dock, travel services. AE, DC, MC, V.* ✦

$$$ 🏨 **Caribbean Villas.** Before they decided to build these two graceful
★ white villas on a lovely stretch of beach about a mile south of San Pedro, Wil Lala was a dentist, and his wife Susan was an artist and an avid birder. Their architectural collaboration has yielded a modern resort, incorporating Caribbean and Spanish styles, in a lush tropical setting. An intelligent and creative design—luggage niches under the built-in sofas and spacious sleeping lofts for six—make these self-catering apartments feel larger than they are. A four-story bird-watching tower has helped make the place a paradise for birders, with as many as 100 species of tropical birds flitting about at any one time, and a tiny artificial reef off the little beach has helped attract schools of fish. This labor of love is a rich and special sanctuary, right near the bustle of San Pedro. There's no restaurant, but two good groceries, Island Supermarket and Rock's II, are nearby for guests who want to do their own cooking. The owners also offer wildlife, fishing, and snorkeling tours. ✉ *Coconut Dr., 1.2 km (¾ mi) south of San Pedro,* ☎ *26/2715; 785/776–3738 in the U.S.,* FAX *26/2885. 10 suites. Kitchenettes, hot tub, beach, dock, bicycles, travel services. AE, MC, V.* ✦

$$–$$$ 🏨 **Mayan Princess.** This three-story building (one of the few in San Pedro), sitting pink and pretty on the water right in the middle of town, offers Florida-style accommodations (rattan furniture, pastel-colored fabrics), with private baths, phones, and cable TV. The studios are decorated with white wicker furniture and colorful bedspreads, and sliding doors open onto verandas where you can eat the meals you've prepared in your well-equipped kitchenette. Off-season, and sometimes even in-season, managers Sheila and Rusty Nale (no kidding) drop room prices here to very low levels; when making reservations, it doesn't hurt to ask for a deal. ✉ *Barrier Reef Dr.,* ☎ *26/2778,* FAX *26/2784. 23 1-bedroom apartments. Air-conditioning, kitchenettes, travel services. AE, MC, V.* ✦

$$ ▦ **Changes In Latitude B&B.** The sign out front, depicting an igloo melting under a tropical sun, represents Canadian owner Lori Reed's move south to Belize to run this little bed-and-breakfast. If you must be directly on the water or have a pool, Changes is not for you, but it's a relaxed and simple spot, with personal attention from the innkeeper and close to San Pedro's restaurants and beaches. The six rooms are all on the small side, but they're clean, with white plaster walls and glass louvered windows, and have private entrances. The three garden-side rooms get the most light; others face a concrete wall. Lori, who lives upstairs, cooks breakfast and serves it in the common room; but you can also prepare your own meals and store beer in Lori's fridge. Diving, snorkeling, and boating trips can be arranged. ⊠ *Coconut Dr., ¼ mi south of San Pedro, beside the Belize Yacht Club,* ☎ FAX *26/2986. 6 rooms. Air-conditioning, travel services. AE, DC, MC, V.* ✇

$$ ▦ **Coconuts Caribbean Hotel.** Operated by the same folks who run Banana Beach (☞ *above*), this motel on the beach stays busy year-round, thanks to attractive rates and perky management. The two-story stucco building has 12 big, airy rooms, with a large L-shape sofa that becomes an extra bed. The bar on the resort's white, sandy beach serves refreshing rum drinks and snacks. David, the manager, is eager to arrange diving and snorkeling trips for you and is a great help with restaurant suggestions. ⊠ *Coconut Dr., ¼ mi south of San Pedro,* ☎ *26/3500,* FAX *26/3501. 12 rooms. Bar, snack bar, beach, snorkeling, bicycles, travel services. AE, MC, V.* ✇

$$ ▦ **The Tides Beach Resort.** One of the island's most-experienced and respected divemasters, Patojo Paz, and his wife Sabrina opened this 12-room hotel in early 1999. The style of the three-story frame structure harks back to the old days on the island, before everybody built with reinforced concrete. If diving is your main interest, you couldn't do better than here—dive packages are available. When you're ready to go get wet, your boat is a few feet away at Patojo's dock, and when you return, there's a beach bar to quench your thirst and swap stories in. Rooms are pleasingly new and attractive, if on the small side, with no-nonsense layouts, two double beds, ceiling fans, bedcovers doubtless purchased from a motel supply catalog. For a few bucks more, you can upgrade to a room with air-conditioning, an in-room fridge, and king-size bed. The best are the four seafront rooms on the second and third floors, with balconies overlooking the beach. The Tides is a little farther north than most resorts, but it doesn't require a water taxi, so you can walk along the beach into town for meals or drinks. ⊠ *Boca del Rio Dr., north of town,* ☎ *26/2283,* FAX *26/3797. 12 rooms. Bar, air-conditioning, refrigerators, dive shop. AE, MC, V.* ✇

$ ▦ **San Pedrano.** Painted mint-green, blue, and white, this is the cheeriest budget hotel in San Pedro. Each of the spotless rooms has crisp linens. The owners, the Gonzalez family, are friendly folks. ⊠ *Barrier Reef Dr.,* ☎ *26/2054,* FAX *26/2093. 6 rooms. AE, MC, V.*

Condo Rental Agencies

You can rent a condo from one of the many condo-resorts on the water, mostly located south of town. All are small, new or nearly new, with lots of space for the money. They usually don't have a restaurant, bar, or room service, and some don't have a pool, but if you're traveling with a group or family they make up for it with extra room and fully equipped kitchens. Most have cable TV, fans, and air-conditioning, at least in the bedrooms. Because they are usually individually owned—the nonresident owners let local managers rent them out when they're not on vacation here—you won't find any cookie-cutter decor. Most are priced around $110–$135 for two persons in-season, and $75 to $100 the rest of the year.

Belizean Reef Suites (✉ Coconut Dr., ☎ 26/2582, FAX 603/288–0774 in the U.S., ✇) is typical, a three-story, six-unit oceanfront condo brokerage just south of town. The one-bedroom suites here are furnished with rattan and mahogany and decorated with local art. There's no pool, but you can take the sun on a small beach.

Casa Solana (☎ 26/2100) has condos just south of town; **Coral Bay Villas** (☎ 26/3003) is a new property, south of town; **Corona del Mar** (☎ 26/2055) also known as Woody's Wharf, is south of town; **Emerald Reef Suites** (☎ 26/2306) is at the north end of town; **The Palms** (☎ 26/3322) is a 12-unit, three-story complex at the south edge of town with a pool and one- and two-bedroom apartments; **Paradise Villas-Tradewinds** (☎ 800/451–7776 in the U.S.) is at the north end of town, and has a pool; **Sunset Beach Resort**(☎ 26/2373) is about 3.2 km (2 mi) south of town, and has a pool.

Outdoor Activities and Sports

BOATING

For sailing, Belize will never rival the British Virgin Islands. The shallow water kicks up a lot of chop, and hidden coral heads and tidal currents pose a danger to even those with local knowledge. Still, you can charter a boat in San Pedro. You'll have to stay inside the barrier reef, but there's a lot of beautiful territory to explore. The name-brand outfit here is **Tortola Marine Management Ltd.** (TMM; ✉ Coconut Dr., ☎ 26/3026 or 800/633–0155 in the U.S., FAX 26/3072, ✇), which has a small fleet of catamarans (sail and new motorized cats) for bareboat and skippered chartering. Rates vary depending on the boat and time of year, but range from around $2,200 to more than $6,000 a week, not including provisions or a $20 per-person sailing fee. Skippers are an additional $100 per day.

SCUBA DIVING

Sensing that their economic future lay in tourism rather than fishing, the people of Ambergris Caye were the quickest to assemble an infrastructure for diving. In terms of the number of dive shops, quality of dive masters, and range of equipment and facilities, Ambergris Caye remains the most obvious base for diving. San Pedro even has a hyperbaric chamber and an on-site doctor to acclimate divers in danger, paid for by contributions from all the dive shops and fees attached to diver insurance—which is highly recommended, since emergency services and transport costs could wipe out your savings in a hurry.

Some of the best local outfitters are: **Amigos del Mar** (✉ On pier off Barrier Reef Dr., near Mayan Princess Hotel, ☎ 26/2706); **Aqua Dives** (☞ SunBreeze Hotel, *above*, ☎ 26–3415 or 800/641–2994, FAX 26–3414); **Larry Parker's Reef Divers** (✉ Spindrift Hotel, Barrier Reef Dr., ☎ 26/3134); **Hustler's** (✉ Boca Del Rio Dr. and Sandpiper St., near Rock's Inn, ☎ 26/4137 or 800/635–7119), **Patojo's** (☞ Tides, *above*); **Ramon's Dive Shop** (☞ Ramon's Village, *above*).

Diving trips are generally run from fast, maneuverable speedboats. There's no bouncing around in Zodiacs here: many of these boats are hand-built out of solid mahogany. As they represent the dive masters' major assets, having cost as much as $14,000 each, they tend to be lovingly maintained. Power generally comes from two hefty outboards mounted on the back, and with the throttle open it's an exhilarating ride. If you don't want to get splashed, sit in the middle.

Most of these dive masters are ex-fishermen, locals from San Pedro who started diving as an adjunct to their work as lobstermen and went on to get certified as dive masters. The best of them are immensely personable and have an intimate knowledge of the reef and a superb eye for coral and marine life. They also have an unusually developed ecological awareness, knowing full well that the destruction of the reef would not only be a great tragedy in itself, but economic suicide for them. It was a group of dive masters who fastened a network of buoys to the bedrock to prevent further destruction of the coral by anchors dropped directly into it. In bad weather, one anchor dragged across the bottom can destroy more coral than a thousand divers.

Dives off Ambergris are usually one-tank dives at depths of 50–80 ft, giving you approximately 35 minutes of bottom time. The general pattern is two one-tank dives per day—one in the morning at 9 and one in the afternoon at 2—though you can vary this depending on your budget. At press time, the following were the prices for diving and snorkeling from Ambergris. Snorkeling: $15–$20 for two hours or $40–$50 for a day trip with lunch; diving: $35–$40 for a single-tank dive, $45–$60 for a double-tank dive, $40–$45 for a single-tank night dive, and $150–$200 for day trips with three-tank dives to Turneffe Atoll or to the Blue Hole at Lighthouse Reef.

Diving is similar all along Ambergris Caye, with only slight variations. You always dive on the windward side of the reef, and the basic form is canyon-diving. For wall-diving, you have to go out to the atolls.

The highlight of the reef is the **Hol Chan Marine Reserve** (Maya for "little channel"), 6 km (4 mi) from San Pedro at the southern tip of Ambergris (a 20-minute boat ride). Basically, Hol Chan is a break in the reef about 100 ft wide and 20–35 ft deep through which tremendous volumes of water pass with the tides. As well as containing rich marine life and exciting corals, the 13-square-km (5-square-mi) park has a miniature Blue Hole, a 12-ft-deep cave whose entrance often attracts such fish as the fairy basslet, an iridescent purple-and-yellow fish frequently seen here. The reserve is also home to a large population of the gloomily named *Gymnothorax funebris,* or moray eel.

Because fishing is off-limits here, divers can see teeming marine life, including spotted eagle rays. You'll identify large numbers of squirrel fish, butterfly fish, parrot fish, and queen angelfish as well as Nassau groupers, barracuda, and large shoals of yellowtail snappers. The fish generally loiter in the canyons, so as you pass over, you have a bird's-eye view of their variety. **Shark-Ray Alley,** a sandbar where you can snorkel with nurse sharks and rays (who gather here to be fed) and even larger numbers of day-trippers, was made a part of the Hol Chan reserve in 1999. Sliding into the water is a feat of personal bravery, as sight of the sharks and rays brushing past you is daunting yet spectacular; just don't show up without food. A night dive here is a special treat: the water lights up with bioluminescence, and many nocturnal animals emerge, such as octopus and spider crabs. You need above-average swimming skills, especially at night; the strong tidal current has caused at least one drowning.

Varying in depth from 50 to 100 ft, Hol Chan's canyons lie between buttresses of coral running perpendicular to the reef, separated by white, sandy channels. Some sides are very steep; others comprise gently rolling undulations. You'll occasionally find tunnel-like passageways from one canyon to the next. Not knowing what's in the next "valley" as you come over the hill can be pretty exciting.

Though Belize doesn't have quite the rainbow variety of coral you'd find on the Great Barrier Reef in Australia—much of it is biscuit-colored—there is nonetheless plentiful brain, antler, and fan coral. Admission to Hol Chan is $2.50, collected at the site by reserve wardens in boats.

San Pedro is the jumping-off point for trips to Hol Chan, but before you go, stop in at the Hol Chan office (⊠ Caribeña St., east of Angel Coral St.) for information on Belize's marine flora and fauna. All of San Pedro's dive operators offer trips to Hol Chan, which generally last about two hours and are reasonably priced (about $15–$20 for snorkeling, $35 and up for a single-tank dive). Ramon's Dive Shop (☞ *above*) and Amigos del Mar (☞ *above*) run glass-bottom-boat tours of the marine reserve, perfect for those who want to see marine life without getting wet.

Nightlife

Barefoot Iguana (Coconut Dr., ¾ km (½ mi) south of town) is the loudest bar on the island, with live music and a light show. **BC's Beach Bar** (⊠ On the beach, just south of SunBreeze Hotel) is a popular beachfront bar with burgers and occasional all-you-can-eat barbecues on Sunday afternoon. **Big Daddy's** (⊠ Barrier Reef Dr., north side of Central Park) is where the action is in San Pedro, with its oversize bar, burgers, and other such fillers for when eating is secondary to drinking. Since it's right on the water, there's a beachside barbecue some nights. The music and real boozing here don't get started until late, around 11. **The Boatyard** (⊠ South of San Pedro, on the lagoon side of the airstrip) is a marina which doubles as a bar and serves smoked ribs and other barbecued fare. It hosts a dance party on Friday evening and bingo on Tuesday. Tucked in beside Big Daddy's disco is **Jambel's** (⊠ Barrier Reef Dr.), serving spicy jerk chicken and other Jamaican dishes. Across Front Street is **Tarzan's** (⊠ Barrier Reef Dr., across from Central Park), a popular San Pedro bar. A few small casinos, some on boats, are in the works. Ask your hotel for information.

Shopping

At **Belizean Arts** (⊠ Fido's Courtyard, off Barrier Reef Dr., ☎ 26/2638) you'll find a selection of works by local painters, plus jewelry and crafts from the region, including hand-painted animal figures from Mexico, masks and fabrics from Guatemala, and brilliantly colored tropical fish made of coconut wood. For island clothing and such, the best gift shop is **D & G Gift Shop** (⊠ Angel Coral St., behind Elvi's, ☎ 26/2069), which also sells custom-made jewelry. About 3 km (2 mi) south of town, **Hummingbird Rattan** (⊠ Coconut Dr., at Mar de Tumbo, ☎ 26/2960) sells high-quality wood-and-rattan furniture made in its factory in Belmopan. At **Sea Gal Boutique** (⊠ Barrier Reef Dr., in the Holiday Hotel, ☎ 26/2431), the owner has an artist's eye, even for T-shirts.

Caye Caulker

13 *8 km (5 mi) south of Ambergris Caye, 29 km (18 mi) northeast of Belize City.*

For many years, Caye Caulker had a reputation as a haven for British "squaddies" unwinding after a tour of duty in Belfast (bar fights were common) and backpackers smoking ganga under the stars. A few traces of those days remain ("No shirt, no shoes, no problem" is a favorite bar sticker), and because Caulker is the cheapest caye, it tends to attract more than its fair share of grunge. But in recent years, the community has made efforts to broaden the island's appeal, including a beach reclamation project, in which sand from the back of the island was pumped to the front to create a larger shore. On the other hand, some of the cabanas are still barely big enough to kennel a St. Bernard, but with the opening of several more-upscale guest houses, Caye Caulker's charms are beginning to shine through. Brightly painted houses on stilts line the white-coral sand streets, and bars and cafés are everywhere. Flowers outnumber cars ten to one (golf carts, bicycles, and bare feet are the preferred means of transportation). The living is easy. This is the kind of place where most of the listings in the telephone directory don't have addresses, just names, or if there is an address it's something like "Near Football Field." There is no beach to speak of—"The Split," a narrow channel at the south end is the closest approximation—but a plethora of dive and snorkel operators offer reef tours (some of them are "cowboys," so make sure you shop around). Plan on spending about $20 for a half-day snorkel trip. If you run out of money, don't worry, you won't be marooned here forever: one of the island's newer amenities is a bank.

Dining and Lodging

$$ ✕ The Sandbox. Whether outside under the palms or indoors in the hardwood room with overhead fans, you'll always have your feet in the sand at this popular spot. Open from 7 AM to 9 PM, the Sandbox serves, among a great many other choices, a lobster omelet for breakfast, a roast-beef sandwich for lunch, and red snapper in a mango sauce for dinner. The chowders are very good, the conch fritters spicy. Prices are reasonable, and the portions are enormous. At night the bar is very lively, filled with the sounds of laughter and the owner's extensive blues collection. Note the names of regulars carved on the backs of the chairs. ✉ *Front St. at the public pier,* ☎ 22/2200. AE, MC, V.

$ ✕ Cindy's Cafe. Cindy, a charming young woman from Whistler, British Columbia, wins the prize for the most attractive sign on Caye Caulker: a hand-painted picture of reef fish. Upstairs on the veranda of this pastel cottage on stilts, Cindy serves organic muesli (no bacon and eggs here), bagels, orange juice, and the best cappuccino in town. If you promise to bring it back, she'll also lend you a book from her well-stocked shelves. Once you've finished breakfast, Cindy's Belizean husband Carlos, the best snorkeling guide on the Caye, will show you the fish. ✉ *Front St. across from the police station,* ☎ 22/2337. *No credit cards. No lunch; no dinner.*

$ ✕ Glenda's. Glenda's has been around for years, and it's still as good as ever for a cheap, filling breakfast or lunch. The classic breakfast is a cinnamon roll, johnnycake (it's not on the menu, but ask), and fresh-squeezed orange juice, and you must have the rice and beans for lunch. ✉ *Back St. toward the south end of the village,* ☎ *no phone. No credit cards. No dinner.*

$ ✕ Syd's. Syd's is a cool, air-conditioned restaurant with Mexican masks on its white walls and a small bar in one corner. The food is basic Belizean and is dirt cheap. There is good seafood, with rice and beans for dinner and burgers or burritos for lunch. On Saturday nights there is a special barbecue for $4 a person, and on both Friday and Saturday you can have a late-night snack here from 10 PM on. ✉ *1 block south of Chan's grocery store, on street behind Front St.,* ☎ *no phone. AE, MC, V.*

$ ✕ YooHoo Deli. This is the best place to grab a Cuban sandwich and a Fanta before your afternoon snorkeling trip. It's open from 10 AM until around sunset. No seating. ✉ *Front St. next to the police station,* ☎ *no phone.*

$$ ⌂ Chocolate's. Chocolate is a very fit 70-year-old Belizean who with his lively American wife Annie rents out the best room on Caye Caulker—a romantic retreat with a large four-poster bed, vaulted mahogany ceiling with fan, and a screened-in veranda that wraps around the room and looks out to the sea. The bathroom has Mexican tiles and a very large shower. Terry bathrobes, halogen reading lamps, a refrigerator, and a coffeemaker are nice little extras. The room is upstairs from Annie's boutique, which has the best women's and children's clothes in Belize, including dresses and sarongs made with fabrics from Bali, some unique silver jewelry, and Guatemalan bags that somehow don't make you look like a backpacker. Chocolate's snorkeling and manatee-watching trip to Goff Caye—or his all-day river and coastal-lagoon boat tour, complete with alligators, spoonbills, and orchids—is terrific. Chocolate says he's planning on building a couple more rooms, since the one he has stays full much of the time. ⊠ *At the north end of Ambergris, near the Split,* ☎ *22/2151. 1 room. MC, V.*

$$ 🏨 **Iguana Reef Inn.** Far and away Caye Caulker's most upmarket lodging, Iguana Reef has just about everything but a concierge. The 12 suites are colorfully furnished with hand-made furniture, tropical spreads on queen beds, and local artwork. Upstairs suites have vaulted ceilings with skylights. The word is that a swimming pool is in the works—it would be the first on the island. Because the inn is on the lee side of the island, you may have the benefit of sunset views from your veranda. Diving trips can be arranged. ⊠ *Near the end of Middle St., toward north end of island next to soccer field,* ☎ *22/2213,* FAX *22/2000. 12 suites. Air-conditioning, refrigerators, travel services. AE, MC, V.* 🐾

$$ 🏨 **Shirley's Guest House.** At the southernmost tip of the caye, Shirley's has four green-trimmed, white wooden cottages on stilts; more rooms in a two-story building, and a cabana with a covered veranda. All of the rooms look out to sea and have refrigerators, fans, and coffeemakers. Shirley's place is quiet and safe because, according to her, she runs a tight ship and no one would mess with her. We have to agree with her there. ⊠ *South end of island, just north of BTIA Resource Center and airstrip, on the waterfront,* ☎ *22/2145,* FAX *22/2264. 10 rooms. MC, V.*

$$ 🏨 **Treetops.** Doris and Terry and their three miniature security guards (Jack Russell terriers) are wonderful hosts at this comfortable hotel. The rooms are a good size and have flowered curtains and bedspreads, ceiling fans, cable TV, and refrigerators; one has a private bath. The white-sand garden has bougainvillea, hibiscus bushes, and palm trees, and is a peaceful place to curl up on a chaise longue and read. Doris is a great help with restaurant suggestions and is happy to arrange water sports and tours. ⊠ *Box 29,* ☎ *22/2008,* FAX *22/2115. 2 rooms with shared bath, 2 with private bath. MC, V.* 🐾

$$ 🏨 **Trends Beachfront Hotel.** The first thing you see when you get off the boat at the pier is this little hotel, painted a tropical pink and green. Thanks to its location and its bright, airy rooms, all with one queen and one double bed (with a higher grade of mattress than you usually get on Caye Caulker), it stays full much of the time, even though it's not on the water. ⊠ *Near Front St., at the public dock, next to the Sandbox,* ☎ *22/2094 or 22/2307,* FAX *22/2097. 6 rooms. Fans, refrigerators. MC, V.* 🐾

Scuba Diving
Frenchie's Diving Services (⊠ Front St., ☎ 22/2234, FAX 22/2074) is a good operator.

Caye Chapel

🔴 *2 km (½ mi) south of Caye Caulker, 10 km (6 mi) south of Ambergris Caye.*

Not since the days of British colonialism has there been a real golf course in Belize. But for traveling duffers, a new course on Caye Chapel, developed by Larry Addington, a wealthy Kentucky businessman, and opened in late 1999, bridges the gap. It's a par-72 course lying beautifully along the Caribbean, flat but long, playing to over 7,000 yards, with four par-5 holes. There has been considerable controversy over the construction of this course, as some environmentalists believe that a golf course—which typically requires large applications of fertilizer and pesticides—could pose an ecological danger to the nearby barrier reef and sea. In return the course uses a special hybrid grass from the U.S. called Paspalum, which requires half the fertilizers, pesticides, and irrigation.

During times when the island isn't reserved for a corporate retreat, visitors can play the course. Rates, which are expected to increase, are currently $75 for 18 holes, including clubs and cart rental but not including transportation to the island. Hotels on Ambergris Caye can arrange for a boat to take you to Caye Chapel, and most water taxis between Belize City and Caye Caulker or San Pedro will stop on demand.

Dining and Lodging

$$$$ ✕🏨 **Caye Chapel Golf Course & Marina.** Accommodations on the island are limited to twelve 3,000-square-ft villas. The villas, which stand at imperial attention along the seafront, are best described as Florida deluxe, similar to what you might see in an exclusive gated development on Key Biscayne or in Boca Raton. Inside, there's every luxury: whirlpool baths, expansive wet bars, kitchens finished with handcrafted cabinets and the latest German appliances. Everything is first class, from the imported linens on the beds to the original art on the walls. Which it should be—these villas go for a whopping $1,000 a night, food not included. Between the back and front nines of the golf course is a 23,000-square-ft clubhouse still in progress at press time. The clubhouse will house a restaurant with indoor and open-air dining, and aims to rival the finest in the U.S., with tile floors, high ceilings, stunning views of the barrier reef and sea, imported fixtures, and a custom-made bar. Plans also call for an Olympic-size swimming pool, fitness center, tennis complex with lighted courts, and basketball arena, all near the clubhouse. Eventually guests will be able to fly in on private jets. ✉ *Caye Chapel (Box 192, Belize City),* ☎ *22/8250,* 🖷 *22/8201, bzgolf£yahoo.com. 12 villas. Restaurant, bar, air-conditioning, pool, tennis court, marina, travel services. MAP. AE, MC, V. Closed to the public when reserved for corporate events.*

St. George's Caye

⓯ *15 km (9 mi) northeast of Belize City.*

This small, relaxed caye, a stone's throw from Belize City, is steeped in history. The state of Belize had its origins here, as St. George's Caye held the first capital of the original British settlement and was subsequently the site of that decisive sea battle with the Spanish. In more recent times, it was a favorite haunt of Her Majesty's forces, and today's resident population is about 20. The trip by boat from Belize City takes about 20 minutes.

Dining and Lodging

$$$ ✕🏨 **Cottage Colony.** These colonial-style beachfront cottages comprise the island satellite community of Belize City's Bellevue Hotel. Off the pretty beach there's excellent snorkeling. All rooms have a Shaker-like simplicity, with wood walls painted white and polished hardwood floors. Meal plans are available. ✉ *c/o Bellevue Hotel, Box 428, Belize City,* ☎ *23/3571 or 21/2020,* 🖷 *27/3253. 13 cottages. Restaurant, bar, air-conditioning, beach, dive shop, snorkeling, boating. AE, DC, MC, V.*

$$$ ✕🏨 **St. George's Lodge.** In colonial days, this long-established resort was a favorite with the British because of its proximity to Belize City. From their Fort George mansions, they kept watch over their territory

capital. Now it's a favorite of American (and other) divers, undoubtedly because of its custom-built dive boats, solid safety reputation, and diving certification program. There are 10 rooms in the main building, which is built of Belizean hardwood (the bar is made of rosewood), and six thatched cottages by the water. Electricity comes from the lodge's own windmills, and your shower water is heated by the sun. The restaurant (meal plans available) churns out homemade bread and terrific grilled snapper or grouper, and coffee is delivered to your door in the morning. ⊠ *Box 625, Belize City,* ☎ *21/2121 or 800/678–6871 in the U.S.,* FAX *23/1460. 6 cabanas, 7 rooms. Restaurant, bar, beach, dive shop. AE, MC, V.* ✨

Scuba Diving
St. George's Lodge (☞ *above*) has a good dive shop.

Turneffe Atoll

⑯ *40 km (25 mi) east of Belize City.*

This chain of tiny islands and mangrove swamps makes up an atoll the size of Barbados. It's the largest and most central of the three atolls, and the draw, of course, is the diving.

Dining and Lodging

$$$ ✕▥ **Turneffe Flats.** The thing here is the view. The reef is only 200 yards away, and the sound of the surf is the only sound audible from the smart, blue-and-white beachfront duplex cabins. The rooms, with their elegant hardwood fittings and large bathrooms, are a far cry from the bare-boards fishing camp that occupied this site the early '80s. Today, you can dive from 31-ft Oceanmasters, but the size of the dive shop (tiny) and the ubiquitous fishing-pole racks suggest that snook, bonefish, and permit are still the dominant lure—indeed, 75% of the clientele comes expressly to fish. If fishing is your passion, you'll love this place; if not, you may feel like a bit of an outsider. ⊠ *Northern Bogue (Box 36, Deadwood, SD 57732),* ☎ *800/815–1304 or 605/578–1304,* FAX *605/578–7540. 6 rooms. Restaurant, bar, air-conditioning, dive shop, snorkeling, fishing. No credit cards.* ✨

$$$ ✕▥ **Turneffe Island Lodge.** White dive tanks poking up out of the sand
★   as fence posts and a rusty anchor from a British warship that foundered on Caye Bokel in 1743 set the tone at this shipshape resort at Turneffe Atoll's south end. Fishing is superb on the nearby flats, under the tutelage of Ron—an easygoing Montanan who honed his skills fly-fishing for trout on his grandfather's river—but diving is the real draw here. This was the first dive lodge to be established on Turneffe, and it bagged the best spot: a few hundred yards from the legendary Elbow (☞ *below*). By the time the other resorts' contingents have reached this exhilarating wall dive, where schools of pelagics patrol the edge of the 1,000-ft drop-off, the Lodge's guests are on their second tank. It's no dive camp, though; the rooms, in attractive yellow cottages with views of the sea and palm trees, have been refurbished without spoiling the cozy ship's-cabin feeling created by the varnished hardwood fittings. The same goes for the two-story colonial-style house, which holds the bar and the dining room. The original mahogany, installed by Mennonite craftsmen in the early '60s, literally glows. Honeymooners may not appreciate the early-morning breakfast bell and family-style dining, and if you don't dive or fish, you may be short a conversation opener. But if you do, this is an ideal place to base yourself. ⊠ *Coco Tree Caye (Box 2974, Gainsville, GA 30503),* ☎ *800/874–0118,* FAX *770/534–8290. 12 rooms. Restaurant, bar, dive shop, snorkeling, fishing. AE, MC, V.* ✨

Scuba Diving

Turneffe is second only to Lighthouse Reef for diving, thanks to several steep drop-offs in its midst. Only an hour from Lighthouse Reef and 45 minutes from the northern edge of Glover's Reef, Turneffe is within day-trip range of Belize's best diving. Turneffe Flats and Turneffe Island Lodge both have good dive services.

Turneffe's highlight, and probably the most exciting wall dive in Belize, is the **Elbow,** at the southernmost tip of the atoll. It's generally considered an advanced dive because of the strong currents here, which want to sweep you out toward the deep water beyond the reef. The drop-off is dramatic: you have the feeling of flying in blue space, your likely traveling companions large groups of eagle rays. Sometimes as many as 50 flutter together, forming a rippling herd that will take your breath away.

Though it's most famous for its spectacular wall dives, the atoll has dives for every level, including novice. **Turneffe's western, leeward side,** where the reef is wide and gently sloping, is good for shallower dives and snorkeling; you'll see large concentrations of tube sponges, soft corals such as forked sea feathers and sea fans, and varied fish, including plentiful permit. Also on the leeward side is the wreck of the *Sayonara.* No doubloons to be scooped up here—it was a small passenger and cargo boat that went down in 1985—but it's a good place to practice wreck-diving.

Lighthouse Reef Atoll

⑰ *80 km (50 mi) east of Belize City.*

If Robinson Crusoe had been a man of means, he would have repaired here for a break from his desert island. It's the most distant of Belize's atolls, but it's the closest you'll get to paradise. Lighthouse Reef is also the most accessible atoll thanks to an airstrip.

The Reef is about 29 km (18 mi) long and less than 2 km (1 mi) wide, and is surrounded by 67 km (42 mi) of coral reef. The Lighthouse Reef system has two of the country's five-star dives: the Blue Hole and the vertiginous walls off Half Moon Caye. Loggerhead turtles, iguanas, and one of the world's two large colonies of red-footed boobies are protected here. The only accommodations are at the Lighthouse Reef Resort, on Northern Caye.

Although difficult to reach and lacking accommodations, **Half Moon Caye National Monument,** Belize's easternmost island, offers one of the greatest wildlife encounters in Belize. Part of the Lighthouse Reef system, Half Moon Caye owes its protected status to the presence of the red-footed booby bird in such stunning profusion that it's hard to believe that the species has only one other nesting colony in the entire Caribbean (on Tobago Island, off the coast of Venezuela). Some 4,000 of these rare seabirds hang their hats on Half Moon Caye, along with more than 90 other bird species, iguanas, lizards, and loggerhead turtles. The entire 40-acre island is a nature reserve, so you can either explore the beaches or head into the bush on the narrow nature trail. Above the trees at the center of the island is a small viewing platform—climb up, and you're suddenly in a sea of birds, which fill the branches of the surrounding trees so completely that it's hard not to be reminded of a certain Hitchcock movie. Several dive operators and resorts arrange day trips and overnight camping trips to Half Moon Caye.

Dining and Lodging

$$$$ ✕▦ **Lighthouse Reef Resort.** If you want to get blissed out in Belize,
★ this is one of the best places to do it. Once a spartan dive camp for afi-
cionados of the reef, it has gradually been transformed into one of the
most exclusive resorts in Central America. Fortunately, "small is beautiful" seems to be the guiding principle of development. You'll find no
clutter or noisy generators here; you'll probably feel like you're the only
person on the island. Lodgings include five brick cabanas and three handsome, British colonial-style villas. Each villa is tastefully furnished in
Queen Anne style and has a modern, well-equipped kitchenette. Stays are
arranged as preset packages of eight days and seven nights, and cost, for
top-of-the-line villa or suite accommodations, about $1,645 per person,
double occupancy, for divers (about $300 less if you don't dive), includ-
ing air transfer from Belize City, meals, and taxes. The setting—white-
coral sand, palm trees, mint-green water—is breathtaking, and the
diving, under expert and friendly supervision, is as good as any in the
world. You won't want to leave. ⊠ *Northern Caye (Box 1435, Dunedin,
FL 33838),* ☎ *800/423–3114 in the U.S.,* ℻ *941/439–2118 in the U.S..
11 rooms. Restaurant, bar, dive shop, fishing. MC, V.* ⊛

Scuba Diving

Less than 2 km (1 mi) from the atoll, the coral reef has precipitous walls
that plummet to 3,000 ft. Great depth doesn't always make for the best
diving, though; many divers say that the best dives happen in less than
50 ft of water. Still, the two most famous dives on Lighthouse Reef are
the Blue Hole and Half Moon Caye Wall, the Grand Canyon and Mat-
terhorn of Belize's underwater world.

From the air, the **Blue Hole,** a breathtaking vertical chute that drops
several hundred feet through the reef, looks like a dark-blue eye in the
center of the shallow lagoon. Formed during an ice age 15,000 years
ago, which exposed the reef's limestone foundations and created vast
subterranean caverns, the Blue Hole was first dived by Jacques Cousteau
in 1970 and has since become a diver's pilgrimage site. Just over 1,000
ft wide at the surface and dropping almost vertically to a depth of 412
ft, the Blue Hole inspires a sensation of swimming down a mine shaft.
It is this excitement, rather than the marine life (of which you'll see
far more at the surface, with a snorkel and flippers), that has led to
suitcase stickers reading "I dived the Blue Hole."

The best diving on Lighthouse is at **Half Moon Caye,** at the southeastern
tip of Lighthouse Reef. The Half Moon Caye Wall is a classic wall dive,
beginning at 35 ft and dropping almost vertically to blue infinity.
Floating out over the edge is a bit like free-fall parachuting. Magnificent spurs of coral jut out to the seaward side, looking like small tunnels; they're fascinating to explore and invariably full of fish. Because
of the great variety of ocean-floor terrain, an exceptionally varied marine life hovers around this caye. On the gently sloping sand flats behind the coral spurs, a vast colony of garden eels stirs, their heads
protruding from the sand like a field of periscopes. Spotted eagle rays,
turtles, and other pelagics also frequent the drop-off. But don't forget
the largest colony of red-footed boobies in Belize; there's nearly as much
activity above water as below it.

South Water Caye

⓲ *23 km (14 mi) southeast of Dangriga.*

South Water is the first caye in the south of Belize to have been developed for tourism. The coral is only a few flipper beats away and makes
for good off-the-beaten-reef diving. A nearby **Smithsonian-run re-**

search institute (✉ Carrie Bow Caye, ☎ no phone) welcomes visitors by appointment; contact the Blue Marlin Lodge for more information.

Dining and Lodging

$$$ ✕🖭 **Blue Marlin Lodge.** This picturesque resort makes an excellent base
Ⓒ for fishing, snorkeling, and diving trips: the reef is only 50 yards away, and the Blue Hole and Glover's Reef are easily accessible. The place is Belizean-run and children-friendly, with games and customized trips to please everyone on your trip. Accommodations, which spread out over half the caye, range from thatched cabanas to larger reef cabins on stilts to rooms in two shingled lemon-yellow buildings. Two of the cabins have air-conditioning. All rooms are close enough to the sea to hear it, and all have private baths, hot water, and electric fans. A restaurant and bar top off the amenities, and meals are included. ✉ *Box 21, Dangriga,* ☎ *52/2243 or 800/798–1558 in the U.S.,* 🖷 *52/ 2296. 16 rooms. Restaurant, bar, dive shop, snorkeling, fishing, babysitting. MC, V.* ⊛

$$–$$$ ✕🖭 **Pelican Beach Cottages.** If you like to snorkel off the beach, get thee to this (former) nunnery. You won't do better in Belize than the houses on South Water Caye owned by the Pelican Beach Resort folks. Pelican's Pouch is a colonial-era house, once a convent belonging to the Sisters of Mercy, with five large rooms on the second floor. There also are two cottages: if you're with a group, you'll want the Osprey's Nest, a three-bedroom house with two large verandas; Heron's Hideaway is a one-bedroom cottage nestled privately away. Accommodations here are on the barefoot comfortable side, not the fancy side. Electricity is solar, sea breezes and fans keep you cool, and the potties are composting. Here on the south end of paradise, you own the best beach, and you can swim and snorkel to your heart's content. The fishing's good, too, and there's diving nearby. Instead of serpents in this garden of Eden, you may occasionally have to resist sandflies and mosquitoes with hard-core DEET. At the center of the island, at what's called the "Pelican's University," student groups (about $65 per person including three meals) are put up in a large house with bunk beds. Anywhere you stay, you can bring your own grub or Pelican Beach's cook will feed you with meals served on the first floor of Pelican's Pouch. All kinds of meal plans can be arranged. ✉ *Box 2, Dangriga,* ☎ *52/ 2044,* 🖷 *52/2570. 5 rooms, 2 cottages, 1 dormitory. Restaurant, dive shop. AE, MC, V www.pelicanbeachbelize.com.*

Glover's Reef Atoll

⑲ *113 km (70 mi) southeast of Belize City.*

Named after the pirate John Glover, this coral necklace strung around a 208-square-km (80-square-mi) lagoon is the southernmost of Belize's three atolls. The diving rates as some of the best in Belize, and there is excellent fishing for permit and bonefish. There are now two resorts here. Visitors to Glover's Reef are charged $2.50 a day or $10 a week, collected by hotels and paid to the Belize Fisheries Department. There's an additional fee of $25 a month for sportfishing around Glover's Reef.

Dining and Lodging

$$$ ✕🖭 **Manta Reef Resort.** This fishing and diving resort, on Southwest Caye on the southern tip of Glover's Reef, is the newer and more up-scale of the atoll's two resorts. You arrive in style, on *The Pelagic,* the resort's custom 50-ft, 850-hp, twin-engine motor yacht, which ferries you to and from Belize City. A two-bedroom house is available for families, and all the cabanas are built of mahogany. You can snorkel in the lagoon, or just kick back, but diving and fishing are the raison d'être here. There's excellent bonefish and permit fishing in flats near the island, and the resort has a small fleet of boats to whisk your party to nearby dive sites at the atoll. ☎ *800/326–1724 in the U.S. 11 cabanas. Restaurant, bar, air-conditioning, room service, dive shop, fishing. AE, MC, V.* ✍

$$ 🏨 **Glover's Atoll Resort.** This budget resort with 12 self-catering cabins (under $200 per person per week), a bunkhouse, and campground is a lesson in laid-back living. Forget that you need running water, a convenience store, and 24-hour electricity to make you happy, and surrender to doing little else but fishing, diving, and cooking your own meals. You bring your tackle for the boat or shore fishing and your own food supplies (and anything else you'll need). This is as close to a Gilligan's Island–style vacation spot as they come. ✉ *Box 563, Belize City,* ☎ *21/ 2016 or 14/8351. MC, V. www.belizemall.com/gloversatoll.*

Scuba Diving

Though most of the finest dive sites are along the atoll's southeastern limb, on the windward side, one exception is **Emerald Forest Reef,** named for its mass of huge green elkhorn coral. Because the most exciting part of the reef is only 25 ft down, it's excellent for novices and snorkelers, and it abounds in healthy corals and fish. It also proves the important point that depth isn't everything.

Long Caye Wall is yet another exciting wall, with a dramatic drop-off to hundreds of feet. Overhangs covered in sheet and boulder coral make it a good place to spot turtles, rays, and barracuda.

Both **Manta Reef Resort** (☎ 23/1895) and Glovers Atoll Resort (☞ *above*) have good dive shops and services.

Southwest Caye Wall, close to the Manta Reef Resort, is a typically dramatic drop-off—an underwater cliff that falls quickly to 130 ft, is briefly interrupted by a narrow shelf, then continues its near-vertical descent to 350 ft. As with all wall dives, this one makes it easy to lose track of depth and time with the exhilaration of flying in blue space, so both ascent and descent require careful monitoring.

The Cayes and Atolls A to Z

Arriving and Departing

BY AIRPLANE

Because an increasing number of travelers transfer directly to Ambergris Caye upon arrival in Belize City, there are regular flights to San Pedro from both the municipal and international airports. The airstrip is right in San Pedro. You'll always find taxis at the airstrip, and the hotels run courtesy coaches. If you're proceeding on foot, it's about two minutes, around the edges of the soccer field, to the hotels in town. There are no buses.

Maya Island Airways (✉ 6 Fort St., Box 458, Belize City, ☎ 23/1140) and **Tropic Air** (✉ Box 20, San Pedro, ☎ 026/2012 or 800/422–3435 in the U.S.) both fly to Ambergris. Round-trip fares for the 20-minute flight are about $48 (municipal) and $88 (international). Flights leave several times daily from both airports.

These two airlines now fly to Caye Caulker as well, and any of the many flights to San Pedro will stop on request. Except for flights to these two islands, there are no scheduled plane connections to the cayes; each resort makes its own arrangements for guests to come out. Lighthouse Reef and Caye Chapel are the only out-islands with airstrips.

BY BOAT

A variety of boats connect Belize City with San Pedro on Ambergris Caye. The cost is $12.50 one-way. The most dependable boats to Ambergris, operated by the Caye Caulker Water Taxi Association, leave from the **Belize Marine Terminal,** on North Front Street, near the swing bridge (☎ 23/1969), unless otherwise noted. The quick open boats leave Belize City at 9 AM, noon, and 3 PM, then depart from San Pedro at 8 AM, 11:30 AM, and 2:30 PM. Kiosk shops and the **Belize City Marine Museum** help kill the time before departure. The *Andrea* departs from the Court House Wharf at 7 AM and returns at 3 PM daily except Sunday. The *Triple J* also leaves from the Court House Wharf, with departures at 9 AM, returning 3 PM daily. The *Thunderbolt* departs from the Texaco gas station, North Front Street, at 3 PM Monday through Saturday, 9 AM on Sunday. Private charter boats around the Belize City swing bridge also make the round trip, but they've been known to rip folks off—agree on a price before heading out and pay the fare only when you have reached your destination.

Boats for Caye Caulker take 45 minutes and cost $7.50 one way to and from Belize City. Departures are every hour-and-a-half from 9 AM to 5 PM, and return from the Public Pier in Caulker from 6:30 AM to 3 PM. The *Andrea, Triple J,* and *Thunderbolt* boats also stop on demand, coming and going, at Caye Caulker.

To reach the more remote cayes, you are basically left to your own devices. You can hire boats for charter in either San Pedro or Belize City, but they're not cheap. The resorts on the atolls run their own flights or boats, but these are not available to the general public. If you're staying at a swanky place, ask your hotel if they provide transportation. If not, ask for some advice on the best way to get there when making your reservations.

For the southern cayes, inquire about boats in Dangriga (☞ Placencia and the South, *below*). Dangriga's Pelican Beach Hotel sends a boat to its resort on South Water Caye, while the Río Mar Hotel runs boats to Tobacco Reef. Neither is usually available to nonguests, but you might be able to catch a ride if there's room. The *Gulf Cruza* (☎ 22/4506) leaves the Southern Foreshore at 6 AM Friday and makes stops at Placencia at 8:30 AM and Big Creek at 10 AM ($25 one way) en route to Puerto Cortez, Honduras, where it arrives at 2 PM ($60).

Getting Around

BY TAXI

If you don't find a taxi at the San Pedro airstrip, you can call a **cab** (☎ 14/9463 or 26/2038).

Contacts and Resources

BANKS

Atlantic Bank (✉ Front St., San Pedro) is open Monday, Tuesday, Thursday, and Friday 8–noon and 1–3; Wednesday 8–1; and Saturday 8:30–noon. **Belize Bank** (✉ 49 Barrier Reef Dr., San Pedro) is open Monday–Thursday 8–1 and Friday 8–1 and 3–6.

EMERGENCIES

On Ambergris: **Ambulance** (☎ 90). **Fire** (☎ 2372). **Police** (☎ 2022).

Hospitals. Lion's Clinic 2073 (✉ Next to the hyperbaric chamber, near the airstrip, San Pedro, ☎ no phone). The **Caye Caulker Health Center** (Opposite Marin Hotel, Caye Caulker, ☎ 22/2166) is open weekdays 8–11:30 and 1–4:30.

Pharmacy. Lopez Drugs (✉ Front St., San Pedro) is open Monday–Thursday 8–noon and 5:30–9, Friday 8–2, and weekends 7 AM–9 PM.

Belize Laundry & Dry Cleaners (⊠ Middle St., San Pedro). **Marie's Laundry Mat** (⊠ Back St., Caye Caulker).

Ambergris Caye's **post office** (⊠ Barrier Reef Dr., San Pedro) is open weekdays 8–noon and 1–5. Caye Caulker's **telephone office** (⊠ Near the Reef Hotel) is open weekdays 8–noon and 1–4, Saturday 8–noon.

THE CAYO

In the early 1980s, when the first jungle lodges began to open in the Cayo district, simply called Cayo locally, not many people thought this wild district on the Guatemalan border would become a magnet for travelers. It seemed too remote, its roads too bad, and its weather too unpredictable. But today more than half of those touring Belize come to the Cayo, making it the country's second-most popular destination, rivaling Ambergris Caye. Comprising more than 5,200 square km (2,000 square mi) of rugged, mountainous land but with fewer than 15,000 inhabitants, the Cayo—whose name originally referred to the peninsula of land between the Macal and Mopan rivers, on which the town of San Ignacio grew up—is both Belize's largest district and one of its least populated. You'll know you are entering the Cayo a few miles west of Belmopan: having run along the side of the Belize River, the road winds out of the valley and heads into a series of sharp bends. In a few minutes you'll see cattle grazing on steep hillsides and horses flicking their tails. If it weren't for the Fanta-orange sunsets and palm trees, this could be the Auvergne.

As in all of Belize, though, the land is never still for long. During a trip to the Mountain Pine Ridge area you can drop, ecologically speaking, from South Carolina to Brazil in the space of a few miles. One minute you're in pine savanna, the next in lush, subtropical rain forest.

Other things change as you enter the Cayo. The heavyset Creoles of the coast give way to light-footed, copper-skinned Mayas and mestizos; Spanish replaces English; and four-wheel-drive vehicles become a necessity. The lost world of the Maya begins to come alive through majestic, haunting ruins. And the Indiana Jones in all of us can now hike the jungle, ride horseback, canoe down the Macal or Mopan rivers, and explore incredible caves.

Most of the wildlife featured on Belize's 20-dollar bill lives in the Cayo—the mountain lions; the jaguar; their diminutive cousin, the beautiful, shy ocelot; and the even smaller margay. Here bird-watchers carry telescopes, cameras, and tape recorders with microphones the size of Larry King's, but for most people a pair of binoculars and some hiking boots will do. Most of Belize's 400-plus bird species can be spotted in the Cayo. Even if you've never been bird-watching, setting off through the jungle in search of motmots, masked tityras, violaceous trogons, and scaly-throated leaf-tossers as the sun begins to burn off the early morning mist will soon have you hooked. Most Cayo resorts offer birding tours.

When you walk in the bush, you have to keep your eyes on the ground. On horseback, however, you can feast your eyes on the surroundings, and at the end of the day it's the horse, not you, who feels tired. Riding has thus become one of the most popular ways of exploring the Cayo's mountain landscape. Many hotels and lodges rent horses by the hour as well as by the day, and several specialist operations rent fine horses, notably Banana Bank Ranch and Mountain Equestrian Trails (☞ *below*).

National Geographic filmed *Journey to the Underworld* in the Cayo's Caves Branch River area, where fascinating limestone caves open from lush tropical forest. Many of these have barely been explored. Resorts such as Caves Branch, Pook's Hill, and Jaguar Paw (☞ *below*) are increasingly arranging cave expeditions for their guests, either by inner tube or by boat; crystal-clear river water, startling darkness, and glistening white columns of stalactites are just some of the highlights. Serious spelunkers can explore with scuba gear. Before trying either, though, inquire about hystoplasmosis, a fungal infection of the lungs that can threaten explorers who venture into caves with large numbers of bats.

As for lodgings, you may be out in the bush, but you won't be roughing it. Indeed, the Cayo has some of the country's finest accommodations, from simple cabanas to beautifully landscaped properties. As usual in Belize, each resort is highly individualized, with a unique ambience created by its owners. All resorts, however, place special emphasis on ecotourism, and nearly all are on what might be called Safari Strip— the Western Highway heading from San Ignacio toward the Guatemalan border. The region's best restaurants are also at the resorts and hotels, and all are open to nonguests.

Numbers in the margin correspond to points of interest on the Cayo and the Deep South map.

Belmopan

⓴ *80 km (50 mi) southwest of Belize City.*

The best way to see Belize's capital is through the rear-view mirror, as you head toward the Cayo. The brainchild of Belize's longest-serving prime minister, George Price, Belmopan was to be Belize's answer to Brasilia and Canberra—a resplendent, modern capital city in the interior. Instead, it's a dreary cluster of concrete office buildings plunked down in the middle of nowhere, proving that cities cannot be created overnight but must come into being over centuries. It's a great shame, because if the money had been spent on revamping Belize City, that somewhat sad and grubby place could have been greatly transformed.

Worth a quick visit on the way out of Belmopan is the **Guanacaste National Park,** named for the huge guanacaste tree that grows here. The park has a rich population of tropical birds and plants. Eight hourly tours run daily, but you can also tour the minipark on your own. ☉ *Daily 8:30—last tour at 3:30.* 🎟 *$2.50.*

Dining and Lodging

$$$$ ✕🏨 **Jaguar Paw.** Though the resort is down 11 km (7 mi) of dirt road
★ on the Cave's Branch River, near Belmopan, it's anything but rustic. Owners Cy and Donna Young poured nearly $1 million into this stylish resort, and it shows. Cresting a hill, you look down at a massive, two-story building with a green, faux-marble entrance. Once inside, you're struck by the eye-popping Maya murals painted by American Pam Braun. Each room has a theme—a Victorian room with country armoire and French curtains, a pioneer room with a pebble-lined shower and rough-hewn wooden bed, and others. The restaurant serves a variety of seafood and tenderloin of grain-fed beef flown in from Kansas; the bar has satellite TV. Surrounding all of this is 215 acres of jungle, river, and caves, through which guests can inner-tube

The Cayo and the Deep South

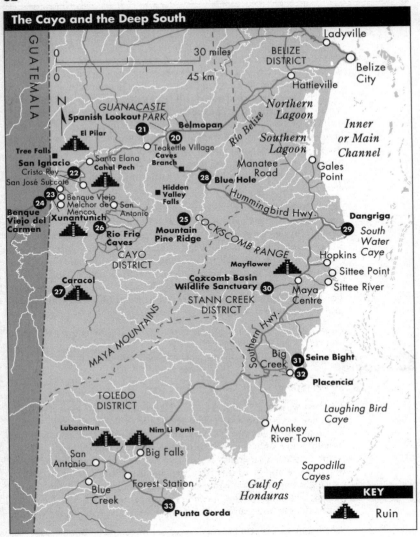

or row. It's not unheard of to clamber into one of these caves with a flashlight (watch out for bats) and find a 1,000-year-old clay pot cradled in a crevice. Several jaguars have also been spotted here, and Donna makes ashtrays from the imprints of their paws—hence, the name. ☒ *Off Western Hwy, between zoo and Belmopan; turn south at Mile 37, and follow dirt road 11 km (7 mi) to lodge (Box 1832, Belize City),* ☏ *81/3023 or 800/335–8645 in the U.S.,* ℻ *81/3024. 16 rooms. Restaurant, bar, pool, travel services. AE, DC, MC, V.* ⊜

\$\$\$ ✕▦ **Banana Bank Ranch.** John and Carolyn Carr—she's a painter from ★ Kansas; he's a rancher and former rodeo cowboy from Montana—are part of the first wave of expats to open lodges in the Cayo. Riding enthusiasts can choose from 25 fine saddle horses to help explore the 5,000-acre estate. A new horse barn is testament to Banana Bank's new emphasis on the equestrian, and John and Carolyn can arrange canoeing and bird-watching trips. The setting, on the bank of the Belize River—Belize's Mississippi—is heavenly. The thatched cabanas, with their curving internal walls, split-level layout, and showers, are simple but pleasant, with 24-hour electricity. Several domesticated wild animals live on the property, including a monkey named Simon and a ravishingly beautiful jaguar, Tika (whose photo was featured in a World Wildlife Fund calendar). Abandoned as a cub, Tika was taken in and lovingly reared by the Carrs. Outside the zoo, she is probably the only jaguar you'll see in Belize. ✉ *Turn north at Mile 48 of the Western Highway and follow dirt road to the Belize River, where a hand-pulled ferry takes you across to the lodge (Box 48, Belmopan),* ☎ *81/2020,* ✉ *81/2026. 5 cabanas. Restaurant. MC, V.* 🐾

\$\$–\$\$\$ ✕⌂ ⚠ **Caves Branch Adventure Co. & Jungle Camp.** Those with Indiana Jones fantasies, look no further. Caves Branch will help you live
★ them out. On a 58,000-acre private estate south of Belmopan, owner Ian Anderson originally offered tents, rustic bunkhouses, and pit toilets, but he's softened a bit and has added comfortable half-screened cabana suites of mahogany and hand-polished bamboo, complete with wicker furniture and flush toilets. (Note: There are no locks on doors.) A budget bunkhouse with eight beds and a riverside spot for pitching a tent are also available. Lighting is provided by oil lamps, but a flashlight is a good idea, too. A look up at the night sky will remind you how many stars you've been missing at home. Late-risers and couch potatoes need not apply: Anderson offers about 14 thrilling eco-adventure caving, waterfall climbing, and hiking trips, open to both lodge guests and day-trippers, with helpful guides who have your safety in mind. On the cave-tubing expedition into Footprint Cave, for example, you'll strap a light onto your head and spend hours alternatively floating into the cave and "parking" your inner tube to crawl past stalagmites into dry chambers. Unbelievable Maya relics are scattered about, seemingly ignored by museums, and just when you think you've left your world behind, your guide will unpack a lunch and you'll eat picnic-style where Maya performed bloodletting rituals. All of this creates much bonding among travelers. When you return from an expedition, cold Belikins await, followed by a delicious homemade meal served family-style. Don't fill up on the delicious fresh-baked bread that precedes dinner; at least two entrées and rice and beans are sure to follow. ✉ *19½ km (12 mi) south of Belmopan (Box 356, Belmopan),* ☎ ✉ *82/2800. 10 cabanas, 6 with shared baths, 8 beds in bunkhouse, camping. No credit cards.* 🐾

\$\$\$ ✕⌂ **Pook's Hill.** When night falls and the lamps are lit on the veranda,
★ this low-key jungle lodge is one of the most pleasant of Cayo abodes. The name comes from Kipling's *Puck of Pook's Hill*; the closest village is Teakettle; and beyond the Roaring River, on whose banks the lodge stands, is a 6,800-acre nature reserve teeming with wildlife, including tapirs and toucans. Owners Vicki and Ray Snaddon used to be beekeepers, but when the African bee wiped out their hives, they decided to become hoteliers. Their solid, stone-and-thatch cabanas are laid out on a sloping, grassy clearing around a small Maya site. The circular ones at the top are smaller, but they make up for it with extra privacy and treetop views. The rectangular and larger cabanas below them sit on a grassy terrace facing the jungle. All have attractive hardwood furniture, window screens, Guatemalan fabrics, and electricity. During the day, you can swim, horseback-ride, bird-watch, or boat up the Roaring River to a series of caves, many of which contain Maya burial sites; then it's back to the veranda, with its beautiful, tiger-stripe floor of polished rosewood, for cocktails before a dinner. If you want a busy social scene, this is not the place. If you want to get away from it all and enjoy the magnificent scenery, you'll never want to leave. ✉ *Turn south at Mile 52 of the Western Highway and go 8 km (5 mi) (Box 14, Belmopan),* ☎ *81/2017,* ✉ *81/2336. 9 cabanas. Restaurant, bar. MC, V.* 🐾

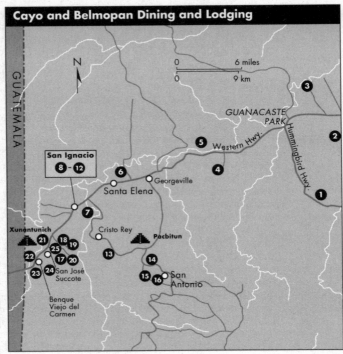

Cayo and Belmopan Dining and Lodging

Spanish Lookout

㉑ *19 km (12 mi) north of Western Highway; follow sign at Mile 59.*

This small hilltop village is one of the centers of the Mennonite community (another is Blue Creek). Blonde, blue-eyed, and seemingly out of place in this tropical country, the Mennonites are in fact one of Belize's most successful ethnic groups. Carpenters and dairy farmers, they build nearly all of the area's resorts, and most of the eggs and milk you'll consume during your stay will have come from Mennonite farms. The women dress in cotton frocks and head scarves, and the men wear straw hats, suspenders, and dark trousers. Many still move about in horse-drawn buggies. The cafés and small shops in Spanish Lookout offer a unique opportunity to mingle with these devout and world-wary people, but note that they do not appreciate being gawked at or photographed any more than you do, and probably less.

San Ignacio

㉒ *37 km (23 mi) southwest of Belmopan.*

When you hear the incredible commotion made by grackles in the trees of the town square at sunset, you'll know that you've arrived in the hub of the Cayo district; it's worth standing still for a moment just to listen to their eerily beautiful sound.

With its well-preserved vernacular architecture, bustling Spanish ambience, and dusty charm, San Ignacio is one of the few Belizean towns where you might wish to linger. Evenings are cool and mosquito-free, there are a few funky and interesting bars and restaurants, though there is little nightlife beyond hard drinking, and the location is excellent for exploring the Cayo. Most accommodations are either in or close to town.

NEED A
BREAK? Not just a bustling café and bar, **Eva's** (✉ 22 Burns Ave.) is a Cayo institution—an Internet café, bulletin board, information center, trading post, and meeting place all in one. The food is honest-to-goodness Belizean fare, with some bacon and eggs, omelets, and sandwiches thrown in for good measure. Mugs of wickedly strong black tea are always available, and no one is in much of a hurry, making this an excellent place to write postcards, catch up on your journal, or just soak up some authentic Belizean atmosphere. Presiding over the colorful chaos is Bob Jones, a garrulous British ex-serviceman, who can tell you everything from where to rent a canoe to what to do if you get bitten by a fer-de-lance (say your prayers) to where to fix a flat or find a room. You can use Eva's computer to catch up on your e-mail.

The **Ix Chel Tropical Research Foundation, Guesthouse, and Wellness Center** (Next to Chaa Creek, ☎ 92/3870, FAX 93/3165, www.ixchel-belize.com ✍ $5.75 to Rainforest Medicine Trail), founded by Dr. Rosita Arvigo (she's a doctor of naprapathy), is a center for traditional Maya medicine. Although she's not a native Belizean, Dr. Arvigo ingratiated herself with Don Elijio Pantí, Shaman of Belize, and in 1985 became his apprentice with the promise to preserve traditional healing practices. The foundation has established itself as a special botanical garden: the beautiful Rainforest Medicine Trail takes you on short, self-guided walk through the rain forest with a chance to study the symbiotic complexities of its plant life. Learn about the healing properties of such indigenous plants as gumbo-limbo and man vine, and see some of the endangered medicinal plants that Dr. Arvigo and her colleagues have rescued and revivified. The shop sells Maya medicinal products like Belly Be Good and Flu Away, as well as Dr. Arvigo's excellent books. As wellness consultants and healers, Dr. Arvigo and her staff have aromatherapy, herbal and mineral-water therapies, Maya massage, manicures, and pedicures for those who stay at the wellness center guest house ($60 per night double occupancy, meals extra) or make appointments. For those who want a real immersion, Dr. Arvigo offers occasional seminars in natural healing and herbalism. Hey, is this Sante Fe or Cayo?

The **Natural History Center and Blue Morpho Butterfly Farm** (✍ $5, ☉ daily 9–4) at Chaa Creek (☞ *below*) draws on a host of contacts made over a lifetime committed to preserving the ecology of Belize (both the Smithsonian and London's Natural History Museum pitched in). The little museum of Belize's flora and fauna has a tiny library, lots of displays from beautiful butterflies to nature's more grim creatures, snakes (thankfully pickled in jars). Just outside is a blue morpho breeding center, a small screened kennel of sorts. If you haven't seen blue morphos in the wild, you can see them up close here and even peer at their slumbering pupae, which resemble jade earrings. Once you're inside the double doors, the blue beauties, who look boringly brown when their wings are closed, flit about or remain perfectly still, sometimes on your shoulder or head, and open and close their wings to what seems like an innate rhythm akin to inhaling and exhaling. Hourly tours are led by a team of naturalists.

Besides thoughtful displays on Cayo ecology, flora, and fauna, **Tropical Wings** (☎ 93/2265, ✍ $2.50), a little nature center, flies 25 butterfly species and rears 20 including the blue morpho, owl, giant swallowtail, and monarch. There's a small restaurant and gift shop.

After crossing the Mopan River near the village of San José Succotz on a hand-pulled, two-car and pedestrian ferry—ask to use the crank yourself, if you'd like—you drive or walk up to **Xunantunich** (pronounced *zoo-nan-too-nitch*), which means Stone Maiden. It's a nice little hike to the ruins: butterflies flit through the air; maidenhair ferns grow in profusion. Near the top, a magnificent avenue of cohune palms announces your arrival at an important ceremonial center of the Maya Classic Period. A visitor center gives the history of the site, and drinks and snacks are available for sale. El Castillo, the massive 120-ft-high main pyramid, was built on a leveled hilltop. Though it's not as well excavated as Altun Ha, it furnishes a spectacular 360-degree panorama over Guatemala and the Mopan River valley for those who clamber to the top. On the eastern wall is a reproduction of one of the finest Maya sculptures in Belize, a frieze decorated with jaguar heads, human faces, and abstract geometric patterns, telling the story of the Moon's affair with Morning Light. Sweep the frieze with your eyes, then pan out across the jungle. It's a great sight. ☎ *$2.50.* ⊙ *Weekdays 8–5, weekends 8–4.*

El Pilar Archaeological Reserve for Maya Flora and Fauna, 13 km (8 mi) west of the village of Bullet Tree Falls (there's a sign just across the Hawkesworth Bridge) is a less-frequented site still being excavated under the direction of Anabel Ford, an archaeology professor at U.C.–Santa Barbara who's known for her unconventional views. Excavations of Maya ruins have traditionally concentrated on public architecture and, shall we say, power structures. At El Pilar, the emphasis is on domestic architecture—reconstructing houses, replanting a garden with crops used by the ancient Maya, and generally creating a sense that people actually lived here. They did so, according to Professor Ford, for 15 centuries, though most of the 25 small plazas and temples date from the last 300 years of occupation, AD 700–1000. Imagine a gated community with swipe cards to gain access to different areas: El Pilar is not quite like that, but the evidence of sentry posts and inaccessible parts of the site suggest that this was a community of high-ranking officials surrounded by a hostile population. Two well-marked trails take you around the site. Because the structures have not been stripped of vegetation, you may feel like you're walking through a series of shady orchards. Don't forget your binoculars: in the 2,000-hectare (5,000-acre) nature reserve there's some terrific bird-watching. Behind the main plaza, a lookout grants a spectacular view across the jungle to El Pilar's sister city, Pilar Poniente, on the Guatemalan border.

Just outside San Ignacio is a third major Maya ruin, the unfortunately named **Cahal Pech** ("place of the tiks"). It was occupied from around 900 BC to AD 1100. At its peak, around AD 600, Cahal Pech was a medium-size settlement, with some three dozen structures in seven plazas. It is thought that it functioned as a kind of guardpost, standing watch over the nearby confluence of the Mopan and Macal rivers. It may be somewhat less compelling than the area's other ruins, but it's really no less mysterious, given that these structures mark the presence of a civilization that we still know so little about. You can try to get some answers at the visitor center and small museum. ☎ *$2.50.* ⊙ *Tues.– Sat. 9–noon and 1–4:30, Sun. 9–12.*

Dining and Lodging
Almost all San Ignacio hotels have restaurants open to nonguests.

$–$$　✕ **Sanny's Grill.** Sanny's starts with basic Belizean favorites such as chicken or pork chops, but then does wonderful things with them, using a hot grill and equally hot spices. Try the champagne shrimp or lime-thyme fish, prepared with red snapper and served with the tastiest, spiciest rice and beans in Cayo. You can dine on a covered deck outside or inside in a casual room. The restaurant's democratic motto proclaims: PRICES ANYONE CAN AFFORD, and they are exceptionally reasonable.

San Ignacio Dining and Lodging

Sanny's is in a house in a residential area off the Benque Road and is hard to find after dark, but it's open until 11 PM. *Going west from San Ignacio, look for a sign on the right just beyond the Texaco station; turn right on the gravel road, go four blocks to a bar, turn left and go to the end of the block. 23rd St., San Ignacio,* ☎ *92/2988. No credit cards. No lunch Sun.*

$$$$ ✕ 🏨 **Blancaneaux Lodge.** You may detect a whiff of Beverly Hills as
★ you sweep down the hibiscus-and-palm-lined driveway of this upscale Mountain Pine Ridge resort and find yourself staring at a well-groomed croquet lawn. This is hardly surprising, as Blancaneaux, once a private getaway, is owned by film director Francis Ford Coppola, who opened its doors to the public in 1993. A small army of gardeners has landscaped the grounds to meet Southern California standards, and the solid mahogany furniture in the bar and expanded dining room glows with polish. Designed by Mexican architect Manolo Mestre, the handsome cabanas were based on local Belizean structures and on houses Coppola had seen in the Philippines while shooting *Apocalypse Now* (the fan in the bar came from the set). Laid out on a hillside above the Privassion River, the lodge's five villas have been featured in *Architectural Digest.* They have soaring thatch ceilings, spacious living rooms, screened porches looking over the river, and Japanese-style tile baths. Francis's own villa, one of the finest of Cayo residences, is available for rent when he's not here. The standard cabanas with decks, while delightful by the standards of most lodges, pale by comparison with the villas. Although you probably won't see Francis, you can sample his personal recipes for pizza and pasta, washed down with a glass of Rubicon wine flown in from his Napa Valley estate. A fleet of Land Rovers waits to take you to remote Maya ruins or on shopping trips to Guatemala; If you have a plane, you can even bring that: Coppola has his own landing strip. ✉ *Chiquibul Rd., from San Ignacio, go 21*

km (12½ mi) to the Mountain Pine Ridge reserve entrance, then another 7½ km (4½ mi), and turn right on dirt road, for approx 1 km (½ mi) to resort (Box B, Central Farm, San Ignacio), ☎ 92/3878 or 800/ 746–3743 in the U.S., ℻ 92/3919. 7 cabanas, 5 villas. Restaurant, bar, horseback riding, travel services. AE, MC, V. ❧

$$$$ ✕⊞ ⚠ **Chaa Creek.** This is the queen of jungle resorts. With more than
★   20 years' experience, owners Mick and Lucy Fleming have Chaa Creek running like a well-oiled Rolls-Royce. Everything about the place, from the quality of the hardwood furniture to the friendliness of the staff of 40, is simply better than it is most anywhere else. The setting, on 330 acres of rolling hills above the Macal River, is magnificent. The whitewashed stone cottages with thatched roofs, Guatemalan decor, and tile floors manage to be both extremely simple and extremely elegant. They have been intentionally left without phones or air-conditioning, although, surrendering to progress, electricity has been installed throughout. Lodgings include 19 cottages; the honeymoon suite, a circular thatched building with the best view; and three luxurious villas. For the budget traveler, Chaa Creek has a tent-free **Macal River Safari Camp** in a clearing above the Macal River, for $45 (per person): small A-frame guestrooms are set up on individual wooden platforms, the bathrooms are spotless, and a gas refrigerator keeps drinks cold. Included in this price are three terrific daily meals prepared by a Belizean chef on a traditional fire hearth, known as a *fogon*. Chaa Creek's new spa, on a hill above the lodge, has an unspeakably gorgeous view of the Mayan Mountains and is by far the best-equipped and most professional spa facility in Belize. Treatments include mud and herbal body wraps, scrubs, and polishes, hydrotherapy, Vichy shower, or traditional massage, and facials. As if all of this weren't enough, Chaa Creek's safari-style tours are among the best in the land. ✉ *From San Ignacio, go 7.6 km (4¾) mi west on Benque Rd. (Western Highway) and turn left on Chial Rd.; follow signs on this unpaved road 6 km (3½ mi) to resort (Box 53, San Ignacio),* ☎ *92/2037,* ℻ *92/2501. 19 cottages, 2 suites, 10 casitas (Macal River Camp). Restaurant, bar, room service, spa, travel services. AE, DC, MC, V.* ❧

$$$$ ✕⊞ **Ek 'Tun.** Owners Ken and Phyllis Dart gave up a life in Boulder, Colorado, to live in a tent while they created this secluded lodge on the lush, green ground above the Macal River. With only two cottages and the highly personal attention of the owners, this is more of a bed-and-breakfast in the jungle than a traditional lodge. After navigating a bumpy road in a Land Rover, you are taken across the river in a skiff. Once on the other side, you step out into a 600-acre grounds with giant capoc trees and flowering shrubs. Both guest cabanas have a large main room plus an airy loft: one is constructed of thatch and hardwood poles, with a magnificent rough-hewn staircase leading up to a sleeping loft; the other has stone walls and a flagstone floor, with a stone staircase. Both have woven floor mats, Guatemalan furnishings, and generous-size bathrooms. If you want to get away from it all, swim in natural mineral pools, ride a horse, hike, go birding and wildlife spotting, this is a perfect place to do it without the distractions of phones and TVs (or, intentionally, electricity). On the extensive network of loop trails, you can see orange-breasted falcons and toucans, and hear the roar of howler monkeys. The excellent meals, included in the price, are served in a stucco-and-thatch dining room overlooking the river. Chilled papaya soup and grouper with *santa hoja* (an anise-flavored Belizean spice) are just two of Phyllis's creations. ✉ *On Macal River, 12 mi upstream from San Ignacio,* ☎ *91/2002 or 303/442–6150 in the U.S. 2 cabanas. Restaurant, bar, beach, mineral pool, mineral baths, travel services. MC, V.* ❧

$$–$$$$ ✕▥ **duPlooy's.** By canoe, this ranchlike ensemble of buildings is only a few minutes upstream from Chaa Creek; by road, you have to drive for 15 minutes over a bumpy track. The bush feeling ends at the gate, where horses, gardens, and stone paths create a beautiful bucolic setting. The location, above a Macal River bend known as Big Eddy, is spectacular—from the deck, 30 ft above the forest floor, you look straight out to a dramatic sweep of limestone cliffs. From the sandy beach below, you can swim and dive off the rocks into the Macal River. Bungalows, all with private baths and electricity, have king-size beds and hardwood Guatemalan furnishings. There are also less-expensive rooms in the jungle lodge, with screened-in porches, and bed-and-breakfast accommodations for the budget traveler in the Pink House, with six airy rooms sharing two baths. A variety of package plans with or without meals are available, but the food is terrific and always includes a vegetarian option. The special work of Ken, an ornithologist, and personable Judy duPlooy of late has been the 45-acre Belize Botanical Gardens, a collection of hundreds of trees, plants, and flowers from all over Central America. Enlightening tours are given by local Maya who can tell you the names of the plants in three languages (Mayan, Spanish, and English) and their varied medicinal uses. An orchid house is being constructed to house the duPlooys' collection of 180 orchid species. *From San Ignacio, go 7.6 km (4¾ mi) west on Benque Rd. (Western Highway) and turn left on Chial Rd.; follow signs on this unpaved road 6 km (3½ mi) to resort,* ☎ *92/3101,* ℻ *92/3301. 3 cottages, 8 rooms, 6 with shared baths. Restaurant, bar, horseback riding, boating, travel services. MC, V.* ✍

$$$ ✕▥ ⛰ **Mountain Equestrian Trails.** If you want a vacation on horseback, the professionals here can't be beat; but even if you can't ride, M.E.T. is a gorgeous place to stay. After a stint in the U.S., owner Jim Bevis, who grew up in Belize, is back in the saddle again. The two attractive two-room cabanas are decked out in Guatemalan furnishings and mahogany fittings, and the well-equipped camp for budget travelers has Eureka tents, each built on a wooden platform and outfitted with two high-quality cots. A huge, hexagonal tent some distance away functions as dining room and kitchen, while meals for full-price guests (various plans available) are served in a pleasant thatch-covered dining room, with bar, at the other end of the property. The setting, in the bottom of a lush valley with views across to the jungle-covered flanks of the Mountain Pine Ridge, is second to none, but it's the riding that makes M.E.T. special. Superbly trained, conditioned, and sure-footed Texas quarter horses pick their way over the resort's 97 km (60 mi) of jungle trails, some of which wind up and down quite precipitous slopes. Though they're quite safe, the horses are no plugs; a flick of the heel and you're off in a cloud of dust. Just across the road from M.E.T., at Mile 8 of the Pine Ridge Road, is Green Hills Butterfly Ranch. ✉ *Western Hwy. to Mile 62.7, turn north onto Mountain Pine Ridge Rd. and continue for 8 mi (13 km) and watch for sign on left. Mountain Pine Ridge Rd., Central Farm,* ☎ *82/3310,* ℻ *82/3505. 4 rooms, tent camp. Dining room, bar, horseback riding. MC, V.* ✍

$$–$$$ ✕▥ **San Ignacio Hotel.** The Queen stayed here when she visited the Cayo in 1994—although there were a lot fewer lodging choices in those days—and if you want to stay in the town of San Ignacio itself, this could be the place for you, too. It doesn't look like much from the outside, and the hallways are cinderblock, but the rooms are large and comfortable, and all have phones, large bathrooms, and verandas facing the jungle. Still, you pay a premium for the convenience of being in town, well into three figures for an unassuming double. There's a small swimming pool and (look no further) an iguana hatchery. The Running W restaurant specializes in steak, and meal plans are available. The staff can arrange birding and other excursions. ⊠ *Box 33,* ☎ *92/2034,* FAX *92/2134. 24 rooms. Restaurant, bar, air-conditioning, pool. AE, MC, V.* ❧

$$ ✕⛿ **Crystal Paradise.** On the Macal River in the village of Cristo Rey, not far from Blancaneaux, this resort is one of the few locally owned Cayo operations. And what a family this is! The Tuts (pronounced *toots*) have 10 children (the tootlets?) and are a roughly equal mix of all three of Belize's main cultures: Creole, Maya, and Spanish. Eldest son Jeronie can identify more than 200 bird species and is an expert on medicinal plants; along with younger brother Evrald, he knows the surrounding jungle of the beautiful Mountain Pine Ridge area about as well as anyone. The Tuts have a good variety of very reasonably priced tours, including jungle camping, river excursions, rafting, spelunking, and horseback trips to Caracol; and rent cars. The cabanas have showers, whitewashed walls, tile floors, and screened and louvred windows. Touches like handmade Guatemalan bedspreads and wall hangings add local flavor. All have private baths and ceiling fans. Breakfast and dinner are included in the rate, and lunch can be bought and packed for outings. ⊠ *Cristo Rey Rd., 6¼ km (4 mi) from San Ignacio, Cristo Rey Village, south of Santa Elena, on road to Cahal Pech,* ☎ FAX *92/2772. 8 cabanas, 12 rooms. Restaurant, bar, horseback riding. MC, V.* ❧

$$ ✕⛿ **Five Sisters Falls and Lodge.** It's unfair to say, as some have, that this lodge in the Mountain Pine Ridge is a poor man's Blancaneaux. Though it is just down the road, it has its own style, and the setting, if anything, is possibly more dramatic here. Perched on a steep hill, it looks down 200 ft to the Privassion River and the falls for which it's named. The lodge's thatched cabanas with electricity, bathrooms, simple bedspreads, decorative mosquito nets, and screened porches with hammocks are owned and run by retired Belizean customs officer Carlos Javier Popper. A tram can take you down to swim in the river if you don't fancy the 286-step path. After your swim, the thatched-roof bar can refresh you further. The restaurant, with a beautiful view of the falls, serves Belizean food. The bar can be occasionally noisy at night. ⊠ *From San Ignacio, go 21 km (12½ mi) to the Mountain Pine Ridge reserve entrance, then another 7½ km (4½ mi), and turn right on dirt road, for approx 1.6 km (1 mi) to resort, Mountain Pine Ridge Reserve, Benque Viejo,* ☎ *92/3184,* FAX *92/3081. 15 cabanas. Restaurant, bar, meeting rooms. AE, MC, V.* ❧

$$ ✕⛿ **Green Heaven.** What's a nice young couple from the South of France doing in Belize? Dominique Agius and Anne-Karine Chappaz say it all started one day in Europe when they were looking for the Costa Rican consulate, found it closed, and stumbled upon a Belize consulate instead. That led to a trip to a country they knew almost nothing about, and eventually to opening this small lodge in 1999. Dominique and Anne-Karine, along with Anne-Karine's parents, frequent visitors from France, provide personal attention to guests who are usually outnumbered by staff and management. The four wood and yellow-stucco cabins with red tin roofs, scattered on a low hill on the Chial Road (the same one that leads to Chaa Creek and duPlooy's), are modestly appointed with hardwood floors and furniture. After the generator shuts down around 11, you can light a romantic oil lamp. There's no river swimming here, but Green Heaven has the nicest swimming pool in Cayo with hammocks under the poolside palapa. Dominique runs the restaurant, La Vie En Rose, serving French classics like beef bourguignon, filet à la Provençale, fruit mousses, and savory crepes. It's open daily from 7 AM to 10 PM. ✉ *Chial Rd., from San Ignacio, go 8 km (4¾ mi) west on Benque Rd. (Western Hwy.) and turn left on Chial Rd.; it's about 1 km (½ mi) farther on right (Box 155, San Ignacio),* ☎ FAX *91/2034. 4 cabins. Restaurant, bar, pool, volleyball, travel services. AE, MC, V.* ☙

$$ ✕▥ **Maya Mountain Lodge.** Bart and Suzi Mickler's hilltop lodge is
★ ☾ not luxurious, but that's not its intention. In recent years, the lodge has focused on family-oriented, educational activities, and although any traveler will also enjoy staying here, the setting is optimal for those who want an active learning experience. Suzi, who has a master's degree in curriculum management, is the "headmistress"; in addition to designing the nature trails (one passes 150 species of edible jungle plants, the other concentrates on ornamentals), she has created a host of courses at different levels, particularly for children, covering everything from Belizean history to ornithology, natural history, and ecology. The lodgings are whitewashed thatched cottages, with newly tiled baths and new furnishings; each has its own patio. A large wooden building offers simpler, budget-conscious rooms. Meals are taken in a pleasant, open-sided dining room near the reception area, and the food is tasty and plentiful. Various meal plans are offered, but alcohol is BYOB. The staff is agreeable, and the grounds are thriving thanks to more than a decade of T.L.C. The tours include everything from horseback riding to mountain biking to Maya ruins. ✉ *Crysto Rey Rd., just outside San Ignacio (Box 174),* ☎ *92/2164,* FAX *92/2029. 8 cottages, 6 rooms with shared baths. Restaurant, pool, travel services. AE, MC, V.* ☙

$$ ✕▥ **Warrie Head Ranch and Lodge.** Upon arrival you're greeted with fresh fruit punch served by Miss Lydia, the personable Creole woman who manages this peaceful lodge. The elegant grounds, with seemingly every tree and shrub flowering, have the look of a botanical garden. It's a short walk across the property to Warrie Head Creek, with its small waterfall, and to the beautiful Old Belize River. A monstrous steam tractor, once used to drag mahogany logs to the river, a horse-drawn sugar mill, and several old chicle pots enhance the historic atmosphere of this former logging camp. Owners John and Bia Searle have stocked the 10 cozy rooms with 18th-century, largely mahogany furniture and antiques. Dinnertime is special at Warrie Head, with guests lining up at the buffet to enjoy big helpings of Miss Lydia's tasty home-style cooking, which draws on Creole, Spanish, and American recipes. ✉ *Box 244, Belize City,* ☎ *27/7185 or 800/815–5019 in the U.S.,* FAX *27/5213. 10 rooms. Restaurant, bar, boating. AE, MC, V.* ☙

$$ ✕▥ **Windy Hill.** You don't have to drive for hours to get to this lodge—it's just outside San Ignacio, on 100 acres. When you see the 25 cabanas, dining room, offices, pool, various sheds and buildings, and rows of tour vehicles, you realize this is quite an operation. It's also an aggressive marketer; all around Belize you see signs touting free rooms at Windy Hill (free in the off-season if you buy a meal plan and take tours). The cabanas, all with verandas and hammocks, are perched on a low hill, across landscaped grounds. Inside, furnishings are custom-made from local hardwoods, and hand-woven Guatemalan rugs adorn the floors. Each also has ceiling fans, a minibar, and 24-hour electricity. The resort runs many tours to Tikal, Caracol, and other destinations. ✉ *Western Hwy. (Benque Rd.) 1⅔ km (1 mi) west of San Ignacio, Graceland Ranch,* ☎ *92/2017 or 800/946–3995 in the U.S.,* FAX *92/ 3080. 25 cabanas. Restaurant, bar, pool, horseback riding, travel services. AE, MC, V.* ☙

$ ✕🖬 **Aguada.** When you can get a clean, attractive hotel room with private bath and a swimming pool to boot, all for $25, go for it. That's the deal at Aguada, a new spot in Santa Elena, San Ignacio's low-key sister town. Run by an American and his Belizean wife, the hotel has a friendly restaurant serving such American standards as burgers as well as Belizean dishes. A large common room has a television and games. If you're carless, it's within walking distance of San Ignacio; you can also take a cab for $2.50, or you can walk 5 minutes to the highway and catch a bus to town ($1). ✉ *Turn north off Western Hwy. at Loma Luz Hospital and go 6 blocks (Box 133, San Ignacio),* ☎ *92/3609. 8 rooms. Restaurant, bar, air-conditioning, pool, travel services. MC, V.* ❧

$ ✕🖬 **Clarissa Falls.** The rumbling falls are the first and last sounds of the day at Clarissa Falls. It's a well-known place that especially attracts Belizeans for a fun Sunday outing, or for a cheap, tasty meal of tacos (40 cents), enchiladas, and *relleno negro* (black bean) soup under the open-air palapa, overlooking the Mopan River. One reason it's so popular is the people who run it: Chena Galvez, the charming owner and manager, her sister, Anna, who creates the simple, delicious food the restaurant serves in copious quantities, and their friendly staff. This is their family ranch, a rolling 900-acre expanse of grassy pastureland and a working cattle ranch, complete with cowboys on horseback herding Brahman bulls. Chena has spent her life on the ranch, and over the years she has built a small colony of homey thatch cabanas with electricity. Two of the units are big enough for large families. Kids love this place, as they can swim, tube, or canoe in the river. There are resident toucans, and the pet parrot, Larry, enjoys drinking coffee. ✉ *Western Hwy., 9 km (5½ mi) west of San Ignacio (Box 44, Santa Elena),* ☎ 🖷 *92/3916. 11 cabanas, 9 with private bath. Restaurant, bar, boating. MC, V.*

$ 🖬 ⚠ **The Trek Stop.** Butterflies, beer, and beds. This B&B covers all the basics: a small butterfly farm and nature center called **Tropical Wings,** a restaurant with cold Belikin and inexpensive Mexican and Belizean dishes, and cheap sleeps in cozy, neat-as-a-pin cabins ($10 per person) with outdoor composting toilets and solar-heated showers. Tents or just tent sites are also available, as is a common kitchen for making your own grub. American expats Judy and John Yaeger and their Belizean partners opened this spot on top of a hill near San José Succotz in 1998. It's a fine find particularly for budget travelers. *San José Succotz village, 9.6 km (6 mi) west of San Ignacio, on the south side of Western Hwy.,* ☎ *93/2265. 6 cabins with shared baths. Restaurant, gift shop. MC, V.* ❧

Outdoor Activities and Sports

CANOEING

The Cayo's many rivers, especially the Mopan and Macal, make it an excellent place for canoeing. Most of the larger resorts, like Chaa Creek and duPlooys (*above*), have canoes, and you can easily rent them in San Ignacio from **Toni Canoes,** at Eva's (☎ 92/2267), or just by asking around.

CAVING

Over the millennia, as dozens of swift-flowing rivers bored through them, the soft limestone of the Maya Mountains became pitted with caves, à la Swiss cheese. The Maya used them as burial sites and, according to one theory, as subterranean waterways that linked the Cayo with communities as far north as the Yucatán. They then fell into a thousand-year slumber, the haunt only of bats, margays, and the occasional grave robber. But in recent years, the caves have been redis-covered by spelunkers. To some people, the best thing about a cave is the circle of light that appears as you approach the exit, but others love that dark, womblike sensation. If you're one of them, contact one of the Cayo's tour operators who have staked out the caves as their own. First on the scene was Ian Anderson, Canadian owner of **Caves Branch Adventure Co. & Jungle Camp** (☞ Belmopan, *above*), who, along with a friendly staff of trained guides, runs exhilarating Indiana Jones–style caving, cave-tubing, waterfall climbing, and hiking trips, for both lodge guests and day-trippers from a tiki-torchlit jungle camp just south of Belmopan. David Simson, of **David's Adventure Tours** (☎ 92/3674,✍) was the first do tours of the now-popular Barton Creek Cave. This trip, and other caving and river trips, costs about $25.

HORSEBACK RIDING

Though the undisputed local experts are Mountain Equestrian Trails and Chaa Creek, **Easy Rider** (✉ 24 Burns Ave., San Ignacio, ☎ 14/8726) also runs equestrian tours of the Maya ruins and other points of interest in the San Ignacio region.

Shopping

Caesar's (✉ On Western Hwy., just east of San Ignacio) has T-shirts, hammocks, postcards, and jewelry for last-minute souvenirs—don't ex-pect a deal. The village of San Antonio is home to the **Tanah Mayan Art Museum** (☎ 92/3310), run by the Garcia sisters, four bright Maya siblings with clever hands and a collective head for business. They've become something of a local legend. At the other end of the village is the Magana family's arts-and-crafts shop, **Magana Zaac-tunich Art Gallery,** which specializes in hardwood carvings. You may want to visit both before buying anything.

En Route Heading southeast from San Ignacio, the road winds up from the Macal Valley through fertile farming country where corn, peanuts, and beans grow in small roadside clearings. Then, a few miles beyond the village of Cristo Rey, the road swings south and southeast away from the river, and the vegetation gets wilder. Cohune palms, trumpet trees, wild papayas, and strangler vines grow in a riot, while here and there a crop of banana or corn cuts into the hillside between them. Shortly before the village of San Antonio, you emerge onto a quasi-plateau with fine views of the Maya Mountains. With its sheep, goats, and orange trees, San Antonio's cluster of brightly painted wooden houses cling-ing to the hillside at 1,000 ft looks like a tropical version of a Greek hilltop community. Past the village, the road begins to climb steeply, and the earth grows steadily redder. In the rainy season, it turns into what looks like mango ice cream. In wet weather, you'll need four-wheel drive, and even then you may get bogged down.

Benque Viejo del Carmen

㉔ *13 km (8 mi) southwest of San Ignacio.*

Benque Viejo del Carmen, the last town before the Guatemala border, until recently offered little for the traveler. While there's still not much to do or see in Benque itself, beyond a drive around the hilly town and a visit to **Cubola Productions,** Belize's top book publisher and record-ing studio, (✉ 35 Elizabeth St., ☎ 93/2083), two new upscale lodg-ing choices have opened here, using Benque as a base for exploring Cayo and Guatemala's Petén.

Dining and Lodging

$$$ ✗⊡ **Mopan River Resort.** Belize's first true all-inclusive resort opened in November 1999 as an answer to visitors' wishes, that meals, tours, drinks, and taxes be included in a reasonable lodging package. Because these services quickly add up, especially at remote jungle lodges where you're locked in to a single provider, Mopan River Resort is a terrific value. Affable globe-trotting owners Jay and Pamella Picon include everything for one package price: transfers from Belize City, room, meals, daily tours (including ordinarily pricey trips to Tikal, Caracol, and Barton Creek cave), local beer and drinks, and even tips and taxes. Seven-day packages are the best deal, although three- and four-day packages also are available. The location is a bit unexpected, across the Mopan River from the back streets of old Benque, but once you've taken the short ferry trip to the resort's manicured 10-acre coco palm–studded grounds, you're in your own private bit of paradise. The outsides of the cabanas look traditional, with thatch roofs and simple porches, but inside they have cable TV, 24-hour electricity, spacious vanity areas, and minibar stocked with complimentary soft drinks and beer. Four of the cabanas are larger suites with full kitchens. Breakfasts are to order, and dinners usually have a theme such as Thai night, with recipes Pam picked up from cooking courses taken at the Oriental Hotel in Bangkok. Over drinks or a barbecue, Jay will regale you with tales of his days as a pilot. *Riverside North, Benque Viejo del Carmen,* ☎ *93/2047,* FAX *93/3272. 7 cabanas, 3 suites with kitchens. All-inclusive. D, MC, V. Closed July–October.* ✿

$$$ ✗⊡ **Royal Mayan Resort and Spa.** If you can get up the stupendously steep hill and get past the closet-size guest rooms of this new resort and spa, which opened in early 2000, you might enjoy this interesting alternative to Cayo jungle lodges. The view—from the top of that darn hill—into Guatemala is nothing short of breathtaking. The hotel, owned by the same people who own Blackbird Caye Resort, has a gorgeous pool, two outdoor hot tubs (one overlooking Xunantunich), and delivers a range of spa services, including massage. Guest rooms are nicely furnished, with custom-made cabinets and designer bedspreads and sheets, which give the rooms an upscale atmosphere. Day trips on mountain bikes are also available for a fee. ⊠ *Between Succotz and Benque Viejo, Benque Viejo del Carmen,* ☎ *888/271–3483 in the U.S.,* FAX *305/969–7946 in the U.S. Restaurant, bar, air-conditioning, pool, spa, exercise room center, travel services. www.royalmayan.com.*

Mountain Pine Ridge

★ ㉕ *24 km (15 mi) southeast of San Ignacio.*

Along with the Cockscomb Basin Wildlife Sanctuary and the Maya ruins at Lamanai, this mountainous, 780-square-km (300-square-mi) nature reserve, a rugged dome of granite and limestone containing some of the most ancient rocks in Central America, is a highlight of any journey to Belize, and an adventure to reach.

Yellow pines mark the transition from lush tropical forest to pine savanna, and the road follows forest tracks that circle the western slopes of the mountains. Baldy Beacon, at just over 3,000 ft, lies to the east. After the heat and humidity of lowland Belize, the cooler air, the smell of pine resin, and the shady pine woods are both enormously refreshing and totally unexpected. It could be Georgia. It could be the country above Saint-Tropez. It isn't at all what you had imagined.

The flora changes dramatically. You'll see lilac-color mimosa, St. John's wort, and occasionally a garish red flower known as hotlips. There's also a huge variety of ferns, ranging from the tiny maidenhair fern to giants the size of small coconut trees, and a fair selection of Belize's 154 species of orchids. Look out, too, for a wild tree called craboo, whose berries are used to make a brandylike liqueur believed to have aphrodisiacal properties. Birds love this fruit, too, so any craboo is a good place to look for orioles and woodpeckers.

The roads—and there are about 2,400 km (nearly 1,500 mi) of them, most unexplored—were built by the British army, who, with U.S. and Belize forces, still use this area for training in jungle warfare. Some of them have names, but most are simply algebraic, like A10. The best way to see this area, of course, is not to bounce around in an Isuzu Trooper but to get on mountain bike or walk.

Hidden Valley Falls, also known as the Thousand Foot Falls (though they're in fact nearly 1,600 ft high) are the highest in Central America. A thin plume of spray plummets over the edge of a rock face into a seemingly bottomless gorge below. All this isn't as appealing as it sounds, since the viewing area is at somewhat of a distance from the falls, and to climb closer requires a major commitment. Be warned: you may be disappointed in the falls. A shelter, some benches, and a public rest room provide comforts.

The nearby **Río On** has flat, granite boulders on which to sunbathe and a series of crystal-clear pools and waterfalls in which to dunk yourself. The village of **Augustine** is home to the headquarters of the forest reserve. It's the only place in the area where you're allowed to camp.

Just outside the reserve proper, but still part of the Mountain Pine Ridge area, are the **Río Frío Caves.** They're only a few miles down a steep track, but these caves are light years away ecologically. In the course of a few hundred yards, you drop from pine savanna to tropical forest. Nothing else in Belize illustrates the country's extraordinary geological variety so clearly as this startling transition. A river runs right through the center and has carved the rock into fantastic shapes over the centuries. Swallows fill the place and at night, ocelot and margay pad silently across the cold, sand floor in search of slumbering prey. From the cool, dark interior, the light-filled world of mosses, birds, and plants outside seems more intense and beautiful than ever. Bisecting the circle of light and rising vertically through the mouth of the cave, like a spar propping up the whole mountain, is a giant hardwood tree, *Pterocarpus officialis,* its massive paddle-shape roots anchored in the sandy soil of the riverbank and its green crown straining toward the blue sky.

Green Hills Butterfly Farm. This is the largest of Belize's six butterfly farms and is across from Mountain Equestrian Trails. A staff of six raises 30,000 pupae a year, flying about 30 butterfly species in a 2,600 square-ft screened flight area. Jan Meerman and Tineke Boomsma are the Dutch partners who operate the farm. Meerman is writing a book on the butterflies and moths of Belize. Tours are conducted daily. ✉ *Mile 8, Pine Ridge Rd.,* ☎ *91/2017.* 🎫 *$4.* ☉ *Tues.–Sat. 8–5.*

Caracol

★ ㉗ *65 km (40 mi) south of San Ignacio, a 3-hr journey by road.*

Caracol ("the snail" in Spanish) is the most spectacular Maya site in Belize and one of the most impressive in Central America. In its heyday, it was home to as many as 200,000 people, almost the population of modern-day Belize. It was a Maya Manhattan, a metropolis with five plazas and 32 large structures covering nearly a square mile. The latest evidence suggests that Caracol gained a crushing victory over the great city of Tikal in the mid-6th century, an idea Guatemala has not quite gotten used to. For centuries, until a group of *chicleros* (collectors of gum base) stumbled on it in 1936, Caracol was buried under the jungle of the remote Vaca Plateau, yet the great pyramid of Canaa is now officially the tallest structure in Belize. Once Caracol has been fully excavated, it may dwarf even Tikal, which lies only a few dozen miles across the Guatemalan border. The road to Caracol is decent—if you want to drive on your own, however, be sure to inquire at your hotel about road conditions first—a visitors center has opened at the site, and many Cayo resorts and tour operators run tours here (around $70 to $80 per person for a full-day tour). *The Archaeological Commission; from the Mountain Pine Ridge reserve entrance (must register), go 14 mi (23 km) to Douglas De Silva Village; turn left (look for sign to Caracol) and go 16 km (10 mi) to the Macal River bridge, where the Chiquibul Forest begins; continue approx. 25 mi (42 km) to Caracol,* ☎ *82/2106.* ✍ *$5.* ☉ *Daily 8–4.*

The Cayo A to Z

Arriving and Departing

BY BUS

Novelo's (✉ W. Collet Canal, Belize City, ☎ 27/7372; 93/2954 in Cayo) has frequent service to Belmopan and San Ignacio from Belize City. The journey takes three hours and costs only $2.50–$3.

BY CAR

Simply follow the Western Highway from Belize City.

Safe Tours Belize (✉ Santa Elena, just east of San Ignacio on the Western Highway, next to the Public Works building, ☎ 02/4262 ✍) is a local Cayo car-rental agency.

BY VAN

Discovery Expeditions (✉ Fiesta Inn; 126 Freetown Rd., Belize City, ☎ 23/0748, FAX 23/0750) picks up at both the International and Belize City municipal airports.

Cayo resorts also provide transportation to and from the airports, whether or not you're staying with them, for about $25 one way. Be sure to call ahead for schedules and reservations: **duPlooy's** (☎ 92/3101, ✍); **Cahal Pech Village** (☎ 92/3740); **Venus** (☎ 92/3203, ✍).

Getting Around

There is limited bus service between the main centers in the Cayo, but since this is wild country, the best way to get around is by four-wheel-drive vehicle, which most of the resorts have. Because of the numerous rivers, touring by canoe is another good mode of transport, as are horses.

Contacts and Resources

EMERGENCIES

Police (☎ 2022).

San Ignacio Hospital (☎ 92/2066).

La Loma Luz Hospital (Santa Elena, ☎ 92/2087).

The Pharmacy (24 West. St., San Ignacio, ☎ 92/2510).

GUIDED TOURS

The best way to get in contact with local tour operators in the Cayo is to check in at **Eva's** (✉ 22 Burns Ave., San Ignacio, ☎ 092/2267), which also sort of doubles as a visitor's center. Most jungle lodges offer tour-inclusive packages and a full range of day trips. Sharon Burns, of

Jute Expeditions (✉ San Ignacio, ☎ 092/2076), conducts excellent guided tours of the region and is retained by many of the lodges.

PLACENCIA AND ENVIRONS

As always in Belize, the transition from one landscape to another is swift and startling. When you approach Placencia by car, the lush, mountainous terrain of the north gives way to a flat plain bristling with orange trees. The Stann Creek Valley is Belize's San Fernando Valley, the place where most of its fruit—mainly bananas, oranges, and grapefruit—is grown. Equally startling is the cultural segue: whereas San Ignacio is strongly Spanish in feeling, this area is strongly Afro-Caribbean. Bananas were the original bumper crop here, but a blight all but eliminated them in 1906. Today, the citrus plantations, which account for 10% of the nation's production, are touted as one of the country's great success stories, even if the labor force is largely migrant workers from Guatemala.

Tourist dollars, the staple of contemporary Belize, have largely passed Dangriga by, but they are rapidly transforming Placencia, the region's most picturesque spot. Seven years ago, there were only three small resorts north of this town. Now there are about 20, stretching up to the village of Seine Bight and beyond. Construction of a new airstrip has made the area more accessible, though roads still consist of red dirt and potholes. Real-estate sales are a driving force here. Indeed, a section of the road down the peninsula was moved west in 1999 so that more land would be on the valuable sea side rather than the lagoon side. Much of the land north of Placencia has been divided up into lots awaiting development; if things continue at this pace, the area will one day rival Ambergris Caye's San Pedro as Belize's top destination.

Numbers in the margin correspond to points of interest on the Cayo and the Deep South map.

Blue Hole

❷❽ *20 km (12½ mi) south of Belmopan.*

Less than half an hour south of Belmopan is this natural turquoise pool surrounded by mosses and lush vegetation, excellent for a cool dip. The Blue Hole is actually part of an underground river system. On the other side of the hill is St. Herman's Cave, once inhabited by the Maya. A path leads up from the highway, right near the Blue Hole, but it's quite steep and difficult to climb unless the ground is dry. To explore the cave, it's best to wear sturdy shoes and bring a flashlight. Some years ago, there were some unfortunate incidents at the site, with tourists robbed and, in one case, raped; but a full-time attendant was subsequently appointed to patrol the area, and the problem has effectively been resolved. ✉ *Hummingbird Hwy.* 🎟 *$4.*

En Route The Stann Creek Valley approaching Dangriga is a study in social contrast. From the road you can see both the simple shacks of migrant Guatemalan workers and the resplendent, three-story villa of one of the main plantation owners, Eugene Zabanay. The villa is on the right just before you arrive in Dangriga.

Dangriga

❷❾ *160 km (99 mi) southeast of Belmopan (2½ hrs of driving, some on bad roads).*

With a population of 10,000, Dangriga is the largest town in the south and the home of the Garifuna (or Black Caribs, as they are also known), perhaps the most exotic and unusual of the many ethnic groups that have found peace and asylum in this tiny country. The Garifunas' story is a bizarre and moving one, an odyssey of exile and dispossession in the wake of the confusion wrought on the New World by the Old. They are descended from a group of Nigerian slaves who were shipwrecked on the island of St. Vincent in 1635 en route to slavery in America. At first, the Caribs, St. Vincent's indigenous population, fiercely resisted the Garifunas' presence, but understanding conquered fear and racial antipathy, and a new African–Native American group was added to the family of man.

In the eyes of the British colonial authorities, the new race was an illegitimate and troublesome presence in one of the Crown's dominions. Worse still, the Garifuna sided with, and were succored by, the French. After nearly two centuries of guerrilla warfare, the British decided that the best way to solve the problem was to deport them en masse. After a circuitous and tragic journey across the Caribbean, during which thousands perished of disease and hunger, the exiles arrived in Belize.

That the Garifuna have managed to preserve their cultural identity is one more example of Belize's extraordinary ability to maintain, rather than suppress, diversity. They have their own religion, a potent mixture of ancestor worship and Catholicism; their own language, which, like Carib, has separate male and female dialects; their own music, African-style drumming with a modern disco variant known as punta rock, which you can hear everywhere in Belize; and their own clannish social structure—they seldom marry outside their own community. In Marcella Lewis, universally known as Auntie Madé, they also had their own poet laureate.

For the traveler, there's not much to see in Dangriga. Imagine the worst parts of Belize City towed down the coast, and you've got it. But for one day each year, November 19, the town is all color and exuberance—this is Garifuna Settlement Day, when these proud people celebrate their arrival in Belize and remember their roots. Dangriga then cuts loose with a week of Carnival-style celebrations.

Dining and Lodging

$$ ☒ **Mama Noots Backabush Resort.** Being Green (or environmentally concerned) doesn't mean you can't also be comfy. Instead of a diesel motor behind your cabana, a combination solar, wind, and hydro system generates electricity. Furthermore, most of the produce served at the open-air cabana restaurant is organic and grown on the grounds. Rooms have firm queen-size beds, ceiling fans, screened windows, mosquito nets, and private baths with hot-water showers. Because the resort is *backabush* (back in the bush), owners Kevin and Nanette Denny advise guests to bring lightweight "jungle clothing," along with a poncho, plenty of insect repellent, and an adventuresome spirit. The only things nearby are the Mayflower reserve and archeological site, where a long awaited excavation and restoration has begun, and miles of jungle trails and waterfalls. Wildlife spotting and birding here are excellent. *From the Stann Creek District Hwy. (Hummingbird Hwy.) junction, take the Southern Hwy. 10 km (6 mi) south; turn right onto an unpaved road (watch for Mayflower and Mamanoots signs) and go 6⅔ km (4 mi) to lodge,* ☒ *Mayflower Archeological Site, Box 165, Dangriga,* ☎ *51/2050. 6 rooms with bath, 2 rooms with 6 beds and shared bath. AE.* ✎

$$ ✕⊞ **Pelican Beach Resort.** This waterfront hotel outside Dangriga might remind you of a tropical version of a Maine boardinghouse, but it's the best one around, and the restaurant serves plenty of fresh seafood. You have easy access to both snorkeling and the Cockscomb Basin Wildlife Sanctuary. Owners Therese (she's from a prominent colonial family and has been a leader in the Belize Audubon Society) and Tony Rath (he's a widely published nature photographer and developer of the award-winning Belize by Naturalight Web sites) and their staff are knowledgeable and helpful. Eight of the rooms have porches and sea views, all have ceiling fans, and the bathrooms have real baths rather than just shower stalls—a rarity in Belize. Rooms are in two reef cabins on stilts and a two-story colonial-style building with a veranda. The resort has an annex on Southwater Caye, 20 minutes from Dangriga by boat (☞ *Cayes and Atolls, above*). ✉ *Northeast Dangriga, on the water, by the airstrip (Box 14, Dangriga),* ☎ *52/2044,* ℻ *52/ 2570. 20 rooms. Restaurant, bar, travel services. AE, MC, V.* ✆

Cockscomb Basin Wildlife Sanctuary

★ ③⓪ *48 km (30 mi) southwest of Dangriga; take the Southern Hwy. to Maya Centre, where there's a dirt road leading into the reserve.*

The mighty jaguar, once the undisputed king of the Central and South American jungles, is now extinct or endangered. But it has a haven in the Cockscomb Basic Wildlife Sanctuary, which covers 102,000 acres of lush rain forest in the Cockscomb Range of the Maya Mountains. Because of the jaguar reserve, as this area is commonly called, as well as other protected areas in the country, Belize has the highest concentration of jaguars in the world.

Jaguars are shy, nocturnal animals that prefer to keep their distance from humans, so the possibility of sighting a jaguar in the wild is almost nil. Still, a visit here is rewarding in other ways. The reserve boasts Belize's best-maintained system of jungle and mountain trails, most of which have at least one outstanding swimming hole. The sanctuary also offers spectacular views of Victoria Peak and the Cockscomb Range, and the chance to see many other endangered flora and fauna, including about 300 species of birds. If you plan to hike extensively, pick up a trail map at the visitor center. Although a visit of any kind requires that you have some serious bug spray with you—Cockscomb is alive with no-see-ums (tiny biting flies) and mosquitoes, and wear a long-sleeved shirt and long pants. The best times to hike anywhere in Belize are early morning, late afternoon, and early evening, when temperatures are lower and more animals are out.

You have to register in a hut by the entrance before proceeding several miles to the reception center. The road climbs up through dense vegetation—splendid cahoune palms, purple mimosas, orchids, and big-leaf plantains—and as you go higher, the marvelous sound of tropical birdsong, often resembling strange wind-up toys, grows stronger and stronger. This is definitely four-wheel-drive terrain. You may have to ford several small rivers as well as negotiate deep, muddy ruts. At the top, you'll find a clearing with hibiscus and bougainvillea bushes, a little office where you can buy maps of the nature trails (notice the marvelous oripendula nests hanging from the rafters), rest rooms, several picnic tables, cabins, and a campground.

In a misguided attempt by an American naturalist to track jaguars' movements in the 1980s, seven jaguars were caught and tagged with radio collars. Special steel cages were built to catch them, since they had smashed several wooden ones to pieces, and a live pig was placed behind a grille and used as bait. A jaguar would enter the cage to catch the pig, trip a door behind it, and find itself captive. What followed was a conflagration of fur and fury of almost unbelievable proportions. The captured jaguars were so powerful that in their desperate attempts to escape, they threw the 300-pound cages around like matchboxes. They sheared off most of their teeth as they tried to bite through the steel. Within a year, all seven had died.

Today there are an estimated 25 to 30 jaguars—8 to 10 mature males, 9 to 10 adult females, and the rest young animals—spread over about 400 square km (154 square mi). This is the world's largest jaguar population and one of Belize's most significant contributions to conservation. In contrast, the jaguar was hunted to extinction in the United States by the late 1940s.

Up to 6 ft long and weighing in just below George Foreman, *Felis onca*— or *El Tigre,* as it's known in Spanish—is nature's great loner, a supremely free creature that shuns even the company of its own kind. The term *jaguar* comes from the Indian word *yaguar* meaning "he who kills with one leap," and that's exactly what a jaguar does, falling on deer, peccaries, or gibnut with a deadly leap and severing the vertebrae in the neck. Except during a brief mating period and the six short months the female spends with her cubs before turning them loose, jaguars live alone, roaming the rain forest in splendid isolation. By day, they sun themselves to sleep; by night, they stalk gibnut, armadillo, and curassow, a kind of wild turkey, with the deadly efficiency of a serial killer. To the ancient Maya, the jaguars were intermediaries between this world and the world of the gods.

Again, you're not likely to see a jaguar, as they have exceptionally good senses of smell and hearing. If you do, you'll be far too close. But walking along these 12 well-marked nature trails is a good way to spend a day. Most are loops of 1 to 2 km (½ to 1½ mi), so you can do several in a day. The most strenuous trail takes you up a steep hill, from the top of which there is a magnificent view of the entire Cockscomb Basin.

Cockscomb Basin has a wonderful array of Belize's wildlife other than the jaguar, including other cats—pumas, margays, and ocelots—plus coatis, kinkajous, deer, peccaries, and, last but not least, tapirs. Also known as the mountain cow, this shy, curious creature appears to be half horse, half hippo, with a bit of cow and elephant thrown in. Nearly 300 species of birds have been identified in the Cockscomb Basin, including the keel-billed toucan, the king vulture, several species of hawks, and the scarlet macaw. And everywhere you walk is the lush, riotous growth of the rain forest—an immense botanical garden with air like that of a sauna. ⊠ *Outside Maya Centre,* ☎ 27/7369. ☞ *$5.* ☼ *Daily 8–5.*

Dining and Lodging

You can camp in the reserve for $5 a night, or for a little more stay in run-down dorms or pleasant new rooms in cabins with solar-generated electricity, but most people stay in or near Dangriga, Hopkins, or Placencia.

$$$$ ✕🖿 **Lillpat Sittee River Lodge.** This lodge, on 50 acres next to the Sittee River, is devoted to a single passion: fishing. And the fishing—on the river, on the flats, or out at Glover's Reef—is superb. Six-night fishing packages, including meals, lodging, boat, and fishing guides who take you where the bonefish, tarpon, permit, and snook are biting, run around $1,900 per person. At these prices, you get a lot more than a fishing shack: native hardwoods and Guatemalan furnishings are used throughout the lodge, and there's satellite TV in a lounge and a beautiful new pool. The curved mahogany table in the dining room, where guests eat family-style after a day's fishing, is a thing of beauty. The co-owner, Dr. Greg Patchett, is the chef. The lodge can arrange bird-watching and snorkeling trips, and diving and dive training are now available through Second Nature Divers (☞ Outdoor Activities, *below*). ⊠ *Sittee River village (Box 136, Dangriga)*, ☎ FAX *51/2019. 4 rooms. Restaurant, bar, pool, fishing. AE, MC, V. EP, MAP, FAP* ☙

$$$ ✕🛏 **Beaches and Dreams.** The Sittee Point/Hopkins area is experiencing a miniboom in lodging, and fortunately for Beaches and Dreams, they've managed to get one of the area's nicest tan-colored stretches of beach. Like many other inn owners here, Sharon and Dave Helgesen, left their jobs elsewhere, in their case at a university in Vancouver, B.C., to build a little beachside dream in Belize. Their tiny seaside inn, completed in late 1998, has two beachside, octagonal duplex cottages, each with 14-ft vaulted ceilings, king beds, and rattan furnishings, plus a small verandah just a few feet from the sea. The restaurant and pub serve good food and cold drinks. Try the seafood and fruit kabobs or the Cajun chicken pizza. Diving trips can be arranged. ⊠ *Sittee Point (Box 193, Dangriga)*, ☎ FAX *53/7078. 4 rooms. Restaurant, bar, travel services. MC, V.* ☙

$$$ ✕🛏 **Jaguar Reef Lodge.** At night, with a row of torches burning on the beach and the palapa-covered dining room glowing in the lamplight, this fine lodge has an East African feel. The setting is quite manicured and right on the coast, just south of the village of Hopkins—and you've got views over the water in one direction, toward the green slopes of the Maya Mountains in the other. Six solid, two-room cottages of whitewashed stone have thatched roofs, and high, pitched ceilings with exposed wooden beams. The rooms are large, airy, and tastefully furnished with Mexican tiles, mahogany furniture, and mini-refrigerators, and they have sea views; the bathrooms have tile baths and mahogany-encased basins. The less essential fixtures and fittings, like the mahogany-and-canvas beach umbrellas and Pawley Island hammocks, are held to the same standard by owner Bruce Foerster, who splits his time between British Columbia and Hopkins. The resort has sea kayaks, and can arrange dive trips, cruises on the nearby Sittee River, or excursions. The food is good, and the mostly Garifuna staff polite and easygoing. The one drawback is the uniformity of the place—it can feel like you're on a cruise ship. Furthermore, sand flies are a ubiquitous problem on this part of the coast, so bring your strongest bug spray. ⊠ *Hopkins Village*, ☎ FAX *21/2041 or 800/289–5756 in the U.S. 12 rooms. Restaurant, bar, air-conditioning, beach, snorkeling. AE, MC, V.* ☙

$ 🛏 **Tipple Tree Beya Inn.** As Hopkins is more like a seaside village in hard times than one flush with the tourist dollars of the Caribbean coast, tiny Tipple Tree Beya provides a comfortable retreat from the culture shock of glamorous resorts along the coast. Two friendly Dutch women run Tipple Tree, which is directly on a good beach, with hammocks for low-key kicking back. Three rooms are unassuming but shiny clean, and a separate private cabin has a kitchenette. Bicycle and kayak rentals are available. ⊠ *Hopkins*, ☎ *51/2006, tipple@btl.net. 1 cabin, 3 rooms, 1 with shared bath. Beach, snorkeling, camping. MC, V www.sites.netscape.net/tippletree/belize*

$ 🛏 **Toucan Sittee.** Neville Collins used to run a store in San Ignacio before he retired to this 20-acre farm. He now grows 10 varieties of mangos and, with his wife Yoli, runs these guest cottages along the river. The four cottages on stilts have either one or two bedrooms with central living and dining rooms, and the bunkhouse sleeps up to five. Neville can arrange all kinds of activities (canoeing, bird-watching, exploratory tours) if you tire of just hanging around in a peaceful place filled with birds and ginger plants. Like all resorts in these parts, this one can get buggy, so bring repellent. ⊠ *Sittee River village,* ☎ *53/7839 or 52/2888. 5 rooms. Fishing, snorkeling. No credit cards.*

Shopping

Near the entrance to the sanctuary is a small gift shop selling woven baskets and fine embroideries of the Maya calendar. **Jaguar Reef Resort** has a fine little gift shop, with pottery and sewn Maya goods as well as Garifuna crafts. The store also carries Marie Sharp's superb hot sauces, New Age music, and drugstore items like sunscreen and the very necessary no-see-um (tiny biting fly) repellents.

Outdoor Activities

The best local diving operation is **Second Nature Divers** (⊠ Sittee River village , ☎ ℻ 53/7038, divers@btl.net, ✆). Jaguar Reef's dive and snorkeling operation is fine, but if not enough people want to dive, the trip may be postponed.

Seine Bight Area

③① *44 km (27 mi) south of Dangriga.*

Like Placencia, its Creole neighbor to the south, Seine Bight is a sleepy coastal fishing village, and Placencia's resorts are increasingly stretching north to this Garifuna hamlet, and beyond it. Though the beach is among the best in Belize, garbage on the beach is a frequent problem. Hotels do rake and clean their beachfronts, and several community cleanups have been held to try to solve this problem. All the resorts and services are off the main road (and the only road) that leads to Placencia.

Dining and Lodging

$　✕ **Mango of Maya Beach.** Owner and chef Chris Duffy is a painter from Connecticut. Her tiny restaurant serves something different every day, all sophisticated by Belizean standards: field greens with Dijon vinaigrette, lobster scampi, tropical fruit fondue. Lunch and dinner are served daily, but if you can, let her know you're coming. ⊠ *Maya Beach, 1 mi north of Seine Bight, on the main road,* ☎ *14/7023. Reservations essential. No credit cards.*

$$$–$$$$　✕🔟 **Inn at Robert's Grove.** Imagine that you've met an attractive, en-
★　ergetic couple named Bob and Risa Frackman, and they invite you to stay at their place on a palm-lined stretch of beach. You can play tennis and swim to your heart's content, either in the Frackmans' beachside pool or in the sea. Bob and Risa's chef, Frank Da Silva, will cook you large breakfasts, pack picnic lunches for boat rides to magical, deserted cayes, and serve dinner in the inn's newly expanded restaurant, with wine from the inn's temperature-controlled wine cellar. Risa, a public relations genius, smooths over any rough spots, and Bob acts as your genial host. This personal attention to your happiness is the essence of this intimate, but growing, resort, which is often full in season. The rooms, in three hacienda-style buildings, each with a rooftop hot tub, have high, pitched ceilings; pretty Guatemalan fabrics and antiques; blue-and-green Mexican-tile bathrooms, and verandas, where you can lie in a hammock and gaze across the turquoise water until it's time for a margarita and the next delicious meal. Two junior suites are worth the extra money, and No. 4, with wraparound deck, is particularly nice. Of course, the Frackmans will arrange whatever activity you fancy. Windsailers, bikes, kayaks, and other sports equipment are complimentary. The hotel has its own PADI dive center with three boats, and a private caye for picnics. ⊠ *1 km (½ mi) south of Seine Bight village,* ☎ *62/3565; 800/565–9757 in the U.S.,* ℻ *62/3567. 18*

rooms, 2 suites. Restaurant, bar, 2 tennis courts, beach, pool, dive shop, snorkeling, fishing. AE, MC, V. ✍

$$$–$$$$ ✕▥ **Luba Hati.** No, there's no relation to Mata Hari: the name means
★ "House of the Moon" in Garifuna. From the widow's walk above the central wing of this U-shape two-story house there's a great view of the lagoon in one direction and the Caribbean in the other. The red-tile roofs and tree-filled courtyard below make it feel a bit like Umbria—no accident, as owners Franco and Mariuccia Gentile are originally from Italy. Franco learned a lot about style in the course of his successful design career in Manhattan; there are no sticks and palapa huts here, but rather a substantial structure of stone and clay. Creative features like staircases supported on giant tree trunks add an unusual touch. Each guest room is individually decorated with African and Guatemalan fabrics and is cool and pleasant, with tiled floors, mahogany fittings, white walls, and a fantastic attention to detail. New air-conditioned beachfront cottages tend to be booked first. You'll eat well here, too: Franco is an excellent chef, and his selection of classic Italian dishes and wines has brought a touch of *la dolce vita* to Placencia. Tours and activities are easily arranged. ✉ *1 km (½ mi) south of Seine Bight village,* ☎ *62/ 3402,* ꜰꜲꜲ *62/3403. 3 cottages, 8 rooms. Restaurant, bar, beach, saltwater pool, snorkeling, fishing. AE, MC, V.* ✍

$$$ ✕▥ **Green Parrot.** This cluster of Mennonite-built cottages on a pretty beach was opened in 1995 by a couple from Saskatoon, Canada, who (have you heard this story before?) cashed out in 1999 and sold to David and Asma Allardice. The new owners seem to be turning things around here, bringing the restaurant back to life and upgrading the little houses. The six original two-level cottages have a ground floor foldaway bed, dining area, and a stocked kitchenette. The sleeping quarters are upstairs, in a loftlike space with a pitched wooden roof and ceiling fans; each has an attractive double bed with a locally crafted bamboo frame and an imported hotel-quality mattress. One nifty feature: an octagonal-shape moving panel in the wall, operated by pulleys, can be opened for a bedside view of the ocean. Two new thatch cabanas with queen beds have outdoor showers (no kitchen facilities). The beachfront restaurant-cum-bar is decorated with high-backed chairs of varnished cane, made by local craftspeople. It's best if you have a car, as it's an expensive $20 cab ride from Placencia; however, in-season at least, a shuttle van ($2.50 one-way, $4 round-trip) runs up and down the peninsula hourly. Meal plans are available. ✉ *North end of Maya Beach, about 6⅔ km (4 mi) north of Seine Bight village, Maya Beach,* ☎ ꜰꜲꜲ *62/2488. 6 cabins and 2 cabanas. Restaurant, bar, beach. AE, MC, V.* ✍

$$$ ✕▥ **Nautical Inn.** The Garifuna fishing town of Seine Bight is a long way from their old home in Phoenix, Arizona, and that's how owners Ben and Janie Ruoti like it. The lodgings are in two-tier octagonal cottages imported from North Carolina, and the management prides itself on offering American-style fixtures, such as hotel-supplied mattresses from Miami and glass-walled showers. As Ben says, "It's not for campers." The Oar House restaurant serves good Belizean home cooking and beach barbecues. The inn has some canoes as well as a dive boat to get you to the reef. If you just want to hang out, a pretty beach awaits your towel, and Janie will show you her baby iguanas, which she raises and releases. On Wednesday evening, the hotel hosts Garifuna drummers and coconut bowling. There's nothing like a milk-filled ball to throw off your game. ☎ *62/3595 or 800/688–0377 in the U.S.,* ꜰꜲꜲ *62/3594. 12 rooms. Restaurant, bar, air-conditioning, pool, beach, dive shop. AE, MC, V. FAP.* ✍

$$ ☎ **Barnacle Bill's.** If you're the independent type and want a self-cater-
ing cottage on the beach, this Maya Beach property has two raised wood
cottages in the palms about 60 ft from the sea. Each cottage has a bed-
room with queen bed, sleeper sofa in the living area, private bath, deck,
and a fully equipped kitchen. ✉ *No. 23 Maya Beach Way,* ☎ *63/7010.
2 cottages with kitchens. No credit cards.* ✎

$ ☎ **Maya Playa.** This is a small, simple budget spot with three 2-story
palapa cabanas and no electricity. Downstairs are the living room and
attractive rustic bathrooms, full of tropical plants; upstairs, the bed-
rooms. You're welcome to cook meals on the shared stove, and a
fresh-vegetable truck drops by specifically for your benefit. ✉ *Maya
Beach,* ☎ *63/7020. 3 rooms. Beach. No credit cards.* ✎

Scuba Diving

Most of the resorts between Placencia and Seine Bight have their own
dive shops, but the best are at **Nautical Inn** (☎ 62/2395) and **Inn at
Robert's Grove** (☎ 62/3565).

Shopping

Painter Lola Delgado moved to Seine Bight from Belize City in the late
1980s. Her workshop, **Lola's Art,** displays her bright, cheerful, well-
executed acrylic paintings of local scenes ($75 to $500), as well as in-
expensive handicrafts. She also sells hand-painted cards and some of
her husband's wood carvings. Espresso and pastries are served. Open
9 AM–10 PM, the workshop is up a flight of steps in a tiny wooden house
off the main street, behind the football field.

Placencia

③② *8 km (5 mi) south of Seine Bight, 52 km (32 mi) south of Dangriga.*

Set in a sheltered half-moon bay with crystal-clear green water and al-
most 5 km (3 mi) of palm-dotted white sand, this incredibly balmy fish-
ing village is straight out of a Robert Louis Stevenson novel. Originally
founded by pirates, it is now peopled with an extraordinary mélange
of peoples. To the west, the Cockscomb Range ruffles the tropical sky
with its jagged peaks; to the east, a line of uninhabited cayes grazes
the Caribbean horizon. From here you can dive, hike into the jungle,
explore the Maya ruins at Lubantuun, or indulge in some of the best
sportfishing in the country; but once you arrive, you'll probably just
want to lie in a hammock under a palm tree, read, sleep, and perhaps
get up long enough to swim.

Placencia is so small that it doesn't even have a main street—it has a
concrete path, just big enough for two. Setting off purposefully from
the south end of town, the path meanders through everyone's back-
yard, passes wooden cottages on stilts overrun with bougainvillea and
festooned with laundry, then peters out abruptly in a little clearing of
coconut palms and white morning glory, as though it had forgotten
where it was headed in the first place. That's the sort of place Placen-
cia is: stroll the sidewalk, and you've seen the town.

Along the path are most of the village's guest houses, and little palapa-
covered cafés on the beach side, serving mainly burgers, rice-and-
beans, and a bit of seafood. But with the creation of more and more
fine, small resorts up the peninsula, Placencia is beginning to compete
with Ambergris Caye in the dining category.

Fences don't exist here, so everybody's backyard and, unfortunately,
garbage is open to public view. In recent years, with more travelers pass-
ing through, this has become something of a problem. The town des-
perately needs a proper garbage-disposal system and a bit of a cleanup.

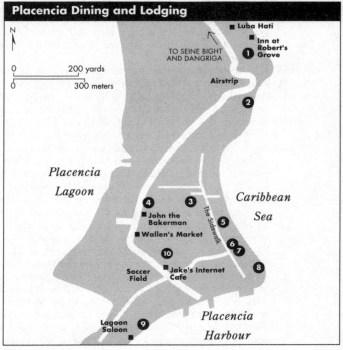

But if you don't mind the dust around the edges, you'll be utterly enchanted by this rustic village, where the palm trees rustle, the waves lap the shore, and absolutely no one is in a hurry.

Yet, even in Placencia, big changes are taking place. A gambling casino in a four-story building is planned for the middle of the village. Lattes and Web cruising have come to town, in the form of an Internet café and coffee shop. And this is a biggie: in December 1999, Wallen's, the peninsula's first grocery, opened a new store complete with air-conditioning and electronic check-out.

NEED A
BREAK?

The Lagoon Saloon, on the water's edge behind the village, is a funky watering hole popular with expats. Under their chili-pepper lights, Americans Bonny and Mike will ply you with Lagoon Monsters (triple-decker rum punches) and some of the best-worst jokes you'll ever hear. They also provide satellite TV, a dart board, and backgammon; it's closed Monday and Tuesday. If your funds start to run dry, the Hokey-Pokey boat (yes, that's its name) will take you across the lagoon to Big Creek for $5.

Dining and Lodging

$ ✕ **Daisy's.** Folks come to Daisy's for the Belize-made Bico brand ice cream, especially the rum raisin flavor. But this diner-style restaurant also serves hearty breakfast burritos, fish sandwiches, conch fritters, and chow mein. It's open from 7:30 AM to 10:30 PM. Just follow the sign on the north end of the sidewalk; look for the building with the tree growing out of its roof. ☏ *No phone. No credit cards.*

$ ✕ **Omar's.** This is the best cheap food in Placencia village. Burritos for breakfast, sandwiches for lunch, and a cold drink anytime. Don't believe the signs—the orange juice *isn't* fresh-squeezed—it's Sunny Delight. *On the sidewalk between the library and Sonny's Resort,* ☎ *no phone. No credit cards.*

$$$–$$$$ ✕▦ **Rum Point Inn.** When they first came to Placencia, George and Coral
★ Bevier had to cut their way through the undergrowth to find the old colonial-style house they'd bought. Today, this beachfront inn is one of Belize's finest resorts. The domelike villas are all about space, light, and air, as though only a thin, tentlike membrane separated you from sea, sky, and palm trees. Each is simply but luxuriously furnished with Guatemalan fabrics and mahogany, and each has a unique arrangement of windows and skylights—some are portholes, others are geometric patterns cut in the walls. Everyone dines together at long, candlelit tables. As the waves lap and the palm trees rustle, the Beviers preside over lively discussions on everything from that day's dive to Maya astronomy to the inside scoop on Belizean politics. The food is cooked by two charming Belizean girls who learned to make such tidbits as lobster and eggplant on English muffins (topped with a layer of grilled Parmesan) from back issues of *Gourmet* magazine. The library has one of Belize's best collections of books on the Maya, piles of novels and magazines, and, in case cultural withdrawal threatens, a raft of CDs and videos. The *Auriga,* the inn's handy, jet-powered dive boat, is extremely seaworthy and, because of its shallow draft, can anchor right by the most remote caye. A cluster of whitewashed two-story buildings have four spacious, high-ceilinged rooms with huge bathrooms equipped with double sinks and Japanese-style bathtubs. Tours and activities abound, including a splendid trip up the Monkey River; but if you just want to kick back, there are few nicer places in Belize to do it. *2.4 km (1½ mi) north of Placencia,* ☎ *62/3239 or 800/747–1381 in the U.S.,* ℻ *62/3240. 22 rooms. Restaurant, bar, beach, pool, dive shop, snorkeling, travel services. AE, DC, MC, V. FAP, MAP.* 🍃

$$–$$$ ✕▦ **Kitty's Place.** Kitty's has stood the test of time while gradually expanding its amenities and activities. Situated on the same beautiful stretch of soft sand as its more upscale neighbor, Rum Point Inn, it offers a mixed bag of accommodations, from single rooms to studios. Some of the nicest rooms are in a spacious, colonial-style house. The upstairs restaurant, with its football pennants and Bob Marley posters, is lively and serves good local fare. Three newer cottages face the sea, each with a king-size bed plus two singles, a dining area, a coffeemaker, and a bathroom with shower and tub. The gift shop sells everything from suntan lotion to Guatemalan crafts, and if you need to check your e-mail, Kitty's functions as one of two local Internet cafés (the other one, the Purple Space Monkey, is in Placencia village.) Sea kayaking, diving, and sportfishing are popular activities, and for $50 per person Kitty will pack you off to a remote caye for the night—you bring the camping gear, Kitty provides the sea kayak and the food. Kitty's also manages six private houses for weekly rental ($300 to $1,000 a week) and offers day and multiday sailings on a 34-ft catamaran, *Ocean Gypsy.* ✉ *Box 528, Belize City,* ☎ *62/3227,* ℻ *62/3226. 3 cabanas, 8 rooms. Restaurant, bar, beach, dive shop, boating, gift shop, travel services. AE, MC, V.* 🍃

$$ ✕▦ **Westwind.** If you want to be hosted by a local Belizean, you can't do better than George Westby, the charming, talkative owner of this gray, two-story guest house on the beach. Westy's family has lived in Placencia for more than 100 years, though he himself only recently re-

turned with his American wife after a 25-year sojourn in Michigan and Texas. With its U.S. fixtures and fittings (proper screened windows and plate-glass sliding doors), the Westwind is now the most substantial structure in the village. The rooms are plain but spotlessly clean, and most have a double bed, ceiling fan, refrigerator, and bathroom with shower. The best rooms are in front, overlooking the sea, but each room has its own porch with beach and sea views. If that's not enough to loosen you up, drop down to the little thatched-roof bank of hammocks on the beach. The restaurant serves good local food, particularly fish— no surprise, as George's cousin is the best fly-fisherman in town (☞ Outdoor Activities and Sports, *below*). Fishing, diving, snorkeling, and other excursions are easily arranged. ☎ 62/3255, FAX 60/3255. 8 *rooms. Restaurant, beach, car rental, travel services. MC, V.* ✍

$–$$ ✕▦ **Sonny's.** This locally run resort is a good value. The larger cabanas, right on the beach, have spacious verandas that look onto the water. The smaller ones, set back from the water, are rather cramped, but all are well-equipped and clean. The restaurant, which has hardwood furniture and cheery tablecloths, serves good local dishes. ☎ 62/3103. *14 rooms. Restaurant, bar, beach. AE, MC, V.* ✍

$ ✕▦ **Barracuda and Jaguar Inn.** This tiny resort is tucked behind the hardware store. One of the four clustered buildings is Canadian owner Wende Bryan's house; another is her jolly, feet-in-the-sand restaurant and bar, the **Pickled Parrot**. Fresh seafood is the main draw, but Bryan also offers a full pizza menu on Friday and a happy hour on Tuesday. The two very reasonably priced cabanas have hardwood fittings, private baths, refrigerators, coffeemakers, and screened porches with hammocks. A two-bedroom apartment was added in 1999. Don't worry, you *will* get some sleep: Wende shuts down the bar at 10 PM and doesn't open the restaurant until noon. ☎ 62/3330. *1 apartment, 2 rooms. Restaurant, bar, beach, snorkeling, fishing. AE, MC, V.* ✍

$$ ▦ **Harry's Cozy Cabanas.** Harry Eiler's three varnished-wood cabanas with screened porches are as nice as Harry is, though they don't have quite as much character. Each has a kitchenette with a fridge. The location is quieter than the main part of the village. *On Placencia harbor, just south of Tentacles,* ☎ 62/3155, harbaks@yahoo.com. *Kitchenettes. No credit cards.*

$–$$ ▦ **Tradewinds.** If you're yearning for a cottage directly on the beach,
★ without neighbors on every side, at a price that's a fourth of what you'd pay for a cabana north of the village, this little cottage colony is for you. Five cabins, painted in Caribbean pastels, are small but pleasant, with private baths and refrigerators. They enjoy about the best location in the village, off to themselves, on the beach at the south point of the peninsula. The hotel also has five rooms in a house. The owner is the village's former postmistress, Janice Leslie. *On the Caribbean side, South Point, Placencia,* ☎ 62/3122. *5 cabins, 5 rooms. Refrigerators, beach. MC, V.*

$ ▦ **Deb & Dave's Last Resort.** Deb Jordan runs this pleasant budget spot in the village, while husband Dave is usually out leading adventure tours. The expat couple also operate Toadal Adventure Tours. As the owners will tell you themselves, this is a budget hotel and there are no amenities, but you get a clean room, access to hot-water baths, and the use of a screened porch with hammocks. It's also near the middle of the village and an easy walk to everything, including the beach. *In the middle of the village, near the road just north of Placencia Market,* ☎ 62/3334. *4 rooms with shared baths. AE, MC, V. Closed September.* ✍

Outdoor Activities and Sports

FISHING

The fly-fishing on the flats off the cayes east of Placencia is some of Belize's best. You'll encounter plentiful tarpon—they flurry 10 deep in the water at times—as well as permit fish, bonefish, and snook. Most of the better hotels can arrange guides; otherwise, if you want local guides, call **Kevin Modera** (☎ 62/3243). Kevin Modera and his partner Mary Toy, a former attorney in the States, have the most informative fishing Web site on Placencia, www.kevinmodera.com. Or ask around for **David Westby** (he knows where the fish are) or call **Kurt Godfrey** (☎ 62/3277), **Earl Godfrey** (☎ 62/3132), or **Egbert Cabral** (☎ 62/3433).

SCUBA DIVING

By the time you get this far south, the reef is as much as 33 km (20 mi) offshore, necessitating boat rides of 45 minutes to an hour to reach dive sites. Because this part of the reef has fewer cuts and channels, it's also more difficult to get out to the seaward side, the best one for diving. As a result, most diving in this region is done from the offshore cayes, which have minireefs around them, usually with gently sloping drop-offs of about 80–100 ft. If you want spectacular wall dives, this isn't the place; you're better off staying in the north or going to the atolls. But there are other boons here—off Moho Caye, southeast of Placencia, are brilliant red and yellow corals and sponges that rarely appear elsewhere in Belize.

Diving costs a little more in Placencia than elsewhere. All-day trips, including two-tank dives and lunch, run $65 with a few people in the boat, including all gear. Snorkeling is about $40 per day.

Most of the larger resorts, like **Nautical Inn** (☎ 62/3595), **Inn at Robert's Grove** ☎ 62/3565) and **Rum Point Inn** (☎ 62/3239), have good dive shops. For been-there-done-that divers, Rum Point also has a new program whereby visitors can take part in R.E.E.F., a marine wildlife survey run out of Key Largo. Divers are asked to fill out survey forms listing the number of bar-fin blennys or mimic triplefin they spot, and the information is forwarded to Florida for cataloging. There are also dive shops in town: Brian Young runs the **Seahorse Dive Shop** (☎ 62/3166 or 62/3356). For snorkeling trips and gear there's **Ocean Motion,** near the grocery store (☎ 62/3363).

Placencia and the South A to Z

Arriving and Departing

BY AIRPLANE

Both **Tropic Air** (☎ 24/5671 or 800/422–3435 in the U.S., ✈) and **Maya Island Air** (☎ 23/1140, ✈) have regular service to and from Belize City (½ hr, $54 from municipal, $64 from international). You can purchase tickets at some of the Placencia resorts, although you might have to ask around to determine which one is acting as ticket agent. The airstrip is about 3 km (2 mi) north of the center of town, so you'll probably want a taxi ($5) if your hotel doesn't provide a shuttle.

BY BUS

For routes south to Belmopan, Dangriga, and Punta Gorda, try **Z-Line Bus Service** (✉ Venus Bus Terminal, Magazine Rd., Belize City, ☎ 27/3937). The Z-Line bus station in Dangriga is seven blocks south of town on the main road, near the Texaco and Shell stations. The main bus stop in Placencia is near the Shell station.

BY CAR

Head southeast from Belmopan on the Hummingbird Highway. Once a pot-holed nightmare, the Hummingbird is now completely paved and easily the best road in Belize, if not in all of Central America. It's also the most scenic road in Belize. On your right rise the jungle-covered Maya Mountains, largely free of signs of human existence except for the occasional clearing of corn and beans.

If you want to go directly from Belize City to Placencia, skipping the Blue Hole, Five Blues National Park, and St. Herman's Cave, take the turnoff at Mile 30 on the Western Highway for Dangriga and the south. The 60-km (36-mi) Manatee Road is unpaved, dusty in dry weather, and sometimes flooded after rains, but unless a bridge is washed out it saves about an hour on the drive south. About 25 mi of the Southern Highway, from Punta Gorda to Big Falls village, is paved.

Along the Placencia peninsula, a shuttle van service operates sporadically, and usually not off-season, between Maya Beach and Placencia ($2.50 one way, $4 round trip). Taxis are available in Dangriga: ask your hotel or call **Neal's Taxi** (1 St. Vincent St., just south of bridge, ☎ 52/3309). Fare from downtown Dangriga to the airstrip at the north end of town is about $3. In Placencia taxis are available (ask your hotel to call one) but are expensive, given the relatively short distances involved: $15 to $20 one way from Placencia to Maya Beach, $5 ($2.50 additional for each person over two in the taxi) from Placencia to the airstrip.

Contacts and Resources
Bank

Atlantic Bank (at the end of the main road in Placencia, across from the Shell station, ☎ 62/3386) is open Mon.–Fri. 8–noon.

CAR RENTAL

Placencia Auto Rental (☎ 63/7001, Debbie Coston) will pick you up at the airstrip. Budget and other Belize City renters will deliver a car to Placencia for a fee of around $65.

EMERGENCIES

Although Placencia now has a nurse, an acupuncturist, a part-time chiropractor, and a natural healer, for serious medical attention you should go to Dangriga or Independence.

Dangriga Hospital (☎ 52/2078).

Dr. John Price Memorial Clinic (Independence, ☎ 62/2167).

VISITOR INFORMATION

The **Placencia Tourism Center** (☎ 62/4045) is upstairs in the post-office building, at the south end of the sidewalk.

TOLEDO AND THE DEEP SOUTH

For many years, poor roads, spotty communications, and the country's highest annual rainfall—as much as 160 inches–kept Belize's "Deep South" off-limits to all but the most adventurous of travelers. The precipitation hasn't changed (you'll need boots and an umbrella in the rainy season), but with improvements to the Southern Highway—the 40 km (24 mi) nearest Punta Gorda has been paved and a section from Dangriga south to past the cut-off to Placencia is scheduled for paving in late 2000—and the opening of new lodges and hotels, the riches of the Toledo district are finally becoming accessible. It's rather like the Cayo district 10 years ago, except that the flora and fauna is even more dramatic here. Toledo is the only part of Belize that has what can truly be described as a rain forest, which hides a plethora of wildlife, including jaguars, margays, and tapirs as well as a teeming variety of tropical birds. The area's rich Maya heritage is only just being unearthed, including a major site currently being excavated by a team from the National Geographic Foundation with help from the Royal Engineers. By all accounts, it dwarfs even Caracol.

Toledo does not have good beaches: the waters of the Gulf of Honduras are invariably muddy from silt deposited by the numerous rivers flowing down from the Maya Mountains. But the cayes off the coast are well worth exploring. The closest are the Snake Cayes; further out are the Sapadillo Cayes, the largest of which is Hunting Caye. A horseshoe bay at the eastern end of the caye has beaches of white coral, where turtles nest in late summer.

Punta Gorda

㉝ *164 km (102 mi) south of Placencia.*

Most journeys south begin in the region's administrative center, Punta Gorda. Founded in 1867 by immigrants from the United States, and subsequently settled by Methodist missionaries from Mississippi, Punta Gorda once boasted 12 sugar estates, each with its own mill. By 1910, however, the town had been almost swallowed by the jungle. Its fortunes revived after World War II, when Britain built an important military base here, but when this in turn closed in 1994, the linchpin of the local economy disappeared. When tourist dollars start to flow, P.G. (as it's affectionately known) will doubtless start to pick up again, but it is currently in hiatus: many of the businesses on its grid of streets lining the bay have closed, and there are only a couple of restaurants in town. And in keeping with its evangelical origins, most of the visitors you see are missionaries, who vie for the souls of the Maya by offering them free dentistry or medicine. But on market days, Wednesday and Saturday, the town comes to life with Guatemalan vendors, who pack the downtown area with colorful fruit and vegetable stands.

Dining and Lodging

$ ✕ **Mangrove Inn.** Basic Belizean dishes are the standards here. The tasty fish dishes are especially good. ✉ *3 Front St., just south of Seafront Inn,* ☎ *73/9910. No credit cards.* ✆ *Closed Sun., Tues.–Thurs. dinner only.*

$ ✕ **Punta Caliente.** This is definitely *the* spot for hearty local fare. The cheerfully homey restaurant has Garifuna pictures and relics mounted on the walls, and the blue plate specials are the typical Belizean mix of fish and chicken dishes, heavy on the rice and beans; but here they're prepared by Garifuna grannies who really know how to make your mouth water. In good weather you can sit at one of the two outside tables. Only slightly off-putting is the smell of an open sewer near the restaurant. *108 José Marina Nuñez St., next to the Z-Line bus station,* ☎ *72/2561. No credit cards.*

$$ 🏨 **Sea Front Inn.** For tourism to have a chance in Punta Gorda, the town needed some good hotels, and the opening of this substantial, four-story property has filled that need. With its pitched roofs and stone-and-wood facade, it looks like a ski lodge in the Swiss Alps—except for the lapis blue galvanized roof. It looks directly over the Gulf of Honduras, with the green humps of the Saddle Back Mountains rising behind it, so the top floors command especially fine views. Inside, on two floors, are single and double rooms and two suites with kitchenettes. For those wanting a good workout, there's a fourth-floor room up a set of steep stairs. Each room is different, furnished with Belizean hardwoods and cable TV. At the back of the original building, owners Larry and Carol Smith, who have been in P.G. for 18 years, have added a group of four apartments, available for hotel guests when not occupied by long-term renters. A third-floor restaurant (now open only for breakfast) has a roof supported by rosewood tree trunks etched with Maya carvings. At the end of the dining room are windows lined with a counter and stools, where you can sit with a drink and look out to sea—if you're lucky, you'll spot a pod of passing porpoises. ⊠ *Front St., Punta Gorda,* ☎ FAX *72/2682. 12 rooms, 2 suites, 4 apartments. Restaurant (breakfast only), bar, air-conditioning, fans, snorkeling, travel services. AE, MC, V.* 🐾

$ 🏠 **Nature's Way Guest House.** Chet Schmidt, who calls himself an "eco-warrior" and once ran a restaurant on Cape Cod, offers an assortment of budget rooms with shared baths in a ramshackle house near the water. Like a hostel, it's a meeting place for budget travelers exploring the frontier or heading on to Guatemala or Honduras. Rooms are white-walled spaces with wood trim, and very, very simple, and there are dorm-style rooms with bunk-bed accommodations for up to four. The breakfast-only menu includes tofu, yogurt, and granola. Chet has been in P.G. for quite a while, and has strong opinions on the Toledo economy, which he is glad to share at length. ⊠ *83 Front St., Punta Gorda,* ☎ *72/2119. 17 rooms with shared baths. Restaurant, travel services. No credit cards.*

$ 🏠 **T.E.A.** The Toledo Ecotourism Association arranges stays in one of 10 participating Maya and Q'eqchí villages. You stay in a simple but clean guest house, then visit Maya homes for breakfast, lunch, and dinner. They speak English and will arrange vegetarian or special meals. In the day, there are walks to the ruins or to waterfalls that empty into bathing pools. For some this is a rare opportunity to learn about a culture, perhaps as an anthropologist might. For others, chickens running in and out and pit toilets may be a bit too authentic an experience. ⊠ *Front St., Punta Gorda,* ☎ *72/2680,* FAX *72/2199. Travel services. No credit cards.*

Outdoor Activities and Sports

FISHING

For bonefish and tarpon there are the estuary flats at the end of the Río Grande. **Fish & Fun** (☎ 72/2670), operated by George Coleman and Ovel Leonardo, Jr., runs fly-fishing, snorkeling, and trips to nearby rivers and to the cayes. The **Sea Front Inn** (☞ *above*) can provide good local guides.

SAILING

Chance Along (⊠ Sea Front Inn, ☞ *above*) is a 33-ft wooden schooner whose owners and captains, Kirby and Tina Salisbury, offer day sails, including lunch, to Port Honduras Marine Reserve for swimming and dingy sailing.

Windsong Charters (Orange Point Marina, Punta Gorda) offers MacGregor 26s, either bareboat or captained. You may find these boats on the light and small side for this type of water, however. The rate for a bareboat charter Sunday to Saturday is $1,850. Provisioning is available from around $225 (☎ 303/983–3739 in the U.S., FAX 303/623–7352).

SCUBA DIVING

This far south, the Reef has pretty much broken up. But individual cayes have their own minireef systems. The best of the bunch is at the **Sapodilla Cayes,** which has great wall dives. The only drawback is that they are 64 km (40 mi) off the coast: a day's dive trip will cost $175 per person. The **Sea Hunt Adventures** (☎ 72/2845) run by Memphis, Tennessee's own Robert Hanggi, can arrange diving and snorkeling trips. He also offers diving/fishing packages and a couple of rooms to stay in.

The Maya Heartland

Drive a few miles out of town and you'll find yourself in the heartland of the Maya. Half the population of Toledo is Maya, a far higher proportion than that of any other region, and they are more cohesive and better organized politically than anywhere else in Belize. The Toledo Maya Cultural Council has created an ambitious network of Maya-run eco-lodges, and in 1995 it initiated the Mayan Mapping Project (MMP), in conjunction with the University of California-Berkeley. By collating oral history and evidence of ancient Maya settlements, the MMP hopes to secure rights to land that the Maya have occupied for centuries but that the Belizean government has seen fit to cede to multinational logging companies.

The Maya divide into two groups: Mopan Maya and Q'eqchí-speaking Indians from the Guatemalan highlands. Most of the latter are recent arrivals, refugees from repression and overpopulation. Each group tends to keep to itself, living in its own villages and preserving its own traditions. The village of **San Antonio,** a market town 56 km (35 mi) west of P.G and the second-largest town in Toledo, is a Mopan Maya center. It was settled by people from the Guatemalan village of San Luis, who revere their former patron saint. The village church, built of stones carted off from surrounding Maya ruins, has a stained-glass window donated by another city with a Luis connection: St. Louis, Missouri. The people of San Antonio have not forgotten their ancient heritage, though, and each year on June 13 they take to the streets for a bacchanalian festival that dates back to pre-Columbian times.

A little further west is the Q'eqchí village of **San Pedro Columbia,** a cheerful cluster of brightly painted buildings and thatched houses. One of the most eye-catching points is a raspberry-red grocery called the "People Little Store." On the way to San Pedro Columbia, don't miss **Blue Creek,** a beautiful stretch of river with turquoise swimming holes and stands of mature hardwood trees. A path up the right-hand riverbank leads to a series of dramatic caves. The Hokeb Ha cave is fairly easy to explore on your own, but others of the many caves that are honeycombed through the limestone here should be visited only with a local guide. International Zoological Expeditions, a Connecticut-based student travel organization (that also operates a marine-ecology center at South Water Caye, off the coast of Dangriga), has established a **jungle lodge** (✉ 210 Washington St., Sherborn, MA 01770, ☎ 508/655-1461 or 800/548-5843 in the U.S., ℻ 508/655-4445) at Blue Creek, with seven rustic cabanas and a restaurant. If you're nearby, you can fax **Ignacio Coc** (℻ 72-2199), a Q'eqchí local who manages the lodge, in advance—he can arrange to pick you up from P.G. and take you to Blue Creek. There's also a jungle canopy skywalk left behind by the Jason Project, which linked schoolchildren in the States to videotaped footage of the rain forest via the Internet. It costs $20 to go up; make sure you have insurance. And don't swim in the river at night—fer de lance snakes like to take nocturnal dips.

Three of Toledo's major Maya sites have already been excavated: Nim Li Punit, Uxbenka, and Lubaantun. **Nim Li Punit** is 37 km (22 mi) northwest of Punta Gorda, off the Southern Highway. A late Classic site, it was discovered in 1976. Twenty-five stelae were unearthed, including one 30 ft tall, the largest ever found in Belize; and in 1986, a royal tomb was excavated. Sadly, few of these artifacts remain on-site.

Lubaantun, which lies beyond the village of San Pedro Columbia, is also a late Classic site. It was discovered in 1924 by German archaeologist Thomas Gann, who coined the name, which means "Place of

ONE LAST TRAVEL TIP:

Pack an easy way to reach the world.

Wherever you travel, the MCI WorldCom Card℠ is the easiest way to stay in touch. You can use it to call to and from more than 125 countries worldwide. And you can earn bonus miles every time you use your card. So go ahead, travel the world. MCI WorldCom℠ makes it even more rewarding. For additional access codes, visit **www.wcom.com/worldphone**.

EASY TO CALL WORLDWIDE

1. Just dial the WorldPhone® access number of the country you're calling from.

2. Dial or give the operator your MCI WorldCom Card number.

3. Dial or give the number you're calling.

Argentina	0800-222-6249
Belize (A)	557 or 815
Brazil	000-8012
Chile	800-207-300
Colombia ◆	980-9-16-0001
Costa Rica (A) ◆	0800-012-2222
Ecuador ÷	999-170
Egypt ◆	7955770
El Salvador (A)	800-1567
Guatemala ◆	99-99-189
Honduras (A) ÷	8000-122
Israel	1-800-920-2727
Mexico	01-800-021-8000
Nicaragua	166
Panama (A)	00800-001-0108
Turkey ◆	00-8001-1177
Venezuela ◆ ÷	800-11140

(A) Calls back to U.S. only.   ◆ Public phones may require deposit of coin or phone card for dial tone.   ÷ Limited availability.

EARN FREQUENT FLIER MILES

Bureau de change

Cambio

外国為替

In this city, you can find money on almost any street.

NO-FEE FOREIGN EXCHANGE

The Chase Manhattan Bank has over 80 convenient locations near New York City destinations such as:

 Times Square
 Rockefeller Center
 Empire State Building
 2 World Trade Center
 United Nations Plaza

Exchange any of 75 foreign currencies

CHASE

THE RIGHT RELATIONSHIP IS EVERYTHING.®

Fallen Stones." Before they fell, Lubaantun must have been an awe-inspiring sight: on top of a conical hill, with views to the sea in one direction and the Maya Mountains in the other, its stepped layers of white-plastered stone would have towered above the jungle like a wedding cake. No one knows exactly what function the structure served, but the large number of miniature masks and whistles found here suggest that it was a center of ceramic production. The central plaza, with tiered seating for 10,000 spectators and three adjacent ball courts, gives rise to images of a Maya Madison Square Garden. In this century, Lubaantun became the scene of the biggest hoax in modern archaeology. After it was excavated in the 1920s, a British adventurer named F. A. Mitchell-Hedges claimed to have stumbled upon what became known as the Crystal Skull. Mitchell-Hedges described the incident in a potboiler, *Danger, My Ally*, in 1951. According to the book, the Crystal Skull was found under an altar at Lubaantun by his "daughter," Anna "Sammy" Mitchell-Hedges. She was not, actually, his daughter, even though he had adopted her as a thirteen-year-old orphan in Quebec, given the fact that she became his lifelong companion. Mitchell-Hedges gave himself out to be a serious archaeologist and explorer: in truth, he was a magazine hack, who was later exposed in England as a fraud and a grave-robber. The Crystal Skull made good copy. Also known as the Skull of Doom, it was supposedly used by Maya high priests to zap anyone they did not care for. Mitchell-Hedges claimed it was 3,600 years old and had taken 150 years to fashion by rubbing a block of pure rock crystal with sand. A similar skull, in the possession of the British Museum, shows signs of having been manufactured with a dentist's drill. Anna Mitchell-Hedges, who today lives in Ontario, has promised to one day reveal the secret: but so far, she has adamantly refused to allow the Crystal Skull to be tested and has denied all requests by the Belizean government to return it. Recently, well into her nineties, she tottered back down to Belize in the company of two publishers. The book should be called *Skullduggery, My Ally*.

Dining and Lodging

$$$ ✕▥ **Fallen Stones Butterfly Ranch and Jungle Resort.** The view from
★ the hardwood terrace behind the restaurant at this excellent small lodge ½ mi from the Maya ruins of Lubaantun is one of the best in Belize: a 360-degree treetop panorama across the jungle to the inky outline of the Maya Mountains, 56 km (35 mi) away. The accommodations, in palapa-covered cabanas laid out on a steep hillside swathed in heliconia, are not quite so spectacular, but the surroundings are so breathtaking that it does not matter much. Two individual cabanas each have a small veranda furnished with clam chairs. The rooms are on the small side, and the bathrooms are modest. As the lodge is only solar-powered, there is no air-conditioning or ceiling fans. Two larger buildings farther down the hillside each have three double rooms. Last, but not least, is the butterfly house. Owner Ray Halberd, a delightfully whimsical Welshman who breaks into song at the slightest provocation, spent his life working as an agricultural botanist for Her Majesty's Overseas Service in such remote corners of the empire as the Gilbert and Ellis islands. But his lifelong dream was to breed butterflies, and Fallen Stones, which opened in 1992, was where he achieved it. At some times, Ray has as many as 3,000 blue morphos in one room, creating a kaleidoscope of flashing neon blue. As well as giving you a personal tour of his magnificent fluttering friends, Ray can arrange trips to nearby Lubaantun or Blue Creek, send you off on a three-hour jungle tour with an excellent guide, or take you canoeing to a bubbling, natural hot spring. Then it's back to the lamplit restaurant for a glass of wine and one of Elsie Halberd's inventive Anglo-Belizean creations: spicy beef stew

with dumplings, chicken soufflé, or coconut blancmange with prune sauce. ✉ *From Southern Hwy. turn left onto the San Antonio road (unpaved) for 2.7 km (1.6 mi) and turn right on unmarked road (look for the sign to Lubaantun); resort is just past the Lubaantun turnoff. Near Lubaantun, between San Pedro Columbia and San Miguel villages (Box 23, Punta Gorda)*, ☎ FAX 72/2167. 8 rooms. Restaurant, bar. MC, V.

Toledo and the Deep South A to Z

Arriving and Departing

BY AIRPLANE

Both **Maya Island Air** (☎ 23/1348, FAX 23/0585) and **Tropic Air** (☎ 26/2012 or 800/422–3435 in the U.S.) fly south to Dangriga, Placencia, and Punta Gorda from both the municipal ($69 one-way) and international ($81 one-way) airports. The P.G. airstrip is on the west side of town; from the town square, walk four blocks west on Prince Street.

BY BOAT

Boat travel between Puerto Barrios, Guatemala, and Punta Gorda, Belize, is not recommended, as the boat hijacking in spring 2000 directly affected this route (☞ Safety *in* Smart Travel Tips). Travelers should consider another form of transportation.

BY BUS

For routes south to Dangriga, Hopkins, Sitee River, Placencia, and Punta Gorda, try **Z-Line Bus Service** (✉ Venus Bus Terminal, Magazine Rd., Belize City, ☎ 27/3937). To Punta Gorda it's about a 10-hour ride for around $11. Road conditions are unpredictable in the rainy season, June–Sept.

BY CAR

The journey to Punta Gorda via the Hummingbird and Southern highways used to be a chiropractor's nightmare: a bone-shuddering, two-day marathon via Belmopan, Dangriga, and Big Creek across some of the worst roads in Belize. It won't be the New Jersey Turnpike, but improvements to the Southern Highway (sadly undertaken to improve logging companies' access to the virgin hardwood forests) will eventually cut that time in half. At press time, however, only the section from Punta Gorda to Big Falls was paved, with preparation for paving underway from Dangriga to Independence and Big Creek.

Contacts and Resources

EMERGENCIES

Punta Gorda Hospital (☎ 72/2026).

GUIDED TOURS

Clive Genus–Taxi, Tour, and Car Rental (✉ 30 Wahima Alley, P.G., ☎ 72/2068). Genus is an incredibly pleasant man with whom to jostle around on bumpy roads visiting ruins, or just traveling the 30 or so miles to a jungle resort. He once stopped halfway and asked a friend if he could pick some of his oranges so that we could taste their sweetness.

VISITOR INFORMATION

Toledo Information Centre (✉ Front St., ☎ 72/2531, ☉ Tues.–Sat. 9–noon and 1–4:30, Sun. 9–noon. Closed Mon.).

BELIZE A TO Z

Arriving and Departing

By Airplane

International flights arrive at **Philip Goldson International Airport** (✉ Ladyville, north of Belize City).

The main airlines serving Belize from the United States are **American** (☎ 800/624–6262), with daily flights from Miami; **Continental** (☎ 800/231–0856), which has two daily nonstop flights from Houston; and **Taca International** (☎ 800/535–8780), which has flights from Los Angeles, Miami, and San Francisco. Taca International offers special baggage concessions to divers and has a modern fleet; the snag is that flights are often late in arriving, which can be a nuisance if you have to make connections later on. It is sometimes cheaper to fly to Cancún and take **Aerocaribe** (☎ 27/5213) for about $200, or switch to a bus to Belize.

By Boat

The future of water-taxi service to and from Puerto Barrios, Guatemala, and Punta Gorda, Belize, is uncertain. For the time being it is not recommended, as the boat hijacking in spring 2000 directly affected this route (☞ Safety *in* Smart Travel Tips). Travelers should consider bus service between Punta Gorda and Belize City, or one of the several daily flights offered.

By Bus

There is daily bus service from the Guatemalan and Mexican borders. Buses cross from Chetumal, Mexico, and stop in Corozal, Belize, where you can catch another bus or a plane to Belize City or elsewhere. Buses from Guatemala (via Flores) stop in the border town of Melchor de Mencos, at the bridge that separates the two countries. Cross the bridge and take a bus or taxi to San Ignacio, 13 km (8 mi) away. Many people commute across the border, so you can probably share a ride if you arrive early in the day; otherwise, it costs $15. From San Ignacio there is regular service to Belize City.

By Car

It's a three-day drive from Brownsville, Texas, to Chetumal, Mexico, on the border with Belize, and then about another 3½ hours to Belize City. On arrival from Mexico, you'll have to hand in your Mexican Tourist Card (and/or car papers, if you have them). On the Belizean side, make sure you get a Temporary Import Permit for your car, or you may be delayed when leaving the country.

Getting Around

By Airplane

Domestic planes in Belize are twin-engine island-hoppers. This means you sit right behind the pilot and, depending on your departure point, may endure several takeoffs and landings. (For example, a flight from Dangriga to San Pedro will likely include three stops.) Most domestic flights leave from the Municipal Airport, near the center of Belize City, which is more convenient than International. The main carriers are Tropic Air and Maya Island Air, both of which fly to San Pedro on Ambergris Caye and Caye Caulker as well as Dangriga, Placencia, Punta Gorda, and nearby Mexican towns to the north. Tropic has the larger and more modern fleet. Domestic flights from and to the municipal airport are between $45–$80, except for those flights arranged on Javier Flying Service, which will take you pretty much anywhere for $170 per hour and has regular flights to Chan Chich Lodge.

By Bus

Although there is no rail system in Belize, there is fairly extensive bus service, run by franchised private companies. The quality of the buses and the roads on which they travel varies considerably (Novelo's is the best company; routes to points south, the worst). Novelo's recently acquired Batty Bros., the competition, so service routes are being consolidated. However, the buses do run according to reliable schedules, are extremely cheap (about $2.50–$15), and remain an excellent way to experience Belize as the Belizeans do. Outside the cities you can flag them down like cabs, and the driver will let you off whenever you want. Expect to ride on old U.S. school buses or retired Greyhound buses. On the Northern and Western Highway routes, there are a few express buses with air-conditioning and other comforts. These cost a few dollars more.

Novelo's buses stop in Corozal, Belmopan, and San Ignacio. Venus Bus Service heads north to Orange Walk and Corozal, while Z-Line Bus Service covers Belmopan, Dangriga, and Punta Gorda.

There is no municipal bus service in Belize City.

➤ BUS INFORMATION: **Novelo's** (✉ W. Collet Canal, Belize City, ☎ 27/7372). **Venus Bus Service** (✉ Magazine Rd., Belize City, ☎ 27/7390 or 27/3354). **Z-Line Bus Service** (✉ Magazine Rd., Belize City, ☎ 27/3937).

By Car

Belize is one of the few countries left in the Americas where off-road conditions are still the norm on many roads. Getting somewhere is never a question of simply going from A to B; there is always a bit of adventure involved, and a few detours to Y or Z.

Only the Northern Highway, to Orange Walk and Corozal, the Western Highway, to Belmopan and San Ignacio, and the Hummingbird Highway from Belmopan to Dangriga, are fully paved. The Southern Highway is being improved, and a 25-mi section near Punta Gorda is paved, with other sections scheduled for surfacing. Once you get off the main highways, distances don't mean that much—it's time that counts. You might have only 20 km (12½ mi) to go, but it can take you a grueling 90 minutes. If you bring your own car, you'll need to buy insurance in Belize. Unleaded premium gasoline costs around $3 per gallon. In remote areas, fill up whenever you see a gas station.

Belize City now has representatives of most major car-rental agencies, as well as several local operators. Prices vary from company to company, but all are exorbitant by U.S. standards ($65–$130 per day). Some of the cars run by the local operators—V8 gas-guzzlers driven down from Texas—will cost you dearly for gas alone, whereas the international agencies have modern, dependable fleets and prices to match. A four-wheel-drive Suzuki, with unlimited mileage from Budget, for instance, costs about $75 per day, though weekly rates are cheaper (about $450). Off-season, rates are lower. For serious safaris, a four-wheel-drive vehicle (preferably a Land Rover or an Isuzu Trooper) is invaluable, and some companies have clauses that bind you not to go off the main highways without one. Most major hotels offer all-terrain vehicles with guides for about $200 per day.

Safety

Belize City got an ugly reputation for street crime in the early '90s, but the government has since made strenuous efforts to clean up the problem, and these seem to be working. Still, take the same precautions you would take in any large city—leave valuables in a safe place, don't wear expensive jewelry on the street, and check with your hotel before venturing into any unfamiliar areas, particularly at night. Dangriga and Orange Walk Town recently have become *less* safe due to the arrival of crack cocaine from Belize City, but everywhere else, you'll find Belize one of the safest, and friendliest, places you have ever visited.

For the time being, boating between Belize and Guatemala is not recommended (☞ Safety *in* Smart Travel Tips).

Contacts and Resources

Car Rentals

Most name-brand Belize City rental-car agencies have locations at the international airport as well as in the city. International airport locations usually are closed on Sundays. Avis also has a location at the municipal airport. Budget, owned by the same people who operate the JMA Motors new-car dealership in Belize City, has a fleet of low-mileage vehicles, and their service is tops in town.

Avis (✉ Radisson Fort George, Marine Parade, Belize City, ☎ 25/2629; Municipal Airstrip, Belize City, ☎ 23/4619; Philip S. W. Goldson International Airport, Ladyville, ☎ 25/2385; Poinsetta Rd., Ladyville, ☎ 25/2629). **Budget** (✉ 771 Bella Vista, Belize City, ☎ 23/2435; Philip S. W. Goldson International Airport, Ladyville, ☎ 23/2435). **Hertz** (✉ 11A Cork St., Belize City, ☎ 23/5395). **National** (✉ Mile 4½, Western Highway, ☎ 23/1650). **Thrifty** (✉ Central American Blvd. and Fabers Rd., Belize City, ☎ 27/1271).

Some local companies are less expensive and just as good. Both also have international airport locations. **Crystal Auto Rental** (✉ Mile 1½, Northern Highway, Belize City, ☎ 23/1600).

Consulates and Embassies

U.S. Embassy (✉ 29 Gabourel La., Belize City, ☎ 27/7161). **Canadian Consulate** (✉ 29 Southern Foreshore, Belize City, ☎ 23/1060). **British High Commission** (✉ Embassy Sq., Belmopan, ☎ 82/2146).There are no Australian or New Zealand embassies or consulates in Central America.

Guided Tours

Many tour companies stick to their local area, but several venture further afield. One of the best is **Discovery Expeditions** (☎ 23/0748, FAX 23/0750), which has several Belize City hotel locations. The staff is friendly and well informed and can help you can arrange expeditions virtually anywhere in the country. **Amigo Travel** (☎ 26/2180), the largest tour company on Ambergris Caye, offers both mainland and island tours and snorkeling excursions. **Melmish Mayan Tours** (☎ 24/5221) and **S&L Travel Services** (☎ 27/7593) are also reputable.

3 GUATEMALA

An extraordinary country with incomparable Maya ruins and spectacular highland markets, Guatemala is the center of the Maya heartland, a landscape colored by costumes of the indigenous peoples, pastel-painted colonial churches, rushing white-water rivers, and expansive stretches of rain forest that hide spider monkeys, toucans, and iguanas among massive mahogany trees draped with mosses, ferns, vines, bromeliads, and rare orchids.

By David
Dudenhoefer

Updated by
Gary Chandler
and Joanna
Kosowsky

GUATEMALA HAS BEEN captivating travelers for centuries. From the time of conquistador Pedro de Alvarado, who stopped between battles to marvel at the beauty of Lake Atitlán, to that of Aldous Huxley, who waxed poetic on the same lake's shores centuries later, this intricate jewel of a country has intrigued and inspired its share of foreigners. The incredible diversity of Guatemala's land and culture means that in a matter of days you can walk the cobblestone streets of an ancient colonial capital, barter with Indians who still speak the tongues of and worship the gods of the ancient Maya, and explore the exotic web of life that is the tropical rain forest.

Perched at the top of the Central American isthmus and anchored below the Yucatán Peninsula, Guatemala is divided politically into a number of departments or states, and divided topographically into a number of distinct regions: the Pacific Lowlands, the Western Highlands, the central Verapaces, the desert of Zacapa, the Caribbean Lowlands, and the northern jungle region of El Petén. With a territory of 108,900 square km (42,046 square mi), Guatemala is slightly larger than Ohio and is home to more than 12.5 million people. Within this relatively small nation are some 19 different ecosystems, encompassing palm-lined beaches, luxuriant cloud forests, 37 volcanoes (several of which are active), rugged mountain ranges, tumultuous boulder-strewn rivers, a scrubby desert valley, and expansive stretches of rain forest chock-full of tropical flora and fauna.

As dramatic as Guatemala's varied landscapes are, its human panorama is even more compelling. Half the population is of indigenous descent, and though the country's Indians have adopted some of the European customs forced upon their ancestors as long as five centuries ago, they remain some of the Americas' most dedicated protectors of indigenous culture.

The first major Maya society dates to 2000 BC, with early traditions and practices drawing from the Olmecs, an established civilization in present-day Mexico. The Maya calendar, a mathematics system (the Mayas invented the first zero), and one of the first writing systems were developed over the next 2,000 years. From about 250 BC to AD 900, Maya societies proliferated and developed complex social systems, agricultural practices, and religious structures, reaching their zenith with the construction of temples like Tikal and Palenque in Mexico. The Maya were particularly adept astronomers, mapping the orbits of the sun, moon, and Venus with incredible accuracy—the Maya lunar cycle differs from today's calculations by only seven minutes. Around AD 1000, the Maya suffered repeated attacks from rival civilizations, followed by a sudden and mysterious period of decline. The arrival of conquistadors like Hernán Cortés and Pedro de Alvarado in the early 1500s, marked the beginning of the subjugation of the Maya throughout Mexico and Central America, which has never really ceased.

Today all of Guatemala's Indians are Maya, but they comprise at least 22 different ethnicities, differentiated by sometimes subtle distinctions in language, dress, and customs. The other half of the population is divided among Ladinos, the Spanish-speaking descendants of Spaniards and Indians; Garífunas, a handful of black Guatemalans descended from escaped African slaves, who live on the Caribbean coast; and the European minority, predominantly of Spanish ancestry, which has maintained its imported bloodline and, accordingly, its colonial lease on power. Though Spanish is Guatemala's official language, it's the mother tongue of only about half the population. Indians tend to speak one of the many indigenous languages, with Spanish as a second language; and most people around Livingston speak Garífuna (pronounced Ga-RI-funa), a mixture of African, Carib, and European languages. These cultures create a human tapestry even more colorful than the Indian weavers' most intricate patterns.

Guatemala's recent history has largely been the story of a struggle for land and political equality in the face of military rule. In 1944 Jorge Ubico, the last of the old-time strongmen, was deposed in a peaceful revolution. Elected in his place was schoolteacher Juan José Arévalo, who promised to modernize the country through education and agrarian reform. Arévalo was succeeded by Jacobo Arbenz, who accelerated land reform by daring to expropriate a small part of the vast holdings of the U.S.-owned United Fruit Company.

In 1954 the U.S. government, anxious to protect American interests in Guatemala, sponsored a successful coup to oust the democratically elected president. The coup effectively closed the door on majority political participation for the next 29 years, as one right-wing government after another staged fraudulent elections.

In 1961 dissident army officers attempted a coup in response to government corruption. Although resistance and eventual revolt was inspired primarily by peasants seeking land reforms and an end to military repression and a oligarchical political system. When their efforts were quickly crushed, this defeat set the stage for a prolonged guerrilla war. By the late 1970s the guerrilla groups had begun to tap into long-held grievances of Guatemala's landless and disenfranchised peasants, most of them Indians. In response to the guerrillas' growing popularity among the landless and poor, the government unleashed a violent campaign of genocidal intensity, not just against the guerrillas, but against innocent civilians.

During the worst years of the violence—the "scorched-earth" campaigns of the early 1980s—some 100,000 mostly poor Indian peasants were raped, tortured, shot, and mutilated as the military razed hundreds of villages throughout the country in an effort to flush out a handful of guerrillas. Tens of thousands more people "disappeared" from military checkpoints and city streets. Some 75,000 escaped to Mexico, and an estimated 30,000 fled into the hostile mountain ranges of the north. Steps toward peace began in the mid-eighties, with open elections resulting in civilian presidents. U.N.-monitored peace negotiations began in 1990 and were expedited by the well-attended 1995 election of Guatemala's current president, Alvaro Arzú. A peace accord, signed in December 1996, put an end to the 36-year civil war that claimed the lives of some 200,000 people.

Guatemala has entered a period of slow recovery. The 1996 peace accord provided for greater legal, linguistic, and educational rights for the indigenous communities, scaled back the military and police, and established a land bank and national property survey to address the claims of landless peasants forced from their communities by the army. (To the dismay of human-rights advocates, however, the accord also includes a controversial amnesty that prevents prosecution of most of the government and military officials responsible for the atrocities.) With peace has come increased international investment and economic growth, evidence of which appears throughout the country in the form of new and improved roads, increased electrification, and better communication systems—all of which not only improve the quality of life, but make Guatemala more visitor-friendly.

With transition, of course, comes uncertainty, and a certain amount of chaos. Robbery and violent bandits, particularly in the Western Highlands, have posed a security problem that some associate with a dismantled military and police force. Keep abreast of current security issues (☞ Health and Safety *in* Guatemala A to Z, *below*) and consider that reasonable precautions may not always be enough to allow comfortable and safe travel. Despite its troubles, Guatemala remains an amazing country that may represent better than any other the beauty and diversity that is the New World.

Pleasures and Pastimes

Archaeological Ruins

The department of El Petén, much of which is covered with tropical rain forest, was the heart of the ancient Maya empire. Only a fraction of the estimated 1,500 ruins have been excavated, and all remain surrounded, if not covered, by jungle. Aside from Tikal, travel to ruins usually involves taking a boat, horseback riding, hiking, mountain biking, or driving a four-wheel-drive vehicle down muddy roads, any of which makes each trip an adventure.

Bird-Watching

More species of birds live in Guatemala than in the United States and Canada combined, and birding is an effortless complement to any day trip or archaeological tour. For hints on what to keep your eye out for, *see* the Wildlife Glossary *in* Chapter 4). Some recommended field guides are *Birds of Mexico,* best purchased before your trip, or *Birds of Tikal,* available in many Guatemalan bookstores.

Caving

An awesome selection of caves awaits the subterranean sportsman. Aktun Kan, in El Petén (at Santa Elena), is very accessible, and Naj Tunich, near Poptún, has underground lagoons and carbon frescoes painted by the ancient Maya. Lanquín, in Alta Verapaz, is an amazing collection of chambers, and the Candelaria River, also in Verapaz, passes through a series of caverns that are only accessible by water a few months of the year. Many other caves remain largely unexplored.

Colonial Architecture

Despite earthquakes, volcanoes, and political strife, such remarkable colonial buildings as Antigua's La Merced and the Church of Santo Tomás in Chichicastenango mark both the country's wounded past and its capacity for endurance.

Dining

The basis of Guatemalan food is corn, usually eaten in the form of a tortilla or as a tamale or on the cob. Black beans accompany most meals, either whole in a broth or mashed and refried. In restaurants, these two items often accompany grilled beef or chicken. *Lomito* is a favorite thin and tender cut of beef from the cow's back; turkey is a popular fowl; and in rural areas you might see *venado* (venison) and *tepezcuintle* (a large, nocturnal rodent) on the menu. (Be aware that tepezcuintle is an endangered species; the more it's ordered, the more it will be hunted.) The most popular fish is the delicious *robálo,* a whitefish known elsewhere as snook, where it's a favored sport fish. Meats are often served in *caldos* (stews) or cooked in a spicy chili sauce. As you travel east, try *tapado,* a traditional Caribbean coconut stew made with plantains, shrimp, crab, and fish. *Queso fundido* (melted cheese with condiments and tortillas), which is sometimes served as an appetizer, is a good choice for light eaters.

Guatemala City has the kind of dining variety you'd expect from a major city, with the finer and more expensive restaurants clustered in the New City, particularly Zona Viva. Antigua also has a remarkable number of good restaurants, and Panajachel and Quetzaltenango have a few good, moderately priced options. Most upmarket restaurants have international menus or specialize in specific foreign cuisines, but a few serve Guatemalan fare. Several Flores restaurants focus on exotic rainforest game. Dining options are more limited in the rest of the country, where the food, though hearty, will evince little enthusiasm from gourmets.

Reservations are recommended at expensive ($$$) restaurants on weekend nights, but dress is informal across the board. Even the more expensive establishments don't require jacket and tie.

CATEGORY	COST*
$$$	over $12
$$	$6–$12
$	under $6

per person for a three-course meal, plus tax and tip. Drinks not included.

✎ *following the text of a review is your signal that the property has a Web site, where you will find details and, usually, images; for a link, visit www.fodors.com/urls.*

Fishing
The Pacific coast offers excellent deep-sea fishing, especially for billfish and mahimahi. The Caribbean coast makes for good snook fishing, and Lake Atitlán is stocked with black bass.

Hiking
Many highland villages are inaccessible by car, so hiking is the only way to explore much of the country. Likewise, many archaeological sites in El Petén are best reached on foot, though lowland hiking is much hotter and muddier than its highland equivalent. A number of active and dormant volcanoes make excellent climbs, some of which can be combined to form overnight trips. Traveling with an adventure-travel company (☞ Guided Tours in Guatemala A to Z, *below*) is a good way to avoid getting lost, robbed, or, in the case of temperamental Pacaya, sprayed with volcanic sand.

Lodging
The level of comfort and quality of facilities ranges from the luxurious suites of the Camino Real to the stark rooms, tiny beds, and cold showers of the ubiquitous budget hotels. In Guatemala City, most of the expensive ($$$) and very expensive ($$$$) hotels are in the New City, whereas most moderate ($$) and inexpensive ($) hotels are in the Old City. With a wide range of quality moderate ($$) and expensive ($$$) hotels, Antigua is close enough to the capital to serve as an alternative, if not preferable, home base; its rooms often fill up on weekends, so make reservations.

Panajachel has the widest and best selection of accommodations in the highlands, and Chichicastenango and Quetzaltenango can claim some creditable lodgings. Chichicastenango's hotels tend to fill up on Wednesday and Saturday nights (for the famous market), so it's best to reserve in advance. Holy Week and other holidays are very busy in most of the popular highland towns. Beyond the towns, little accommodation exists; most remote highland villages offer only inexpensive, spartan lodging, if any at all.

El Petén and the Caribbean coast have several luxury hotels ($$$$), though options also exist for roughing it in the several well-kept and inexpensive ($) backpackers' havens.

CATEGORY	COST*
$$$$	over $75
$$$	$45–$75
$$	$20–$45
$	under $20

All prices are for a standard double room, including 10% VAT and 10% tourist tax.

✑ *following the text of a review is your signal that the property has a Web site, where you will find details and, usually, images; for a link, visit www.fodors.com/urls.*

River Trips

Guatemala is filled with white-water rivers, many of which have never been run, as well as slow-moving lowland rivers that have been navigated for thousands of years. Adding to the adventure, most of the popular rivers flow through lush tropical forests bursting with wildlife.

Rivers are rated on a scale of I to VI. Class I signifies no rapids; Class II, small rapids; Class III, difficult rapids with waves; Class IV, very difficult or advanced; and Class V, violent hydraulics for experts only. Class VI rivers are unrunnable. White-water rivers in Guatemala include: Chiquibul, Coyolate, Motagua, and Naranjo (Class II–III, year-round) and Cahabón and Rio Los Esclavos (Class III–IV, year-round). The Candelaria (Class III–IV, March–May) takes you through virgin forest and caves. Alternatively, canoes, kayaks, or *kayukos* (locally made canoes fashioned from the trunk of tree) paddled by a local guide can be rented at Río Dulce and El Boqueron (in El Estor) for a more leisurely navigation.

Shopping

Guatemala presents a mind-boggling selection of traditional handicrafts at remarkably low prices. The work of local artisans and weavers is usually called *típica,* roughly translated as "typical goods." Every touristed town has an overabundance of típica shops, but many of those in Antigua and Guatemala City have finer quality, more expensive wares, often refashioned for contemporary tastes and uses. If you're looking specifically for a good deal, stick to the street. Bargaining is the modus operandi of street vendors and is also common in the markets and shops; asking prices are sometimes rather high, so be patient.

Nearly all of Guatemala's handicrafts come from the highlands, so the highlands themselves are a shoppers' paradise. Most famous are the handwoven fabrics—in every highland village you'll see women weaving the local traditional patterns derived from pre-Hispanic motifs. But Guatemala's indigenous population creates countless other kinds of handicrafts; just as each region has its traditional fabrics, it has other specialties, such as baskets, toys, tinwork, glassware, statues, bags, or hats. The highland town most famous for shopping is Chichicastenango, but you'll usually get the lowest prices in the areas where the handicrafts are made.

Guatemala's public markets are a wonderful way to witness the everyday lives of the population. Vendors lining a jumble of narrow, warrenlike passages hawk fruits and vegetables, flowers, meat, nuts, candles, incense, toiletries, and gaudy, U.S.-made T-shirts. Markets are held on the following days:

Monday: Antigua, Chimaltenango, Zunil
Tuesday: Sololá
Wednesday: Chimaltenango
Thursday: Antigua, Chichicastenango, Nebaj, Quetzaltenango, San Juan Atitlán, San Lucas Tolimán, Santa Cruz del Quiché, Todos Santos Cuchumatán
Friday: Chimaltenango, Sololá, San Francisco El Alto
Saturday: Antigua, Totonicapán
Sunday: Antigua, Chichicastenango, Momostenango, Nebaj, San Lucas Tolimán, Quetzaltenango, Todos Santos Cuchumatán

If you forget to buy something in the highlands, don't worry; the market in Guatemala City's Zona 1 has a little bit of everything, at prices as low as you'll find anywhere else. A general note: it's illegal to take pre-Columbian and colonial artifacts or antiques out of Guatemala. Only postcolonial works—anything made after 1820—can be exported.

Exploring Guatemala

Great Itineraries

Guatemala is a rugged country where major roads (read: paved roads) are few and far between and superhighways such as you find in Mexico don't exist. Since there are only two airports—one in Guatemala City, the other in Flores—most domestic travel takes place on roads, such as they are. For this reason, a trip to Guatemala should last no less than five days, during which span you can take in the most popular sights and still get off the beaten path. Eight days allows a better look at Tikal and El Petén, and 10 days adds a trip to the Caribbean coast.

All but the hardiest travelers will want to base themselves in the country's few cities and tourist towns (where the lodgings are) and explore the more isolated regions on day trips; the road system simply doesn't lend itself to rotational touring. Most of the more charming villages are on roads that end in the mountains, necessitating a lot of doubling back. Make sure your trip includes a Thursday or Sunday—market days—in Chichicastenango. In addition to filling your luggage with típica, a market will infuse your trip with more of Guatemala's vivid colors and living traditions, and leave a lasting impression of a place that's moving into the 21st century while respecting its past.

Numbers in the text correspond to numbers in the margin and on the maps.

IF YOU HAVE 5 DAYS

Consider **Guatemala City** ①–⑩ your transportation hub and make for **Antigua** ⑪–㉓, Guatemala's prettiest colonial city, as soon as you're rested. Spend at least two nights here. While in Antigua, plan an early morning excursion to the mountain village of **Chichicastenango** ㉛ and its exuberant, colorful market (Thursday and Sunday), where the region's best handicrafts are laid out. On day four, take an early-morning plane from Guatemala City to **Flores** ㊾, a tiny pastel-painted El Petén town with a few good restaurants and shops, and head straight to the Maya ruins at **Tikal** ㊾. (You'll want to get there before the midday heat and humidity descend.) If this is your first trip to Tikal, you might want to sign up for a day tour from Antigua or Guatemala City, as the site itself is huge, and it's convenient to have ground transportation waiting for you in Flores. Depending on your schedule, you may choose to spend the night in Tikal, so as to see the ruins in the morning (a must for birders), or 40-minutes away in Flores, where you'll be closer to the airport for your flight back to Guatemala City.

Spend the first night in **Guatemala City** ①–⑩ to acclimatize, visit the museums, and have dinner in Zona Viva. On day two, head for **Antigua** ⑪–㉓, and tour the remarkable ruins of 16th-, 17th-, and 18th-century monasteries and convents. Spend two nights here, and on your fourth day, head for lakeside **Panajachel** ㉔. Spend day five visiting the villages surrounding picture-perfect Lake Atitlán or head to the renowned market in the colonial highland village of **Chichicastenango** ㉛. After shopping and visiting the churches here, take a half-hour hike up the hill behind town to the sacred carved-stone image of a Maya deity. On day six, return to Guatemala City and take a mid-day flight to **Flores** ㊾, in El Petén. Spend the afternoon in Flores shopping, strolling, and sipping cappuccino. That night, make arrangements for a morning taxi at your hotel—you'll want to leave before dawn for the breathtaking Maya site of **Tikal** ㊳. Try to arrive about an hour before sunrise, and bring a flashlight and bird-watching binoculars. At the gate, you can hire a guide to lead you through the jungle to Temple IV, the highest temple—climb the rustic ladder to the top, then relax and watch the dawn unfold over the rain forest that engulfs the ancient city. It's unforgettable. If you're not a morning person, you might want to spend the night at one of the Tikal hotels and split your tour of the ruins over a few days. You can spend the last morning hiking the terrific trails of the **Biotopo Cerro Cahuí** ㊹ before returning in late afternoon to the Flores airport and Guatemala City. Or return to the capital for a white-water excursion on the Coyolate River (☞ Sidetrip: Pacific Coast, *below*).

Those who've come for relaxation should follow the seven-day itinerary above, staying in **Guatemala City** ①–⑩, **Antigua** ⑪–㉓, and **Panajachel** ㉔ or a highland village, with a trip **Tikal** ㊳, and add additional days to the highlands for a tour of the Lake Atitlán villages or perhaps a trekking excursion to Volcan Pacaya from Antigua. The adventurous and energetic also should follow the seven-day itinerary but continue on the road from the El Petén region for a trip south. Travel by bus or car to **Río Dulce** ㊹, once an important trading river for the Maya, check into a hotel, and sign up for a river trip to the Castillo de San Felipe. (If you brought a car, you can leave it at your hotel and pick it up on your way back to Guatemala City.) The next day, take an early-morning boat ride to the **Chocón Machacas Wildlife Reserve** ㊻ for a tour, then an afternoon boat ride farther east to the colorful Garífuna community of **Livingston** ㊼. Spend the night here. On the last morning, take a ferry to the banana port of **Puerto Barrios** ㊽, where you can swim or explore the waterfront. By early afternoon, start heading back to Guatemala City.

When to Tour Guatemala

Most come to Guatemala in summer (June–August) or winter (January–April). The busiest time of year is Holy Week (Palm Sunday to Easter Sunday), for which hotels in Antigua, Panajachel, and Chichicastenango are fully booked months ahead of time. The rainy season runs from May to November, with a few dry spells in July and August. A typical day in the rainy season is sunny in the morning, cloudy at midday, and pouring throughout the afternoon and evening. Guatemala's climate depends more on altitude than season. The coasts and El Petén are hot and humid, while the mountains are drier, with warm days and cool nights. The higher you go, the colder it gets. August through October is hurricane season, and while this may not interrupt your stay in Guatemala, it may slow or delay your air transportation plans to and from the area.

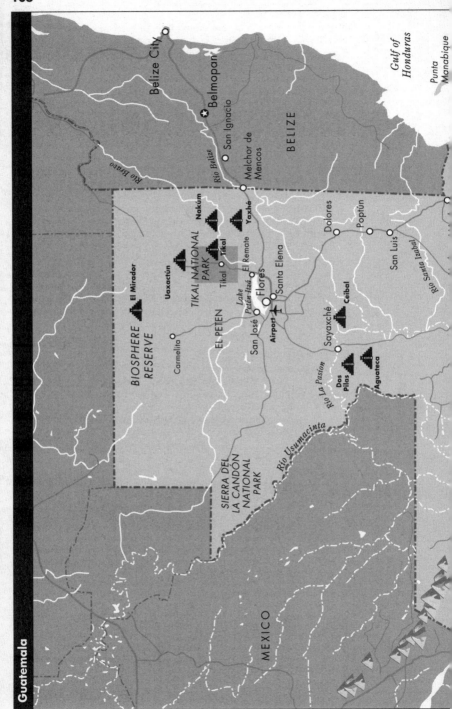

Guatemala

Belize City

Belmopan

San Ignacio

BELIZE

Gulf of
Honduras

Punta
Manabique

Río Bravo

Río Belize

Melchor de
Mencos

BIOSPHERE
RESERVE

El Mirador

Uaxactún

Nakúm

Yaxhá

Dolores

Poptún

San Luis

Río Santa Izabal

TIKAL NATIONAL
PARK

Tikal

El Remate

Santa Elena

Carmelita

EL PETEN

Flores

Lake
Petén Itzá

San José

Airport

Ceibal

Sayaxché

Dos
Pilas

Aguateca

Río La Pasión

SIERRA DEL
LA CANDÓN
NATIONAL
PARK

Río Usumacinta

Río Usumacinta

MEXICO

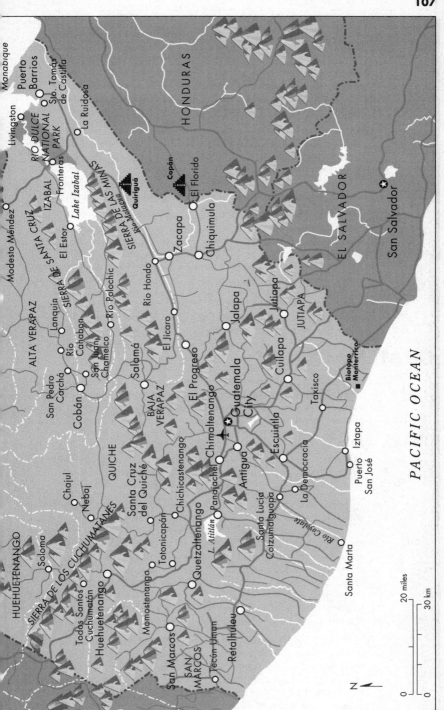

PACIFIC OCEAN

The best time of the week to visit any highland village is on its market day, when the streets are packed with families from the surrounding countryside. The liveliest time of year for each town, however, is the week or several days of its annual festival, which surrounds the feast day of the town's patron saint. Festivals are an interesting mixture of religious ritual and carnival commotion, with processions, live music, and traditional dancers in costumes that depict animals, gods, and conquistadors.

Important highland festivals occur in Huehuetenango (July 12–17), Santiago Atitlán (July 23–27 and Holy Week), Momostenango (July 21–August 1), Nebaj (August 12–15), Santa Cruz del Quiché (August 14–19), Quetzaltenango (September 9–17), Totonicapán (September 24–30), Panajachel (October 1–7), Todos Santos (October 21–November 1), Zunil (November 22–26), and Chichicastenango (December 13–21).

In Antigua, the Biennial Cultural Festival (February 2001, 2003, 2005) includes a variety of artistic events held in the city's ruins and ancient buildings. Antigua also plays host to series of processions during both the Christmas season and Holy Week, when residents stage colorful religious parades and reenact Christ's last days in Jerusalem. On All Saints' Day (November 1), huge kites fly from the cemetery of Santiago Sacatepéquez, near Guatemala City; and Guatemalans nationwide celebrate Independence Day (September 15) with traditional music, dances, and costumes. The village of San Felipe de Jesús, just north of Antigua, hosts a saint's day celebration (August 30).

GUATEMALA CITY

The capital is a big, busy, and, let's face it, ugly city. With few of the country's most captivating draws—no Maya ruins, flamboyant markets, or spectacular birding—there's little reason to stay longer than necessary. Still, as it's the principal transportation hub, you can't avoid passing through, so you may as well make the most of it. Fortunately, Guatemala City or Guate (pronounced Guat-TAY), as it's called by locals, has some decent restaurants and hotels, as well as several excellent museums, a healthy nightlife, and all the modern services that have yet to be introduced to the less-developed interior.

A sprawling metropolis with 2.5 million inhabitants and 21 different zones may seem intimidating at first, especially since there's another division of the capital into Old and New cities. But there is virtually no reason to stray from four central zones, which makes getting around—and getting your bearings—quite manageable. The Old City spans Zona Uno (Zone 1) and beyond to the north, and the New City spans Zona Nueve and Zona Diez (Zones 9 and 10) in the south. Between them is Zona Cuatro (Zone 4) notable only for its transitional location between the Old and New cities and because it contains the bus terminals. Otherwise, its dirty, a bit seedy, and best avoided.

In the Old and New cities, numbered *avenidas* (avenues) run south to north, increasing in that direction. Similarly, numbered *calles* (streets) run west to east, increasing in that direction. Addresses are usually given as a numbered avenida or calle followed by two numbers separated by a dash: the first number is a nearby cross street or avenue and the second is a specific building. The building numbers increase as they approach the higher-numbered cross streets, and then start over at the next block, so 9 Avenida 5–22 is on 9 Avenida between 5 and 6 calles, and 9 Avenida 5–74 is on the same block, only closer to 6 Calle. A word of warning: make sure you're in the right zone. Different zones often contain identical addresses.

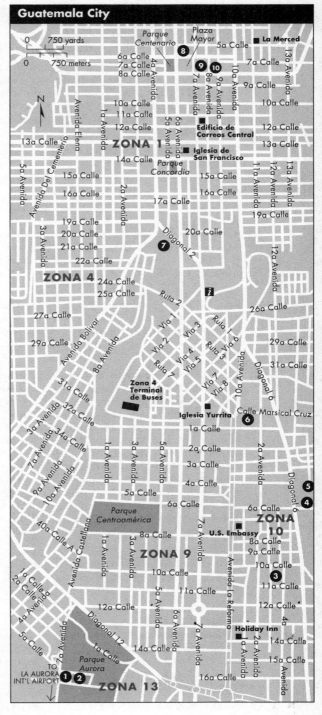

Guatemala City

The city's major arteries are 6 and 10 avenidas: 6 Avenida runs through the center of Zona 1 (via Zona 4) into the heart of Zona 9, passing three series of identically numbered calles; 10 Avenida runs through Zonas 1 and 4 and becomes Avenida La Reforma.

Comfort-seekers tend to stick to the New City, while those interested in bargain shopping and seeing the city's unvarnished goings-on head for the Old City. As with shopping and sightseeing, hotels and restaurants tend to follow the same pattern. With the exception of the big market downtown, in the Old City, shop hours are weekdays 10–1 and 3–7, Saturday 10–1.

Numbers in the text correspond to numbers in the margin and on the Guatemala City map.

The New City

Whereas the Old City is the real Guatemala, the New City's modern look and pace are reminiscent of upscale districts in North American cities. This is especially the case in Zona Viva, the posh center of Zona 10, where dozens of smart restaurants, bars, and clubs stay open long after the rest of the city goes to bed. During the day, the New City's museums and cultural sites draw an equally affluent and savvy public.

Avenida La Reforma splits the New City down the middle, with Zona 9 to the west, and Zona 10 (and Zona Viva) to the east. To save confusion, always check which zone your destination is in before heading there.

A Good Tour

Begin at the **Museo Nacional de Arqueología y Etnología** ①, for a crash course in Maya history. Next door, the **Museo Nacional de Arte Moderno** ② will ricochet you into the present with exhibitions of contemporary Guatemalan art. Taxi over to **Zona Viva** ③ for lunch at one of the several terrific restaurants. Afterward, head east on 6 Calle and down a long hill (you could also stop in somewhere to call for a taxi), past 6 Avenida to **Museo Ixchel** ④, arguably the city's best museum, where the traditional Maya textile arts are beautifully emphasized, and then to neighboring **Museo Popol Vuh** ⑤ for a survey of remarkable archeological objects from the Pre-Classic era through colonialism. From here, the **Jardines Botánico** ⑥ is about seven blocks away: walk north on 6 Avenida to 1 Calle and turn left. It's a great way to wind up your predusk day, before heading back to your hotel for a predinner rest.

TIMING

If you visit all the museums and stop for lunch, this tour will easily fill a day. Since the Zona 13 museums are somewhat far from the rest of the attractions in the Zona 10 environs, you'll likely want to get a lift. A taxi is about $5.

Sights to See

⑥ **Jardines Botánico** (Botanical Gardens). At the northern end of Zona 10, the small but lovely gardens contain an impressive collection of plants and a little Natural History Museum, both maintained by the University of San Carlos. ⊠ *Just off Avenida La Reforma on 0 Calle, Zona 10,* ☎ *331–0904.* ☜ *5¢.* ☉ *Weekdays 8–4.*

④ ★ **Museo Ixchel.** The city's best museum focuses on textiles and costumes of Guatemala's indigenous community. An impressive array of handwoven fabrics from 120 Highland communities, some of which date from the 19th century, is displayed here, as well as sculpture, photographs, and paintings, including work by Andres Curruchich, an important and influential Guatemalan folk painter. Multimedia and interactive weaving displays make it engaging for all ages, and there's a café, bookstore, and terrific gift shop, too. The only drawback is its location—at the bottom of a long hill at the Francisco Marroquin University. ⊠ *End of 6 Calle, at 6 Avenida, Zona 10,* ☏ *331–3634.* ⊡ *$2.50.* ☉ *Weekdays 8:30–5:30, Sat. 9–1.*

★ ❺ **Museo Popol Vuh.** Though much smaller than other museums, Popol Vuh has an interesting display of stone carvings from the Pre-Classic period, the earliest pieces of which date from circa 1500 BC. Religious figures wearing headdresses, animals, and mythological half-animal–half-man creatures bear common representational Maya motifs—stolid eyes, hawkish nose, and fierce poses. These are among the best-preserved, and detail is surprisingly intact. Statues range widely in size, but some are quite big, which is particularly impressive given that they were cut from single stones. Also look for the "painted books," which were historical records kept by the Maya. The most famous is the museum's namesake, the Popol Vuh, which was lost (and recovered) after it was transliterated using Roman letters and then translated into Spanish. ⊠ *End of Calle 6, at 6 Avenida, Zona 10,* ☏ *361–2301.* ⊡ *$2.* ☉ *Mon.–Fri. 8–5:30, Sun. 9–1.*

NEED A
BREAK?
You can sip a cappuccino and satisfy your sweet tooth on the porch of **Cafe Zurich** (⊠ 6 Avenida 12–58, Zona 10, ☏ 334–2781), a former colonial home. The menu has specialty coffees, sandwiches, chocolate, and more chocolate.

★ ❶ **Museo Nacional de Arqueología y Etnología** (National Museum of Archaeology and Ethnology). Dedicated to the ancient and modern Maya, it has a large and excellent collection of Maya pottery, jewelry, masks, and costumes, as well as models of the ancient cities themselves. ⊠ *Edificio 5, La Aurora Park, Zona 13,* ☏ *272–0468.* ⊡ *$5.* ☉ *Tues.–Sun. 9–4.*

❷ **Museo Nacional de Arte Moderno** (National Museum of Modern Art). Surrealism and multimedia work are among the wide range of styles represented here by many of Guatemala's most distinguished artists. Efraín Recinos and Zipacna de León are two of Guatemala's most famous artists, and both have permanent displays here. ⊠ *Edificio 6, La Aurora Park, Zona 13,* ☏ *331–0703.* ⊡ *$2.* ☉ *Tues.–Fri. 9–4.*

❸ **Zona Viva.** Lots of upscale restaurants and several nightclubs have popped up here around the towering international hotels. This is undoubtedly the most cosmopolitan area of town, where people dress up, flaunt their appearances and accessories (cell phones and expensive cars are commonplace), and could be residents of any large North American city. The daytime crowd is mostly businessmen; it's at night that the scene is particularly lively. Streets accommodate displaced pedestrians overflowing from the insufficiently tiny sidewalks, where some restaurants have introduced alfresco seating; lines extend from popular discos and bars, and the music inside mixes with the felicitous percussion of the neighborhood. Although Los Proceres shopping mall is nearby, the shops and boutiques that characterize San Salvador's Zona Viva are simply not here; but by simply looking, it's safe to say that things are headed in that direction.

Dining

Virtually every street in the Zona Viva has two or more tempting restaurants, making it almost impossible to go wrong. Some tried-and-true favorites are listed below, but expect newcomers to the neighborhood. Fortunately, Zona Viva is small enough that you can stroll around until you find that perfect place.

CONTEMPORARY

$$ ✕ **Siriacos.** This cheerful bistro serves pasta, seafood, and steak in a vaguely art deco setting, with tall black chairs, modern art on the walls, and tablecloths in primary colors. The Caesar salad and pasta of the day are especially recommended. ✉ *1 Avenida 12–12, Zona 10,* ☎ *334–6316. AE, DC, MC, V. Closed Sun. No lunch Sat.*

ECLECTIC

$$$ ✕ **Jake's.** If you can only go out once to eat in Guatemala City, come
★ here. Jake Denburg, a painter-turned-restaurateur, has used his creative talents to produce a unique international menu, ranging from hand-made smoked chicken tortellini to robálo in a green-pepper sauce. The crowning achievement is the robálo *Venecia royal,* (with a creamy shrimp sauce over a bed of spinach). The setting in which these complex, carefully prepared meals are served is a beautiful converted farmhouse with hardwood ceilings and tile floors. The wine list is quite possibly the best in Central America, and Jake's is the exclusive Guatemala distributor of several top cigar brands. ✉ *17 Calle 10–40, Zona 10,* ☎ *368–0351,* FAX *363–0115. AE, DC, MC, V. Mon.–Sat. 12–3, 7–10:30; Sun. 12–4.*

FRENCH

$$$ ✕ **Jean François.** Even without a sign, this restaurant has been popu-
★ lar since its opening day. Embroidered chairs, hand-carved wooden cherubs on the walls, and gold stars on the ceiling contribute to the dining room's charm; outside, on the patio, candlelit tables provide a more intimate setting. The rich Provençal menu starts you off with such mouthwatering appetizers as shrimp soufflé or chicken mousse. For the main course, try the mushroom and chicken ravioli or the delicate robálo *le classique,* sautéed in butter, fresh green herbs, and spices. ✉ *Diagonal 6, 13–63, Zona 10; look for whitewashed walls, and enter through passage on right,* ☎ *333–4785. DC, MC, V. Closed Sun. No dinner Sat.–Tues.*

GUATEMALAN

$$$ ✕ **Hacienda Real.** Warming the open-air dining room are enchanting,
★ small stone pedestals containing hot coals, so even on a rainy day you needn't pass up the upscale, authentic cuisine. Choose from platters of robálo, shrimp, steak, and pork loin, which are served with a variety of savory condiments, like fresh salsas and pickled carrots and jalapeños. The attentive servers bring endless baskets of warm tortillas, but try not to eat every last one—an after-dinner must is the truly incomparable caramel flan. ✉ *13 Calle 1–10, Zona 10,* ☎ *335–5409. AE, MC, V.*

$$$ ✕ **Los Ranchos.** The pretty blue colonial facade welcomes you with big
★ picture windows to Guatemala's top steak house. Most of the meats, including the rib-eye and chateaubriand, are U.S. imports, but the signature dish is *churrasco Los Ranchos* (the house skirt steak), hailing from Argentina. Appetizers include cassava cream soup and fried pork rinds, and desserts range from tiramisu to the very Guatemalan *tres leches* (cakes injected with three types of milk: sweetened condensed, evaporated, and cream). The excellent wine selection represents Chile and France, among others, and every Saturday there is a ceviche lunch buffet with shrimp, clams, black conch, crab, and squid. ✉ *2 Avenida 14–06, Zona 10,* ☎ *363–5028. AE, DC, MC, V.*

$$$ ✕ **Romanello's.** A classy but popular Zona Viva spot, Romanello's serves
★ a limited but well-prepared selection of the country's best meat and seafood, with both local and Italian influences. The decor is simple but elegant, with pink stucco walls, wooden floors, arched doorways, and

a few antiques. One table in back overlooks an attractive shopping nook with a small garden. There is no menu; you can normally choose from tenderloin, robálo, lobster, and a pasta dish, all of which can be prepared with a number of different sauces. ⊠ *1 Avenida 12–70, Zona 10,* ☎ *368–0690. AE, DC, MC, V. Closed Sun.*

$$ ✕ **Hacienda de los Sanchez.** This steak house is a Zona Viva favorite thanks to its quality cuts of meat, yet the atmosphere alone has won over more than one vegetarian. Guatemala and the old American West meet in the canopied dining room and cozy yet airy patio. The brick floors and copious plants complement the picnic tables and old saddles. Grilled and barbecued meat dominate the menu, but chicken and seafood round it out. There's a full-service bar and a decent wine list. ⊠ *12 Calle 2–25, Zona 10,* ☎ *360–5428. AE, DC, MC, V.*

ITALIAN

$$$ ✕ **Enzo e Lorenzo.** Part of Guatemala's small but growing cadre of remarkable Italian restaurants, this newly opened family establishment treats its guests to great food and a friendly, understated atmosphere. The moment you sit down, a glass of wine and an appetizer are set before you (pray for the *caponata*–it's brilliant), which tide you over while you peruse the menu of classic Italian dishes. The *casarecce* (a sautéed eggplant and mushroom dish), lasagna, and risotto are all excellent choices, and for dessert try the homemade lime sorbet, served in hollowed lime halves, or the *affogato al caffe,* a scoop of vanilla ice cream floating in a cup of strong hot coffee. (Note the Zona 9 address.) ⊠ *7 Avenida 13–01, Zona 9,* ☎ *331–9346. AE, DC, MC, V.*

$$$ ✕ **Tre Fratelli.** Owned by three hip Guatemalans, this flashy, busy restaurant caters to the city's young professionals, serving up cuisine and atmosphere that are part Italian, part new American, and part exotic Guatemalan. Fettuccine *frutti di mare* (with seafood), ravioli *alla Bolognese* (with a variety of meats), and the *quattro stagione* (four season) pizza are house favorites, and fresh oven-baked bread accompanies all meals. Top your meal off with chocolate mousse, homemade ice cream, or just a cappuccino or espresso, brewed in Italian coffee urns. ⊠ *2 Avenida 13–25, Zona 10,* ☎ *366–2678. AE, MC, V. No dinner Sun.*

LATIN

$$$ ✕ **De Mario.** Though firmly rooted in traditional Spanish cuisine, the menu here is one of Guatemala's largest and original, including such entrées as roast suckling pig and a traditional Spanish paella. Mario's robálo with a special mushroom sauce is a standout. The restaurant changed ownership recently, but the present service seems to be living up to the old (and excellent) reputation. ⊠ *13 Calle and 1 Avenida, Zona 10,* ☎ *332–1079. AE, DC, MC, V. Closed Sun.*

MIDDLE EASTERN

$$ ✕ **Olivadda.** The cozy Hotel Santa Clara proffers an ideal lunch spot for tasty Mediterranean fare. A tranquil patio setting, with a melodic fountain, is surrounded by flowers and hummingbirds. Follow traditional Middle Eastern appetizers, such as tabbouleh, baba ghanouj, and falafel, with a chicken-breast sandwich with cumin dressing or *kafta* (delicately spiced beef patties, served in pita bread with tahini). Finish your meal with an orange-and-honey baked apple stuffed with almond and cinnamon. ⊠ *12 Calle 4–21, Zona 10,* ☎ *339–1811. AE, DC, MC, V.*

PIZZA

$$ ✕ **Pizzeria Vesuvio.** The pizza here is baked in an open brick oven, making it Guatemala City's best. Vesuvio has three locations, but this one, in Zona 10, is the most comfortable with its living-room-like setting.

Choose from a variety of pizza creations, or one of several pasta dishes. All of the pasta is made in-house. The grand pizza, sufficient for two people, ranks as one of the city's best cheap meals. ⊠ *18 Calle 3–36, Zona 10,* ☎ *337–1697. DC, MC, V.*

Lodging

$$$$ ⊞ **Camino Real.** Affiliated with the Westin chain, the Camino Real has
★ every service imaginable and a staff that aims to please. It has hosted many celebrities and heads of state. The spacious reception area lies just beyond a long, subdued foyer with a low ceiling, wood-and-mirror walls, and overstuffed leather chairs. The rooms are done in dusty rose, green, and brown and furnished with stately, carved French provincial–style pieces. All rooms have tile baths, cable TV, and three phones. The three executive floors have roomier units with work areas and double French doors from which you can see the volcanoes. ⊠ *14 Calle and Avenida La Reforma, Zona 10,* ☎ *333–4633; (800) 228–3000 in the U.S. and Canada,* FAX *337–4313. 388 rooms. 2 restaurants, 3 bars, minibars, in-room safes, 2 pools, spa, 2 tennis courts, 8 shops, concierge, business services, travel services. AE, DC, MC, V.* ✑

$$$$ ⊞ **El Dorado Marriott.** Though its facade is hardly attractive, El Dorado's beauty is in its location, near Zona Viva. Inside, a spacious reception area and lounge offer rest to the weary; guests plop down in the couches and armchairs and order cocktails while jazz tunes play on. Beyond the lobby are the bar, restaurants, shops, offices, and the Cabaña Club, a spa and sports facility open to all guests. Rooms are carpeted, with pink, purple, and green floral drapes and bedspreads. Each has a small balcony, cable TV, and tile bath. Note that this is in Zona 9, not Zona 10. ⊠ *7 Avenida 15–45, Zona 9,* ☎ *331–7777; (800) 228–9290,* FAX *332–1877, dorado@guate.net. 385 rooms. 3 restaurants, bar, minibars, pool, spa, meeting rooms, travel services. AE, DC, MC, V.*

$$$$ ⊞ **Hotel Residencial La Casa Grande.** This comfortable hotel in a stately former residence is a wonderful New City lodging choice. A classical statue greets you just inside the iron gates, while the small reception area opens into a comfortable lounge with a fireplace. The restaurant is in the former courtyard; its cast-iron chairs are surrounded by stout pillars and arches and dangling philodendrons. Rooms have tile floors and are furnished with Guatemalan antiques and reproductions. Front units open onto a balcony, but back rooms are quieter. ⊠ *Avenida La Reforma 7–67, Zona 10,* ☎ *332–0914* FAX *336–7911. 28 rooms. Restaurant. AE, DC, MC, V.*

$$$$ ⊞ **Mansión San Carlos.** Formerly the owner's own home, this modest colonial hotel puts a little space between you and the bustling Zona Viva. Ceiling-to-floor windows in the reception area look onto a sunny courtyard with statues and a fountain-cum-pool. Low sloping stairs lead up to seven elegant and individually decorated rooms with hardwood floors and doors, and colonial furnishings. The shapes of the rooms go beyond the basic box. Other rooms in an inviting annex beyond the courtyard are newer but more predictable, resembling chain hotel rooms, with prefabricated furniture. Internet access is available. ⊠ *Avenida La Reforma 7–89, Zona 10,* ☎ FAX *362–9077/9076, hscarlos@gua.net 21 rooms. Restaurant, business services. AE, DC, MC, V.*

$$$$ ⊞ **Meliá Guatemala.** At this business-class hotel on the city's south side, two giant glass elevators in the atrium-style lobby ascend to a dizzying view of the city and the surrounding volcanoes. Meliá caters to large conventions, with 22 meeting rooms, 16 ballrooms, and 24-hour office services, from copy machines to secretaries. The bright, modern rooms have comfy beds, minibar, and cable TV; special business suites come with two telephones and an ironing station. Rooms on the south side have the most impressive views of the Agua (inactive) and Pacaya

(active) volcanoes—even the 6th-floor exercise gym has great views. Its location is near the airport just 3 km (1.9 mi) away, along with shops and some restaurants, but you'll be quite a distance from Zona Viva. ✉ *Avenida Las Américas 9–08, Zona 13,* ☎ *339–0666; 800/339–3542 in the U.S.,* FAX *339–0690. melia.guatemala@solmelia.es. 194 rooms, 2 suites. 2 restaurants, exercise room, sauna, spa, car rental. AE, DC, MC, V.* ✇

$$$$ 🏨 **Stofella.** For those looking for a small-scale and classy business hotel in Zona 10, Stofella is a real find. A short staircase at the end of a long walkway leads to a small, flower-filled reception area decorated in soothing earth tones. A similar color scheme is carried out in the rooms, which have double beds and a small alcove/sitting room off the bedroom. You can rent a cellular phone, fax, and computer. A Jacuzzi, gym, and cozy bar are available for après-work. ✉ *2 Avenida 12–28, Zona 10,* ☎ *334–6191,* FAX *331–0823. 28 suites. Bar, exercise room, laundry service, business services. AE, DC, MC, V.*

$$$ 🏨 **Cortijo Reforma.** Don't be put off by its drab, T-shape, 16-story high-rise towers: Cortijo is a largely relaxing and comfortable place to set up camp, especially if you get a kick out of 1970s-style decor. Each suite has a double bed and sofabed (easily sleeping four in total), full kitchen, and minibar. Most have 1½ bathrooms. Many rooms have volcano views, and north-facing units overlook the Torre del Reformador, a scaled-down version of the Eiffel Tower that lights up at night. The staff is experienced and friendly. ✉ *Avenida La Reforma 2–18, Zona 9,* ☎ *332–0712; 800/344–1212 in the U.S.; 0800/951–000 in London;* FAX *331–8876. 150 suites. Restaurant, bar, barbershop, beauty salon, meeting rooms, travel services. AE, DC, MC, V.*

$$$ 🏨 **Hotel Santa Clara.** This colonial house-turned-hotel has the atmosphere and character that more modern hotels in the city lack. Ivy-covered walls giving way to a small carpeted reception area mark the entrance, and most rooms surround a breezy interior corridor overflowing with potted plants and wood carvings. Others have a shared balcony with spiral staircase, overlooking a small outdoor corridor. The rooms are softly lit, have wooden paneling and tiled floors, and nice touches like dried flowers and rustic paintings. The Middle Eastern restaurant ☞ **Olivadda** is particularly recommended. ✉ *12 Calle 4–51, Zona 10,* ☎ *339–1811,* FAX *332–0775. santaclara@pronet.com.gt 14 rooms. Restaurant, room service. AE, DC, MC, V.*

Nightlife

The Zona Viva is the city's nightlife center, with everything from quiet bars to fashionable discos. All of the following can be found here. **The Brass Beer Company** (✉ 3 Avenida 12–48) serves a variety of excellent in-house brews to a mellow crowd. **Guiseppe Verdi** (✉ 14 Calle at Avenida La Reforma) is an upscale bar at the Camino Real Hotel. **Sesto Senso** (✉ 2 Avenida 12–81) draws an international crowd with indoor and outdoor seating, and once-weekly live music ranging from Guatemalan classics (ranchero or folksy) to classic rock. Discos come and go, but the good ones of the moment are **Loro's** (✉ 1 Avenida 13–27), **Rich and Famous** (✉ upstairs at Los Proceres Mall, on Avenida La Reforma and Blvd. de los Proceres), and **Status** (✉ 4 Avenida 3–49). **El Establo** (✉ Avenida La Reforma 14–32) and **Shakespeare's** (✉ 13 Calle 1–51) are good places to meet travelers and American expats, although the former is a bit sketchy.

Outside of the Zona Viva, there are a number of bars on Avenida Las Américas, between 4 and 9 calles, that are hip and youthful without being sophomoric. Movies listed in local papers are most often in Spanish with English subtitles.

Shopping

With the exception of the big market in the Old City, shop hours are weekdays 10–1 and 3–7, Saturday 10–1.

ART

You can buy artwork by contemporary Guatemalan painters at **Arte 21 Galería** (⊠ Plaza Colonial, 1 Avenida 12–47, Zona 10), **Galería Ríos** (⊠ Calle Montufar 0–85, Zona 9), and **Sol de Río** (⊠ 5 Avenida 10–22, Zona 9).

BOOKS

Sophos (⊠ Avenida La Reforma 13–89, El Portal shopping square) is the best place for new books in English (and German and French) in Zona 10, with everything from travel guides to Toni Morrison, and for a cup of coffee while you peruse. In Zona 9, **Librería el Pensativo** (⊠ 7 Avenida 13–01) and **Cervantes** (⊠ Avenida La Reforma 13–70) have new titles in English. Used English-language paperbacks (including Westerns) are sold and lent in a bar called ☞ **El Establo**, *above*. The gift shop at the ☞ **Popol Vuh Museum** *above* has interesting art, folk objects, and history books. The **IGA** (Instituto Guatemalteco Americano, ⊠ Ruta 1, 4–05, Zona 4, ☎ 331–0022) has an extensive English-language lending library and moderately priced Internet access.

JEWELRY

Jades S.A. (⊠ Camino Real, 14 Calle and Ave. La Reforma, Zona 10) is a branch of the well-known Antigua jade factory and retail shop. **La Esmeralda** (⊠ Camino Real, 14 Calle and Ave. La Reforma, Zona 10) specializes in, you guessed it, emeralds. **Joyería el Sol** (⊠ 13 Calle 2–75, Zona 10) is another of the city's better jewelers. **L'Elegance** (⊠ Camino Real, 14 Calle and Ave. La Reforma, Zona 10) sells exquisitely crafted silver trays, jewelry boxes, vases, and place settings by the Italian design family Camusso.

LEATHER

Shops with fine leather products include **Arpiel** (⊠ Avenida La Reforma 15–54, Zona 9; ⊠ Avenida Las Américas 7–20, Zona 13), **Boutique Mariano Riva** (⊠ 12 Calle 1–28, Zona 9; ⊠ Avenida La Reforma 15–54, Zona 9), and **Tata** (⊠ Avenida La Reforma 12–81, Zona 10).

TÍPICA

An above-ground source for típica is the **handicrafts market** (⊠ 6 Calle in La Aurora Park, Zona 13). A number of stores sell handicrafts and European styles mixed with traditional weaving. **Sombol** (⊠ 14 Calle and Ave. La Reforma, Zona 9) has an impressive collection of clothing, textiles, and paintings. The smaller **El Gran Jaguar** (⊠ 14 Calle 7–49, Zona 9) is across the street and down a bit; the much bigger and grander **San Remo** (⊠ 14 Calle 7–61, Zona 9) is next door and **Típicos Reforma Utatlán** (⊠ 14 Calle 7–77, Zona 13) is on the same block. Across Avenida La Reforma, in Zona 10, there are several small típica shops at the corner of 1 Avenida and 13 Calle. One block south is **Bizzarro** (⊠ 14 Calle and 1 Avenida, Zona 10). **Belloto** (⊠ Avenida La Reforma 11–07, Zona 10) has a creditable selection, as does the elegant **Casa Solares** (⊠ Avenida La Reforma 11–07, Zona 10).

The Old City

Older and grittier than Zona 10, the Old City (Zona 1) can be both hustle and bustle in the way of many Central American capitals. But sightseeing on foot (or bus) is easily managed. A walk through the **Parque del Centenario and Plaza de las Armas** (⊠ between 6–8 calles and 5–7 avenidas) will lead you past clusters of historical landmarks that survived the 19th century's earthquakes. At one end of the park is a huge band shell, where military bands and other musicians perform; the adjacent plaza is expansive, with a fountain in the middle, and bordered immediately by park benches, then by the National Palace, the main cathedral, and the central market, a semi-underground arcade packed with vendors.

A Good Walk

History buffs will want to begin at the **Centro Cultural Miguel Angel Asturias** ⑦, but those on the fly should head for the Plaza de las Armas where the **Palacio Nacional** ⑧, **Catedral Metropolitano** ⑨, and **Mercado Central** ⑩ are clustered.

TIMING
A few hours should suffice to see the Old City sights.

Sights to See

❾ **Catedral Metropolitano** (Metropolitan Cathedral). The intriguing edifice has ornate altars, statues, and colonial religious art, including the *Assumption of the Virgin,* or the Patron Saint of Guatemala. Built between 1782 and 1868, a rare example of pre-earthquake architecture in the Old City, it stands solidly on the east end of the Plaza de las Armas. A marble fence around the building also serves as a memorial. ⊠ *8 Calle and 7 Avenida,* ☎ *no phone.* ☜ *Free.* ۞ *Daily 8–6.*

❽ **Centro Cultural Miguel Angel Asturias.** The imposing Teatro Nacional, the open-air Teatro del Aire Libre (a former military amphitheater), and a small museum of antique arms largely constitute this multibuilding cultural center named for the Guatemalan Nobel Prize–winning novelist. Asturias opposed the dictatorship—and subsequently spent much of his life in exile—which used the Teatro Libre for its public proclamations and rallies. ⊠ *24 Calle 3–81, Centro Cívico,* ☎ *332–4042.* ☜ *Free.* ۞ *Weekdays 10–4.*

❿ **Mercado Central** (Central Market). The underground market is a seemingly endless maze of passages where handicrafts from throughout the country are hawked from overstocked stalls. Compared to the open-air markets in Antigua or Chichicastenango, the mercado is ugly and less inviting, but the wares—leather, wood masks and statuary, clothing and blankets—are often cheaper here. A peep at the colorful and exotic fruit stands on the first floor can be wonderful cultural and sensory experience, although the perishable yet nonrefrigerated items for sale means that farther in it can also be a little too sensory. ⊠ *8 Calle and 8 Avenida,* ☎ *no phone.* ۞ *Mon.–Sat. 9–6, Sun. 9–noon.*

If religious art and architecture are one of the reasons you're here, pop inside **La Merced** (5 Calle and 11 Avenida), consecrated in 1813, to see its baroque interior. It's just a few blocks east of the Mercado Central. Many of these elaborate paintings and sculptures once decorated Antigua's original La Merced but were moved with the capital to Guatemala City. It's open daily 6 AM–7 PM.

Sure, you can mail things from your hotel, but as one of the city's prettier buildings, the cantaloupe-color **Edificio de Correos Central** (Main Post Office: 7 Avenida 12–11, ☎ 332–6101) is worth a visit if you have something to drop in the slot. It's four blocks south of the Catedral Metropolitano and open weekdays 8–7 and Saturday 8–3.

The **Iglesia de San Francisco,** (6 Avenida and 13 Calle) built between 1800 and 1851, has an ornate wooden altar and small museum. Across the street from San Francisco is the church of **Santa Clara** (6 Avenida and 13 Calle), notable for its purple lace hangings and blue walls. The wildest church of them all is the neo-Gothic **Iglesia Yurrita** (Ruta 6, between 7 Av. and Av. La Reforma), with bizarre stained-glass windows and weird carvings where you'd expect the Addams Family would go for Sunday Mass.

⑧ Palacio Nacional (National Palace). The grandiose palace built during the presidency of Jorge Ubico between 1939 and 1944 once held the offices of the president and his ministers, but now its five floors and 320 rooms house a fine **art museum.** The collection of paintings and sculptures by well-known Guatemalan artists was moved here from Antigua after that city's devastating earthquake. Look for Alfredo Galvez Suarez's mural above the entry. The palace's ornate stairways, stained glass, fountains, and quiet courtyards form a pleasant contrast to the city outside its walls. The guards will lead you to the presidential balcony off the banquet room for a *propina* (tip). ⊠ *6 Calle and 7 Avenida,* ☎ *221–4444, ext. 1133.* ☞ *65¢.* ☉ *Weekdays 9–5:30, weekends 9–4:30.*

OFF THE
BEATEN PATH

RELIEF MAP – Created in 1904, this cement map depicting Guatemala's precipitous topography is so immense that you have to view it from an observation tower. ⊠ *Minerva Park, at end of Avenida Simon Cañas, Zona 2,* ☎ *no phone.* ☞ *Free.* ☉ *Daily 8–4.*

KAMINALJUYÚ – From 300 BC to AD 900, an early Maya city of some 50,000 people flourished in what is now the heart of Zona 7. Though most of this city is buried beneath today's urban sprawl, this impressive site, which includes several pyramid bases, offers a glimpse of the area's prehistory. Some of the objects found here are on display at the archaeological and Popol Vuh museums (☞ New City, *above*).

Dining
American/Casual

$ ✕ **Europa Bar and Restaurante.** Judy Strong, an Oregon native, created this long-standing hangout for travelers and American expatriates. The second-floor bar has a welcoming atmosphere where you can relax, play backgammon, or watch a sports event on cable TV. Expect American mainstays like hamburgers, chili, *pollo migado* (breaded chicken), and mashed potatoes, and a diner-style breakfast of pancakes or eggs, bacon, and hash browns. ⊠ *11 Calle 5–16, Zona 1,* ☎ *253–4929. No credit cards. Closed Sun.*

Café

$ ✕ **Café de Imeri.** Follow your craving for wonderful cakes, pies, and coffee to this elegant eatery in an old house with a barrel-tile roof and wooden balcony. Predessert items, such as sandwiches and soups are also available. You can dine indoors or in a luxuriantly planted courtyard with a small fountain at one end, but the tables on the balcony above the courtyard are the best of them all. ⊠ *6 Calle 3–34, Zona 1,* ☎ *232–3722. No credit cards. Closed Sun.*

Guatemalan

$$ ✕ **Arrin Cuan.** Ask a local to recommend a restaurant in the Old City, and most will send you to this spirited and classy Guatemalan restaurant decorated with bright handwoven fabrics, wooden masks, and soda-bottle flower vases. The flavorful cuisine is typical of the Cobán area: choices include *kak-ik* (a spicy turkey stew), *gallo en chicha* (chicken in a slightly sweet sauce), the more adventurous *sopa de tortuga* (turtle soup), and roasted tepezcuintle. On Friday and Saturday nights, you'll dine to live marimba music. ⊠ *5 Avenida 3–27, Zona 1,* ☎ *238–0242/ 0172. AE, DC, MC, V.*

$ ✕ **Mi Comedor.** Pictures of the Last Supper, fish tanks, and fake flowers adorn this bright and friendly mom-and-pop eatery. Daily breakfast and lunch specials are straight-up Guatemalan: eggs, beans, homemade cheese, chorizo, and tortillas—most for under $3. Order the fresh-squeezed O.J., if you like it nice and tart. And no one speaks English, so brush up on your "Huevos, por favor" on the way over. ⊠ *10 Calle, between 8 and 9 Avenidas,* ☎ *no phone. No credit cards.*

Mexican

$$ ✕ **Los Cebollines.** The decor is rather banal, but the attraction here is the wide selection of delicious Mexican food. There are two menus: a drink menu, with cocktails, Mexican beers, and sangria; and a food menu, with traditional tacos, burritos, fajitas, and, less predictably, *caldo tlalpeno de pollo* (a chicken stew with chickpeas and avocado). A sister restaurant in the New City has the same name and menu, but a touch more elegance. ⊠ *6 Avenida 9–75, Zona 1,* ☎ *232–7750;* ⊠ *1 Avenida 13–42, Zona 10,* ☎ *368–0663. AE, DC, MC, V.*

$$ ✕ **El Gran Pavo.** You can't miss El Gran Pavo—it's a pink building with a gaudy neon sign on top, and the inside is just as flashy as the facade. Bright colors bedazzle the innocent initiate, and mirrors, plants, Mexican hats, and blankets add to the sensory load. The food is authentic Mexican, with the standard *taquitas* (tacos), enchiladas, and *moles,* but you'll also run across items like *aujas nortenas* (grilled beef strips covered with a red sauce and surrounded by avocado slices) and *camarones siempre joven* (shrimp in a spicy black chili sauce). The restaurant is open past midnight and has live music, including mariachis, who can also perform private concerts for a small fee. ⊠ *13 Calle 4–41, Zona 1,* ☎ *232–9912. AE, DC, MC, V.*

Spanish

$$ ✕ **Altuna.** This popular restaurant in an old house a block from 6
★ Avenida serves a predominantly Spanish menu in a pleasantly bustling atmosphere. Waiters move briskly about in white jackets and ties in the main dining area—a covered courtyard surrounded by a wooden railing and potted plants—or in several adjacent rooms decorated with Iberian paintings, photographs, and posters. The menu is fairly limited; consider the calamari, filet mignon with mushroom sauce, or paella. Prices lean toward the low end of moderate. ⊠ *5 Avenida 12–31, Zona 1,* ☎ *251–7195, 232–0669. AE, DC, MC, V. Open noon–11 PM, closed Mon.*

$ ✕ **El Mesón de Don Quijote.** A colorful restaurant in the heart of the Old City, Don Quijote serves respectable northern Spanish cuisine—Asturian, to be exact—at reasonable prices. It's a favorite late-night spot (open until 1 AM) with Guatemalan old-timers. The long bar is adjoined by several dining rooms, and hosts live music at night under a flashy painting of a flamenco dancer. The large menu is filled with such palate pleasers as seafood casserole, cold cuts of Spanish ham, lentils with sausage, baked lamb, and paella (for four people or more). On weekdays, the four-course executive lunch can't be beat. ⊠ *11 Calle 5–27, Zona 1,* ☎ *232–1741. AE, DC, MC, V. Closed Sun.*

Lodging

$$$ ▥ **Pan American.** Truly the grande dame of downtown hotels, the Pan
★ American was the most luxurious lodging in town in the mid-20th century. To step into the lobby of this former mansion is to leave the confusion of the city and busy address behind. The lobby is a spacious, covered courtyard with attractive wrought-iron chandeliers and tables spilling out from the restaurant, whose servers dress in traditional highland costumes. The rooms are small but attractive, with tile floors, throw rugs, highland bedspreads, and walls adorned with traditional weavings and paintings. The Old World charm is complemented by the technology of the New World, with Internet access for guests. ⊠ *9 Calle 5–63, Zona 1,* ☎ *232–6807,* ℻ *232–6402, panamhot@invovia.com.gt.*

56 rooms. Restaurant, concierge, travel services, airport shuttle. AE, DC, MC, V.

$$ ▦ **Chalet Suizo.** This quiet hotel has been popular with budget travelers for more than 40 years. Most of the rooms face a series of small courtyards and are fairly plain, with tile floors and small beds with thin mattresses; but the place is clean, friendly, and will store extra luggage while you travel around the country. An attractive courtyard behind the reception area has carved wooden pillars and a few tables and chairs. ⊠ *14 Calle 6–82, Zona 1,* ☎ *251–3786,* ▯▯ *232–0429. 47 rooms, 15 with bath. Restaurant, travel services. No credit cards.*

$$ ▦ **Fortuna Royal.** The Fortuna Royal has succeeded where few others have: It combines American-style comfort and cut-rate prices in the middle of the Old City. The lobby's marble floors and wood paneling give way to wall-to-wall carpeting and floral wallpaper in the rooms, all of which are spacious and immaculately clean. ⊠ *12 Calle 8–42, Zona 1,* ☎ *230–3378,* ▯▯ *251–2215. 20 rooms. Restaurant, room service. AE, DC, MC, V.*

$$ ▦ **Hotel Colonial.** Although it occupies a lovely 19th-century town house, this hotel doesn't live up to the expectations raised by its facade. Nevertheless it's a pleasant enough place with a few exceptional rooms—ask for one of the larger, well-furnished rooms or one with a view. The reception area overlooks an enclosed patio full of potted plants and small tables, and the small lounge is furnished with antique reproductions. The rooms have wooden floors, colonial-style decor (including fake fireplaces), and small modern baths. ⊠ *7 Avenida 14–19, Zona 1,* ☎ *232–6722 or 232–2955,* ▯▯ *232–8671. colonial@infovia.com.gt 42 rooms. Breakfast room. AE, DC, MC, V.*

$$ ▦ **Hotel Spring.** All the rooms in this Spanish colonial–style hotel have
★ high ceilings, carpeting, and firm beds, and most face a large, pleasant courtyard filled with potted plants and cast-iron tables and chairs. There's a small café behind the courtyard, and several rooms on the second floor share a balcony that overlooks the avenue. The Spring is a good deal, but note that the shelter next door is a refuge for street children, so keep your eyes open for those tempted to pickpocket a less-than-alert tourist. ⊠ *8 Avenida 12–65, Zona 1,* ☎ *232–6637,* ▯▯ *232–0107. 40 rooms, 22 with bath. AE, DC, MC, V.*

$$ ▦ **Posada Belén.** This little bed-and-breakfast on a quiet side street is
★ exceptional, thanks to the couple who run it. Built in 1873, the building is the family's former home and has been renovated just enough to combine Old World charm with modern comfort. Rooms have tile floors, handwoven bedspreads, and walls decorated with Guatemalan paintings and weavings. Family-style meals are made to order by the owners, who are also a fount of information about the city and getting around it. ⊠ *13 Calle "A" 10–30, Zona 1,* ☎ *232–9226,* ▯▯ *251–3478. 10 rooms. Dining room, library, travel services, airport shuttle. AE, DC, MC, V.*

$ ▦ **Hotel Ajau.** This basic and somewhat run-down hotel is built in the Spanish style, with an interior courtyard and three floors of balconied rooms. The rooms are clean, and have tile floors and a few pieces of cheap wooden furniture; those with bath also have cable TV. Rooms facing away from the street are quieter. ⊠ *8 Avenida 15–62, Zona 1,* ☎ *232–0488,* ▯▯ *251–8097. 43 rooms, 23 with bath. No credit cards.*

Nightlife

Old City nightspots have more character than those in the New City, so they shouldn't be passed up just because the area isn't the greatest. Walking alone at night isn't a good idea, especially south of 15 Calle; although the nightspots listed here are all north of here, you'll still see shady characters. It's best to take a cab for any destination more than a few blocks away, especially for those staying in the New City, since after 8 PM many New City buses only go as far as the Calle 18–Avenida 5 bus stop, which is a notoriously seedy area, although the bus stop itself is well lit.

Folksy and intellectual, **La Bodeguita del Centro** (⊠ 2 Calle 3–55, ☏ 230–2976), has live music, poetry readings, and good beer. If you're just looking for beer, visit **Europa Bar** (⊠ 11 Calle 5–16, Zona 1) or, if you feel like dancing, go to **El Gazabo** (⊠ 6 Calle at 3 Avenida, Zona 1). **El Mesón de Don Quijote** (⊠ 11 Calle 5–27, Zona 1) is open until 1 AM and has live music that draws a 30-and-up crowd.

Shopping

If you're looking for handicrafts and aren't headed for Antigua or the Highlands, the best place for them here is in Zona 1 at the **Mercado Central** (☞ *above*), where you'll find jewelry, leather, and handwoven fabrics. If the passages of the Central Market make you claustrophobic, try the vendors of the **Portal Comercio** (⊠ Commercial Arcade, south of the Plaza de las Armas) or stroll through the **Plaza de las Armas** (⊠ 6 Calle and 7 Avenida) on Sunday for a look at the wares.

Specialty típica shops in Zona 1 include **Maya Modern** (⊠ 7 Avenida and 9 Calle), **Lin Canola** (⊠ 5 Calle 9–60) and **La Momosteca** (⊠ 7 Avenida 14–48).

Side Trip: The Pacific Coast

For white-sand beaches, head to the Caribbean. For outdoor adventure, head southwest of the capital for the Monterrico natural reserve, white-water rafting on the Coyolate River, or world-class billfishing for sailfish, marlin, and tuna.

The **Biotopo Monterrico** (Monterrico Nature Reserve: 48 km south of Guatemala City) encompasses 6,916 acres of seashore, mangrove swamp, and dense tropical forest, and is home to more than 100 species of migratory and indigenous birds. Bird-watching boat tours are $9 and best done in the very early morning. Turtles swim ashore from July to February, and you can often see them digging nests for their eggs at night. The village of Monterrico even has a decent beach, but be careful: the ocean can be rough.

Guatemala's southern coast is arguably the most productive billfishing spot in the world, especially during fall and spring, and several world records have been set here. The targets are enormous 80–150-lb sailfish, but 100-lb yellow tuna and 400-lb blue marlin are often caught in the outer waters. **Artmarina** (☞ Fins 'n Feathers Inn, *below*) and **Marina El Capitan** (⊠ ☏ 881–4403/4397) are the best fishing companies in the area, with single and multiday excursions from the Iztapa area. The fishing is great, but this isn't a sport for the financially needy.

On an exhilarating **white-water rafting trip** down the Rio Coyolate (June through October), you'll pass iguanas sunning themselves on overhanging branches, flitting morpho butterflies, and warm waterfalls. Trips are safely run by Area Verde and Clark Tours (☞ Guided Tours, *below*) with English-speaking guides. Routes on the Coyolate have Class II and III rapids, perfect for beginners, although both companies have more difficult routes elsewhere, too. Transportation (from Antigua or Guatemala City), breakfast, and lunch on the riverbank following the trip are included in the $85 per-person price.

Dining and Lodging

There are several moderately priced hotels along the seashore in Monterrico, most of which are little more than concrete rooms with mosquito netting. They have no addresses but are easy to find along the small beach. **Hotel Baule Beach** (☎ 473–6196 in Guatemala City) has a good restaurant. Farther down are well-kept, pastel-color bungalows rented by **Pez de Oro** (☎ no phone).

$$ ✕ **Divino Maestro.** You may as well eat at the best restaurant in Monterrico, a simple place with a thatched roof in an open-air room. There is no fixed menu, but you can choose from four types of fresh fish as well as crab, shrimp, meat, or chicken. The *caldo de mariscos* (seafood stew) is delicious. ⊠ *Aldea of Monterrico,* ☎ *no phone. No credit cards.*

$$$$ ▥ **Fins 'n Feathers Inn.** Operated by the Miami fishing outfit Artmarina, the Fins 'n Feathers Inn is an oasis of luxury in the droopy, former port town of Iztapa. With an outdoor restaurant, in-room Jacuzzis, and a bulbous pool, it's designed for maximum relaxation after a long day at the rod and reel. Four spacious villas have kitchenettes, living rooms, and sun decks, while the restaurant specializes in imported steaks and, of course, freshly caught fish. ⊠ *Iztapa, 12 mi east of San José,* ☎ *881–4035/4956; 800/882-4665 or 305/663–3553 in the U.S.,* ℻ *305/666–6445 in the U.S., fish@artmarina.com. 4 suites. Restaurant, bar, pool, fishing, airport shuttle. AE, DC, MC, V. www.artmarina.com.*

$$$ ▥ **Hotel Turicentro Martita.** This large, modern hotel has cool rooms and enticing swimming pools, both welcome services in the typically hot and muggy climate here. Though somewhat sterile and overpriced, Martita is Puerto San José's best hotel and is popular among middle-class Guatemalan families and foreign embassy employees on vacation from their posts in the capital. They also have Internet access. ⊠ *Route 9, just north of the central plaza, Puerto San José,* ☎ *881–1337/ 1339 in San José, 474–1189 in Guatemala City;* ℻ *881–1246 in San José, 474–1126 in Guatemala City. 38 rooms. Restaurant, bar, air-conditioning, 2 pools, travel services, airport shuttle. AE, DC, MC, V.*

Getting Here

By Bus. Buses depart from the main bus station in Guatemala City for Taxisco and Puerto San José every half hour. Microbuses depart from Taxisco regularly for La Avellana, where there's a ferry to Monterrico Beach. In Puerto San Jose, taxis and local buses can take you to Iztapa.

By Car. Take the highway to Escuintla from Guatemala City. At Escuintla, head east toward Taxisco, and follow the road to La Avellana and the Moterrico ferry. For Puerto San José, continue south on Highway 9 past Esquintla until it ends at a truck depot. From there, San José is to the right, and Iztapa is to the left.

Guatemala City A to Z

Arriving and Departing

BY AIRPLANE

Less than a mile from Zona 9 or 10, **La Aurora Airport** (☎ 332–6084, 332–6085, 332–6086, or 332–6087) is a bit too close for comfort, but it's where planes for quick trips to Tikal (Flores Airport) and international flights are based. A taxi to the airport from downtown runs $6–$8.

BY CAR

All roads lead to Guate, or so it would seem. If you enter by land, it's easy to drive (or hop a bus) to the capital.

Getting Around

BY BUS

The bus system seems chaotic, but buses are cheap and plentiful, if somewhat run-down. Locals are usually happy to point you to the one you need. The No. 82, No. 83, and No. 101 cover the essential routes, including La Reforma (Zona 9/10), the main bus terminal (Zona 4), and 10 Avenida (Zona 1). Other buses also serve La Reforma and say REFORMA on the windshield; likewise, buses that say TERMINAL all pass by the main bus station in Zona 4. Only the No. 83 buses marked AEROPUERTO go to the airport. Bus service pretty much ends at 8 PM. Watch your belongings (especially the ones containing your money) while boarding, riding, and exiting the bus.

BY CAR

Tabarini Rent-a-Car (⊠ 2 Calle A 7–30, Zona 10, ☎ 331–2643 or 331–2707, ℻ 334–1925; La Aurora Airport, ☎ 331–4755), a local agency, with six branches in Guatemala, lets you pick up a car in one city and drop it off in another.

BY TAXI

Taxis park throughout the city—usually near major hotels, parks, or intersections—and can usually be flagged down on major streets. Most do not have meters, so negotiate a price before getting in. Within the same zone, a ride should cost $2–$3; between zones, expect to pay $4–$6.

Contacts and Resources

EMERGENCIES

Ambulance (Red Cross, ☎ 125). **Fire** (☎ 122 or 123). **Police** (☎ 120).

Hospitals. Hospital Herrera Llerandí (⊠ 6 Avenida 8–51, Zona 10, ☎ 334–5959 and 332–5455) and **Centro Médico** (⊠ 6 Avenida 3–47, Zona 10, ☎ 332–3555).

Pharmacies. If you're a little out of sorts, there's no reason to leave your hotel, because **Farmacias KLEE** (☎ 360–8383) will deliver to your room 24 hours a day. **El Sauce Las Américas** (⊠ Calle 23 and Avenida Las Américas, Zona 13, ☎ 331–5996) is also open 24 hours a day, but doesn't deliver. **Farmacia Americana** (Zonas 9, 10, 13, 14, and 15, ☎ 360–2914) offers free delivery to hotels 8 AM–7 PM daily. **Farmacia San José** (⊠ 5 Avenida 16–56, Zona 1, ☎ 232–5314) closes at 6 PM.

GUIDED TOURS

Many major tour operators offer half- and full-day city tours as well as day trips and adventure trips to outlying sites and towns. **Area Verde** (☎ 832–3383 or 832–6506 in Antigua, 🖎) has white-water rafting and kayaking day trips and excursions. **Clark Tours** (⊠ Hotel Camino Real, Zona 10, ☎ 368–2056; ⊠ Hotel Las Américas, Zona 13, ☎ 339–0676; ⊠ Zona 1, ☎ 251–4172; and ☎ (800) 707–5275 in U.S.). **Jaguar Tours** (⊠ Edificio Topazio Azul, 13 Calle 2–60, Zona 10, locale 1, ☎ 334–0421). **Tropical Tours** (⊠ 4 Calle 2–51, Zona 10; ⊠ 6 Avenida "A" 10–52, Zona 1, ☎ 334–5893). **Turansa** (⊠ Km 15 Carretera Roosevelt, Zona 11, locale 69, ☎ 595–3575). **Unitours** (⊠ Hotel Camino Real, Zona 10, ☎ 337–2858, 337–2861, or 333–4633, ext. 6939, ℻ 337–2861; ⊠ 7 Avenida 7–91, Zona 4, ☎ 331–4199 or 331–4103, ℻ 334–2001).

VISITOR INFORMATION

Guatemala's ever-helpful government tourism office, **INGUAT** (⊠ 7 Avenida 1–17, Centro Cívico, Zona 4, ☎ 331–2995 or 332–7628), is open weekdays 8–4 and Saturday 8–1.

ANTIGUA

45 km (28 mi) west of Guatemala City.

Guatemala's most Spanish town, Antigua is filled with vestiges of its past—cobblestone streets, enchanting convents, and vine-covered ruins—and is surrounded by the three looming (and sometimes smoking) volcanoes, Agua, Acantenango, and Fuego. Founded in 1543, the city was initially called Santiago de los Caballeros de Guatemala (St. James of the Knights of Guatemala), after the patron saint of the Spanish conquistadors. For 200 years it was the capital of an area that is now Central America and the Mexican state of Chiapas and was, along with Lima and Mexico City, one of the three great cities of the Americas.

By the late 18th century, Santiago had been destroyed by earthquakes and rebuilt several times, and was a major political, religious, intellectual, and economic center. It had 32 churches, 18 convents and monasteries, a university, seven colleges, five hospitals, beautiful private mansions, wide cobblestone boulevards, and many small parks with fountains. However, late in 1773, powerful tremors struck again, reducing much of the city's painstakingly restored elegance to rubble. Reluctantly, the government relocated to a safer site in the Ermita Valley 45 km (28 mi) east, where Guatemala City now stands

Razed and haggard as it was, Santiago was further violated by the relocation project. Gradually, all that could be stripped and carried—art, furniture, doors, tiles, columns—was moved to the new capital. Even the city's name was lost; renamed La Antigua (Old) Guatemala, it's most commonly called simply "Antigua."

Ironically, it is because Antigua was abandoned that it retains so much of its colonial character. Only the poorest inhabitants stayed put after the capital was moved, and being of limited means they could only repair the old structures, not build anew. In the 1960s protective laws took effect, limiting commercial development and requiring all development to remain in keeping with the city's colonial architecture; and in 1972 the National Council for the Protection of Antigua Guatemala was formed to restore ruins, maintain monuments, and rid the city of such modern intrusions as billboards and neon signage. Recent restoration projects, both private and public, have beautified if not transformed this once-rustic hamlet into a hip and trendy—but still captivating—destination.

Today you'll find a mountainside enclave of culture and the arts that is vastly more pleasant and sophisticated than Guatemala City. Antigua seems to better combine the charmed remnants of its colonial past with amenities of the modern world than the capital. Its luxuries and higher prices mean that many native peoples cannot afford to live here, however, and instead many travel to the city daily to sell their wares. An ever-increasing influx of visitors, both foreign and domestic, has led to increased tourist services as well as some of Guatemala's finest hotels and restaurants, a plethora of shops and galleries, and several dozen Spanish-language schools that attract students from all over the world. Antigua is a favored escape for wealthy Guatemalans, and many foreigners live here permanently, running small lodgings and restaurants.

The most spectacular time to be in Antigua is Semana Santa (Holy Week), from Palm Sunday to Easter Sunday, which brings a series of vigils, colorful processions, and reenactments of Christ's last days in Jerusalem. You'll see Roman centurions charging through the streets on horseback, boulevards carpeted with colored sawdust and flowers, and immense hand-carried floats wending their way through throngs of onlookers. INGUAT has schedules and maps with procession routes; just be aware that Antigua's hotels are booked for this event months ahead of time.

Numbers in the text correspond to numbers in the margin and on the Antigua map.

A Good Walk

Begin your walk at the lively **Casa K'Ojom** ⑪, where the instruments used in indigenous musical traditions are displayed. Before heading west to the ruins of **La Recolección** ⑫, explore the two mercados near the bus station; the covered market to the south of the bus station, Mercado des Artisans, is arranged around a terrace and has better-quality wares. From the markets, walk north on Amaeda de Santa Lucía and turn right onto 1 Calle Poniente for the yellow-stuccoed **Nuestra Señora de La Merced** (Our Lady of Mercy) ⑬ and its beautiful fountain, and the **Convento Santa Catalina** (Convent of St. Catherine) ⑭ across the street. Next, take a tour of the manicured grounds and labyrinthine ruins of the **Convento de las Capuchinas** ⑮, 3 blocks east at 2 Avenida Norte and 2 Calle Oriente. Leave the convent for the heart of Antigua where the **Ayuntamiento** ⑯ or city hall stands on the north side of **Plaza Mayor** ⑰. Like all other Central American cities and towns, the plaza is a public gathering place where lazing the day away is perfectly acceptable. To the south is the **Palacio de los Capitanes Generales** ⑱, which has been a government administration building for centuries and now houses the IN-GUAT tourism office and to the east is the **Cathedral de San José** ⑲. Across 5 Calle Oriente from the cathedral is the **Museo de Arte Colonial** ⑳, with religious art dating from the 17th century and more recent representations of the popular Holy Week festivities held in Antigua. Between 2:00 and 4:00 you can visit **Casa Popenoe** ㉑, a private residence and a restored and beautifully furnished colonial mansion, two blocks east. Close by are the ruins of **Convento Santa Clara** ㉒, with hidden passages and mysterious underground rooms, and the **Monasterio San Francisco** ㉓, where you can knock on the tomb of Friar Pedro de San José de Betancur to have your prayers answered.

Timing

As you wander Antigua's ancient avenues, you will continually be surprised by its restrained pace and by its tiny, private nooks and sanctuaries. Take the time to explore picturesque streets and rest in places that have views of the volcanoes. This tour, taken at a leisurely pace, can fill a day. To get and keep your bearings, remember that at Plaza Mayor, the streets and avenues switch from *Norte* to *Sur* and *Oriente* to *Poniente* in relation to it. A useful navigation tip: the northeast corner of Plaza Mayor is at 4 Avenida and 4 Calle, while the southwest corner is 5 Avenida and 5 Calle.

Sights close promptly at 5 and some ruins are closed on Sunday and Monday.

Sights to See

⑯ **Ayuntamiento** (City Hall). Today, as in colonial times, the ayuntamiento was the seat of the city council. It also houses two museums, the **Museo de Santiago** (Museum of St. James) and **Museo del Libro Antiguo** (Museum of Antique Books). The former displays colonial art and artifacts and adjoins what was once the city jail in back; Central America's first printing press is in the latter, along with a collection of ancient manuscripts. ⊠ *4 Calle Poniente, on north side of Plaza Mayor.* 🎫 *Museums: 40¢.* ☉ *Tues.–Fri. 9–4, weekends 9–noon and 2–4.*

126

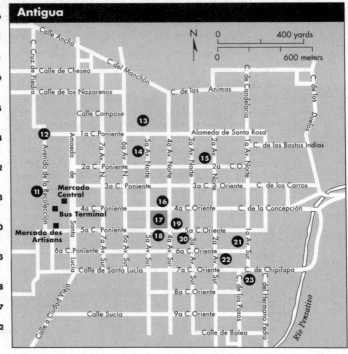

NEED A
BREAK?
Wander over to **Cookies, ETC.** (✉ 4 Calle Oriente and 3 Avenida), a four-table café and pastry shop serving 15 different kinds of homemade cookies filled with nuts, chocolate, coconut, oatmeal, and spices.

---

⑪ Casa K'Ojom. "K'Ojom" means "music" in three different indigenous languages, and this very modest "house of music" highlights the depth of musical traditions within Guatemala's vastly diverse indigenous population. An interesting 15-minute documentary film set to music is a good introduction for the newcomer touring the center's collection of musical instruments and artifacts. There's even an effigy of San Simón, a notorious beatified bad boy known to offer advice only when bribed with cigars and liquor. A gift shop sells well-made crafts, including masks, CDs, and simple instruments. At press time, Casa K'Ojom was considering a relocation; call ahead or contact INGUAT (☞ Visitor Information *in* Antigua A to Z, *below*). ✉ *Calle de la Recoletos 55, at 5 Calle Poniente,* ☎ *832–3087.* ✍ *$1.* ⊘ *Mon.–Fri. 9:30–12:30 and 2–5, Sat. 9:30–12:30 and 2–4, closed Sunday.*

㉑ Casa Popenoe. A short loop through this beautifully restored colonial mansion takes you through courtyards and several rooms containing decorative household items, including original paintings, fine ceramic dishes, and ornate wood doors and paneling, most of which have been in the house since its original construction. An English-speaking guide is usually available. Since it is a private home, there are no public rest rooms, and open hours are limited. ✉ *1 Avenida Sur at 5 Calle Oriente.* ✍ *70¢.* ⊘ *Mon.–Sat. 2–4.*

⑲ Cathedral de San José. Only two chapels remain in the cathedral, which was completed in 1680 but mostly destroyed in 1773. As in most other Latin American churches, the cross and altar are toward the east, so that worshipers face the Holy Land. ✉ *4 Avenida Sur, on east side of Plaza Mayor.*

OFF THE BEATEN PATH	**ARTESANIAS UNIDAS** – A 10-minute drive southwest of Antigua brings you to San Antonio Aguas Calientes, a dusty little Indian village built around an ancient church and hot springs, frequented mostly by locals. It's worth a special trip here for Alida Perez's textiles museum and shop, Artesanias Unidas, for its incomparable selection of handmade place-mats, fabrics, and huiples. These articles are the real thing and don't come cheap: Huiples start at about $50. For the price of admission you can watch the pieces being made and can try on costumes. Call IN-GUAT (☞ Visitor Information *in* Antigua A to Z, *below*) for directions and information. *San Antonio Aguas Calientes, on the main street, No. 4-16,* ☎ FAX *832-3169 or 831-5950.* ✒ *$3.*

★ ⓯ **Convento de las Capuchinas.** The Capuchin nuns founded Antigua's largest and now best-preserved convent in 1736. The nuns arrived from Madrid 10 years earlier, and their new convent quickly grew in size because, unlike other convents, the women did not need to pay dowries to undertake the religious life. After the earthquake of 1773, it was abandoned, though damage to the structure was relatively light. In the 1940s the convent was restored and opened as a cultural site. The ruins are quite nice and include several lovely courtyards and gardens, former bathing halls, an acoustically enhanced cellar, and a low, round tower lined with the nuns' cells—two of which illustrate cloistered life with rather eerie mannequins. Climb to the roof for a memorable view of the surrounding landscape. ✉ *2 Avenida Norte at 2 Calle Oriente,* ☎ *no phone.* ✒ *$2.* ◷ *Daily 9–5.*

⓮ **Convento Santa Catalina** (Convent of St. Catherine). The only remnant of the once enormous convent is a beautiful yellow arch that spans 5 Avenida Norte, known at that location as Calle de Santa Catalina. It was founded in 1613 with only four nuns and modest facilities, but by 1693 the nunnery's growing popularity forced it to expand across the street. The arch was built to allow the sisters to pass from one side to the other unseen, and was virtually the only part of the convent left standing after the 1773 earthquake. ✉ *5 Avenida Norte and 2 Calle Poniente,* ☎ *no phone.*

㉒ **Convento Santa Clara** (Convent of St. Clara). Shortly after it was founded in 1699, the convent became a rather elaborate complex and a home to 46 nuns. It was never so active again, however, as it was destroyed by an earthquake in 1717 and was then rebuilt with the intention of exceeding its former glory in terms of size and complexity only to be struck by violent tremors again in 1773. Once again the convent collapsed and this time was finally abandoned. The arches and garden courtyards of the ruins make for pleasant roaming, though; keep an eye out for hidden passages and underground rooms. Across the street, a large water basin with beautiful magenta arches (actually a public laundry area) stands at the head of a palm-lined park, where vendors sell a variety of goods and crafts. ✉ *2 Avenida Sur at 6 Calle Oriente,* ☎ *832-3185.* ✒ *$1.50.* ◷ *Daily 9–5.*

NEED A BREAK?	Near the Santa Catalina arch is the **Posada Don Rodrigo** (✉ 5 Avenida Norte 17), a colonial mansion that is now a first-class hotel. Even if you don't stay here, you can wander around the courtyards and gardens, listen to the marimba players, and visit the restaurant for a drink or the Antiguan flan, layered with figs and sweet potato. You'll want to come back for dinner.

❷❸ **Monasterio San Francisco** (Monastery of St. Francis). The tomb of Friar Pedro de San José de Betancur, who lived in the 17th and 18th centuries and was beatified by Pope John Paul II for his good works, has imbued this 1579 monastery with quite a bit of local importance. Many miracles are ascribed to Friar Pedro, and until recently, petitioners had only to knock gently on the casket containing his remains to have their prayers answered. The actual remains have since been moved to a more finely rendered receptacle to the left of the main altar, but the original tomb still serves the purpose, and is covered with letters, photos, and plaques from grateful believers, and from those still seeking the good brother's grace. The remainder of the monastery, now in ruins, is worth a visit for the second-story views of Antigua and the surrounding areas. Enter through a small path near the right-rear corner of the church. ⊠ *7 Calle Oriente and 1 Avenida Sur,* ☏ *no phone.* 🎟 *30¢ for ruins, church is free.* ☉ *Daily 9–5.*

❷⓪ **Museo de Arte Colonial** (Museum of Colonial Art). On the former site of the University of San Carlos, the museum, its cloisters left largely intact through the shakier centuries, has mostly 17th-century religious paintings and statues commissioned by the Castilians and a year-round photography display on the Holy Week celebrations. ⊠ *Calle de la Universidad and 4 Avenida Sur.* 🎟 *$4.* ☉ *Tues.–Fri. 9–4, weekends 9–noon and 2–4.*

★ ⓭ **Nuestra Señora de La Merced** (Our Lady of Mercy). The ancient church and monastery of the Mercedian fathers is one of Antigua's brightest attractions, with its decorative yellow stucco facade. It was built in 1548, destroyed by the earthquake of 1717, and finally inaugurated in 1767, six years before a second massive earthquake forced the city itself to be abandoned. La Merced survived the 1773 quake intact, however, thanks to architect Juan Luis de Dios Estrada. Estrada designed the church to be earthquake-resistant, with a squat shape, thick walls, and small, high windows. The church has a decorative interior, a wide stone esplanade, and the attached monastery has an immense fountain and excellent views of surrounding volcanoes. There are remnants of unfinished restoration projects here and the fountain never seems to flow, but this doesn't interfere much with its beauty, particularly at sunset or when the bougainvillea is in bloom. ⊠ *Corner of 1 Calle Poniente and 6 Avenida Norte,* ☏ *no phone.* 🎟 *25¢ for monastery, church is free.* ☉ *Monastery, daily 9–noon and 3–6.*

⓲ **Palacio de los Capitanes Generales** (Palace of the Captains General). It has not been fully restored since it housed royal colonial offices, but today the building, easily recognized by its stately archways, houses the INGUAT tourism office and other government headquarters, including the police department and an army barracks. ⊠ *5 Calle Poniente, on south side of Plaza Mayor.*

⓱ **Plaza Mayor.** A well-kept city center with a pretty fountain surrounded by old colonial buildings, the plaza is where locals and travelers alike pass quiet afternoons on tree-shaded benches, although most public events are also staged here. ⊠ *Between 4 and 5 calles poniente and 4 and 5 avenidas sur.*

⓬ **La Recolección.** Despite opposition from the city council, which felt the town already had plenty of monasteries, this one dating from 1700 was destroyed by a major earthquake that hit the same year inauguration was finally won (1717). Like many others, it was rebuilt only to be shaken to the ground again in 1773. A stone arch still graces the church stairway, but the ceiling did not fare so well—it lies in huge jumbled blocks within the nave's crumbling walls. The monastery is in better shape though, with spacious courtyards, low arches, and thick walls. Enter via a small path to the left of the church. To get here, head west on 1 Calle Poniente to the dead end; the ruins unmarked are across the street. ✉ *1 Calle Poniente at Calle de la Recolección,* ☎ *no phone.* 🎫 *$1.30.* ☉ *Daily 9–5.*

OFF THE
BEATEN PATH

ANTIGUA SPA RESORT – About 3 km (2 mi) from Antigua in the village of San Pedro El Panorama is a perfect getaway for those who want to be pampered. With massages, facials, and a series of package deals, some of which include an overnight stay in a suite, you'll be glad you made this part of your trip. Free transportation to and from Antigua is available. ✉ *3 Avenida 8–66, Zona 14,* ☎ *832–3960,* FAX *832–3968, kascott@usa.net.*

Dining

$$$ ✕ **El Asador de Don Martín.** This exclusive restaurant serves upscale Guatemalan cuisine in the elegant atmosphere of a restored colonial home. Ring the bell at the entrance and you'll be led to a table in a small garden courtyard, or to one of two rooms with corner fireplaces and paintings by local artists. The menu includes choice grilled meats and lomito, robálo, and venison dishes. You can count on impeccable service. Since this is a decidedly adult place, it's best not to bring the kids. ✉ *4 Avenida Norte 16,* ☎ *832–0501. AE, MC, V. Closed Mon., Tues.*

$$$ ✕ **La Casserole.** The chef at this restaurant-gallery serves up French and European cuisine with subtle Guatemalan influences, incorporating local flavors and products into classic gourmet dishes. Although the menu changes every 10 days, there are a few constants: seafood bouillabaisse, cooked in a slightly spicy tomato sauce, and steak tenderloin with *chiltepe* sauce are two standouts. The gallery, El Picarón, and restaurant are in a renovated colonial house with fountains and peach and gold walls lined with rotating exhibits of paintings and photographs. ✉ *Callejón de la Concepción 7, around the corner from the Hotel Santo Domingo,* ☎ *832–0219. AE, DC, MC, V. Closed Monday, no dinner Sunday.*

$$$ ✕ **Mesón Panza Verde.** The rich sauces and scrumptious desserts of
★ this fantastic restaurant will make you thankful that it's a 15-minute walk from the city center. Part of a first-class hotel by the same name, the Mesón Panza Verde has thoughtfully prepared dishes and impeccable service in a quietly elegant setting. The meat dishes are particularly good, such as the lomito bourguignonne with escargot, and the dessert menu offers drink suggestions with each entry. Choose from tables in two well-lit dining rooms, or from those set up along the hotel's beautiful interior courtyard. To get here, head south for four long blocks on 5 Avenida, which runs along the west side of Plaza Mayor; the restaurant in on the left, past 9 Calle Oriente ✉ *5 Avenida Sur 19,* ☎ FAX *832–2925. AE, DC, MC, V.*

$$$ ✕ **Welten.** Welten's owner says she wants her customers to feel like
★ guests in her home, and until the bill arrives, it's easy to fall under the illusion. (You even have to knock to get in.) Take your pick of seating locales: on a plant-filled patio with hammocks and cascading orchids; by a small pool and garden out back; or in one of the elegant dining rooms. The menu includes handmade pasta, such as a spunky anolini with creamy pepper and cognac sauce, as well as fish and meat dishes with a variety of sauces. All the vegetables are organic, and the bread is homemade. Save room for the rich and tasty desserts. ✉ *4 Calle Oriente 21,* ☎ *832–0630. AE, DC, MC, V. Closed Tues.*

$$ ✕ **Fonda de la Calle Real.** An old Antigua favorite, this place now has two locations, both serving the same Guatemalan and Mexican menu. The original space is just off the Plaza Mayor, on 5 Avenida Norte, and

has upstairs seating with pleasant views, though the space is slightly cramped. The new branch around the corner on 3 Calle is in a large colonial home and is more spacious and attractive with both indoor and outdoor seating. The menu includes queso fundido and a famous *caldo real* (a hearty chicken soup). The 3 Calle branch has live music on weekends. ⊠ *3 Calle Poniente 7,* ☎ *832–0507. Daily noon–10;* ⊠ *5 Avenida Norte 5,* ☎ *832–2696. Daily 7:30 AM–9:30 PM. AE, DC, MC, V.*

$$ **✕ El Mediterraneo.** Step into this tiny restaurant and you step into North-
★   ern Italy, and the source of some of Antigua's finest Italian food. Antipasti, delicate homemade pastas, and an affordable wine selection will ensure your satisfaction. The atmosphere and decor are low-key with just the right amount of class. ⊠ *6 Calle Poniente 6-A,* ☎ *832–7180. V. Closed Tues.*

$$ **✕ Nicholas.** Across the street from La Merced, this cozy restaurant offers savory Spanish fare in the congenial atmosphere of an after-hours piano bar. The owner-chef is a Basque-trained Guatemalan, who doubles as bartender and waitress now and then. The seafood dishes are universally great, as are the lomito Roquefort and the ravioli. Don't pass on the fig bisque for dessert. A rotating collection of local and expat musicians provides surprisingly good live jazz on Friday and Saturday. ⊠ *1 Calle Poniente 3,* ☎ *832–0277. No credit cards. Closed Wed., no dinner on Sun. No lunch.*

$ **✕ Café Condesa.** Homemade pies and pastries and light, tasty meals make this spot a popular one. Breakfast is served all day starting at 6:45, with daily specials, like toast topped with strawberries, papaya, or mango and sprinkled with sugar, and omelets with fresh vegetables. For lunch try the daily quiche specials or the brie plate. You can eat in the cafe's airy dining room and courtyard, or get a cappuccino and a sweet roll to go at the Café Condesa Express next door. ⊠ *West side of Plaza Mayor, inside Casa del Conde,* ☎ *832–0170. MC, V.*

$ **✕ Café de la Fuente.** This popular vegetarian café is in the courtyard of La Fuente, a fairly classy collection of shops in a renovated colonial estate. Classical music, hanging plants, and white patio furniture create a peaceful atmosphere. The international breakfasts, served until 11, range from New York bagels and cream cheese to Mexican tofu *rancheros* (with salsa). La Fuente also makes one of the best desserts in town: *pie de lodo* (mud pie), a decadently rich, heated chocolate brownie topped with coffee ice cream and chocolate syrup. It's open until 7. ⊠ *La Fuente, 4 Calle Oriente 14,* ☎ *832–4520. No credit cards.*

$ **✕ Café Flor.** This homey restaurant switched from Mexican to Thai cuisine in 1996 and never looked back. The friendly proprietors now serve a Pan-Asian menu that includes curries, Chinese noodles, and vegetarian Indian dishes. On weekends it's open until midnight. Be careful though—some of the food, especially the curry, is quite spicy. ⊠ *4 Avenida Sur 1,* ☎ *832–5274. AE, MC, V.*

$ **✕ Doña Luisa Xicotencatl.** Named after the adored mistress of Span-
★   ish conquistador Pedro Alvarado, Doña Luisa's is one of the most popular breakfast spots in town and something of a local institution. A multitude of tables are scattered throughout a dozen rooms and on the balcony and terrace of this former colonial residence, but it's still not easy to get a seat. Early morning specialties include fruit salad, pancakes, and very fresh bread (the bakery is right downstairs); sandwiches and light fare make for ample lunch and dinner options. The service can be slow, but the ambience and eclectic decor make the wait pleasant. Incidentally, the bulletin board downstairs is an excellent source of information for travelers. ⊠ *4 Calle Oriente 12,* ☎ *832–2578. MC, V.*

$ ✕ **Frida's Cocina Mexicana.** Looking for good food in a festive cantina setting? This is the place. Fill up on classic Mexican fare, including taquitos, enchiladas, and burros, the diminutive siblings of the American-style burrito. At night, the margaritas and nachos are fodder for a fiesta among friends, especially when the mariachi band shows up. ✉ *5 Avenida Norte 29, near the arch,* ☎ *832–0504. No credit cards.*

$ ✕ **Quesos y Vino.** Both of these small Italian restaurants serve homemade pasta, pizzas baked in a wood-burning oven, and a variety of cheeses and home-baked breads. The newer location, on Calle Oriente, has a more polished atmosphere than the original but is less intimate. Choose from an impressive selection of imported wines sold by the bottle. ✉ *5 Avenida Norte 32 and 2 Calle Oriente 22,* ☎ *no phone. No credit cards. Closed Tues.*

Lodging

$$$$ 🏨 **Casa Santo Domingo.** In 1992, a truly elegant hotel was built around
★ the ruins of the ancient Santo Domingo monastery. Long mellow passageways and snug little courtyards and gardens recall a bygone era. Dark carved-wood furniture, yellow stucco walls, and iron sconces preserve the monastic atmosphere throughout. Fountains, hanging plants, and colonial furniture decorate the public rooms. Luxury amenities abound, without detracting from the historical feel; guest rooms have antique fireplaces, cable TV, and deep bathtubs with Jacuzzis. The food at the hotel restaurant, however, is considerably less inspiring. Internet access is available. ✉ *3 Calle Oriente 28,* ☎ *832–0140,* 🅵🅰🆇 *832–0102. 97 rooms. Restaurant, bar, pool, massage, sauna, spa, concierge. AE, DC, MC, V.*

$$$$ 🏨 **Hotel Antigua.** As a tasteful combination of colonial elegance and
★ modern comfort, this hotel succeeds where others fail. Guest rooms are furnished with fireplaces and cable TV and surround a large lawn and pool, while one- and two-level suites can house a whole family quite comfortably. The oldest part of the hotel is a colonial-style building with a restaurant, small bar, and a beautiful sitting room. Weddings are sometimes held in a sunny esplanade overlooking the church of San José. Internet services are available. ✉ *8 Calle Poniente 1 at 5 Avenida Sur,* ☎ *832–0288/0331,* 🅵🅰🆇 *832–2807, hainfo@hotelant.com.gt. 60 rooms. 2 restaurants, bar, pool, playground, convention center. AE, DC, MC, V.*

$$$$ 🏨 **Posada del Angel.** You'd never know from the somewhat ramshackle
★ entrance that you're at the threshold of Antigua's classiest establishment. It's all part of the ruse at this unassuming yet supremely discreet hotel, whose five rooms have seen their fair share of celebrity guests, including Bill Clinton, former Guatemalan President Alvaro Arzu, and former Canadian Prime Minister Pierre Trudeau. The rooms are spacious and luxurious, with high ceilings, large fireplaces, overstuffed beds, ornate decor, and tile bathrooms. An airy sitting room has a massive fireplace on one side and a long gorgeous reflecting pool on the other, and the restaurant, bar, and library are imbued with genuine class and charm. Every service imaginable is available for guests of this truly angelic inn. ✉ *4 Avenida Sur 24A,* ☎ 🅵🅰🆇 *832–0260, or* ☎ *800/934–0065 in U.S., elangel@ibm.net. 5 rooms. Restaurant, bar, room service, concierge, travel arrangements, airport shuttle. AE, DC, MC, V.* 🕭

$$$ 🏨 **Casa Azul.** There aren't many hotels whose comment book is filled with recommendations of specific rooms, but the spectacular volcano views from Casa Azul's second floor make this hotel one such place. With sitting rooms that open onto a pleasant courtyard and modern fountain, Casa Azul, just half a block from Plaza Mayor, has a serene and artistic atmosphere. The rooms are decorated in washes of red and, of course, blue; those upstairs are more expensive, but they're larger and brighter, and have those gorgeous views. Complementary Continental breakfast is served beside the small pool. ⊠ *4 Avenida Norte 5*, ☎ *832–0961/0962*, FAX *832–0944, casazul@guate.net. 10 rooms. Bar, Jacuzzi, pool, sauna. AE, DC, MC, V.* ✎

$$$ 🖬 **Quinta de las Flores.** In one of Antigua's newer luxury hotels, the
★ colonial and the whimsical combine for a beautiful sanctuary. Although the look is that of a 19th-century hacienda, the grounds and rooms are decorated with modern renditions of Guatemalan crafts. The gardens and the hotel's open-air restaurant have superb views of all three volcanoes. All rooms have high ceilings, fireplaces, and TVs. The bungalows, which sleep up to five people, are quaint and fully furnished, from barbecue patio to toaster oven. Because it's quite a way outside of town, this hotel is best suited for those with a car, for those in search of peace and quiet, or for those who don't mind a healthy walk. ⊠ *Calle del Hermano Pedro 6, just past the white stone church,* ☎ *832–3721/3722,* FAX *832–3726, qflores@infovia.com.gt. 9 rooms, 5 bungalows. Restaurant, bar, minibars, pool, playground. MC, V.* ✎

$$ 🖬 **Hotel Aurora.** This genteel hotel, run by the same family that opened it in 1923, is slightly overpriced but has an unbeatable location in the heart of the city. The comfortable, if somewhat dark, colonial-style, tile-floor rooms face a huge and beautiful garden, which is in turn surrounded by a tile portico strewn with plenty of cool rattan chairs. The effect is that of an oasis in the midst of the hubbub. Rooms have wooden furniture and old-fashioned armoires, and all have bathtubs and phones. Breakfast is included. ⊠ *4 Calle Oriente 16,* ☎ FAX *832–0217/5515, haurora@conexion.com.gt. 15 rooms. V.*

$$ 🖬 **Hotel Convento Santa Catalina.** This aptly named hotel was built
★ among the ruins of the old Spanish convent whose only remaining structure is the often-photographed arch crossing 5 Avenida Norte. The front rooms are spacious, if somewhat dimly lit, and tastefully decorated with *típica* and handwoven bedspreads. Most face a verdant courtyard with a fountain, where a smattering of tables and chairs encourages leisurely cocktail-sipping. The modern rooms in the annex stray from traditional Guatemalan decor, but they're bright and have kitchenettes. All rooms have cable TV and phones. ⊠ *5 Avenida Norte 28,* ☎ *832–3879,* FAX *832–3079, hotelconvento@conexion.com.gt. 18 rooms. Restaurant. No credit cards.* ✎

$$ 🖬 **Hotel Posada Los Búaros.** The decorative fountain that gives this hotel its name is set against a wall in the courtyard, and is just one of many touches that make this new hotel attractive and comfortable. The rooms have firm beds, red-tile floors and iron-lattice settings, and a full kitchen and bright breakfast room are available for general use. The owner and staff are extremely friendly, and frequently offer discounts to students, groups, long-term guests, or even those who simply balk at the somewhat inflated rates. There are plans for a sitting room, with couches and reading lamps. ⊠ *7 Avenida Norte 94,* ☎ FAX *832–2346. 10 rooms. Breakfast room. V.*

$$ 🖬 **Posada San Sebastián.** These two sister hotels have simple, comfortable rooms, an unassuming atmosphere, and a friendly staff. The posada on 2 Avenida is the more attractive—it's an older, colonial home with a colorful bar—but the more modern hotel on 3 Avenida has a central location. ⊠ *3 Avenida Norte 4,* ☎ *832–2621, 7 rooms;* ⊠ *2 Avenida Sur 36A,* ☎ *832–3282, 9 rooms. ardisis@hotmail.com. Bar. No credit cards.*

$ 🖬 **Hospedaje Santa Lucía.** Although they don't live up to the fancy facade outside, the rooms at the Santa Lucía are simple, clean, and won't empty your pocket. There's actually no sign or number outside, so look for a white arch over the door, next to a paper store. Inside, red-tile floors, high ceilings, and heavy, wood furniture lend a certain in-room charm. The bathrooms are absolutely spartan and hot water is only available for a few hours at a time (6 AM–9 AM and 6 PM–9 PM). Also, ask for a room in the back, as 6 Avenida can get busy. During your stay, be sure to climb the roof for a memorable view of La Merced and the surrounding area, especially in early morning and after dark. ☒ *6 Avenida Norte 43,* ☏ *no phone. 20 rooms. No credit cards.*

$ ☷ **Posada Asjemenou.** You may have heard enough about charming hotels in former colonial mansions, but the difference here is the bargain price. The rooms are clean and comfortable, and the staff friendly and eager. The small café serves breakfast and snacks, and if you hanker for more substantial victuals, you can walk over to the owners' larger restaurant (off the Plaza Mayor), which specializes in pizza. ☒ *5 Avenida Norte 31,* ☏ FAX *832–2670. 12 rooms, 9 with bath. Café. AE, DC, MC, V.*

$ ☷ **Villa San Francisco.** A block north of the San Francisco ruins, this low-key hotel is a great value for the money. An upstairs walkway has nice views of its namesake church, and, if the Monday wash is not in the way, all three volcanoes. The rooms are modestly furnished and clean, and the proprietors have plans to add more rooms and a rooftop café. Maya Bike Tours (☞ *below*), a small but well-run adventure tour operator, is based in the hotel lobby and offers traditional travel services as well as a variety of two-wheeled trips. International phone and fax service is also available. ☒ *1 Avenida Sur 15,* ☏ FAX *832–3383, mayanbikeone@conexion.com.gt . 10 rooms, 4 with bath. Travel services. MC, V.* ☙

$$$ ✕☷ **Hotel Posada de Don Rodrigo.** A night in this restored colonial mansion, some 250 years old, is a journey into colonial antiquity. All of the rooms have high ceilings and gorgeous tile floors and are furnished with antique armoires; two lovely courtyards and several small gardens enhance the grounds. The dining room has a tile fountain, a fireplace, and a terrace whose garden is lit at night. Just off the terrace, a woman prepares tortillas on a grill, and marimba music in the courtyard enlivens every meal. The menu has Guatemalan favorites, a few Continental choices, and pasta. Light sleepers, beware: the festivities can sometimes go long and lively into the night. This hotel has an excellent sister establishment in Panajachel (☞ *below*), and reservations and transportation for both can be arranged in either city. ☒ *5 Avenida Norte 17,* ☏ FAX *832–0291 in Antigua, chotelera@c.net.gt. 35 rooms. Restaurant, bar. AE, DC, MC, V.*

$$$ ✕☷ **Mesón Panza Verde.** A beautiful courtyard just inside the main
★ entrance has a fountain, garden, and spacious corridors along its circumference, setting the stage for your relaxing respite here. The elegant downstairs guest rooms open onto small gardens, while the romantic suites upstairs have four-poster beds, down comforters, large bathrooms, and ample patio space with chairs and hammocks. The rooftop patio is wonderful in late afternoon or early morning, and the restaurant is one of the best in town (☞ *above*). It's a bit of a walk from the city center, but with food and furnishings this good, you may not want to leave. Breakfast is included. ☒ *5 Avenida Sur 19,* ☏ FAX *832–2925, mpv@infovia.com.gt. 3 rooms, 3 suites. Restaurant. AE, DC, MC, V.*

Nightlife and the Arts

THE ARTS

The **Biennial Cultural Festival** in February of odd-numbered years, is a relatively new venture but is expected to become an important event. It features a mélange of plays, art exhibits, street performances, and films. Throughout the year, various **musical and artistic productions,** including opera, are staged in the city's ruins, churches, and galleries.

Check with INGUAT (☞ Visitor Information *in* Antigua A to Z, *below*) for current programs.

You won't have trouble finding a bar in Antigua. For jazz, head to **Nicholas** (⊠ 1 Calle Poniente 3), a homey piano bar in front of La Merced, or **Jazz Gruta** (⊠ Calzada de Santa Lucía Norte 17), an intimate jazz club with music every day but Sunday. **Al Afro** (⊠ 6 Calle Poniente 9, ☎ 832–3188) serves up fondue and a daily happy hour to the sounds of salsa and Latin jazz. The ever popular **La Chimenea** (⊠ 4 Calle Poniente and 7 Avenida Sur) caters to a young Spanish school crowd with its pop music and small dance floor. **Picasso's** (⊠ 7 Avenida, at 2 Calle Poniente) also has a youngish clientele. All sorts of people show up at the frequently and festively crowded **Macondo Pub** (⊠ 5 Avenida Norte, under the arch). **Monoloco Sports Bar** (⊠ 2 Avenida Norte 6B, upstairs) has it all: giant burritos, pints of micro-brew, and satellite coverage of various sporting events. If you want to dance the night away (or at least until 1 AM), **Casbah** (⊠ 5 Avenida Norte 45) has Latin and rock rhythms in Antigua's only true disco.

Video parlors that run mostly bootlegged American movies are popular since the local movie theater tends to run second-rate films. Try **Cinemaya** (⊠ 6 Calle Poniente 7, at 5 Avenida) and **Cinema Bistro** (⊠ 5 Avenida Sur 14), both of which serve refreshments and alcohol. Weekly schedules are posted on the town's many community bulletin boards.

Outdoor Activities and Sports

From white-water rafting and mountain-bike tours to volcano hiking and rock climbing, Antigua has plenty of fresh air activities. For adventure trips, it is always best to go with a tour operator (☞ Guided Tours, *below*), rather than head out solo. In fact, spend a little more and use an established and registered agency—the service is typically better and, in the event of problems, the INGUAT office can help mediate, and even get your money back. Don't count on having the same luck with the kids selling volcano trips in Plaza Mayor.

The most popular volcano trip is to Pacaya, the only active one of the four accessible from Antigua (although Fuego smokes fairly often). Pacaya erupts with some frequency, so always ask about conditions *before* signing up. Typically Pacaya's crater is awhirl in steam, sulfur gas, and radiated heat; it's not toxic, but a handkerchief is nice to have along. Absolutely do not wear sandals on Pacaya or any other volcano hike, as lava rock can be razor sharp.

A number of working coffee and macadamia *fincas* (farms) southwest of Antigua, on the road to San Antonio Aguas Calientes, are fun to visit. To get to the fincas, head south on Calle a Ciudad Vieja, an extension of Alameda Santa Lucia. **Finca Los Nietos** (⊠ 6 km/3.6 mi from Antigua, ☎ 831–5438, 🎫 $5.25) is a working coffee farm. To get to **Finca Valhalla** (⊠ 7 km/4.2 mi southwest of Antigua, 0.5 km before San Miguel Dueñas, ☎ 831–5799, 🎫 $1), a macadamia farm, continue on Calle a Ciudad Vieja south, past the Old City, which is little more than a few unkempt church ruins; if you reach San Miguel Dueñas, a tiny village, you've gone too far. Call **Finca Francisco Falla** (⊠ ☎ 832–0409, 🎫 $25) for reservations and directions to this coffee and macadamia farm. Depending on the season, some plantations make better visits than others. Check with INGUAT (☞ Visitor Information *in* Antigua A to Z, *below*) before heading out.

Shopping

BOOKS

Thanks to its sizable expatriate population, Antigua has Guatemala's best selection of English-language reading material. **Casa Andinista** (⊠ 4 Calle Oriente 5) sells travel guides, some hard-to-find titles, note cards, and posters. **La Galería** (⊠ 5 Avenida Sur 4) sells books on Plaza Mayor's west side. **Hamlin & White** (⊠ 4 Calle Oriente 12A, in Jades, S.A.) sells international newspapers, new and used books, and current magazines. **Nim Po't Centro de Textiles Tradicionales** (⊠ 5 Avenida Norte 29B) has a huge selection of used books alongside its traditional textiles. You can try the smallish **Un Poco de Todo** (⊠ 5 Avenida Sur 10) for a few things to read. The **Rainbow Reading Room** (⊠ 7 Avenida Sur 8) has a decent selection of English titles.

GALLERIES

El Sitio (⊠ 5 Calle Poniente 15), **Galería El Carmen** (⊠ Calle del Chagón 19D), **Wer Art Gallery** (⊠ 6 Calle Oriente 8), **Galería de Artes Integradas "Los Nazarenos"** (⊠ 6 Calle Poniente 13), and **Estípite** (⊠ Avenida el Desengaño 22) all carry works by local artists, including oils, ceramics, and wood carvings. Rumor has it that the last two may be closing.

HANDICRAFTS

Antigua is home to some of the finest merchandise in Guatemala, though not necessarily at bargain prices. The single largest concentration of crafts is in the **Mercado de Artisanias** (⊠ end of 4 Calle Poniente, next to the bus terminal). Closer to the Plaza Mayor, you'll find dozens of shops all up and down 5 Calle Norte and 4 Aveninda Poniente, from high-end boutiques to family-run stores packed with inexpensive típica.

La Boutique (⊠ 5 Calle Poniente 13) carries a variety of contemporary clothing woven in traditional patterns. **La Casa de los Gigantes** (⊠ 7 Calle Oriente 18) has a good selection of quality trinkets, including genuine antique festival masks. For handpainted pottery, try **Casa Sol** (⊠ 5 Avenida Sur 14). For embroidery, try **Colibrí** (⊠ 4 Calle Oriente 3). **The Gift Shop** (⊠ 3 Calle Poniente 3-B) carries a full range of kitchenware, from ceramics to beautiful hand-blown glassware. **Ixchel** (⊠ 4 Calle Oriente 20) specializes in hand-spun wool rugs and blankets. **The Kashlan Pot** (⊠ La Fuente, 4 Calle Oriente 14) has an excellent selection of *huipiles* (embroidered blouses). **La Máscara** (⊠ 5 Avenida Sur 4A) specializes in festival masks and wooden statuettes. Owned by expats, the **Casa de Las Bosas** (⊠ 4 Calle Oriente 22) and **Que Barbara** (⊠ 4 Calle Oriente 37) are shops that have adapted local handicrafts to North American and European tastes.

JEWELRY

Jade is mined all over the country but worked almost exclusively in Antigua. Most of the jade shops offer free tours of their facilities, where you can see the stones being cut, carved, and polished. It's beautiful work and very affordable by most U.S. and European standards. Still, expect to pay top-end prices for the very best items. Perhaps the best place to watch workers carving jade into jewelry is the main factory and showroom of **Jades S.A.** (⊠ 4 Calle Oriente 12 and 4 Calle Oriente 32, ☎ 832–3841), where President Clinton visited and bought a necklace (for Chelsea, of course). **Platería Típica Maya** (⊠ 7 Calle Oriente 9) is also top-notch retailer. Smaller emporiums include **Casa del Jade** (⊠ 4 Calle Oriente 3), **Jades Imperio Maya** (⊠ 5 Calle Oriente 2), and **The Jade Kingdom** (⊠ 4 Avenida Norte 10).

Antigua A to Z

Arriving and Departing

BY AIRPLANE

There is no airport in Antigua. Guatemala City's La Aurora Airport is about an hour's drive away.

BY BUS

A variety of companies, including **Transportes Turisticos Atitrans** (✉ 6 Avenida Sur 7, ☎ 832–3371 in Antigua; 332–5788 in Guatemala City) and **Turansa** (✉ 5 Calle Poniente 11B, ☎ 832–4691) run several daily shuttles between hotels in Guatemala City and Antigua, stopping at La Aurora Airport. It's best to call ahead for reservations and pickup, but you can also purchase tickets ($7–$10) on board.

Buses leave Guatemala City (✉ 18 Calle and 4 Avenida or 15 Calle between 3 and 4 avenidas, Zona 1) for Antigua every 15 minutes from 6 AM until about 6 PM. From Antigua, buses depart from the market area (when they're full) on a similar schedule. The trip takes about an hour; in the evening it's slower and the buses are more crowded.

To get to the Western Highlands, either reserve a spot on one of the above shuttle buses ($12 to Chichicantenango, $12 to Panajachel, $25 to Quetzaltenango, $35–$50 to the Mexican border) or catch a public bus at the terminal, which is slower, crowded, but a lot cheaper. There are only one or two direct buses to Panajachel and Quetzaltenango each day, usually at 7 AM ($2). Direct service to Chichicastenango ($2) is more frequent with five or six trips per day. It's best to double-check at the tourist office a day prior to leaving.

BY CAR

To reach Antigua, drive west out of Guatemala City via the Calzada Roosevelt, which becomes the Interamerican Highway, winding up into pine-covered hills with excellent views. At San Lucas, turn right off the highway and drive south to Antigua. If you're coming from the Western Highlands, turn right just after passing Chimaltenango.

BY TAXI

A taxi between Guatemala City and Antigua should cost about $25. Regular service is available between La Aurora Airport and Antigua. As usual, you'll have to haggle with drivers.

Getting Around

Antigua is not a large city and has no intracity service. People walk or take taxis, which are plentiful, cheap, and easy to flag down or get in the Plaza Mayor or near the bus station, behind the market. Remember to do a bit of haggling and to agree on a price before beginning your ride.

Contacts and Resources

CAR RENTALS

Tabarini Rent-A-Car (✉ 2 Calle Poniente 19A, ☎ FAX 832–3091).

EMERGENCIES

Hospital: Pedro de Betancourt Hospital (✉ Calle de Los Peregrinos and 4 Avenida Sur, ☎ 832–0301).

Pharmacy: Farmacia Roca (✉ 4 Calle Poniente 11, ☎ 832–0612).

Police (West end of Palacio del Capitán, ☎ 832–0251) for serious crimes.

Tourist Police (✉ Palacio del Ayuntamiento, enter on 4 Avenida Norte, ☎ 832–7290/0532), 24-hour hot line for free escorts, information, and minor matters.

INTERNET SERVICE

With its sizable foreign-student and expatriate population, Antigua has ample Internet access at very low prices. **Cybermania** (⊠ 5 Avenida Norte 25B, beneath the arch) has fast computers and hip decor, while the simpler **Cybermundo** (⊠ 5 Avenida Norte 15A) is just down the street. Others include **Conexion** (⊠ 4 Calle Oriente 4, in La Fuente shopping center) and **C@fe.net** (⊠ 6 Avenida Norte 14), which serves good coffee. Fax and international telephone services are generally available for very low prices. Expect to pay 80¢ per half hour of e-mailing, and about the same per minute for international calls to North America (more to Europe and Australia).

GUIDED TOURS

Independent tour guide Elizabeth Bell offers personalized trips, from walking tours of Antigua to three-day Tikal excursions, through her company, **Antigua Tours** (⊠ 3 Calle Oriente 28, in the Hotel Casa Santo Domingo, ☎ FAX 832–5821, elizbell@guate.net, ✍).

Antigua's best volcano tours are offered by **Eco-Tours "Chejos"** (⊠ 3 Calle Poniente 24, ☎ 832–5464, FAX 832–2657, ecotour@hotmail.com) whose friendly owner has climbed Pacaya volcano more than 1,800 times in 15 years. His prices are higher than most, but the tours are quite good, and generally have fewer people. **Sin Fronteras** (⊠ 3 Calle Poniente 12, ☎ 832–1017, FAX 832–2674, sinfront@infovia.com.gt) and **Voyageur** (⊠ 4 Calle Oriente 14, inside La Fuente shopping center), ☎ 832–4237, FAX 832–4247, info@travel.net.gt) are also reputable outfits.

The rolling hills and wide valley floor that surround Antigua make for great mountain biking. These tour agencies include bikes, helmets, and water bottles. **Mayan Bike Tours** (⊠ 1 Avenida Sur 15, in Villa San Francisco Hotel, ☎ 832–3383, mayanbikeone@conexion.com.gt, ✍) offers a wide range of half-day trips to advanced multi-day trips. **Old Town Outfitters** (⊠ 6 Calle Poniente 7, ☎ 832–4243, pueblo_viejo@hotmail.com) caters to more of a backpacker crowd, its rides are suitable for people of all ages and abilities. Old Town also rents rock climbing and camping equipment.

INGUAT (☞ *below*) can also find you a qualified tour guide.

TRAVEL AGENCIES

There are a great number of travel agencies here, most of which are perfectly fine for making simple travel arrangements. Among the better known are **Rainbow Travel Center** (⊠ 7 Avenida Sur 8, ☎ 832–4202, FAX 832–4206, myers@gua.gbm.net), **Sin Fronteras** (⊠ 3 Calle Poniente 12, ☎ 832–1017, FAX 832–2674, sinfront@infovia.com.gt), **Vision Travel** (⊠ 3 Avenida Norte 3, ☎ 832–3293, FAX 832–1955, vision@guatemalainfo.com, ✍), and **Turansa** (⊠ 5 Calle Poniente 11-B, ☎ 832–4691).

VISITOR INFORMATION

The tourist office, **INGUAT** (⊠ 5 Calle Poniente, Palacio de los Capitanes Generales, on south side of Plaza Mayor, ☎ 832–0763), is open daily 8–noon and 2–5.

THE WESTERN HIGHLANDS

The Western Highlands—or *el Altiplano* in Spanish—are bounded to the south by a chain of volcanoes that begins near Guatemala City and stretches nearly to Mexico. A series of rugged mountain ranges form the region's northern border, the Atlantic lowlands mark the eastern edge, and Chiapas and the Mexican border form the western boundary. The altiplano's high altitudes and lowlands create a contradictory

The Western Highlands

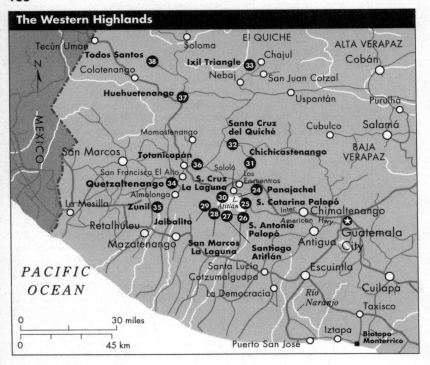

yet spectacular landscape of grumbling volcanoes and silent granite peaks, broad alpine lakes and narrow river ravines, lush tropical valleys and eerie cloud forests, pine-draped hillsides and wide pastoral plains. Many come to the Highlands to experience its natural beauty, and they are rarely disappointed.

But the landscape is not the only source of contradiction—or conflict—in the Altiplano. This is home to the majority of Guatemalan's indigenous people (of which there are 23 distinct ethnic groups), most of whom live in small villages punctuating the region's valleys and hillsides. The villages are typically colorful agricultural communities with a mix of traditional and postcolonial practices, held together by an economy based on crop cultivation, handicrafts, and a series of weekly markets. In stark contrast to Guatemala's elite and fast-growing middle class, the lives of most indigenous people are extremely modest. As crop cultivation becomes less viable (forcing indigenous people to the cities), and mainstream Guatemala outgrows its urban borders, the ways and worlds of very different peoples come increasingly into contact, and nowhere does this happen more frequently in Guatemala than in the Western Highlands. With foreign travelers and expatriats jumping into the mix, the area is truly a grab bag of culture, language, and privilege.

Sadly, for Guatemalans the coming together of varied traditions has been more contentious than cooperative. Their country holds the dubious distinction of fighting the longest continuous civil war in the west at 36 years. Much of that war, which officially ended in 1996, was fought in the Western Highlands, and at its center was a struggle over the preservation and protection (or lack thereof) of indigenous lifestyles and institutions. Although many issues remain unresolved, the people of the Western Highlands are now weary of fighting, and most, regardless of their wartime sympathies, simply want peace and prosperity. With a little openness and humility, travelers should find most people in the Altiplano kind and attentive, whether in large towns like Quetzaltenango or small indigenous towns in the Ixil Triangle.

It would be hard to say where the "heart" of the Western Highlands is, but Lake Atitlán is certainly on the shortlist. At the foot of three massive dormant volcanoes—San Pedro (9,920 ft), Tolimán (10,340 ft), and Atitlán (11,560 ft)—the lake has inspired all who've seen it, including John L. Stephens, Aldous Huxley, and even conquistador Pedro de Alvarado, whose troops named the lake "place of great waters" in their Nahuatl tongue. Early in the morning and on calm nights, the lake's water is as smooth as glass, capturing the huge volcanic cones in its reflection like an immense terrestrial mirror. But in the early afternoon, a wind known as the *xochomil* blows across the lake, and the surface turns choppy and defiant. The xochomil can turn Atitlán's waters violent in a hurry, so water sports and trips in paddleboats are advisable only in the morning. Another curiosity of the lake is its lack of outlets—water drains exclusively through underwater fissures. In 1976, an earthquake broke open a gigantic underwater chamber, causing the surface level to drop a whopping 6 ft in a matter of hours.

About 13 towns on its shores range from tacky tourist traps to charming indigenous villages. The latter are quiet agricultural communities, with proud, independent, and conservative residents; most women and men wear traditional costumes, which vary from town to town. Nearly everyone speaks one of two Maya languages (Tzutujil to the south, Cakchiquel to the north).

To the north, Chichicastenango represents what for many is the best part of the Western Highlands: the markets. Throughout the region, small towns hold weekly or biweekly markets, where locals and travelers alike come to buy, sell, and trade. Four hours west of Lake Atitlán is Quetzaltenango, Guatemala's second-largest city. Sierra de Chuacús, a string of active and dormant volcanoes just outside the city limits, makes this a place from which outdoor excursions are often based. It also has a number of Spanish schools, and is an alternative to Antigua in that respect.

Farther north and west lie the Cuchumatanes Mountains, which are also excellent for hiking, especially in the areas of Todos Santos and the Ixil Triangle. You can get topographical maps from the **Instituto Geográfico Nacional** (✉ Ave. Las Américas 5–76, Zona 13, Guatemala City, ☎ 332–2611), but if you want to climb volcanoes, it's best to go with a guide, or at least consult one before ascending, since certain areas, particularly on Guatemala's volcanoes, harbor bandits. (☞ Health and Safety *in* Guatemala A to Z, below).

Guatemala has been dubbed "the land of eternal spring," and it's fitting for the most part, with cool nights and warm afternoons. Still, the Western Highlands are not the Central American tropics of sun-lover dreams—Quetzaltenango and other high-altitude towns can get downright cold at night, especially in the winter. There's no need to overpack (most towns shut down pretty early anyway) but a sweater or warm jacket is essential.

The first towns outlined below are those that rim Lake Atitlán. Those that follow are part of ventures farther north and west into the highlands. Highways run between the principal towns and roads to more remote villages radiate from these hubs; and while they have improved greatly in the last few years, many roads remain in poor shape.

*Numbers in the text correspond to numbers in the margin and on the
Western Highlands map.*

Panajachel

㉔ *110 km (68 mi) northwest of Antigua.*

A few decades ago, Panajachel was just a quiet Cakchiquel village on
the northern shore of Lake Atitlán (Lago Atitlán in Spanish), but it has
since grown into somewhat of a hangout for foreigners who came to
visit and never left. And who can blame them? Pana's setting is highly
dramatic, bordered by three volcanoes that drop off into the crystalline
waters of Atitlán. A mild climate, spectacular scenery, and an abundant
selection of hotels (expect to see new ones virtually popping up around
you), restaurants, and visitor services make Pana an extremely popular
destination for international travelers of all kinds, as well as a favorite
weekend getaway for Guatemalans from the capital. Large numbers of
visitors have reduced Pana's indigenous character, and the cultural landscape can be tiresomely bohemian. Fortunately the old part of town, up
toward the valley, hasn't lost its charm, and the traditional pueblos nes-
tled in the hills nearby, where the visitor-to-resident ration is righted, have
retained much of their unique traditional character. And during Sunday
markets, Pana looks much like any other highland village.

Pana's main drag is **Calle Santander**, which runs in three long blocks
from the lakeshore to its intersection with **Calle Principal** and **Avenida
de los Arboles.** The former is where public buses drop off and pick up
passengers, and the latter is essentially an extension of Calle Santander
to the north. There are two banks at the intersection, and most shops
and restaurants are either down Calle Santander, or up Avenida de los
Arboles.

The **Reserva Natural Atitlán** (✉ 2 km/1 mi west of Panajachel, next
to Hotel Atitlán, ✆ $7 general, $3.50 students) has a walking trail that
loops through a small river canyon, crossing suspended foot bridges
and passing spider-monkey and coatimundi enclosures. There's also a
large butterfly atrium, a herb garden, and a private beach for a bit of
post-educational relaxation. It's best to arrive in the morning, when
the animals and butterflies are most active. Free transportation by catamaran is available from the San Pedro–bound ferry dock.

NEED A
BREAK?

The otherwise nondescript **Cafeteria Las Palmeras** (✉ West side of Calle
Santander) has fantastically good cappuccino and *café helado,* a tall
glass of coffee with a dollop of vanilla ice cream in it. **The Deli 2** (✉ End
of Calle Santander) is a great spot for breakfast, lunch, or a snack by
the lake. It has good coffee, fresh bagels, pastries, and an unusual
menu that includes falafel and hummus.

Dining and Lodging

$$ ✕ **El Bistro.** This small Italian restaurant, among the best Panajachel
★ has to offer, is hidden behind a low wall and an iron gate where the
main drag hits the lake. A few tables are set up in a garden, where hum-
mingbirds dart among flowering vines, and inside are two cozy, inti-
mate dining rooms. All of the simple but delicious food, from the tasty
bread to the fresh pasta, is homemade. Two standout specialties are
the fettuccine *arrabiata* (with a slightly spicy tomato sauce) and the
steak *au poivre,* cooked in a wine sauce and served with fresh vegeta-
bles and black pepper. ✉ *End of Calle Santander,* ☎ *no phone. No
credit cards. Closed Tues.*

$$ ✕ **Casablanca.** This main-street restaurant is Pana's most elegant. The wood-trimmed and white-walled dining room has Guatemalan artwork and windows overlooking the street. A few tables on the upper level are more intimate. The menu is ample, if somewhat overpriced, and includes a few seafood standouts—the lakefish and lobster are good choices—and salad, pasta, and meat dishes offer variety. Musicians occasionally entertain. ✉ *Calle Prinsipal 0–93, at Calle Santander,* ☎ *762–1015,* FAX *762–2025. AE, DC, MC, V.*

$$ ✕ **Al Chisme.** This popular, American-owned restaurant serves good, casual, Americanized food in a relaxed atmosphere. You can sit on a covered terrace or in the main dining room, with a fireplace, a bar, and a soundscape of jazz or rock-and-roll. Many of the regulars attest to the town's reputation as a hippie hangout. As a popular breakfast spot, Al Chisme serves homemade bagels and pastries, but the lunch and dinner menu is even better, with a selection ranging from chicken *cordon bleu* (filled with cheese and ham), to shrimp-curry crepes to three-cheese lasagna. ✉ *Avenida de los Arboles,* ☎ *no phone. AE, MC, V. Closed Wed.*

$$ ✕ **La Laguna.** The slightly dark, candlelit interior and mellow jazz or Latin American music on the stereo make Laguna the perfect place for a romantic dinner. Seating is on the porch or scattered throughout rooms decorated with wooden masks and other local handicrafts in what is a comfortable former residence, surrounded by a large lawn. Selections range from the traditional *pepian de pollo* (chicken in a spicy sauce) to black bass from Lago Atitlán. The fixed-price menu is a good deal. ✉ *Calle Principal between Calle Santander and Avenida de los Arboles,* ☎ *762–1231. DC, MC, V.*

$ ✕ **El Patio.** Although it's identifiable by the patio from which it takes its name, most of the restaurant's tables are indoors, in a large dining room with little ambience. Nevertheless, it's a fairly popular spot for breakfast, but the lunch and dinner menus offer greater variety, with items such as filet mignon, chicken à la king, roast pork, and a barbecue special on Sunday. ✉ *Calle Santander,* ☎ *762–2041. AE, DC, MC, V.*

$
★ ✕ **Pájaro Azul.** Tired of *huevos y frijoles* for breakfast every day? The outstanding crepes at this classy pastel-painted café will come to your rescue. Choose from a small but creative menu of savory veggie-filled dinner crepes to sweet dessert crepes, or pick your favorite combination of ingredients. It opens at 7 AM, and has a pile of back-issue magazines (including the *New Yorker*), and there's not a single frijole in sight. ✉ *Calle Santander, next to the post office,* ☎ *no phone, no credit cards.*

$$$$
★ ✕⊡ **Hotel Atitlán.** The area's most luxurious hotel is on a quiet cove about a mile east of town. An older, Spanish-style inn, it consists of a main building flanked by two-story wings that form a semicircle around a pool and gardens. The extensive grounds border a long stretch of beach and the Reserva Natural Atitlán (☞ *above*), a wooded butterfly and nature reserve crossed by footpaths and hanging bridges. Rooms have tile floors, carved wooden furniture, and handwoven bedspreads, and each has a balcony or patio with a lake and garden view. Even if you don't stay here, it's worth stopping by for a meal or drink, as the view of the water from both the bar and restaurant is wonderful, especially at sunset. The food is reliable, if a bit overpriced, with a standard menu of baked chicken, decent cuts of meats, and simple pastas. ✉ *2 km (1 mi) west of Panajachel, look for a large sign on the S-curve as you leave Panajachel for Sololá,* ☎ FAX *762–1441 in Panajachel;* ☎ *360–8405/0641 and* FAX *334–0640 in Guatemala City (call here for reservations), hotinsa@infovia.com.gt. 64 rooms. Restaurant, bar, pool, tennis court, beach, shop. AE, DC, MC, V.*

$$$ ✕🖭 **Cacique Inn.** This quiet hotel is an assemblage of several little buildings about one block off the main street, and though it doesn't have a view of the lake, it has an excellent restaurant, a swimming pool, and a lovely garden. Spacious though sparsely decorated rooms occupy several of the two-story buildings, and have large sliding-glass doors that open to the pool and garden. The rooms may seem a bit cool thanks to the tile floors, but they also have working fireplaces that can warm you up in a snap. The hotel grounds are surrounded by a wall, which makes the terraces and patios by the pool a relaxing, private haven. The Cacique's restaurant is one of the best in town, serving an ample selection of international and Guatemalan dishes. Cacique's agreeable chefs will sometimes even prepare dishes that aren't on the menu. ⊠ *Calle del Embarcadero, near Calle Principal,* ☎ 𝖥𝖠𝖷 *762–1205. 35 rooms. Restaurant, bar, pool. AE, DC, MC, V.*

$$$$ 🖭 **Barceló del Lago.** This six-story building behind the public beach is Panajachel's biggest and most modern hotel. With its gaudy exterior and uninspired contemporary decor, the Barceló lacks the character of smaller hotels, but it's comfortable, conveniently located, and has first-class service and great lake views. Rooms feature wall-to-wall carpeting, firm double beds, cable TV, large bathrooms, and either balconies or patios (first floor) with Atitlán vistas. An airy, plant-filled bar is welcoming and a huge restaurant next door looks onto the pool. ⊠ *End of Calle Rancho Grande, at Calle Buenas Nuevas,* ☎ *762–1555/ 1560,* 𝖥𝖠𝖷 *762–1562;* ☎ *361–9683/9685 in Guatemala City, barcelol@infovia.com.gt. 100 rooms. Restaurant, bar, pool, hot tub, massage, sauna, exercise room, meeting rooms. AE, DC, MC, V.*

$$$ 🖭 **Hotel Dos Mundos.** With its high thatched roofs, colorful gardens, and immaculate pool, this is a classy hotel without the hefty price tag of most deluxe accommodations. The rooms are medium size, with simple and tasteful furnishings. Most open right onto the attractive patio and pool, where you can relax on lounge chairs with a drink and a book. The restaurant has a certain elegance, with tables set beneath a soaring thatched roof, and a menu full of well-made pasta and wine. ⊠ *Calle Santander 4–72,* ☎ *762–2078/2140,* 𝖥𝖠𝖷 *762–0127, dosmundos@atitlan.com. 21 rooms. Restaurant, pool, travel services. AE, DC, MC, V. www.atitlan.com.*

$$$ 🖭 **Hotel Posada de Don Rodrigo.** All the way at the end of Calle Santander, this excellent hotel has large rooms, friendly service, and easy access to the lake. The rooms are tastefully decorated with handwoven bedspreads and dark-wood headboards and chairs, and have big bathrooms with luxuriously strong showers. The restaurant, with beautiful lake views, serves good standard fare, and yet never seems crowded. Of course, the view would be even better if the Don's giant waterslide wasn't in the way. A huge grassy field out back is bordered on one side by an open-air corridor filled with chairs and hammocks. ⊠ *End of Calle Santander,* ☎ *762–2326/2329;* ☎ *331–8017/5562,* 𝖥𝖠𝖷 *331–6838 in Guatemala City; chotelera@c.net.gt 28 rooms. Restaurant, pool, sauna, squash. AE, DC, MC, V.*

$$$ 🖭 **Müllers Guest House.** On the quiet street parallel to Calle Santander, a block from the Old Town, this simple four-room hotel is reminiscent of a European bed-and-breakfast, with pretty grounds and a garden. The rooms are immaculate and very un-típica, with blond-hardwood floors and ceilings and pastel colors. Breakfast in the comfortable, homey sitting room is included in the price, as is wine and cheese in the late afternoon. Reserve well in advance in high season and on weekends. ⊠ *Calle Rancho Grande 1–82,* ☎ *762–2442/2392;* ☎ *363–1306 reservations (Guatemala City). htmuller@amigo.net.gt 3 rooms, 1 bungalow. No credit cards.*

$$$ ⊡ **Rancho Grande Inn.** In the early 1940s, a German immigrant by the name of Milly Schleisier opened this bed-and-breakfast comprised of a series of bungalows flanking the street. In so doing, she created perhaps the most charming of Pana's accommodations, melding the designs of country houses in her homeland with the colorful culture of her adopted residence. Since 1975 Rancho Grande has belonged to Marlita Hannstein, who has maintained the level of comfort and service established by Schleisier. Every room is unique, but all are spacious with comfortable, king-size beds, A-frame wood ceilings, white stucco walls, tile floors, and locally woven rugs and bed covers. They also have porches and are separated by lawns and gardens. Some bungalows can sleep up to five, and the suite has a fireplace, phone, and cable TV. Breakfast is included, and is served family style every morning. ⊠ *Calle Rancho Grande, between the beach and Old Town,* ☎ *762–1554,* FAX *762–2247. hranchog@quetzal.net 11 bungalows, 1 bungalow suite. Breakfast room. AE, DC, MC, V.*

$$ ⊡ **Hotel Montana.** Set back in the older, calmer part of town near the cathedral, the unassuming Montana is bright, clean, and reasonably priced. What the rooms lack in lake views is made up with an expanse of verdant mountainside. The rooms are small, but they have comfortable beds, reliable hot water, and cable TV. This is the cheapest of the moderate ($$) hotels, and though it's within easy walking distance from Calle Santander, the neighborhood here is quiet, attractive, and seldom visited by tourists. ⊠ *Avenida de los Arboles, across from the cathedral,* ☎ *762–0326/0333,* FAX *762–2180 montana@atitlan.com. 15 rooms. No credit cards.*

$$ ⊡ **Hotel Regis.** Although it's conveniently located in town, Regis isn't quite as attractive or quiet as the competition, but it's cheaper. A group of bungalows is spread out around smallish but well-tended grounds, which include a small playground and two outdoor thermal hot springs. The room decor is an attempt at the popular colonial motif. Several bungalows have fireplaces, and some can sleep six. If you pay with a credit card, you'll be levied a 10% surcharge. ⊠ *Calle Santander, at Calle el Chali,* ☎ *762–1149,* FAX *762–1152, regis@atitlan.com or hotelregis@hotmail.com. 20 bungalows. Hot tub, playground. AE, DC, MC, V.*

$ ⊡ **Hotel Galindo.** Rooms are small and somewhat dumpy at Galindo, conveniently located in town behind its own spacious restaurant, but they surround a lush garden courtyard. Behind the courtyard are several suites, which are considerably larger and have separate sitting rooms and fireplaces. The restaurant is breezy and attractive, but better food can be found nearby. Note: the hot water is unreliable. ⊠ *Calle Principal,* FAX *762–1168. 14 rooms, 4 suites. Restaurant. No credit cards.*

$ ⊡ **Hotel Maya Kanek.** On the main street at the edge of the Old Town, this place is in a quiet area with fewer foreigners than on the tourist side of Pana. Arranged like a miniature motel, rooms surround a paved parking area. They're rather small and have little decor to speak of, save for some bright blue paint and occasional brickwork. Still, they're clean and have firm mattresses. Hot water is available 6 AM–9 AM and 6 PM–9 PM only. The owner is a friendly fellow and has assembled a thorough list of local boat and bus schedules in the lobby. ⊠ *Calle Principal,* ☎ *762–1104,* FAX *762–0084. 20 rooms, 15 with bath. No credit cards.*

Nightlife and the Arts

Since Pana approximates a resort town, it probably has the liveliest nightlife in the highlands. Most night spots are clustered near the intersection of Avenida de los Arboles and Calle Principal. The **Circus Bar** (⊠ Avenida de los Arboles, ☎ 762–2056) is a popular spot for locals and travelers alike, and also serves good food. There's often a short set of live music. **Chapiteau Disco** (⊠ Avenida de los Arboles), a dim bar and disco playing a mix of mostly American and Latin rock. A cluster of other bars less frequented by the backpacker crowd are in the same area. On Calle Santander, the mellow **Sunset Café** (⊠ at the lakefront) has great views and nightly live music. **Grapevine** (⊠ Calle Santander) has both a video lounge and a happy hour, from 7 to 9. Or join the locals at **El Blabla,** a bar-disco, or **Socrates,** for dancing to salsa and merengue, or head to the cantinas on Calle Rancho Grande for a beer.

Outdoor Activities and Sports

As Panajachel evolves from an isolated Guatemalan village into a booming lakeside resort, water sports are becoming more popular, giving Lago Atitlán a Club Med feel. That said, you might as well get involved. Rent a kayak or canoe at the public beach for $3 an hour or $10 a day. **Diversiones Acuáticas Balom** (⊠ between Santander and Satiago ferries, look for a red Marlboro kiosk, ☎ 762–2242) handles them all, as well as private boat tours of the lake. It's best to get out early and be back by noon, as the afternoon winds can be fierce.

For exploring on land exploring, you can rent a mountain bike at **Moto Servicio Quiché** (Avenida de los Arboles, at Calle Principal) and pedal over to nearby villages. Rental rates are about $1 per hour, $7 for 8 hours, or $9 for 24 hours.

You can also explore the exhilarating landscape with a hike. INGUAT has maps, ferry schedules, and can hook you up with a guide, which is recommended since all routes—up the Volcán Atitlan or over the lake to the nearby villages of San Pedro and Santa Cruz—are definitely off the beaten path.

If you want to swim, your best bet is to head to one of the smaller towns, such as Santa Cruz, San Marcos, or San Lucas (☞ *below*). They all have nice docks from which to swim, and the water is cleaner. In Pana, the best place for swimming is the **public beach** on the far east side of town (to your left, facing the water). To get here, cut over the river beyond the Santiago–bound ferry dock, and follow the dirt road to beach, indicated by various docks.

Shopping

There is no shortage of things to buy, or places to buy them here. Handicrafts and artesanía of all sorts are sold by locals and expats alike, in stores and on the street: Calle Santander is lined with **vendors** who hang their wares from fences and makeshift stalls. The large **Tinimit Maya** outdoor market (⊠ East side of Calle Santander, halfway down) is easily the best place for reasonably priced, quality típica. **Casa Alegre** (⊠ East side of Calle Santander, near Calle 15 de Febrero)) is a large boutique with a varied selection and good prices. **Mayan Relics** (⊠ Calle Monte Rey) sells a variety of local and other goods at a bargain. **Ojalá Antiques** (⊠ Comercial Pueblito, east side of Avenida de los Arboles) has a small but excellent selection of fine goods and antiques. **Galería** (⊠ Calle Rancho Grande) sells both antiques and contemporary art.

BOOKSTORES

The Comercial Pueblito shopping square on Avenida de los Arboles has two bookstores: **Xibalba** (⊠ Comercial Pueblito, downstairs) has a fairly mixed selection, and **Get Guated Out** (⊠ Comercial Pueblito, upstairs) carries mostly romance, mystery, and sci-fi titles, and is your best bet for English-language newspapers.

Telephones and Internet Service

MayaNet (⊠ Calle Santander) and **Interp@na** (⊠ Edificio Rincón Saí shopping square, second floor, Calle Santander at Calle Principal) are Pana's best. Both are open daily until 9 PM, and charge $2 per hour.

Compare rates on international phone calls and faxes from here; they may be lower than you'd pay at TELGUA.

TELGUA (Calle Santander, halfway between lake and Calle Principal) is open daily 7 AM–midnight. Unfortunately, international calls are expensive from Panajachel: $2 per minute and up. If you can wait, it's much cheaper in Quetzaltenango and Antigua.

The **post office,** open weekdays 8–4, is opposite the police station on a side street facing the church. For packages, it's safer to use one of the many businesses that specialize in shipping; try **Get Guated Out** (⊠ Comercial Pueblito, upstairs) or **DHL Worldwide Express** (⊠ Calle Santander, in Rincón Saí complex, ☏ 762–1474). In addition to international shipping, DHL has a courier service that runs to and from Guatemala City—the price ranges from $5 to $20, but it'll save you a trip.

Visitor Information

The folks at the **INGUAT** (Calle del Lago, ☏ 414–0090) tourism office in Panajachel are very helpful. The office is located on the lakefront, in a blue kiosk, near the Barceló hotel. Unfortunately, it's quite a walk from the bus stop. To get here, walk all the down Calle Santander; take a left on Calle Buenas Nuevas and a right on Rancho Grande toward the water.

EMERGENCIES

The **police station** is near the end of Calle Principal next to the municipal building. **Panamedic Centro Clínico Familiar** (⊠ Calle Principal 0–72, ☏ 762–2174) offers 24-hour medical attention—Dr. Francisco Ordoñez and his wife, Dra. Zulma Ordoñez, both speak English. **Farmacia Nueva Unión** (⊠ Calle Santander, 1 block below Calle Principal) is open daily 24 hours.

Santa Catarina Palopó

25 *4 km (2½ mi) east of Panajachel along a dirt road.*

You'll be surrounded by the brilliant blues and greens of traditional native *huipiles* (embroidered blouses) as you walk down the cobblestone streets of this picturesque town. The hotel Villa Santa Catarina, at the lakeside entrance to town, has magical views of the water and volcanoes. Some of Guatemala's greatest contradictions are also visible in Santa Catarina, with ramshackle homes standing within eyesight of luxury chalets, whose owners arrive as often by helicopter as they do by car.

Dining and Lodging

$$$ ✕🏨 **Villa Santa Catarina.** This well-located hotel is housed in a long, two-story yellow building with an adobe tile roof. Guest rooms are small, with hardwood floors, exposed ceilings, peach walls, and típica bedspreads; each has a private balcony, most with a view of the lake. The restaurant serves typical Guatemalan dishes such as *pepian de pollo* (chicken in a spicy sauce) and robálo. The hotel has a game room and a pool, and windsurfing and a series of natural hot springs are only a few feet away. ⊠ *Calle de la Playa,* ☏ FAX *762–1291, stpvillas@pronet.net.gt 36 rooms. Restaurant, bar, pool, waterskiing. AE, DC, MC, V.*

San Antonio Palopó

26 *6½ km (4 mi) east of Santa Catarina Palopó.*

Slightly larger than its sister village, Santa Catarina Palopó, San Antonio is a hill town with the feel of a quiet fishing village. Women dress in white blouses with colored stripes, and this is one of only a handful of regions in Latin America where men still dress in traditional costume on a daily basis—their pants are designed with geometric motifs and calf-length woolen wraparounds fastened by leather belts or red sashes. Village life here still consists mainly of farming, weaving, and attending church services.

A beautiful adobe colonial **church** in a stone plaza marks the center of town. The interior is spacious and peaceful, and its tall whitewashed outer walls are particularly pretty when lit up at night. During the day, the steps are used as a social meeting ground, where all passersby are sure to stop for a while.On the main drag, between the church and the school at the entrance of town, is an excellent **women's textile cooperative,** where you see master weavers in action. The process is fascinating, and the results are stunning. Although most are exported, there's a small shop on site, and the proceeds (or a small donation) help sustain the cooperative.

Lodging

$$ 🏨 **Terrazas del Lago.** This very basic but charming hotel overlooks the town's public beach and is decorated with floral-pattern stone tiles. Large guest rooms have stone walls, wood tables, and iron candlesticks; those in front have patios with lake vistas. A small restaurant on top of the hotel serves simple breakfast and lunch fare, while the several terraces are perfect for a quiet cup of coffee or tea. ✉ *Calle de la Playa,* ☎ *762–0037. 12 rooms. No credit cards.*

En Route Halfway between San Antonio Palopó and Santiago Atitlán is the tiny village of San Lucas Tolimán, and the hotel that recommends making a stop here.

$$$$ ✕🏨 **Pak'Ok Marina and Resort.** The centerpiece of the truly magnificent Hotel Pak'Ok is its elegantly decorated restaurant, where the dinners, from Continental dishes to Guatemalan favorites, and desserts are exquisite, and a bank of two-story windows provides a spectacular view of the San Lucas harbor. The rooms are similarly classy, with colonial-style furnishings, and they surround a sloping grass courtyard with hammocks, pool, extensive gardens, and an outdoor bar. Many rooms have private verandas, and kitchenettes, and the hotel has its own grocery across the street. Individual Spanish lessons, water sports, and tours can be arranged. Several discounted rooms are located in a comfortable annex across the street. ✉ *Calle Principal,* ☎ *206–7561,* FAX *334–6075, sonya@infovia.com.gt. 25 rooms. Restaurant, bar, pool, tennis court, kayaks, laundry service. AE, DC, MC, V.* ⌘

Santiago Atitlán

★ ㉗ *1-hr boat ride from Panajachel, 21 km (13 mi) west of San Antonio Palopó, 31 km (19 mi) from Panajachel.*

Across the lake from Panajachel, fascinating Santiago is the capital of the proud and independent Tzutuhil Indians, who resisted political domination during the country's civil war. Contradictorily, it's also a popular location for wealthy Guatemalans from the capital, who've built their second homes here on the lake. Nevertheless, with a population of 48,000 (among which only a few dozen are gringos or Ladinos), it's one of the largest and most vital indigenous towns in Guatemala, a town that has roused a number of activists. Many of these activists and residents were killed or "disappeared" during the war, and during this time the military stationed themselves nearby, no doubt to minimize dissent. Much local history derives from Santiago's resistance to military oppression and its strong belief in civil rights for indigenous people, including a peaceful march held on December 12, 1991, in which the village protested the army's presence and the military responded with gunfire.

The desire to preserve indigenous culture and traditions has also made Santiago well-known for the quality of its weaving, and most people still wear the striking traditional costume, including, for women, a headdress resembling a bright red halo. It's also one of the few places where people actively worship Guatemala's cigar-smoking Maximón, a Maya god masquerading as a Catholic saint, and remain contentedly unresolved in their contradictory Maya (or pagan) and Catholic beliefs. As you get off the boat, small children may offer to lead you to see Maximón in exchange for a few quetzales. If not, ask for a guide at the tourist office, which is uphill from the dock.

The **Santiago church** in the main plaza is unique for the Tzutuhil deities featured in the pulpit woodwork. It was on this very pulpit that Oklahoma-born priest Father Stanley Francis Rother was assassinated by right-wing death squads in July 1981 for his outspoken support of the Tzutuhil cause, demanding accountability for "disappeared" residents, and an end to the army's presence. (A base was located just outside of town, near where the Parque de la Paz now lies.) Beloved by the local parishioners, he is remembered with a plaque near the door.

On the road west to San Pedro, past Posada Santiago, **Parque de la Paz** commemorates 13 Tzutuhiles, including several children, who were killed when the army garrison open fired on a peaceful demonstration that protested the military presence here. The massacre drew national outrage, and President Serrano Elías himself apologized and withdrew military forces from Santiago. The memorial is a sober reminder of Guatemala's tortured past.

Horseback riding on the lake is offered by two Americans, Jim and Nancy Mattisson, and their company **Aventura en Atitlán** (⊠ 10 km/6 mi from town, on the road to San Pedro, ☎ 201–5527). Various rides, including an exhilarating torchlit nighttime outing, wind through lush lowlands and spectacular cloud forests. A terrific meal at the ranch house awaits the end of every ride. The prices here are significantly higher than at other outfits, but their service and safety record are immeasurably better. Reservations are recommended.

Dining and Lodging

$$ ✕🏠 **Bambú.** Run by a Spanish expat with a penchant for gardens and fine food, the Bambú has beautiful spacious grounds, an excellent restaurant, and bright comfy bungalows. The bungalows are simple but charming, with red-tile floors, thatched roofs, and a private patio. Immaculate stone pathways loop through a series of taxonomically arranged gardens (cacti in one, flowers in the next, and so on), while most of the restaurant's fruits, vegetables, and herbs are cultivated out back. The restaurant serves mostly Spanish food in an A-frame dining room with exposed beams, excellent views, and a crackling stone fireplace. Canoes are available for paddling around. ⊠ *1 km (½ mi) east of town, on the road to San Lucas Tolimán,* ☎ *721–7197, 201–8913. 5 bungalows. Restaurant, bar, boating. AE, DC, MC, V.*

$$ ✕🏠 **Posada de Santiago.** With northern Californian friendliness and
★ flair, this longtime Santiago icon has deluxe accommodations in private bungalows, excellent food, and fabulous lake and volcano views. Bungalows have carved-wood doors, stone walls, fireplaces, and thick wool blankets on the beds. The restaurant serves exquisite specialties, such as smoked chicken píbil in a tangy red sauce and Thai coconut shrimp, and has an extensive wine list to boot. Also on the premises

is a small store, and canoe and mountain-bike rentals are available. A 10% surcharge is added if credit cards are used for payment. ⊠ *Road to San Pedro, 1 km (½ mi) south of town,* ☎ *702–8462,* ☎ FAX *721–7167, posdesantiago@guate.net. 12 bungalows. Restaurant, boating, mountain bikes. AE, DC, MC, V.* ♨

San Marcos La Laguna

㉘ *15 mins by boat from Panajachel; by car, exit Interamericana Highway at Km 148 (direction Quetzaltenenago).*

Tranquillity is imparted in the lakeside setting and the relaxation services at **Las Pirámides** (⊠ private dock, ☎ 205–7151, 205–7302), a live-in meditation center and yoga retreat offering day-, week-, and month-long courses. (The course cycles begin and end on the full moon.) Rates begin at $8–$10 per day, depending on length of stay. The price includes room, vegan or vegetarian board, instruction, and use of the sauna, library, and kitchen. It's easy to find, as every structure is either a pyramid or an A-frame.

You can get a decent **massage** at the **Hotel Unicornio** (⊠ behind Las Pirámides) where the decor is dominated by various wooden, ceramic, and fuzzy unicorns.

Lodging

$ 🏨 **Posada Schumann.** A bit of old-fashioned class in this otherwise sleepy town, Posada Schumann has cozy rooms and bungalows, a decent restaurant, and a narrow swath of garden stretching down to the lake. Exposed stonework and unfinished wood paneling lend a slightly rustic feel, while típica and festive colors add Guatemalan flavor. Note that the hot water can be unreliable. ⊠ *Posada Schumann dock,* ☎ *202–2216. 4 rooms, with shared bath; 3 bungalows. Restaurant. No credit cards.*

Jaibalito

㉙ *10-min boat ride west of Panajachel.*

Jaibalito has two inexpensive and excellent hotels, even though it's so small that it rarely appears on Lake Atitlán maps. Santa Cruz La Laguna is a 30-minute walk east, but it is otherwise quite isolated. In fact, there's nothing else around and no boat service after 6 PM—but for those seeking genuine peace and quiet, this is the best of the undisturbed lakeside retreats.

Dining and Lodging

$–$$ ✕🏨 **The Vulcano Lodge.** Amid a forested coffee plantation five minutes from the lakeshore, the Vulcano has smallish rooms with firm beds, tasteful decor, and private patios. Well-kept gardens with hammocks make for peaceful relaxation, and the restaurant serves decent European cuisine. Intriguing artwork by local artist Guido Bondioli is displayed throughout, and can even be bought right off the walls. Though slightly overpriced and lacking lake views, this is still a fine hotel for those seeking quiet seclusion. ⊠ *Four-min walk from Jaibalito dock, follow the signs and yellow arrows,* ☎ *no phone,* FAX *762–0092. vulcanolodge@hotmail.com 54 rooms, 1 suite. No credit cards.*

$ ✕🏨 **Casa del Mundo.** Built on a clifftop overlooking the water, where you can navigate the hotel's kayaks, gorgeous Casa del Mundo has unquestionable claim to Lake Atitlán's best view. Every single room has a stunning view, but Nos. 1 and 3 are the most breathtaking. If you can drag your eyes away from the windows, you'll notice the beautiful wood beam ceilings, red-tile floors, stucco and stone walls, and artsy decor. The restaurant has large windows, and meals are served family style. ⊠

Jaibalito dock, ☎ *204–5558,* ℻ *762–0092. casamundo@yahoo.com 8 rooms, 4 with bath. Boating. No credit cards.*

Santa Cruz La Laguna

③⓪ *10-min boat ride west of Panajachel.*

It's a steep walk up to the village, but the hardy are rewarded with a glimpse into a town unmarred by hordes of visitors—or any at all, for that matter. A highlight of this little village perched on a hill is a small but beautiful **adobe church** in the main plaza, whose walls are lined with carved wooden saints. Santa Cruz is also the starting point of a wonderfully scenic four-hour walk west to **San Marcos de La Laguna,** which passes through several tiny villages and along gusty bluffs overlooking the lake.

Because Lake Atitlán affords divers with "mile-high" waters and rich underwater archaeology, an **ATI Divers** (⊠ Hotel Iguana Perdida, main dock, ☎ 762–2646, santacruz@guate.net) PADI-certified diving school is based in Santa Cruz. ATI has courses for all levels, from basic certification (4-days, $160) to dive master (price varies according to experience).

Dining and Lodging

$$ ✕⛺ **Arca de Noé.** This rustic lakeside hotel has magnificent views, friendly owners, and delicious home cooking. The guest rooms, housed in several attached wood and stone bungalows, are small but neat, with low ceilings. Electricity is solar-generated, and there is no hot water. Meals are served family style in the main building, which resembles a New England farmhouse. The menu changes constantly, but each meal comes with fresh vegetables and bread right out of the oven. ⊠ *Main dock,* ☎ *306–4352,* ℻ *762–0092. thearca@yahoo.com. 10 rooms, 6 with bath. Restaurant, boating. No credit cards.*

$ ✕⛺ **La Iguana Perdida.** The Lost Iguana is part hotel and part summer camp. There's no electricity and no hot water, and the toilets are glorified Port-A-Potties. Still, the thatched bungalows are brimming with character, and the grass-mat walls and kerosene lamplight add distinct character. For groups, the dorm-style rooms can hold five to eight of your traveling pals. The restaurant serves good family-style meals, and owners Deedle and Mike are very friendly. The guests tend to be fairly young, and most are here for ATI diving courses (☞ *above*). ⊠ *Main dock,* ☎ ℻ *762–2646. santacruz@guate.net 3 dorm-style rooms; 3 cabins, with shared baths. Dive shop, sauna. No credit cards.*

Chichicastenango

③① *37 km (23 mi) north of Panajachel, 108 km (67 mi) northwest of Antigua.*

★ The main attraction in Chichicastenango, a colorful and accessible highland town, is the **market** in the main plaza. One of the largest in the country, it's held every Thursday (5:30 AM to 1:30 PM) and Sunday (5:30 AM to 3 PM) and, like all other highland markets, was originally the basis of local commerce. Since its fame has grown, however, the local market has been pushed to the periphery. The bulk of today's business is conducted between tourists—arriving en masse twice weekly—and indigenous merchants from throughout the highlands, who come to sell their wares to the foreigners. The evening before market day is in many ways more intriguing than the event itself—and hotels tend to fill up quickly on Wednesday and Saturday nights, the days before the big market—as vendors set up their stalls with pleasant anticipation, and the town still belongs to the Indians.

All the buying and selling tends to overshadow the fact that "Chichi" would be well worth visiting even if there were no market at all. On a small hill surrounded by pine forest, Chichi is an anomaly of sorts in that the Catholic Church openly accepts local pagan rituals, and an elected indígena council works hand-in-hand with the church to administer the city. The council leaders, known as *cofrades* (loosely meaning brothers), are locally appointed. The cofradía is the most prestigious position in town, but like most good things, it comes at a heavy price. The cofrades have to pay for all of Chichi's holiday celebrations and fiestas out of their own pockets. This is especially costly during the town's grand fiesta, **Dia de Santo Tomás,** on December 13–21, when the city explodes with parades and dances. During the festivities, the cofrades wear elegant silver costumes and carry staffs topped by a magnificent sun medallion.

This mixing of Catholicism with Maya ritual is much in evidence at the church of **Santo Tomás** (⊠ Plaza Mayor), in the heart of the market. Chichi is still considered the Holy City of Quiché. The elaborate Catholic dias santos (saints' days) processions are followed by equally elaborate Maya religious rituals, which unfold on the church steps. Built in the mid-1500s, right on the site of a Maya altar, Santo Tomás is busy with worshipers all day and late into the night; its steps are usually engulfed in a cloud of copal incense, which worshipers burn while performing rituals before entering the church. You can enter through a door on the right side of the church; just remember that picture-taking is not allowed inside.

Unfortunately, the indígena are not totally free from Christian persecution. The shrine to the deity **Pascual Abaj,** on the hilltop outside of town, is often wrecked by zealous Christians. Each time, the elongated stone face of the waist-high carved idol is restored, and believers continue their daily prehispanic rituals with incense, candles, and offerings of flowers. Since it's one of the most accessible of the highland Maya shrines, respectful visitors have often turned out to watch. (Be sensitive about taking photographs if you go.) Brujos, the local shamans, preside over these ceremonies, and the villagers recite special prayers and offer candles, food, alcohol, and the occasional slaughtered chicken. To see the shrine, follow 9 Calle until you see the signs for the narrow footpath up the hill. Boys hanging around the plaza will guide you to the shrine for a small fee and can tell you when the rituals take place.

Capilla de Calvario (Calvary Chapel, ⊠ across the plaza from Santo Tomás) doesn't attract the attention that its neighbor does, but it has a nice view of the market. A little **museum** of pre-Columbian artifacts (⊠ next to Santo Tomás) displays the private collection of a local priest.

The beautiful and colorful **cemetery** (⊠ west end of 8 Calle) has mostly aboveground sarcophagi, painted in brilliant shades of teal, yellow, and orange. Since the cemetery drapes over a low hilltop, the colors and shadows look particularly pretty in late afternoon.

Dining and Lodging

$ ✕ **Las Brasas.** Pine boughs cover the floor and an eclectic collection of típica brightens the walls of this excellent second-floor steak house. The chef, formerly of the Hotel Santo Tomás, grills up a great steak, but there are plenty of other options, including a giant plate of beans, eggs, *longaniza* (a spicy sausage similar to chorizo), vegetables, cheese, and tortillas, as well as a few vegetarian dishes. Music and a full bar keep things lively, but not intrusively so. ⊠ *6 Calle 4–52, second level,* ☎ *756–1006. AE, DC, MC, V.*

$ ✕ **Café-Restaurante La Villa de los Cofrades.** With two locations within a block of each other, it's hard to miss this longtime Chichi eatery. The smaller of the two has patio seating right on the plaza, where you can people-watch and plot your market day while feasting on Belgian waffles or sipping one of the finest cappuccinos in the country. The other restaurant, a block down 5 Calle, has a larger dining room and less traffic. The lunch and dinner menus at both consist mainly of fish, meat, and pasta, but the plaza-side location has more vegetarian dishes (and in hefty portions). If you're in a hurry to get to the market, beware: the service can be miserably slow. ✉ *Northeast corner of plaza; 5 Calle and 6 Avenida;* ☏ *no phone. No credit cards.*

$ ✕ **La Fonda del Tzijolaj.** The narrow balcony of this second-floor restaurant overlooks the plaza and is an especially good place to watch the vendors set up on the eve of a market. Of the mostly traditional menu items, the chicken *chimichurri* (chicken in an herb sauce) is an excellent choice, but there are a few surprises, too, such as spinach gnocchi. Most entrées come with soup, a salad, and a soda. ✉ *Centro Commercial Santo Tomás, north side of plaza, second level,* ☏ *756–1013. AE, MC, V.*

$$$ ✕▥ **Hotel Santo Tomás.** Built in the Spanish style, in which the rooms surround a courtyard, Santo Tomás places second in the running for the town's best hotel. Breezy outdoor passageways lead from the beautiful courtyard with two fountains to guest rooms and are lined with hundreds of plants growing from rustic clay pots. Rooms are spacious and decorated with traditional textiles and antique reproductions, and each has a fireplace. The back of the hotel is quieter and has views of the surrounding Quiché countryside, whereas front rooms overlook the town. The large restaurant has a lunch buffet on market days, and on the upper level of the hotel are a heated pool and small exercise room. Attendants wear traditional garb and leave you to your own devices unless you call upon them. ✉ *7 Avenida 5–32,* ☏ *756–1316/1061,* FAX *756–1306. 43 rooms. Restaurant, bar, pool, hot tub, sauna, exercise room. AE, DC, MC, V.*

$$$ ✕▥ **Mayan Inn.** The genuine adobe construction and original wood-
★ work make the luxurious Mayan Inn one of the most unusual hotels in the country. Built and operated by the Clark family (of Clark Tours) since 1932, the Mayan Inn is a veritable historical site, and most locals regard it as a town treasure. A tour is highly recommended, even if you stay elsewhere. Rooms are furnished with fireplaces, antiques, and Guatemalan weavings and art, and surround a series of beautifully maintained garden courtyards or overlook the forested hills around town. Particularly nice are the rooms built into the hillside at different levels; the lower the level, the more likely you'll have a view of the town's colorful, vibrant cemetery and the surrounding pine forests. Service is excellent—an attendant in traditional costume is assigned to each room and does everything from lighting the fire to serving dinner. Meals are taken in stately old dining halls with fireplaces, with a set menu that changes daily. The restaurant is open from 7 to 9 AM, noon to 2 PM, and 7 to 9 PM. ✉ *3 Avenida at 8 Calle, behind Capilla de Calvario, one block west of the plaza,* ☏ *756–1179/1202,* FAX *756–1212;* ☏ *reservations: 339–2888,* FAX *339–2909 in Guatemala City. 30 rooms. Restaurant, bar. AE, DC, MC, V.*

$$ ✕▥ **Hotel Chuguñilá.** This enjoyable hotel is in an older building a few blocks north of the plaza. A variety of rooms face a nice cobblestone courtyard, which is unfortunately used for parking. The tile portico from which most rooms lead off has some chairs, tables, and potted plants. Rooms are furnished simply; the more expensive ones have fireplaces. The oddly shaped and warmly lit dining room is perhaps the hotel's best feature, especially since its windows look out onto the relaxed main drag or the hotel's courtyard. Lunch and dinner menus offer mostly standard fare: meats, pasta, sandwiches, and salads. ✉ *5 Avenida 5–24,* ☎ FAX *756–1134. 31 rooms, 5 with shared bath, 2 suites. Restaurant. AE, DC, MC, V.*

$$$ 🏨 **Hotel Villa Grande.** This large luxury hotel at the entrance to town offers the modern amenities absent from most other Chichicastenango hotels, but it unfortunately also lacks their charm. The hotel consists of five unattractive buildings, most of which have panoramic views of town. The air-conditioned guest rooms are small, with peach walls and típica bedspreads, and the more spacious suites have fireplaces. ✉ *Cantón Pachoj Alto, Km 144 on road to Antigua,* ☎ *756–1053,* FAX *756–1140. 67 rooms. 2 restaurants, bar, indoor pool, hot tub. MC, V.*

$ 🏨 **Hospedaje Salvador.** Somewhere between the Gingerbread House and Chutes&Ladders, this big colorful mishmash of a hotel is a favorite among budget travelers. Rooms are aligned along three and four levels of curved incongruous breezeways, with steep stairs zigzagging all about. In the middle of it all is a large cobblestone courtyard decorated with statues and potted plants, and facing the entrance is a small shrine shared by the Virgin Mary and a Maya god. Though rooms are a bit musty, beds a bit lumpy, and hot water is available only for a couple of morning hours, what the Salvador lacks in comfort it compensates for with low rates and lots of character. ✉ *10 Calle at 5 Avenida, three blocks south of the plaza,* ☎ *756–1329. 46 rooms, 10 with bath. No credit cards.*

$ 🏨 **Hotel Chalet.** Sans the snowy Alps, a small sun-splashed breakfast room is at the heart of this cozy little hotel, whose yellow walls and friendly service somehow make the name work. The rooms and bathrooms are smallish but not cramped. Masks and other handicrafts adorn the walls, and mellow jazz plays in the breakfast and sitting rooms. At press time an outdoor terrace was also in the works. The hotel is down a small unpaved road intersecting with 7 Avenida. A 5.5% surcharge is levied for credit cards. ✉ *3 Calle C 7–44,* ☎ FAX *756–1360. 7 rooms. AE, MC, V.*

$ 🏨 **Posada El Arco.** This is a great little hotel in its price range with a homey feel. The spacious rooms, with their hardwood floors, wood-frame beds, and slightly corny decor, are happily reminiscent of a 70s-style rec room. The owners, Don Pedro and Doña Emilsa, speak English and are friendly and helpful. All rooms have fireplaces, bathrooms, and hot water around the clock. A washing machine and dryer are available for a small fee. To get here, climb up the stairs at the foot of the arch, and turn left. (Don't be fooled by kids who may try to divert you to other hotels by telling you El Arco is closed: these folks work for the competition.) ✉ *4 Calle 4–36,* ☎ *756–1255. 7 rooms. No credit cards.*

Nightlife

Nightlife in Chichi is pretty much limited to the hotel bars. The best entertainment on a Wednesday or Saturday night is to wander around town, visit the church, and watch the vendors set up their stalls.

Shopping

Although the selection of goods from around the country at the Thursday and Sunday **markets** is overwhelming, the prices rise the moment the first tour bus rolls into town. The purchasing possibilities are endless: gorgeous huipiles from Nebaj, made-for-tourist "típico" clothing, wooden masks, wool blankets, woven bags, baskets, machetes, metates (a corn-grinding stone), jade, pottery, and everyday necessities from soap to cassette tapes to produce. Although the city tries to centralize the frenzied shopping activity around the plaza, surrounding streets are inevitably blocked off by the overflow. If it's any kind of reassurance, the town is famous for its ability to accommodate masses of people on market day. Try to come to Chichi early the day before market day: not only will you get better deals the evening before while the vendors are setting up, but part of the fun is to see the transformation of the lovely, sleepy town into a grand bazaar. Late afternoon of market day, when the big spenders have moved on, is also a good time for getting good deals. Still, the prices on quality textiles and wood masks are among the best you'll find anywhere.

Arriving and Departing

Buses leave Chichicastenango from the corner of 5 Calle and 5 Avenida virtually all day. Those headed north, down 5 Calle, are going to Santa Cruz El Quiché, while those headed east on 5 Avenida are likely headed for Guatemala City. You may have to change buses in Los Encuentros to get to Quetzaltenango, Sololá, and Panajachel, or in Chimaltenango for Antigua.

Shuttle service to most highland towns can be arranged through the friendly **Servicios Turísticos Chichicastenanga** (✉ 3 Calle C 7–4, ☎ FAX 756–1360) in the Hotel Chalet, whose guests get discounts, and by **Chichi Tours** (✉ 5 Calle 4–42, ☎ 756–1017/1008). Prices are generally $5–$7 to Panajachel, $12 to Antigua, $20 to Guatemala City, and $15 to Quetzaltenango.

Getting Around

All of Chichi's hotels, restaurants, and sights are within walking distance of Plaza Mayor, which is between 7 Calle and 8 Calle on 5 Avenida. The main strip is 5 Avenida, where you'll also see the Santo Tomás church and the Arco Gucumatz. From the bus stop, at the corner of 5 Calle and 5 Avenida, it's two blocks south to the plaza, past the Arco Gucumatz, at 4 Calle. (Calle numbers increase southward; avenida numbers increase to the east and decrease to the west.) Most of the hotels, restaurants, and artesanía stores lie near the central plaza on 6 Avenida and 6 Calle. The TELGUA and post offices are on 7 Avenida, two blocks east of the plaza.

Santa Cruz del Quiché

③② *19 km (12 mi) north of Chichicastenango.*

Adventurous travelers may want to continue north from Chichicastenango for further glimpses of the department of El Quiché, which offers more fine scenery and traditional villages. A half hour north of Chichicastenango lies Santa Cruz del Quiché, the provincial capital, which isn't as attractive as Chichicastenango but has inexpensive accommodations, a bank, and several restaurants on the main plaza. Adventurers should be aware, however, that the remote Quiché roads, once known for intense guerrilla activity, were recently the site of some ugly roadside assaults on buses and cars.

"Quiché," as the town is commonly called, has a pretty white church on the east side of the Parque Central. Municipal buildings sandwich the church on either side, one of which has a nice clock tower. To reach the Parque Central from the bus terminal, walk north (uphill) on 1 Calle for five blocks, then head west for one block.

OFF THE
BEATEN PATH

UTATLÁN – Also called K'umarcaaj, which was the ancient capital of the Maya-Quiché kingdom, this once-magnificent site was destroyed by Spanish conquistadors in 1524. The Maya ruins that remain haven't been restored, but they are frequently used for traditional celebrations. You can get a taxi to and from the ruins for about $5. You can also walk the pleasant 3 km (2 mi) without much difficulty—just follow 10 Calle out of town, where it turns into a dirt road. A tight S-curve is the half-way point; later, a long curving downhill forks at the bottom, and the ruins are to the right.

Dining and Lodging

$ ✕ **Comedor Flipper.** A lively cage of birds lends a cheerful atmosphere to this small eatery, which serves good Guatemalan fare. The *avena* (a warm wheat-derived beverage) is delicious, especially on a cold morning. There is no sign of the restaurant's trusty cetaceous namesake, though a ceramic sailfish atop the refrigerator comes close. ⊠ *1 Avenida 7–31, around the corner from Hotel San Pasqual,* ☎ *no phone. No credit cards.*

$ 🏨 **Hotel San Pasqual.** It's not the Holiday Inn by any means, but the San Pasqual has a certain charm, and the couple who run it are engaging and friendly. The medium-size rooms have simple decor (a few have handwoven bedspreads) and surround a sunny courtyard with clotheslines stretching to the roof next door. The shared baths are clean, but hot water is available only in the morning. Televisions can be rented, in case the Quiché nightlife doesn't cut it. ⊠ *7 Calle 0–43, Zona 1,* ☎ *755–1107. 37 rooms, 11 with bath. No credit cards.*

Arriving and Departing

Buses leave Chichicastango for Quiché every 15 minutes, and return on the same schedule, from 3 AM to 5 PM. Buses depart from Quiché for Nebaj six times daily starting at 7 AM ($1.55, 4 hours), and for Uspantán seven times daily starting at 9 AM ($1.20, 4 hours).

Ixil Triangle

③③ *95 km (59 mi) north of Santa Cruz del Quiché (5 hrs by bus).*

An interesting although somewhat inaccessible part of El Quiché is the Ixil Triangle, which comprises the villages of **Nebaj, San Juan Cotzal,** and **Chajul.** It's a fantastic area for hiking. Nebaj is the most accessible of the three, but Cotzal is serviced by sporadic buses, and Chajul can be hiked or driven to. The Ixil Triangle is home to many indigenous groups, including the Ixil Indians, a proud and beautiful people who speak a unique language and preserve a rich culture. Rigoberta Menchú, a Quiché woman who won the 1992 Nobel Peace Prize, was born and raised in San Miguel Uspantán, a tiny village near Chajul. A longtime activist and organizer, her book, *I, Rigoberta Menchú* (1983) is a summary of Menchú's life and work, narrated after she fled Guatemala and lived in exile. In fact, the entire region was the scene of intense combat during the early 1980s, when the army razed dozens of villages. Though things are quiet now, a frightening number of widows and orphans populate the area, and the friendly nature of the locals belies the nightmare they lived just a decade ago.

Quetzaltenango (Xela)

③④ *91 km (56 mi) southwest of Chichicastenango.*

Though Quetzaltenango is Guatemala's second-largest city, it's little more than an overgrown town. In a valley surrounded by rich farmland, the city has long had an economy based on agriculture, but it is also a significant industrial center known for its textiles and glassware. Travelers come to the area to relax by the luxurious hot springs before or after working themselves into a frenzy shopping. Tons of shops throughout the city sell woven goods, and local fabrics are known for their high quality. The first Sunday of each month is the main market day, and the Parque Centroamérica becomes a shopper's heaven. Even if the shop-

I, RIGOBERTA MENCHÚ . . . MOSTLY

IN 1992, the Nobel Peace Prize was awarded to Rigoberta Menchú (b. 1959), a woman raised in the tiny highland village of San Miguel Uspantán. Menchú was born just before a string of military dictators usurped control of Guatemala for 43 war-filled years, and she grew up as dozens of opposition and guerrilla groups rose to resist them. Along with many of her family members, Menchú opposed the dictatorship by organizing unions, work-stoppages, and peaceful demonstrations, which included peasants from various regions. She was eventually forced into exile, and continued opposing Guatemala's military rule by touring the world, drawing international attention to the repression there, and addressing the United Nations numerous times. In 1983, her testimonial *I, Rigoberta Menchú: An Indian Woman in Guatemala* was published, and the plight of Guatemala's indigenous people—and the brutality of the military regime—was revealed in wrenching detail. In her book, Menchú describes losing two brothers to malnutrition on a coffee plantation, and the razing of her village by wealthy land-prospectors. Most disturbingly, Menchú relates the story of a third brother, who was kidnapped by the army, tortured, and then burned alive in the plaza of a nearby town.

In 1999, American anthropologist David Stoll challenged Menchú's account with the publication of *Rigoberta Menchú and the Story of All Poor Guatemalans*. His research suggested that the conflict over Menchú's village's lands was actually a long-running dispute between her father and his in-laws, and that while Menchú's brother was unquestionably kidnapped, tortured, and murdered by the military, it was probably not carried out as Menchú suggests. While still a potent symbol of indigenous rights, Menchú—and the indigenous cause, by association—is now viewed by some with incredulity. More than a few have called for her Nobel Prize to be revoked.

Whether or not Menchú personally witnessed the events she describes, it is indisputable that hundreds of indigenous workers, particularly children, died of disease, malnutrition, or outright abuse on the plantations; that indigenous people were (and are) forced or cheated out of their lands; and that the military committed innumerable acts of brutality, including public executions. In 1998, the UN-sponsored Guatemalan Truth Commission, whose research dug much deeper than Stoll's, denounced the military's actions during the civil war as genocide. If Menchú's account wasn't wholly her own, but included incidents suffered by other indigenous men and women, does that diminish the horror of what occurred? If she included the experiences of others to draw attention to a conflict the international community had ignored for over 20 years, can anyone really blame her?

Stoll himself admits Menchú is fundamentally right with respect to the army's brutality, though he downplays it considerably no doubt to bolster his own book's more dubious claims, that it was the guerrillas, not the ruling generals, who were responsible for igniting political violence in the highlands. But it is the debunking of Rigoberta Menchú that he will be remembered for, and which will forever endear him to Guatemala's war criminals, many of whom remain in public life. Stoll may claim he's playing the devil's advocate, but in this case, the devil really doesn't need his help.

—Gary Chandler

ping thing isn't for you, you can watch the weaving process in many of the small villages in the area. Quetzaltenango is also a choice place to study Spanish, with several excellent programs that are widely considered more rigorous than those in Antigua. Word spreads fast, however, and Quetzaltenango has recently become the most popular "alternative" site to study Spanish. The steady influx of foreign students has its advantages and can be a lot of fun, but Quetzaltenango is no longer the place to go if you really want to avoid speaking English.

The city received its name, which means "place of the quetzal," from the language of the Mexicans who fought with Alvarado. The conquistador defeated the great Indian warrior Tecún Umán in the area and destroyed the nearby Quiché city of Xelaju. But local Indians have never gotten used to the city's foreign name and instead refer to Quetzaltenango as Xela (pronounced *shay*-la), which is the name you'll find on buses.

With a few reference points, Xela is not too hard to navigate. Always be sure you're in the right zona. The central park is in Zona 1 at the intersection of two main roads: 4 Calle and 12 Avenida. North of the park (uphill), the calle numbers decrease; they increase south of the park. The avenidas decrease to the east and increase to the west. Most of the listings here are in Zona 1, but for those in Zona 3, simply walk up 15 Aveninda "A" until you hit Rodolfo Robles, where the *calle* numbers start over.

The central plaza, **Parque Centroamérica,** is surrounded by architectural masterpieces. The **cathedral** on the park's west side has soaring walls and a crumbling facade, which are often under some form of reconstruction. The **Casa de la Cultura** to the south, is an interesting building on the outside, but its contents aren't really worth the $1 entry. A more interesting way to spend a dollar is at the nearby **Museo del Arte,** whose eclectic art collection ranges from realist oils to abstract and multimedia works. Use the same ticket to get into the **Museo del Ferrocarril** (Railroad Museum) if you like. Enter at 7 Avenida 12–12.

NEED A BREAK?	The inexpensive **Café Baviera** (⊠ 5 Calle and 12 Avenida), just off the plaza, has an ample selection of excellent coffees and fresh pastries, quiche, and hot croissant sandwiches.

The big, bustling **Minerva market** next to the bus terminal is the best of Xela's four markets. But watch your pockets—groups of skillful thieves prey on tourists coming to and from the buses.

In Zona 3, the lovely **Parque Benito Juarez** is where many Xelan families spend their Sunday afternoons, with ice cream and food stalls in glorious abundance. Two very unusual **churches** are nearby: the incongruous blue Baroque structure across from the park, and the lime-green church down one block (15 Avenida A and 2 Calle, Zona 3), whose enormous freestanding concave altar has a Picasso-esque rendition of angels and saints.

Dining and Lodging

$$ ✕ **Da Valentino.** Blond-wood tables and chairs, white tablecloths, and white walls sparsely adorned with pencil or watercolor pieces yield a calming and neutral setting. This leaves the food to speak for itself—which includes handmade egg noodles and delicious gnocchi with rich sauces. Valentino bills itself as "High Quality Italian Slow Food," and for good reason: expect to wait a while for the plates to come. ⊠ *14 Avenida A 1–37, Zona 1,* ☎ *761–4494. No credit cards. Closed Monday.*

When it Comes to Getting Local Currency at an ATM, Same Thing.

Whether you're in Yosemite or Yemen, using your Visa® card or ATM card with the PLUS symbol is the easiest and most convenient way to get local currency. For example, let's say you're in France. When you make a withdrawal, using your secured PIN, it's dispensed in francs, but is debited from your account in U.S. dollars. This makes it easy to take advantage of favorable exchange rates. And if you need help finding one of Visa's 627,000 ATMs in 127 countries worldwide, visit **visa.com/pd/atm**. We'll make finding an ATM as easy as finding the Eiffel Tower, the Pyramids or even the Grand Canyon.

It's Everywhere You Want To Be.

SEE THE WORLD
IN FULL COLOR

Fodor's Exploring Guides bring all the great sights vividly to life with hundreds of photographs, fascinating historical background, and colorful anecdotes. Detailed maps and practical information keep you headed in the right direction.

Pair a **Fodor's** Exploring Guide with your trusted Gold Guide for a complete planning package.

$$ ✕ **Royal Paris.** This restaurant caters to the numerous foreigners who are in Xela to study Spanish, so consequently it offers a wide selection of interesting dishes, such as chicken curry and vegetarian sandwiches, prepared with a French bistro flair. It also has a bar, an extensive wine list, and breakfast fare. The ambience is definitely imported, and the feeling is dark and slightly bohemian, courtesy of Parisian cabaret scenes on the walls and jazz on the stereo. ✉ *Calle 14A 3–06, Zona 1,* ☎ *761–1646. AE, DC, MC, V.*

$ ✕ **El Kopetin.** Aside from the two big hotels, this restaurant serves the best food in Zona 1. It's not large or fancy, but somehow it's comforting and familiar, with its wood paneling and long polished bar. The menu has a number of appetizers, like queso fundido, and a selection of meat and seafood dishes, some of which get smothered in rich sauces. Good food and service at reasonable prices have made this place popular with the locals, so it can be tough to get a seat later in the evening. ✉ *14 Avenida 3–51, Zona 1,* ☎ *761–8381. AE, DC, MC, V.*

$$$ ✕🏠 **Hotel Villa Real Plaza.** The Villa Real surrounds a spacious, covered courtyard illuminated by skylights. All of the rooms are large and have wall-to-wall carpeting, double beds, and fireplaces, but the "newer" ones (added in 1994) are generally superior to the dimly lit older ones. Ask for a room upstairs and away from the bar, as the night crowd can be noisy. The restaurant has an interesting selection that ranges from cordon bleu to a variety of stews and pastas, plus a small sampling of vegetarian dishes. There is also a large bar. ✉ *4 Calle 12–22, Zona 1,* ☎ *761–6270,* 🅵🅰🅇 *761–4045/6180. 50 rooms. Restaurant, bar. AE, DC, MC, V.*

$$$ ✕🏠 **Pensión Bonifaz.** Don't be fooled by the term "pension" in its name: This is Quetzaltenango's most upscale hotel. Inside a stately old yellow edifice at the central plaza's northeast corner, the Bonifaz isn't quite as grand as its exterior, but it is a comfortable, well-run establishment. Rooms are large and carpeted, with modern decor and cable TV. The nicest rooms are in the older building, and if you don't mind a little noise, the ones on the street have small balconies with nice plaza views. The rooftop garden makes a nice afternoon reading spot. The hotel's café has light lunch fare, while the restaurant has a Continental menu; both share a devilishly tempting pastry cart. ✉ *4 Calle 10–50, Zona 1,* ☎ *761–4241/2184,* 🅵🅰🅇 *761–2850. mbonifaz@guate.net 74 rooms. Restaurant, bar, café, pool, hot tub. AE, DC, MC, V.*

$$$ 🏠 **Casa Mañen.** Mixing modern designs with colonial decor, the Casa Mañen is a beautiful new hotel just west of the central plaza. The rooms are spacious and homey, with gorgeous wall hangings and throw rugs and an occasional rocking chair. On the roof is a two-level terrace with seating and a fantastic view of the city. Breakfast comes with the room and is served in a small dining room downstairs. Service can be somewhat reluctant, but by no means inattentive. A 10% surcharge is levied with credit card payment. ✉ *9 Avenida 4–11, Zona 1,* ☎ *765–0786,* 🅵🅰🅇 *765–0678, casamannen@xela.net.gt. 9 rooms. AE, DC, MC, V.*

$$ 🏠 **Hotel Modelo.** Founded in 1883, the Modelo is a great family-run establishment whose wizened but spunky manager was actually born on the premises. Over the years, it has maintained its distinguished appearance and a tradition of good service. Much of the hotel's furniture is antique, and the rooms have wooden floors and stucco walls decorated with traditional weavings. Rooms surround a few small courtyards with porticoes leading off the lobby. There's a fine colonial-style restaurant, and a nearby annex where several newer rooms can be rented for less. ✉ *14 Avenida A 2–31, Zona 1,* ☎ 🅵🅰🅇 *763–1376. 24 rooms. Restaurant. AE, DC, MC, V.*

$ ▦ **Casa Kaehler.** This quiet, ramshackle pension a few blocks off the plaza is run by a friendly family of German descent and is a popular spot with travelers on a budget. Rooms are on two floors of a converted residence and face a small courtyard overflowing with plants. Though the rooms are simple, they're clean, and the hotel has a separate lounge where guests gather to read, relax, or chat. There's only one room with a private bath and a double bed, but the shared baths are well maintained and have plenty of hot water. ✉ *13 Avenida 3–33, Zona 1,* ☎ *761–2091. 7 rooms, 1 with bath. No credit cards.*

Nightlife

Aside from the lounges in the big hotels, there are only a few nightspots in Xela. A luxurious little bar operates at the **Casa Grande** (✉ 4 Calle and 16 Avenida, Zona 3), which sometimes has live music on weekends. Right off the park, the **Salon Tecún** (✉ Pasaje Enrique, connecting 11 and 12 Calles) is a small pub catering to a student crowd. **Cinema Paraíso** (✉ 14 Avenida 1–04) is a small video-café that shows both mainstream and art-house films. If you feel like dancing, try **El Garage Club** (✉ Blvd. Minerva).

Shopping

Handiwork from most of the villages in the region can be found in the **new market** (✉ 1 Calle and 15 Avenida, Zona 3), and since there are few shoppers, prices tend to be low. Another **market** (✉ near the plaza, Zona 1) has a limited selection of típica. **ADEPH** (✉ Rodolfo Robles Calle 15–63, Zona 1) is an outlet for a local artisans' association. **AJ Pop** (✉ 14 Avenida A 1–26) is one of many típica shops. **Vitra** (✉ 13 Avenida 5–27, ☎ 763–5091) is a famous glass store, with occasional factory tours and excellent hand-blown pieces at very affordable prices.

Telephones and Internet Service

Maya Communications (✉ Above Salon Tecún, Pasaje Enrique, connecting 11 and 12 Calles) and **Casa Verde/Green House** (✉ 12 Avenida 1–40, Zona 1)) have both telephone and Internet services.

Books

At **VRISA Bookshop** (✉ 15 Avenida 3–64, Zona 1, ☎ 761–3237) you're free to read current magazines and newspapers without purchase. They also have a fairly large collection of new and used books and coffee and espresso.

Mountain Biking

There's great **mountain biking** through the hills and villages surrounding Xela. **VRISA Bicycles** (✉ info at VRISA Bookshop, 15 Avenida 3–64, Zona 1, ☎ 761–3237) rents both on-road and off-road bikes by the day or week, and has maps for self-guided tours for riders of all abilities.

Trekking

Quetzaltrekkers (✉ Casa Argentina, Diagonal 12 8–67, Zona 1, ☎ 761–2470, quetzaltrekkers@hotmail.com, ✍) is a nonprofit company that supports three major social-service programs by coordinating truly unforgettable hiking trips. The 2-day/3-night trek from Xela to Lake Atitlán, and a 2-day/1-night ascent of the Tajamulco volcano both pass through spectacular countryside and several remote villages. Although certainly quite strenuous, people of all ages and hiking abilities have completed both trips. Equipment is provided.

En Route   In Almolonga, 5 km (3 mi) south of Quetzaltenango, you'll find women wearing bright orange huipiles and beautiful headbands. At the busy Wednesday and Saturday markets, you can buy fruits that are cultivated in the area. A few kilometers beyond town are several hot springs, where private tubs can be rented for a few dollars.

Zunil

★ ㉟ *9 km (5½ mi) south of Quetzaltenango.*

Zunil is a radiant highland village at the base of an extinct volcano surrounded by the most fertile land in the valley. Mud and adobe houses are arranged around a whitewashed colonial church that marks the center of town. Monday is market day, and women with flashy purple shawls crowd the indoor marketplace hawking fruits and vegetables that come straight from their own gardens. Zunil is another good place to pay your respects to San Simón. Here the idol has become a tourist attraction, and foreigners are charged 50¢ or so to see him. Everyone in town knows where he is, and almost everyone asks a favor of him at some time or another. Don't forget to bring a small gift.

High in the hills above Zunil and tucked in a lush ravine, the wonderful hot springs of **Fuentes Georginas** draw locals and tourists alike. There are four pools, two of which remain (for the most part) in their natural basins; all four vary from tolerable to near-scalding. The area is in the middle of a cloud forest, and besides the views, some beautiful hikes begin and end here. If you reserve a cabin, you can hike in the morning and soak all night. To get here by car, take the first left off the main road after passing Zunil. Otherwise Zunil buses leave Xela from the Monumento de la Marimba every 20 minutes; catch a taxi from there to the hot springs (20 min, $6 for up to four people).

Lodging

$ ⬚ **Fuentes Georginas.** There are a dozen bungalows and a restaurant, and though the cabins are rather run-down, they do have fireplaces and decent furnishings. The draw is 24-hour access to the hot springs, which close to the public at 5 PM. Since there's no phone, you're stuck if you arrive and they're full, but this is a risk usually confined to weekends. ⊠ *First left past Zunil, 8 km (5 mi) from main road,* ☏ *no phone. 8 bungalows. Restaurant. No credit cards.*

En Route   San Francisco El Alto, 14 km (9 mi) northeast of Quetzaltenango, in the department of Totonicapán, has one of the country's largest livestock markets, held every Friday, and commands great views of the valley below and the surrounding volcanoes.

San Miguel Totonicapán

★ ㊱ *30 km (18 mi) northeast of Quetzaltenango.*

Hop a bus behind the cathedral in Xela to get to this traditional village famous for its wooden toys, hand-loomed textiles, tinwork, wax figures, and painted and glazed ceramics. Market day is Saturday.

Shopping

All the villages in the Quetzaltenango area have weekly markets where típica can be purchased, but Totonicapán is full of **workshops** where a wide variety of handicrafts are actually produced. The **tourist office** (⊠ Casa de Cultura, 8 Avenida 2–17, next to the Hospedaje San Miguel, Zona 1 (Palín), ☏ 𝔽𝔸𝕏 766–1575) organizes tours of various workshops—call in advance. The tourist office also produces a map for self-guided tours, but studios aren't always prepared for walk-in visits.

En Route   Momostenango is 35 km (21 mi) north of San Francisco El Alto, along a dirt road. An extremely traditional village and the center of an important wool-producing region, the village displays its famous blankets and ponchos woven on foot looms at a Sunday market.

Huehuetenango

③⑦ *94 km (58 mi) north of Quetzaltenango.*

Huehuetenango, just off the Pan-American Highway, at the foot of the
Cuchumatanes mountain range, was once part of the powerful Mam
Maya kingdom that dominated most of the highland area. It wasn't
until much later that the Guatemalan Quiché came into the area to stir
things up, pushing the Mam Maya up into the Cuchumatanes Mountains and as far north as Chiapas, Mexico. Huehue is a quiet town today,
without any real attractions of its own; it is mostly a gateway to the
magnificent Cuchumatanes and the isolated villages scattered across
them. The town is centered on a large plaza with a band shell, surrounded
by government offices and a few banks. A couple of blocks to the east
is the central market, where local handicrafts can be purchased.

OFF THE   **ZACULEU –** These restored ruins served as the political hub of the Mam
BEATEN PATH   people, a little understood Maya group that dominated this region well
                 into the second millennium. Spanish troops led by Pedro de Alvarado's
                 brother, Gonzalo, were unable to defeat the Mam militarily, so they laid
                 siege to the capital; after 45 days, the starving Mam surrendered. The
                 United Fruit Company restored the ruins in the 1940s but did a pretty
                 heavy-handed job, leaving the site looking somewhat artificial. Never-
                 theless, it's a tranquil spot with views of the surrounding pine-draped
                 hills, and a modest museum offers some insight into the world of the
                 Mam. Minibuses leave for the ruins from the corner of 2 Calle and 7
                 Avenida. To walk the 4 km (2½ mi) here, go down 2 Calle to the T inter-
                 section, turn right, and continue until the the road splits at a triangle-
                 shaped store. Bear right, and then turn right at the first corner onto an
                 unpaved road. Stay on this main road the whole way, but ask for *las ru-
                 inas* if you're unsure.

Dining and Lodging

$ ✕ **Las Brasas.** This little steak house is probably Huehuetenango's best
restaurant. The decor is unassuming enough, with lots of wood and
simple red-and-white tablecloths, but since it's the only restaurant in
town that has anything remotely resembling atmosphere, it is a fairly
reassuring sight. The house specialty is grilled meat, but the menu is
fairly ample and even includes Chinese food, which you sure won't find
anywhere else in town. ⊠ *2 Calle 1–55,* ☎ *764–2339. AE, MC, V.*

$ ✕ **Jardín Café.** This colorful little corner restaurant serves decent food
in a bright, friendly atmosphere, and consequently it's popular with
the locals. It opens daily at 6 AM for breakfast (the pancakes are excellent), and the lunch and dinner menus include basic beef and chicken
as well as a few Mexican dishes. ⊠ *4 Calle and 6 Avenida,* ☎ *no phone.
No credit cards.*

$ ✕ **Pizza Hogareña.** Although the ambience is nothing to speak of, you
★ can build your own pizza from a long list of fresh ingredients or opt
for spaghetti, grilled meat, or sandwiches. ⊠ *6 Avenida 4–49,* ☎ *764–
3072. No credit cards. Closed Mon.*

$$$ ⌂ **Hotel Casa Blanca.** Who would've thought little old Huehue-
nango would have such a classy hotel? Large rooms, excellent service,
and a central location make it the town's best lodging option. Third-
floor rooms have great views, and the hotel's bougainvillea is spectacular
when in full bloom. The restaurant has tables in a cozy dining room
with a fireplace, as well as in a shady courtyard out back. ⊠ *7 Avenida
3–41,* ☎ FAX *769–0777. 15 rooms. Restaurant, conference room. V.*

$$ ⌂ **Hotel Zaculeu.** This older hotel off the main square is a longtime
Huehue favorite. The entrance leads into a lush garden courtyard, which
is surrounded by a portico and the hotel's older rooms. A passage on

the other end of the courtyard leads to the newer rooms, which are built on two levels and surround an enclosed parking area. The older rooms are graced with local weavings and other handicrafts but can be noisier, especially those along the street. The newer ones have wall-to-wall carpeting, modern bathrooms, and TVs, but are more expensive and lack character. ⊠ *5 Avenida 1–14,* ☎ *764–1086,* 𝖥𝖠𝖷 *764–1575. 38 rooms. Restaurant. No credit cards.*

$ 🖾 **Hotel Mary.** This four-story hotel in the heart of town offers clean, spartan accommodations at a good price but not much more. Though not terribly attractive, Hotel Mary is conveniently located across the street from the post and TELGUA offices. Most rooms have cable TV. Ask to see a few different rooms, as some are much better than others. ⊠ *2 Calle 3–52,* ☎ *764–1618. 27 rooms. No credit cards.*

En Route   A short drive north of Huehuetenango, the dirt road begins to wind its way up into the Cuchumatanes Mountains, where traditional villages are set between massive, rocky peaks. There's a *mirador* (scenic view) near the town of Chiantla, 6 km (4 mi) from Huehuetenango. From there it's up, up, up for quite a while.

Todos Santos Cuchumatán

38   *50 km (31 mi) north of Huehuetenango; turn left at the Paquix junction, some 20 km (12 mi) outside Huehuetenango.*

Although it takes about three hours to cover the 40 km (24 mi) separating Huehuetenango and Todos Santos, the bumpy, uphill ride is probably the best way to experience the tremendous height and mass of the Cuchumatanes Mountains. The winding dirt road is too narrow for oncoming buses to pass, and the ride can be especially anxiety-provoking when one side of the road drops off into a 200-foot ravine. Despite the arduous journey, Todos Santos is the most frequently visited mountain village, especially during the big local festival, October 21 to November 1, which celebrates the Day of the Dead (All Saints and All Souls days) the longest village festival in Guatemala. The high point of the celebration is a horse race done bareback. Market day year-round is Thursday, where you can see the men in their traditional red candy-cane striped pants and pinstriped shirts with long embroidered collars. The women wear stunning red, pink, and purple huipiles with dark blue skirts.

Hiking

Todos Santos is a popular base for hiking, which accesses both beautiful mountain scenery and quaint nearby villages like San Juan Atitán, Santiago Chimaltenango, San Martín, and Jacaltenango. If you're adventurous, head farther north to Soloma, a larger town with markets on Thursdays and Sundays, or on to San Mateo Ixtatán, a small village known for its traditional Chuj Indian inhabitants and a small Maya site. Market days—Thursday and Sunday—are the best time to visit San Mateo. At Barillas, to the east, the mountains begin to drop down toward the rain forests.

The Western Highlands A to Z

Arriving and Departing

BY AIRPLANE
Both Xela and Huehuetenango have small airports with service to and from the capital on **TACA** (☎ 261–2144).

BY BUS
To Panajachel, **Transporte Rebuli** (☎ 251–3521) leaves Guatemala City (⊠ 21 Calle 1–34, Zona 1) hourly from 5 AM to 4 PM daily. Buses

leave Panajachel hourly from 6 AM to 3 PM daily. The 6 AM and 3 PM buses are Pullmans—they're more expensive but much more comfortable. Count on a four-hour trip.

To Chichicastenango and Santa Cruz del Quiché, **Veloz Quichelense** (☎ no phone) operates hourly buses, departing from the capital (✉ Terminal de Autobuses, Zona 4) on the half hour between 5 AM and 6 PM and returning from Santa Cruz on a similar schedule.

To Quetzaltenango (Xela), **Galgos** (☎ 232–3661) buses leave Guatemala City (✉ 7 Avenida 19–44, Zona 1) at 5:30, 8:30, and 11 AM, and 12:45, 2:30, 5, 6:30, and 7 PM. They depart from Quetzaltenango (✉ Off Calzada Indepedencia, Zona 2) at 4, 5, 8:15, 9:45, and 11:45 AM, and 2:45 and 4:45 PM. The trip takes four hours.

To Huehuetenango, you can choose from two bus services for the five-hour run from Guatemala City. **Los Halcones** (✉ 7 Avenida 15–27, Zona 1, ☎ 238–1979) has departures at 7 AM and 2 PM. **Rápidos Zaculeu** (✉ 9 Calle 11–42, Zona 1, ☎ 232–2858) runs buses at 6 AM and 3 PM.

Transportes Velasquez (✉ 20 Calle 1–37, Zona 1; 20 Calle 2–43, Zona 3, ☎ 221–1084) also has daily departures.

From **Antigua,** there are a few direct buses each morning to Quetzaltenango, Chichicastenango, and Panajachel, or else take any bus to Chimaltenango and then catch a connecting bus on the Interamerican Highway. Anything heading north will stop at Los Encuentros, in case you need to transfer again. A shuttle service between Panajachel and Antigua leaves Antigua about 8 AM and Panajachel around noon daily. Tickets can be purchased at the big hotels, or most travel agencies.

BY CAR

The Interamerican Highway—more country road than highway, really— heads northwest out of Guatemala City, where it is called the Calzada Roosevelt. It passes through Chimaltenango (km 56) before reaching a crossroads called Los Encuentros (km 127), which is marked by a two-story, blue, traffic-police tower. Here the road to El Quiché (Chichicastenango, Santa Cruz del Quiché, and the Ixil Triangle) splits off to the right. To the left is the Interamerican Highway. You'll pass a turnoff to Sololá and Panajachel 3 km (2 mi) later on the left, and then shortly after, the exit at Km 148 leads to the west side of Lake Atitlán and the towns of Santa Clara, San Marcos La Laguna, and San Pedro. The Interamerican Highway continues over some impressive ridges and then descends to a crossroads called Cuatro Caminos, about 200 km (124 mi) from the capital. Here the road to Quetzaltenango, 27 km (17 mi) south, heads off to the left. Staying on the highway about 60 km (37 mi) north of Cuatro Caminos, the road to Huehuetenango cuts off to the right. Many roads to the north of Huehuetenango and Santa Cruz del Quiché are unpaved and pretty rough—this is nerve-racking mountain driving relieved intermittently by memorable views.

Getting Around

BY BOAT

With the exception of the Panajachel–Santiago line and package tours, Lake Atitlán's public ferry service has been replaced by private boat taxis. Although they don't follow a schedule, the private boats are much faster and more numerous, and they cost the same. Panajachel has two primary docks, one at the end of Calle del Embarcadero and one at the end of Calle Rancho Grande. The first is for private boats on the San Pedro route, including Santa Cruz, Jaibalito, San Marcos, Santa Clara, and San Pedro. It's $1.30, no matter where you get off, and boats leave when they fill up. The other dock is for ferries to Santiago ($1.30,

1 hr), with departures at 8:30, 9, 9:30, and 10 AM, and 4 and 5 PM, and returns at 6 and 11:45 AM, and 12:30, 1, 2, and 5 PM. Private boats occasionally take passengers to Santiago, as well ($2, ½ hour). The IN-GUAT office has a daily excursion that leaves for Panajachel at 9 AM, stopping for an hour or so in San Pedro, Santiago, and San Antonio Palopó, and returning around 4 PM, for $5.20. And, of course, you can always negotiate with a driver for a private tour.

BY BUS

Daily buses leave Panajachel for Chichicastenango at 7, 8, 9, and 10:30 AM, and 1 PM; for Quetzaltenango at 5:30 and 11:30 AM, and 2:30 PM; for San Lucas Tolimán at 6:30 AM and 2 PM; and for Santa Catarina and San Antonio Palopó at 9 AM. Hourly buses operate between Quetzaltenango and Huehuetenango (a 2½-hour trip), and sporadic service is available between Quetzaltenango and Chichicastenango, but it's often quicker to switch buses at Los Encuentros. Service from Quetzaltenango to Panajachel runs at 6 AM, noon, and 1. Buses to both San Francisco and Momostenango leave Quetzaltenango from the Minerva bus station, in Zona 3, while those to Almolonga and Zunil depart from the area behind the cathedral, in Zona 1. Buses to the Ixil Triangle leave Santa Cruz around 8 and 9 AM and return at 12:30 and 3. There is also early-morning bus service between Huehuetenango and Sacapulas. Buses leave Huehuetenango (✉ 4 Calle and 1 Avenida) for Todos Santos at 11:30 AM and 12:30 PM, returning at 5 and 6 AM, or you can hike down from Todos Santos to the Interamerican Highway via San Juan or Jacaltenango and catch one of the regular buses coming from the Mexican border.

Contacts and Resources

EMERGENCIES

National Police (Panajachel, ☎ 762–1120). **Medical emergencies** (Panajachel, ☎ 762–1258).

Pharmacy. Farmacia Nueva (✉ 6 Calle and 10 Avenida, Zona 1, Quetzaltenango, ☎ 762–4531).

TRAVEL AGENCY

Guatemala Unlimited Travel Bureau (✉ 1 Calle and 12 Avenida, Quetzaltenango, ☎ 761–6043).

VISITOR INFORMATION

INGUAT offices are in Panajachel (✉ Edificio Rincón Saí, at beginning of Calle Santander, ☎ 762–1392), open daily 8–12, 1–5; in Quetzaltenango (✉ South end of Parque Centro América, ☎ no phone); and in San Miguel Totonicapán (✉ Casa de Cultura, 8 Avenida 2–17, next to Hospedaje San Miguel, Zona 1, ☎ 766–1575).

THE VERAPACES

In the departments of Alta Verapaz and Baja Verapaz, northeast of Guatemala City, you'll find a mountainous region covered with lush forests and coffee plantations, drained by wild rivers, and pierced by deep caverns. The smaller Baja Verapaz is drier than Alta Verapaz, to the north, where deluges are common and mist-covered mountains the norm. The area's humid climate, which often comes in the form of a misty rain called *chipi-chipi,* has made it the cradle of Guatemala's cardamom spice and coffee production.

The Verapaces retain a mystical air, particularly enhanced by the presence of the mysterious quetzal bird, found only in the mist-covered cloud forests. The male has a spectacularly long tail and shiny blue-green feathering, the inspiration for weaving designs and paintings all over

Guatemala, as the Maya royalty wore the feathers in their crowns. The pride Guatemalans feel for this bird and its significance in their culture and history is recognized in the name of the currency, which is also called the quetzal.

The region's inhabitants are predominantly Pokomchí and Q'eqchí Indians, who over the years have lost much of their territory to expanding coffee plantations and have, as a result, abandoned some of their traditional ways to sustain themselves. The region's largest city, Cobán, has an almost completely indigenous population and a handful of businesses that cater to visitors, making it a good base for exploring sights and surrounding villages.

Numbers in the text correspond to numbers in the margin and on the Verapaces and Atlantic Lowlands map.

Quetzal Reserve

★ ㊴ *164 km (102 mi) northeast of Guatemala City, 75 km (46½ mi) north of El Rancho; from Guatemala City, take the Carretera Atlantíca to El Rancho (km 84), and turn left toward the mountains.*

A 2,849-acre tract of cloud forest along the road to Cobán, just south of the village of Purhulhá, the reserve was created to protect Guatemala's national bird, the resplendent quetzal, which is endangered by the indiscriminate destruction of the country's forests. Also called the Mario Dary Reserve, the area was named after the Guatemalan ecologist who fought for its creation and was a victim of the political violence of the early 1980s.

The elusive but beautiful quetzal has been revered since the days of the ancient Maya, who called it the winged serpent. Though the Maya often captured quetzals to remove their tail feathers, which grow back, killing one was a capital offense. The quetzal has long symbolized freedom, since it is said that the bird cannot live in captivity. Although the female quetzal is attractive, the male is as spectacular a creature as ever took to the air, with its crimson belly, bright, metallic-green back, and 2-foot-long flowing tail feathers. Its unforgettable appearance notwithstanding, the quetzal remains difficult to spot in the mist and lush foliage of the cloud forest. The reserve offers the chance to see the resplendent quetzal in its natural habitat during its mating season, between April and June. The best place from which to see the birds is not in the park itself, oddly enough, but in the parking lot of the hotel Ranchito del Quetzal, 1½ km (1 mi) north. Since it is easier to spot quetzals around dawn or dusk, it's worth spending a night in the area. Even if you don't catch a glimpse of the legendary quetzal, there are plenty of other species to spot, and the luxuriant greenery of the cloud forest is gorgeous in its own right.

The Quetzal Reserve is also one of the last cloud forests in Guatemala and represents a vital source of water for the region's rivers. A walk along its trails gives the sense of being in a giant sponge. Water, evaporated from Lake Izabal and the Honduran Gulf, comes down in the form of rain and condensed fog, which is then collected by the towering old-growth trees and verdant, dense vegetation. The loss of cloud forests such as this one is turning adjacent lowland areas into desert.

Once inside the forest, breathe deep; the air is rich with moisture and oxygen. Epiphytes, lichens, hepaticas, mosses, bromeliads, ferns, and orchids abound. If you're lucky, you can see (and hear) howler monkeys swinging above the two well-maintained trails: Los Helechos ("the ferns"), which takes about an hour, and Los Musgos ("the

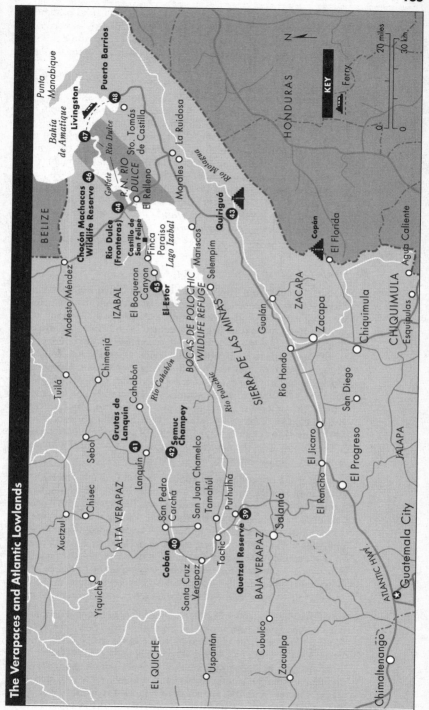

The Verapaces and Atlantic Lowlands

Punta
Manabique

Bahía
de Amatique

Puerto Barrios

48

Livingston **47**

Río Dulce

Sto. Tomás
de Castilla

Gólfete

46 **44** P. N. RÍO
DULCE

El Relleno

La Ruidosa

Chacón Machacas
Wildlife Reserve

Morales

Morales

Río Motagua

BELICE

Río Dulce
(Fronteras)

Castillo de
San Felipe

Finca
Paraíso Lago Izabal

Quiriguá **43**

HONDURAS

IZABAL

El Boquerón
Canyon **45**

Mariscos

Copán

El Florida

Modesto Méndez

El Estor

Selempím

ZACAPA

Agua Caliente

Chimenjá

BOCAS DE POLOCHIC
WILDLIFE REFUGE

Gualán

Zacapa

CHIQUIMULA

Tuilá

Río Cahabón

Río Polochic

SIERRA DE LAS MINAS

Río Hondo

Chiquimula

Sebol

Chisec

Grutas de
Lanquín

Cahabón

San Diego

Esquipulas

Xuctzul

41
Lanquín

42 Semuc
Champey

San Pedro
Carchá

San Juan Chamelco

Tamahú

Purulhá

Salamá

El Jícaro

El Progreso

JALAPA

Yiquiche

ALTA VERAPAZ

Tactic

39

El Rancho

ATLANTIC HWY.

Santa Cruz
Verapaz

Cobán **40**

Quetzal Reserve

BAJA VERAPAZ

Guatemala City

Uspantán

EL QUICHE

Cubulco

CHIMALTENANGO

Zacualpa

KEY

- - - Ferry

N

0   20 miles

0   30 km.

moss"), which takes two hours and makes a short detour past a series of beautiful waterfalls. The last part of both trails crosses a river with concrete bathing pools where you can take a swim if you don't mind the cold. An interpretive guide is available at the stand at the trailheads. ☎ *No phone.* ☑ *Free.*

Dining and Lodging

$$ ✕⌂ **Posada Montaña del Quetzal.** This comfortable country lodge near
★ the Quetzal Reserve is the area's best hotel. You may choose from small rooms within the main building and spacious bungalows, each with two bedrooms, a sitting room, and a fireplace. The restaurant overlooks the swimming pool and serves a limited selection of Guatemalan and Continental cuisine, and even if you don't spend the night, this is a good spot for a meal or snack. Wander the trails nearby—you might catch a glimpse of a quetzal. ☒ *4 km (2½ mi) south of the Quetzal Reserve at Km 156.5 along the Carretera a Cobán,* ☎ *335–1805 in Guatemala City. 8 rooms, 10 bungalows. Restaurant, bar, coffee shop, pool, hiking, fishing. No credit cards.*

Cobán

⓴ *50 km (31 mi) north of the Quetzal Reserve.*

Cobán is in many ways the city that coffee built. During the 19th-century coffee boom, Cobán functioned almost independently of Guatemala City, exporting its products and dealing directly with Germany, where most of its prominent citizens immigrated from. Though German influence declined during World War II, when the U.S. government pressured Guatemala to expel most of the region's German residents, traces of their historical influence remain. At the **Finca Santa Margarita** (3 blocks from Parque Central, 3 Calle 4–12, Zona 2, ☎ 952–1286) you can take a 45-minute walking tour of an operating coffee farm and witness the process of planting, growing, harvesting, and processing coffee beans weekdays 8–12:30 and 1:30–5, Saturday, 8–noon. Owned by the Dieseldorff family, with 110 years of coffee-growing experience in the Coban area, the plantation has an Old World feel with slatted wooden buildings and simple, by-hand processing.

A large group of people gathered in a circle in Cobán's central hilltop plaza indicates the presence of a street performer charming snakes, breathing fire, or walking on broken glass. Teenagers from all over the region come to secondary school here, and during the school year they hang out in the park in their uniforms. The **cathedral,** with blue-gray and yellow trim and bordering the plaza to the east, is worth peeking into; it's actually one of the more understated church decors you'll see. The porch of the two-story **municipal building** to the north sometimes houses special events, like book fairs and photo exhibits, as well as a large group of homeless peddlers and travelers who sleep here at night.

The longtime residents of Cobán are the Q'eqchí Maya, a people who for the past few generations have been migrating down the Polochic River valley for fertile land and now live as far away as the Atlantic coast. Though the Q'eqchí are never featured in the colorful Guatemalan brochures, many women still wear traditional clothing, though the style is different from those of the highlands. *Corte* (woven skirts), each made of eight meters of fabric, are gathered and usually worn to just below the knees. They are worn with embroidered huipiles fashioned from a rectangular piece of fabric, with a hole cut out for the neck and the sides sewn up. Following in the traditions of the ancient Maya, the Q'eqchí are religious people mixing modern theologies with older rituals and beliefs. Many caves around the region serve as houses for religious ceremonies involving candle and incense burning.

The **Museo El Principe Maya** (Museum of Maya Artifacts; 6 Avenida 4–26, Zona 3, ☎ 952–1541), a 10-minute walk from the plaza, has a private collection of ancient Maya artifacts, mostly recovered from El Petén. Though the collection is relatively small, the variety and exquisiteness of the pieces are impressive. See masks, giant sacrificial pots, a reconstructed tomb, jade jewelry, statues, instruments, and weapons. The $1.50 entrance fee includes a guided tour with the collection's knowledgeable owners.

The eighty-something eccentric Otto Mittelstaedt, a Guatemalan of German descent, founded and runs the magnificently beautiful **Viveros Verapaz Orchid Farm** (Carretera Antigua, 3 km outside of Cobán, on the old road to the capital, ☎ 952–1133). It's worth a trip to the town's outskirts, as Otto clearly enjoys sharing his passion with visitors, pointing out breathtaking blossoms and describing the painstaking process of coaxing the orchids to bloom. Typically, orchids bloom in late November and early December, the height of the season culminating in Cobán's **International Orchid Festival** held annually in early December in the cathedral complex off the plaza. Orchid-cultivators from as far as Japan come to show off their flowers and discuss orchid life and politics, including whether aroma is a valid criterion for judging an orchid's beauty. Tours are casual and offered daily: be sure to take notice of the *monja blanca*, Guatemala's national flower.

OFF THE BEATEN PATH	**SAN PEDRO CARCHÁ** – An interesting daily market is the highlight of this traditional little town 6 km (4 mi) east of Cobán. Nearby Las Islas, with a waterfall and pool, is a popular spot for picnics and swimming.

Cobán's more than respectable national soccer team, Cobán Imperial, plays regularly in the hilltop **soccer stadium,** five blocks northwest of the bus station in the Estadio Verapaz, where bleacher and grassy hillside seating is available. Look for the sandwich board in the plaza for events information. Tickets are about $3. Every year on the second Sunday in May, Cobán fills up with runners and spectators for the 21-km **International Cobán Half Marathon,** over and around the area's beautiful green hillsides. About 2,800 runners from around the world participate annually. Runners can register at the municipal building (☎ 952–1369).

A small, well-organized group of businesses is interested in promoting the area's wealth of tourism potential. Though it is still relatively unexplored by tourists, Cobán may become the second Antigua, especially if the paving project of the road from Coban through Sayaxché to Flores is completed, creating a new easy-to-travel route between the capital and the Petén. A good place for information is the **Internet Café** (☎ 951–4040), off the park, which not only has computer access, but also information on tours to Salachichaj lagoon and waterfall, Semuc Champey, Rey Marco Cave, Chicoy Cave, El Salto waterfall, and other points of interest. **Scenic Eco-Flights** (☎ 951–0332) has affordable custom-designed private air tours of the region including trips to the hard-to-access Laguna La'chua. Casa de Acuña and Hostal Doña Victoria (☞ *below*) both have tours and travel services.

Dining and Lodging

$ ✕ **Café El Tirol.** Milly, the owner of this popular café and daughter of Otto Mittelstaedt, the orchid man, grew up on a coffee plantation near Cobán. Duly qualified, she serves the largest selection of caffeine drinks in the coffee growing region. Hot coffee, cold coffee, coffee with liquor, coffee with chocolate, and a wide assortment of teas make up most of the six-page drink menu. She also whips up the best breakfasts in town. ⊠ *Off the park, opposite the church, 1 Calle 3–13, Zona 1,* ☎ *no phone. No credit cards. Closed Sun.*

$ ✕ **Kikoe's Tasca Bar and Restaurant.** The one-eyed gray-haired boisterous owner Kikoe is happy to chat about anything from his career as a mineralogist to beer (excluding American varieties), and provides a home away from home for many travelers and locals. Clean and well-built, with a wraparound bar and fireplace, Kikoe's is the only real bar in Cobán, serving 12 kinds of beer and 150 kinds of liquor. The place doesn't get hopping until late and stays open until one in the morning. It's also the place for *Eisbein* (smoked pork leg), *Rippchen auf Kraut* (smoked pork chop), *Szegedin* (Hungarian goulash), and cheese fondue, a small but savory menu particularly for meat lovers. ⊠ *2 Avenida 4–33, Zona 2,* ☎ *952–1248. V. Closed Sun., Mon.*

$$ ✕🖬 **Hotel La Posada.** True charm, the kind communicated by way of
★ nonchalance, pervades La Posada, an attractive colonial inn with a front-porch café overlooking Cobán's central plaza. Rooms have wood floors and exposed beam ceilings and are furnished with antiques and Guatemalan handicrafts, as are the porticoes and hallways. Some rooms have fireplaces, wardrobes, and writing desks. Blue chairs and cloth hammocks fill the porch overlooking the small garden. Inside are a TV lounge and a cozy restaurant with a fireplace serves mostly Guatemalan food. ⊠ *1 Calle 4–12, Zona 2,* ☎ ᶠᴬˣ *952–1495. 14 rooms. Restaurant, café, Ping-Pong. AE, DC, MC, V.*

$ ✕🖬 **Casa D'Acuña.** The Restaurante Casa D'Acuña is a necessary stop when you're in Cobán, whether you're a guest of the hotel or not. Sit inside or in the garden and enjoy a variety of Italian dishes and desserts. Lasagne is a cheesy favorite. Homemade carrot cake and a cup of locally grown coffee make a great after-dinner dessert or midday snack. A small and clean bunk bed–style hostel operates in conjunction with the restaurant; one room with a double bed is also available. The proprietors—the lovely Guatemalan–American Acuña family—are not only an invaluable local resource but take a personal interest in each of their guests. They also run excellent two- to five-day eco-adventures, including package tours from Antigua to the Quetzal Reserve, Candelaria (an ancient sacred Maya 30 km-long cave), Tikal, and other Guatemalan sights. ⊠ *4 Calle 3–11, Zona 2,* ☎ *951–0482,* ᶠᴬˣ *952–1268. 7 rooms with shared bath. Restaurant, café, travel services. AE, MC, V. Restaurant closed Mon.* ✆

$ 🖬 **Hostal Doña Victoria.** First built as a convent over 400 years ago, the Doña Victoria is decorated in colonial style with antiques and statues. A stone porch encircling a thick, lush garden is lined with hammocks, rocking chairs, and stuffed couches. Rooms are spacious and clean with wood ornaments, firm mattresses, and thick bedding for the cold Cobán nights. All rooms are quiet and have TVs; baths have hot water (although avoid No. 4, with its tomblike bath tub). ⊠ *3 Calle 2–38, Zona 3,* ☎ *951–4214,* ᶠᴬˣ *951–4213. 9 rooms. Restaurant, travel services. AE, DC, MC, V.* ✆

En Route   Tiny **San Juan Chamelco,** 16 km (9 mi) southeast of Cobán, was the first church to be built in Alta Verapaz, surrounded by its hilly streets blooming with flowers. Chamelco is easy to get to, with buses running back and forth from Cobán on the paved road all day.

Rediscovered and opened in the past year, **Grutas de Rey Marco** (⊠ 8 km/5 mi from San Juan Chamelco, in Aldea Santa Cecilia) are relatively untouched caves. Tours take you in only a few hundred yards, but the potential for further exploring is untold, as the cave stretches for many miles beneath the Sierra Yalijux mountains. The entrance is narrow, and you should expect some crawling and a river crossing that can be waist high in the rainy season. Entrance fee ($3) includes a hard hat and a (weak) head lamp, plus a guide with a high-powered light of his own. Plan on getting muddy, and proceed at your own risk: the rocks are slippery and you'll have to watch your head. Unlike caving elsewhere, no real safety precautions exist, and don't expect a scientific tour from the guides. Cave interpretation doesn't go beyond "This formation looks like an alligator. This one, like a tower." Tours from Cobán can be arranged through the Internet Café (☞ *above*).

Lanquín

63 km (39 mi) northeast of Cobán.

This village with rustic accommodations is on the doorstep of some impressive natural wonders. Stop by the hilltop municipal offices and arrange to have someone turn on the lights and let you into the nearby

㊶ Grutas de Lanquín caves, for which there is a small charge. The subterranean chambers and underground rivers are easy to explore with the "no boundaries" policy, though this means that most of the stalactite formations have long been carried off as souvenirs. Visit the caves toward sunset and sit at the entrance for the spooky bat show when thousands upon thousands of the creatures leave their dark day dwellings for the starry, insect-filled night sky. As for going in, there are no trails or guides here, so you're on your own. Beware the slippery rocks and rickety ladders, and ignore the graffiti.

㊷ Often praised as the most beautiful spot in Guatemala, **Semuc Champey** appears to be simply a series of emerald pools surrounded by dense forest. The pools, as you'll find, are perfect for swimming. Upon further investigation you'll notice that the pools are actually the rooftop of a natural land arch, the water originating from the raging Cahabón River that disappears with a torrential smashing of white water and mist into the depth of a mysterious cavern. Local legend has it that various explorers have tried to enter the underground passage by lowering themselves over the lip of the arch, many to turn back right away, and several to be swallowed up, their bodies never to be recovered downstream where the river returns to daylight and its calm meandering rhythm. Semuc Champey is only 10 km (6 mi) south of Lanquín on a dirt road, but you'll need a four-wheel-drive vehicle to reach it or about three hours to make the hike. You can get directions at the municipal offices or rent a pickup and driver from the children in town who solicit visitors for the trip.

Dining and Lodging

$$ ✕🖪 Hotel El Recreo Lanquín Champey. This large hotel at the mouth of the Lanquín caves is a good place for swimming. Lodgings are in clean albeit concrete rooms in the main building and in several bungalows out back. The restaurant was built with the expectation of more diners than it typically garners; it serves decent, typical Guatemalan food. ⊠ *Across from Lanquín River,* ☎ *951–4160,* 🖷 *951–2333. 12 rooms, 4 bungalows. Restaurant. No credit cards.*

White-Water Rafting

Expeditions companies are based in Guatemala City or Antigua, and they provide transportation. Rafting trips on the Cahabón River (Class III–IV depending on the season) lasting from one to three days can be arranged through **Area Verde Expeditions** (⊠ 4 Avenida Sur 8, Antigua, ☎ 🖷 832–3863; ⊠ Box 476, Salida, CO, 81201, ☎ 🖷 719/539–7102, heesaker@areaverde.com) or **Maya Expeditions** (⊠ 15 Calle 1–91 Zona 10, Guatemala City, ☎ 363–4965 or 832–1017 in Antigua).

The Verapaces A to Z

Arriving and Departing

BY BUS

Transportes Escobar/Monja Blanca runs direct, comfortable Pullman buses between Guatemala City (⊠ 8 Avenida 15–16, Zona 1, ☎ 238–1409) and Cobán (⊠ 2 Calle 3–77, Zona 4, ☎ 952–1536), passing the Quetzal Reserve. The driver will let you off, if you ask. Buses depart every hour or so from 4 AM to 4 PM at both ends of the route, and the trip takes four hours. Buses stop near El Rancho at the Villa del Sol for food and restroom breaks.

Typical buses leave Cobán at 5, 8, and 11 AM for the seven-hour bumpy, dusty trip down the Polochic River Valley to El Estor, on Lake Izabal's north shore. Periodic bus service is also available through Lanquín and Cahabón to El Estor. Though the views are spectacular, this trip is only for travelers who can bear discomfort in the pursuit of high adventure. A rustic road connecting Cobán with El Petén has sporadic bus service, so very few choose this route. Rumor has it that this road will soon be paved.

BY CAR

From Guatemala City, take the Carretera Atlantíca to El Rancho, where you'll take Rte. 17 north for the Quetzal Reserve, Cobán and Lanquin destinations. Everything is off this highway and is marked with signs. Be aware that there are not many gas stations before Cobán.

Getting Around

BY BUS

Buses run regularly between Cobán and San Pedro Carchá, where there is sporadic service to Cahabón via Lanquín. Buses also run regularly between Cobán and San Juan Chamelco.

BY CAR

Several agencies rent cars in Cobán for about $50 a day, which is a great option if you want to spend some time exploring the area. Reserve ahead of time, especially for the weekends. **Geo Rental** (⊠ In the same building as Café El Tirol, off the plaza, 1 Calle 3–13, ☎ 952–2059); **Inque Renta Autos,** ⊠ 3 Avenida 1–18, Zona 4, ☎ 952–1994; **Sears** (⊠ 8 Avenida 2–36, Zona 4, ☎ 952–1530); or **Tabarini** (⊠ Avenida 227, ☎ 952–1504).

EMERGENCIES

Police (☎ 951–1306).

Hospital (☎ 952–1315 in Cobán).

Pharmacy: Farmacia Central (☎ 951–0581 in Cobán).

THE ATLANTIC LOWLANDS

Guatemala's small, humid stretch of Caribbean coast was immortalized by the country's famous Nobel Prize–winning writer, Miguel Ángel Asturias, in *Viento Fuerte* (1950), *El Papa Verde* (1954) and *Los Ojos de los Enterrados* (1960), popularly known as The Banana Trilogy. Today, Dole and Chiquita own huge plantations in the region's lowlands. From the port in Puerto Barrios, gigantic freight liners leave daily with enormous shipments of bananas stacked like children's blocks. Life and livelihood in this region is arranged around the crops, and groups of men traveling together can be spotted along the roadside, each carrying nothing more than a knit bag or a small backpack: they are banana farm workers. Typically men from one village organize and seek work as a group to increase their chances of being hired.

Although the minimum wage is about $3.50 a day, some will work for as little as $2, and return home only on Sunday, the one day they don't live and work on the farms.

Though the indigenous culture is not as striking as what you encounter in the highlands, the Q'eqchí Indians include many who speak only their native Q'eqchí language. They have migrated down the Polochic Valley from Cobán and inhabit the region, which includes hard-to-access areas like the Sierra Santa Cruz and the Sierra de las Minas mountain ranges. Some mountain villagers walk a full day or more to get to market. In the larger towns are a wide variety of indigenous and Ladino peoples. The coastal towns of Livingston and Puerto Barrios are home to the Garífuna, Afro-Caribbean peoples who speak a language of the same name.

Traces of the Maya empire, such as the impressive Quiriguá ruins and the ancient Maya city of Copán, just over the border in Honduras, mark the movement of the Maya through the lowlands. Because it's still a somewhat unsettled and undiscovered area, however, the only well-traveled route is the lush Río Dulce canyon, connecting the town of Río Dulce with Livingston. Otherwise, the region is practically untouched by tourism, particularly the stunning Lake Izabal, the largest lake in Guatemala, which sits in a tropical valley bordered by the Sierra de las Minas to the south (which reach a stunning height of 10,000 ft) and the Sierra Santa Cruz to the north.

The heat and sun in the lowlands is intense. Be prepared with a good sun hat, light-weight, long-sleeve shirts, and light pants or long skirts. (Shorts just don't protect legs from the sun, tall grass, insects, and dust.) Also pack plenty of sunscreen and insect repellent. The best time to visit is in November and December—the end of the rainy season when temperatures are springlike. You will also greatly improve your experience in the lowlands if you adapt the local rhythm of life. Wake at sunrise and do most of your activities in the morning. With a good book in hand, find a hammock in which to relax over the noon hours. Then hit the street again in the late afternoon and evening, which is a wonderful time of day to be out and about. It is best to avoid the area during March, when the heat is at its apex and farmers are burning their fields, leaving the skies hazy and thick and the great views obliterated.

From Guatemala City, most arrive and depart here via the Carretera Atlantíca (Atlantic Highway), and those heading overland to El Petén will pass through this region. The bus ride is about five hours to Río Dulce or Puerto Barrios on a good day. Descending the mountains, the road is curvy, and as you descend you will feel the temperature and humidity rising. A new intra-country airline service, Inter Airlines, flies to both Río Dulce and Puerto Barrios.

Numbers in the text correspond to numbers in the margin and on the Verapaces and Atlantic Lowlands map.

Quiriguá

★ **43** *186 km (115 mi) northeast of Guatemala City, and 96 km (60 mi) southwest of Puerto Barrios, on the Carretera Atlantíca; turn at km 205 and head south 3 km (2 mi). Look for small roadside signs indicating a Maya temple.*

In ancient times an important Maya trading center stood here, on what was then the banks of the Motagua River (the river has since changed its course), and for many years was closely linked to the city of Copán. Quiriguá is famous for its beautiful and intricate carving, similar to that found at Copán, and especially for its massive and amazingly well-preserved stelae, which are the largest in the Maya world, some over 30-ft tall. Unlike the hazy remnants of images you see at most other sites, in which the art has been worn away over the centuries by wind, rain, and sun, the carvings here emerge from the rock faces in three dimensions. The stelae depict Quiriguá's most powerful chiefs, especially Cauac Sky, who was probably the city's most influential leader. Several monuments, covered with interesting zoomorphic figures, still stand, and the remains of an acropolis and other structures have been partially restored. The ruins are surrounded by a lush stand of rain forest—an island of untouched wilderness in a sea of agricultural production in the heart of banana country. This is an excellent spot for birding as well. There is no bus service down the dirt road leading to the ruins from the highway, and walking can be very uncomfortable, especially during the dry season when the heat and sun are intense and the road extremely dusty. Fortunately, there are vehicles traveling between the ruins and the highway. ☎ *No phone.* ⊠ *$3.* ⊙ *Daily 8–4.*

Side Trip: Copán, Honduras

238 km (147½ mi) northeast of Guatemala City, in Honduras via El Florido. Take Carretera Atlántica to Río Hondo; south on CA 10 to Vado Hondo (9 km/5 mi south of Chiquimula); CA 11 east for 48 km/30 mi to El Florido; continue on CA 11 for 11 km/7 mi to ruins.

Lying in the jungles of western Honduras, the ancient Maya city of Copán is one of the pinnacles of Maya achievement. The amazing pyramids, freestanding stelae of various rulers, a hieroglyphic staircase with the longest Maya epigraph discovered to date, and other relics left by this highly advanced civilization are a must-see. Remarkably well-preserved and ornate, the ruins are arranged around an expansive, neatly groomed central plaza. A small **Museum of Mayan Sculpture** (⊠ $5) nearby contains facades (one of ball court), temples (and replicas of temples), and benches over 1,500 years old. The museum was closed for about a year due to a damaged roof, though it's possible that there was more to the museum's closing than a few simple leaks. Tensions between the locals and the University of Pennsylvania and Harvard archaeologists who are responsible for the majority of the excavations make restoration complicated. Since the discovery of Copán by archaeologists in the 19th century, some of the locals have become master excavators and artists, passing their skills learned from the universities down through their family lines. The skilled locals claim that the Spirit of Margarita destroyed the museum roof when her sacred tomb was opened.

Copán reached its apex during the eighth century, when it controlled much of the Maya empire's southern realm and experienced an intensification in artistic development, the remnants of which can be seen today. The fifth-century ruler Yax Kúk Mo began a written history of Copán and was the first of a dynasty of 17 rulers who governed during its golden age. Yax Kúk Mo's tomb, which was discovered beneath a pyramid in 1993 by a University of Pennsylvania research team, will eventually be exhibited to the public. In fact, only a small portion of Copán's estimated 4,000 buildings have as yet been excavated.

The attractive nearby town of Ruinas de Copán has a variety of accommodations. **La Casa de Café** (☎ 504/651–4508, ✍) is a reasonably priced bed-and-breakfast inn with three guest rooms and a shared bath. **Plaza Copán Hotel** has air-conditioned rooms and a swimming pool (⊠ Bolevar el Centro, across from the town plaza, ☎ 504/651–4278, ✍). The **Copán Museum**, on the main square, specializes in artifacts, including the burial of a scribe. From Guatemala City, take the

Carretera Atlántica to Río Hondo; then head south past Chiquimula to Vado Hondo, where a dusty road heads off to the left to the border post of El Florido and on to the nearby ruins. Many Guatemala City travel agencies offer one- or two-day tours to Copán. An easy, if more expensive, daily shuttle goes directly to Copán Ruinas from Guatemala City or Antigua. The five-hour trip costs $25. Flights from Guatemala City are available to San Pedro Sula (☞ Guatemalan Carriers *in* Smart Travel Tips), the airport closest to the ruins. Note: crossing back over this border into Guatemala with a rental car is notoriously frustrating. Have documents handy and be prepared for delays. ⊠ *Copán Ruinas, Honduras,* ☎ *no phone.* 🎟 *$10.* ⊙ *Daily 9–5.* 🐾

Río Dulce

★ ⓐ *30 km (19 mi) northwest of La Ruidosa, where the road to El Petén leaves the Carretera Atlantíca.*

Though the town of Fronteras, known more commonly as Río Dulce these days, sits on the shore of a beautiful waterway, it sadly falls short of its potential. Overdevelopment and traffic make it difficult to experience its otherwise prime location on the water. In fact, it's the junction of several travel routes, thanks to the country's longest (cement) bridge, which spans the foot of Lake Izabal connecting El Relleno and the Atlantic Highway to the south with Río Dulce, and beyond, to El Petén, to the north. West are the Castillo de San Felipe and the road leading to the lakefront town of El Estor, and to the east is Bahí de Amatique. Río Dulce has little in the way of dining and lodging, although quality places accessible by boat are nearby, thanks to the large expat boating community and wealthy Guatemalans who dock their boats at the many marinas. The *launcheros* (boat drivers) parked outside of Río Bravo Pizzeria will take you anywhere in the area for under $5.

The Río Dulce was an important Maya trade route and later became the European colonists' main link with Spain. Because Spanish ships regularly exported Guatemala's products via the river, it was also frequented by pirates, who attacked both the ships and the warehouses on the shore of the lake. In hopes of curtailing forays by pirates, 17th-century colonists built a series of fortresses on the river's north bank, at the entrance to the lake. The forts were repeatedly razed by pirates only to be rebuilt bigger and better. In the 1950s the Guatemalan government reconstructed the ruined castle of **Castillo de San Felipe** (☎ no phone, 🎟 $1), named after King Philip II of Spain, to resemble its last version, and the result is an attractive landmark in a small national park. From 1655 to 1660 it was used as a prison. You can reach it by the road leading west from Río Dulce or by a short boat ride.

Dining and Lodging

$$$$ ✕🏨 **La Ensenada Hotel and Yacht Club.** Although La Ensenada (formerly the Marimonte) has less character than the competition—sparse grounds and simple rooms—it is easy to reach. Rooms surround a large pool, and a three-story bar-and-restaurant complex overlooks the water. Many new buildings a good distance from the river have several modern rooms each (11 have air-conditioning), but the older bungalows, which are slightly run-down, have much better views of the river. Windsurfers are available for rent, and river trips can be arranged. ⊠ *1½ km (1 mi) east of El Relleno, Km 275 Carretera á Peten,* ☎ *947–8585 in Río Dulce; 367–5444 in Guatemala City,* 🖷 *366–1236. 38 rooms. Restaurant, bar, pool, windsurfing, travel services. AE, MC, V.*

$$$ ✕🏨 **Catamaran Island Hotel.** On the north bank of the river a few miles
★ east of the bridge, this hotel complex takes advantage of its waterfront location with a series of one-room bungalows and a restaurant built

right over the water. Spacious and insect-proof bungalows make the most of the riverside breezes, but perhaps their nicest feature is their porches, which are perfect for watching boats plying the river. Cheaper landlocked rooms aren't nearly as nice. The restaurant and bar are in an immense open-air thatched building with lovely views. The specialties are steaks and grilled fish, including the delicious robálo plucked from the river. The hotel arranges boat trips to surrounding attractions and to Livingston. ⊠ *5 km (3 mi) east of bridge,* ☎ *947–8361,* ℻ *367– 1633, hcatamaran@guate.net. 28 bungalows. Restaurant, bar, air-conditioning, fans, pool, travel services. MC, V.*

$ ✕🏨 **Bruno's.** A popular hangout for the yachting crowd, Bruno's has recently built a hotel addition to its restaurant. Rooms are clean and big and two include private bath, TV, air-conditioning, and a kitchen. A tiny pool sits between the hotel and restaurant, which serves sandwiches and drinks. The big TV in the restaurant draws a crowd for American football games. E-mail service is available next door to the restaurant. ⊠ *Under the bridge, on the Río Dulce side,* ☎ *930–5178, rio@guate.net. 9 rooms, 4 with shared bath. Restaurant, pool. AE, MC, V. www.mayaparadise.com.*

$ ✕🏨 **Hacienda Tijax.** Partially built over the water, this hotel offers a number of different accommodations, from birdhouse-shape doubles with shared bath to large two-story rustic town houses with a kitchen and private bath designed for bigger groups. A series of swinging bridges over a mangrove swamp connects the lodge with a jungle reserve and rubber-and-teak plantation. With Tijax as your base you can go on a hike, learn how rubber is extracted at the plantation, swim in a natural jungle pool, or take a horseback ride. Tijax is also well known for their restaurant, which serves a variety of Italian dishes including homemade pesto. ⊠ *2-minute boat ride from Río Dulce. Ask at the Tijax Express office, next to Río Bravo in Río Dulce for free transportation,* ☎ *902–0858,* ℻ *902–7523. 9 rooms, 2 with shared bath. rio@guate.net*

$ 🏨 **Mini Hotel Yair.** If you get stuck in Río Dulce and just need a clean place to spend the night, the Hotel Yair is definitely your best bet. All rooms have single beds, and two rooms (at press time) have TV and air-conditioning. The service is friendly and attentive and the location makes it easy to catch an early bus. ⊠ *One block from town center, on the road leading to Castillo de San Felipe,* ☎ *930–5132. 11 rooms. No credit cards.*

River Trips

One of the most beautiful boat trips in the country is the two- to three-hour ride on the **Río Dulce** between the town of Río Dulce and Livingston. *Collectivos* (public launches) leave from Río Bravo Restaurant in Río Dulce or the public dock in Livingston usually with no fewer than eight people and cost about $9 per person each way. (The launcheros will keep you waiting all afternoon if the boat is not full.) It's best to arrive early in the morning; 9 AM is the earliest they leave from Livingston. There's usually a morning trip from Río Dulce, too; however, boats tend to leave only when full, and not according to a schedule. Private trips to and from Livingston and Río Dulce can be arranged at the docks in both towns and allow you the freedom to stop where you want along the way. They can run you $100 or more. Don't fall into the trap of paying more for a "guided tour" because they simply don't exist. All public launches stop at Bird Island, a roosting place for several hundred cormorants; Flower Lagoon, a small inlet covered in bobbing water lilies; and *aguas calientes* (hot water springs), a small, hot sulfurous waterfall pouring into a shallow river. Definitely bring your bathing suit.

When you're negotiating your private boat trip, tell the launchero that in addition to the usual stops you want to go to *Ak'tenamit* and **Río Tatin More**, two truly insider destinations. Ak'tenamit (☎ 902–0608 in Río Dulce or 254–1560 in Guatemala City), Q'eqchí for new village, is a clinic, school, and garden project on the river's north shore at the canyon's entrance. The brain child of sharp and witty Steven Dudenhoefer, the organization is run by Q'eqchí and expatriate volunteers and is an interesting place to visit for local culture.

Río Tatin is one of the smaller rivers that drain into the Río Dulce, and, by rowing or motoring down it you can get closer to the jungle, which drapes over the riverbanks. A short distance upriver is **Finca Tatin** (☎ 902–0831, fincatatin@centramerica.com), a small rustic bed-and-breakfast and Spanish school, run by a friendly Argentinean family. They will rent you their canoes, which is a great way to see the river without the loud roar of a motor.

El Estor

㊺ *40 km (24 mi) west of Río Dulce, on the northwest shore of Lago Izabal.*

A small trading post for coffee exporters called "The Store" gave El Estor its name. Q'eqchí comprise 85% of the town's population, but there's also a decidedly Caribbean influence, mostly described as *tranquilo*, Spanish for easygoing and laid-back, and its truth becomes evident as you stroll around town, which the now-defunct nickel mine just west of town helped to create. The mine laid out the central plaza, lakeshore walk, municipal dock, and brick streets, and developed the potable water system. Although El Estor lacks luxury accommodations, it does offer a variety of eco-adventures, with bird-watching on the lake— El Estor's on a migratory path, so thousands of species can be spotted here—and magical sunrises and sunsets from the Sierra Santa Cruz mountains lookouts. The two banks in town change money and traveler's checks but do not give credit card advances. El Estor has one gasoline station, bicycle rental, a daily market, and several decent hotels and restaurants, though as of yet no public Internet service.

You can watch how the beautiful weavings of Guatemala are made at the **Q'eqchí Women's Weaving Workshop** (✉ Free, ⊙ Mon.–Sat. 8– noon and 3–5), four blocks north of the central plaza, one block north of the soccer field. Every year a small group of young women leave their villages to come live on the grounds of the workshop, and they spend 12 months learning the age-old craft of loom and belt weavings. Every woman who successfully completes the course is given a loom to take back to her village and encouraged to make a living from her craft and to teach other women how to weave. You can ask for directions at the workshop store, on the main street across from the Corpobanco.

OFF THE BEATEN PATH

BOCAS DEL POLOCHIC WILDLIFE REFUGE – Declared a protected area in 1996, this Polochic River delta wetland on the western end of Lago Izabal has rich plant and animal life, including 250 species of birds. The refuge, made up of marshlands, rain forests, lagoons, small bays, and rivers, is over 51,000 acres, a third of which is aquatic. A Guatemalan-run NGO, Defensores de la Naturaleza, manages the area and runs a remote ecological lodge (reached by boat) at the base of the Sierra de las Minas mountain range, at the southwest end of the lake. The rustic two-story thatched-roof lodge has bunk beds with bedding along with mosquito nets, a full service kitchen, solar-powered lights, and dry composting toilets. Guided trips are arranged through the Defensores office in El Estor (next to the police station, one block up from the public dock) and include a guided boat trip to and from the station, preset meals in the station prepared by Q'eqchí women from the local community of Selempím, a visit to the village, a tortilla-making lesson, and hikes to a mirador overlooking the refuge. Interpretative land and aquatic trails make this an especially compelling trip for nature enthusiasts. Often spotted are blue herons, kites, kingfishers, snowy egrets, and, if you are lucky, a rare motmot or manatee. A midnight thunderstorm is magical here, but regardless of the weather you'll hear the din of howler monkeys long into the night. Rates are $25 with meals per night, plus the boat trip. *Defensores de la Naturaleza,* ☎ *949–7237 or 369–7777 in Guatemala City. rbocas@defensores.org.gt.*

The new northshore road from Río Dulce to El Estor has put the ferry boat from Mariscos out of commission and has made getting to El Estor easier than ever. To get here, you're best off renting a private car, taxi, or van in Río Dulce, because the road is bumpy (and the public buses worse than other bus lines in Izabal, and more expensive). The hour-long ride takes you past an expansive banana plantation as well as cattle ranches. Look for the massive ceiba trees, the sacred trees of the Maya—the only reason they were left to stand when the rest of the forest was cleared for cattle grazing. Also try to spot the strangler fig trees, which wrap themselves around the trunks of palms. Eventually, they supplant the palms, and the trees die from lack of sunlight.

Dining and Lodging

$ ✕ **Restaurante Chaabil.** *Chaabil,* the Q'eqchí Maya word for "beautiful," is an apt name for the best restaurant in El Estor. Built on the water, Chaabil is the perfect place to catch an afternoon breeze, an undisturbed morning view of the majestic Sierra de las Minas, or a spectacular sunset. You may even get an opportunity to snap a photo of a fisherman delivering the catch of the day. Make reservations ahead of time to enjoy a bowl of seafood tapado, or stop by anytime for lake perch or river robálo, two personal favorites served with rice and mixed fresh vegetables. For dessert, try the pineapple or papaya smoothie. A two-minute walk west of the central plaza, Chaabil is easy to spot, a traditional open-air ranchon made with tropical hardwoods and a tightly woven palm-leaf roof. ⊠ *West of town center,* ☎ *no phone. No credit cards.*

$ ✕🏨 **Hotel Marisabela.** This lakefront two-story hotel has clean, simply furnished rooms with double beds, good ventilation, views of the lake, and optional cable TV. A third-floor balcony is filled with wooden lounge chairs and is the best place in town for a siesta. Owner Isabel de Mane speaks Italian and English as well as Spanish. Though the restaurant always looks closed, it's not. Just open the gate and call out "Buenos tardes!" until one of the workers appears. The Italian dishes are authentic and filling. ⊠ *Two blocks east of the municipal building on the lakefront,* ☎ *949–7206. 7 rooms. Restaurant. No credit cards.*

$ 🏨 **Hotel Vista al Lago.** This building was once the original store from which El Estor derived its name. Run by the loquacious Oscar Paz, the hotel has clean, small rooms with single beds and private bathrooms. The wide street-side wooden balcony is a great place to take in the town's waterfront and watch the slow comings and goings at the town offices next door. Before checking in, make sure that the town hall next door has no plans for a dance; otherwise the thumping music will keep you up until 4 AM. Note: reservations are not always honored. ⊠ *Lakefront, next to the town hall,* ☎ *949–7205. 16 rooms. No credit cards.*

El Boqueron Canyon

El Boqueron Canyon is perhaps the most beautiful natural wonder in Guatemala. The narrow limestone canyon walls reaching heights of 600 ft are covered in jungle plants and hanging tree moss. Hummingbirds dance around blooming flowers, blue morpho butterflies dart in front of your boat, and kingfishers dive at minnows. Sometimes howler monkeys visit the trees at the entrance to the canyon. Listen for their howls in the late afternoon. All along the canyon you can climb rocks, explore caves for bats clinging to rock faces, or see if you can pick out the Balancing Rock. (It's about a 15 minute canoe ride from the canyon entrance.) The water is clean and cool and great for swimming except during periods of heavy rain, when all the local rivers turn a muddy brown. The entrance to the *balneario* (swimming beach) is on the El Estor side of the bridge. Close to the canyon entrance on the other side of the bridge is a turnoff past a giant ceiba tree that leads to several thatched huts right on the river: the proprietors, Antonio or Miguel, provide low-sitting, roughly fashioned *kayuko* (canoe) rides up the canyon for about $1 a person. On hot weekend afternoons, the base of the canyon tends to fill up with locals, making it a somewhat noisy family affair. It's 3 mi east of El Estor; 10-minutes by bus or taxi or 30 minutes on bike.

Finca Paraiso

Known for its hot-water waterfall, think of Finca Paraiso as a natural spa and soak for the grungy traveler. Don't be dissuaded from these hot springs even if it is 100 degrees outside: the natural hot stream falls 20 ft over rocks into a clean cold river. A trail leads from the front gate upriver about 200 meters to the falls. From here, it's a short yet somewhat rocky climb from the shore to the waterfall—and rocks can be very slippery—but you won't regret the effort once you've waded in. If you have goggles or a snorkeling mask, carefully explore around the waterfall where small caves under the rocks create natural sauna rooms. You can also hike upstream (for about a half hour) to the narrow cave at the source of the cold river. (If you hike on the path, drop down to the river when the path starts to go up.) The rock formations here are otherworldly, and swimming through the cave in the dark is a heart-racing experience. Bring a waterproof flashlight if you plan to go in, you'll need it.

On the lake, 2 km (1 mi) downstream from the hot springs is the **Turicentro El Paraiso**, where a simple restaurant serves breakfast, lunch, and dinner, and pretty little thatched-roof cabañas with private baths are for rent. Tractor service is available to take you to and from the hot springs, which is free when you spend the night. To get here, follow the small road across from the the gate for 2 km (1.3 mi) to the lake. ⊠ *10 mi east of El Estor on the road to Río Dulce,* 🎫 *$1.*

Chocón Machacas

46 *45-min boat ride from Río Dulce.*

The northern banks of the Golfete, a wide body of water between Lago Izabal and Río Dulce canyon are covered by the 17,790-acre **Chocón Machacas Wildlife Reserve,** or *manatee biotopo* (natural manatee park), as it's locally known. Among the stretches of virgin rain forest and the extensive mangrove swamp here are gentle manatees—shy marine mammals, also known as sea cows for their enormous size. (They're so large, in fact, that you can see them from a low-flying plane.) The manatee is as elusive as the quetzal bird, however, and as you boat through the reserve you're more likely to see the surroundings, otters, and several bird species, such as pelicans, cormorants, and American coots. Some of the creeks go through thick forest, under giant mahogany, ceiba, and mangrove trees, which hang over the water to form tunnels so thick they block sunlight. A tiny island surrounded by the park's dozens of creeks and lagoons has a well-maintained on-land trail of a ½ mi or so that is easily walked for those with stiff boating legs. The trail has such interesting examples of old-growth trees as the San Juan, a tall, straight tree with yellow blossoms, and such rain-forest plants as orchids and bromeliads.

The only way to get to the reserve is by boat, and most launches up and down the river will stop at the park entrance if requested, but rarely do they enter the park. Most of the major hotels on the Río Dulce rent boats with guides for individual or group tours ($100). A visitor's center at the park entrance has interpretive pamphlets (some in English) that can be purchased when in stock.

Livingston

★ **47** *37 km (23 mi) northeast of Lago Izabal; take a boat downriver from Río Dulce or a ferry from Puerto Barrios.*

Situated on the Gulf of Honduras at the mouth of the Río Dulce, Livingston or *La Buga* (the Mouth, in Garífuna) might as well be its own Caribbean island—the only way to get to or from the town is by boat, and the culture is closer to that of Jamaica than the rest of Guatemala. Livingston is home to the Garífuna people. They are descendants of Arawak Indians and Africans, who came originally from St. Vincent, an island in the Lesser Antilles. After 20 years of resisting British encroachment, the Garífuna were forcibly removed from their homeland and deposed on Roatán, Honduras. The Garífuna migrated to the mainland, settling all along the Caribbean coast from Belize to Nicaragua. Each year on November 24 to 26, Livingston hosts a festival to celebrate the arrival of the Garífuna on the coast of Guatemala. A number of sailboats reenact the original voyage from Roatán. Garífuna from Honduras, Belize, and the United States turn out, and the town rejoices with traditional music and dancing, parades, and soccer matches. The Feast of St. Isidore May 13–15 is another huge celebration, which is dedicated to corn, as Saint Isidore is the saint of corn planting. The best time to visit is during these energetic holidays.

Livingston's single paved street is the only evidence left of its heyday as a large port for the Guatemalan coffee-exporting boom of the late 19th century. Today, Livingston's residents make their living mostly from fishing or the tourist industry. Once you arrive, lay down your worries and settle under a coconut palm. Reggae, ganja (not a good idea for tourists; you might end up doing time in an infamous Guatemalan prison), and the soft lick of waves measure out the slow pace that draws visitors to this small, laid-back community. At night, roving bands of Garífuna musicians and dancers perform for crowds of tourists. The Garífuna are famous for their punta dancing—they may grab you out from the crowd and teach you some moves you didn't know your body could make.

Anyone expecting pristine white sandy beaches and blue Caribbean waters, however, is bound to be disappointed. The narrow **beach** that stretches north from the river mouth is lined with shacks for several miles and is not very clean near town. A 1½-hour walk or short boat ride to the north, however, takes you to a gorgeous little jungle river called **Siete Altares,** with a series of deep pools and rainy-season waterfalls that are ideal for swimming. Rather than heading out on your own (robberies have been reported in the past), try to arrange for a guided walking tour with the cheery and enthusiastic **Rogelio Franzua** (☎ 947–0406), who speaks some English and knows a great deal about the history and culture of the area. A bag lunch is provided. Tours are about $7. Or arrange a tour through Restaurante Bahía Azul (☞ *below*). A little more than halfway to the falls, just past the river is **Salvador Gaviota Restaurant and Lodge,** a rustic little joint whose shaded dock and fish-and-chips might interest you for lunch or dinner.

If you are not up for the trip to the falls, the beach is a great place to explore with its several bars and a little shop where Pablo Marino sells handmade drums, shakers, and wood carvings. Afternoon breezes off the ocean make resting on the beach a good place to pass the torrid afternoons.

Day trips by boat up the Río Dulce to the Chocón Machacas wildlife reserve (☞ Chocón Machacas, *above*) and Castillo de San Felipe (☞ Río Dulce, *above*) or to the local Siete Altares, Playa Blanca (one hour northwest by boat), and Río Crocoli (30 minutes northwest by boat) can be arranged at the public dock, through the Hotel Tucán Dugú, Casa Rosada, or Bahía Azul (☞ *below*).

Be aware that young men wait on the town dock to "escort" tourists to their hotel. You can accept their offer or refuse, either way, they will follow you and ask for money. "Tipping" them to leave you alone is your prerogative.

Dining and Lodging

$ ✕ **Pizzeria Rigoletto.** For a combination of decent pizza, wacky stories, and Mexican lemonade, try this small restaurant run out of Maria's house. A cook by profession and writer by hobby, Maria has *plenty* to say about her cooking and her life experiences. Ask her about once catching one of America's Most Wanted. When not spinning yarns, she prepares about 15 varieties of pizza, which you're advised to stick to, and various Italian dishes. It's a good idea to preorder your pizza early in the afternoon. ✉ *Head left from the public dock; it's about 200 yards down the road on the right,* ☎ *no phone. No credit cards.*

$ ✕ **Restaurante Bahía Azul.** Bahía Azul is the most popular tourist restaurant in town—the walls are covered with travel information and you can often arrange tours and trips here. Located at the curve on main street, its porch seating is a great place to people watch. The large menu includes everything from lobster and sandwiches, to Chinese dishes and breakfast fare. Most nights include live drumming and dancing by a local band. ✉ *Main St., up the hill from the public dock,* ☎ 947–0049, 🖷 947–0136. MC, V..

$ ✕ **Restaurante Margoth.** This mainstay of Livingston run by the well-respected and large Doña Margoth serves the usual fare of seafood and fish dishes. The restaurant is most famous for its seafood tapado with plantains. The meal is delicious but a challenge to eat, so tuck your napkin in your shirt collar. The ambience is that of a bright and bustling cafeteria. The Doña keeps a sharp eye on her workers and the service is speedy. ✉ *A light green building halfway down the secondary commercial road,* ☎ 947–0019. AE, MC. Closed 3 PM–7 PM daily.

$$$$ ✕🏠 **Hotel Tucán Dugú.** Livingston's only first-class hotel, the hilltop ★ Tucán Dugú has some great views of the Caribbean. Extensive grounds stretch over the hillside and overflow with lush tropical foliage. Rooms are in a long, two-story, thatch-roof building, and all of them are spacious and have views of the gulf, so you won't miss the absent TV. The large pool, one of the best in Guatemala, is surrounded by palm trees, lounge chairs, and a bar. If you're staying elsewhere, you can pay 25 quetzales to use the pool all afternoon. The restaurant serves decent local seafood such as coconut shrimp and robálo, but is almost always

empty. Trips up the Río Dulce and to spots around the bay can be arranged. ✉ *Main St., up the hill from the public docks,* ☎ 947–0072 *or 334–5064 in Guatemala City,* ℻ *334–5242 in Guatemala City, tukansa@guate.net. 46 rooms, 4 suites, 4 bungalows. Restaurant, bar, pool, beach, travel services. AE, DC, MC, V.*

$ ✕▥ **African Place.** This whitewashed restaurant and hotel geared toward backpackers resembles a castle out of an eccentric fairy tale. It was designed and built in 1980 by owner Israel Alcalde, originally from the Basque region of Spain. However, he calls the hotel's design "Poor Arabic Style" because the tile work, which, in the Middle East, would cover the bottom half of the walls, is here only two tiles high. Note the stars of David worked into the floors and walls. For eats, the restaurant carries all the inexpensive Livingston favorites, including seafood soups, fried fish, and rice and beans. Breakfast is also served. ✉ *Turn left where main street connects with the secondary commercial road; it's 3 blocks down, between the church and the cemetery,* ☎ 947–0221. *No credit cards. Closed 4 PM–7 PM daily.*

$ ✕▥ **Casa Rosada.** This casual waterfront bungalow hotel can best be
★   described as Guatemala's most luxurious way to rough it. Each of the 10 basic bungalows is furnished with bright highland furniture and a pair of twin beds covered with mosquito nets. Don't be scared off by the shared bathrooms; they're clean and comfortable, and the shower inside the main building has hot water. The main building houses a restaurant that serves excellent meals and snacks and has a fine patio overlooking the water. American-style breakfasts are available all day. The dinner menu changes daily but always includes lobster, steak, fish, and a vegetarian plate. All dinners include salad, coconut bread, and dessert and are served at 7 PM sharp on candlelit tables. Call or stop by to put in a reservation by early afternoon. Owner Cathey Lopez, a Berkeley expat, arranges river trips from Rosada's private dock. The place fills quickly, so reserve ahead if possible or arrive early in the day. ✉ *Down the street to the left of the public dock,* ☎ 947–0303, ℻ 947–0304. *10 bungalows with shared bath. Restaurant, boating, laundry service, travel services. AE, DC, MC, V.*

$ ▥ **Hotel Garífuna.** Clean, simple, and secure, the Hotel Garífuna run by the cordial Livingston natives Enrique and his family, puts you in the heart of a Garífuna neighborhood. In this two-story brick building, all the rooms have private baths and open onto a porch overlooking the street or its tree-filled backyards. ✉ *Turn left where main street connects with the secondary commercial road. Two blocks down, look for the signs to turn right. Halfway down the street on the left,* ☎ 947–0183, ℻ 947–0184. *6 rooms. Laundry service. AE, DC, MC, V.*

Nightlife

Residents of Livingston are famous for their weekend bashes, mostly centering around several beachfront discos. Bariques Place and Playa Ocho are the two lively spots at the end of main street, but it's also a good idea to ask around town. Punta rock pulls everyone out onto the dance floor, although you'll hear other stuff, too. You may not realize that everyone is hard at work on the dance floor until you look at their hips, the focal point of the punta, a Caribbean dance with African roots. On some nights, drummers wander the town center in an unorganized fashion playing for quetzales. The **Ubafu,** a Rasta-inspired shack (note the Bob Marley posters) is sometimes open for a late-night jam if there are enough beer-drinking customers.

Puerto Barrios

48 *295 km (183 mi) from Guatemala City at end of Carretera Atlantíca, or 2 hours by ferry (or 45 minutes by launcha) from Livingston.*

Low on attractions but with plenty of hotels and restaurants, this port town is a good way station if you're headed to or from Belize, Livingston, or Punta Manabique.

Dining and Lodging

$$ ✕ **Restaurante Safary.** The best-known restaurant in Puerto Barrios, the Safary is one of the few businesses located right on the water. On a hot afternoon or steamy night, the ocean breezes are a tremendous relief from the stale air of town center. Especially since it's a large *ranchon,* an open-air structure with a grass roof. The food is not first class and you sit on wooden benches, but lots of locals eat here. ✉ *End of 5 Avenida at the water,* ☎ *948–0563. AE, DC, MC, V.*

$$$$ ✕🏨 **Cayos del Diablo.** Opened in 1991, this first-class Best Western hotel on Bahía de Amatique (Amatique Bay) brings luxury accommodations to a spectacular natural setting. Rooms are in a series of thatched bungalows, with colorful decor, air-conditioning, and cable TV. Tropical gardens beautify the grounds surrounded by rain forest, and directly in back is a forest-draped hill with a small waterfall. The hotel has a pool and private beach, and trips on the bay and up the Río Dulce can be arranged. Hourly hotel boats make pickups at the dock in Puerto Barrios. ✉ *13 km (8 mi) west of Puerto Barrios, Km 8 Carretera a Livingston, near Santo Tomás de Castillo,* ☎ *948–2361; 948–0263; 333–4633 in Guatemala City through the Hotel Camino Real; 800/528–1234 in the U.S.,* 📠 *948–2364; 331–5720 in Guatemala City through the Hotel Camino Real. 50 rooms. Restaurant, bar, pool, beach, waterskiing, meeting rooms, travel services. AE, DC, MC, V.*

$$$ ✕🏨 **Hotel Puerto Libre.** This place stands at a crossroads outside of town and resembles a U.S. motel, with large, modern, simply furnished rooms built around a parking area and swimming pool. Since the noise of traffic can rattle the light sleeper, it's worth asking for rooms in the far left corner, which are quieter and have views of the woods and a small stream. You can leave your car here if you overnight in Livingston. ✉ *Crossroads for Santo Tomás de Castilla,* ☎ *948–3065,* 📠 *948–3513, htptolib@gua.net. 30 rooms. Restaurant, air-conditioning, pool. AE, MC, V.* 🐾

The Atlantic Lowlands A to Z

Arriving and Departing

BY AIRPLANE

In-country air service is available through Inter Airlines with flights to Puerto Barrios and Río Dulce (Fronteras) on twin-engine 12-seater prop planes. Flights leave daily between Puerto Barrios and Río Dulce, except for Friday and Saturday when there are two flights. The trip costs $40. You can book flights through **Inter Airlines/Business Travel Management** (✉ 7 Avenida 14–44, La Galeria, 2nd floor, Zona 9, Guatemala City, ☎ 360–1363 btm@infovia.com.gt).

BY BOAT

Boats leave from Livingston for Puerto Omoa, Honduras, and for Punta Gorda, Belize, on Tuesday and Friday morning when there are enough passengers. From Puerto Barrios, boats leave daily for Puerto Omoa and Punta Gorda. The 2½-hour trip to Omo costs $35. The 1½-hour trip to Punta Gorda costs $10. Before you go, you must get your passport stamped. The Livingston immigration office (7 AM–9 PM) is on the left side of the street on the hill leading up from the public dock. The immigration office in Puerto Barrios, open 7 AM–noon and 2–5, is two blocks north of the public dock on 9 Calle. You will be charged a $10 exit tax.

Boat travel between Guatemala and Belize has historically been safe, however in May 2000, passengers aboard a water taxi traveling from

Puerto Barrios, Guatemala, to Punta Gorda, Belize, were shot at from another boat. Six were killed, and one American aboard was injured. Increased border tensions are rumored to be the cause, although at press time this had not been confirmed, nor had anyone been arrested in conjunction with this incident.

BY BUS

For Puerto Barrios, comfortable Pullman buses leave the capital hourly from 6 AM to 5 PM, but be sure to ask for the *especial* bus, **LITEGUA** (✉ 15 Calle 10–40, Zona 1, Guatemala City, ☎ 232–7578 or ✉ 6 Avenida 9–10, Puerto Barrios, ☎ 948–1002). Trips to the capital from Puerto Barrios also leave hourly. LITEGUA also has a direct bus to Río Dulce from the capital. The trip in each direction takes about six hours and costs $5. Sporadic bus or prompt taxi service is available between Carretera Atlantíca and the nearby ruins of Quiriguá.

The Linea Dorada (Dorada Line) is a direct bus that runs between Guatemala City and Flores, in El Petén, that passes through Río Dulce. Linea Dorada leaves the capital every day at 10 AM and 9 PM, however, the late bus is not recommended if you are getting off in Río Dulce. From El Petén, Linea Dorada passes through Río Dulce on the way to the capital at about 2 PM. The price is $21 for one-way service to and from Río Dulce and the capital.

For Río Dulce (Fronteras), you can also take a Puerto Barrios–bound LITEGUA bus and get off at La Ruidosa junction to catch a another bus (on the Linea Dorada) that will take you the remaining 45 mi north. All LITEGUA buses stop about halfway at the Valle Dorado, near Río Hondo, for a lunch and bathroom break, and all Flores-bound buses (on the Linea Dorada) pass through Río Dulce. Note: Fuentes del Norte, which runs from the capital to Flores and to El Estor, is not recommended because of its bad service and run-down, dirty buses. However, at press time it was the only bus service between Río Dulce and El Estor: the trip costs $2 and takes about 1 bumpy hour.

For Copán, hourly buses leave Guatemala City (18 Calle and 9 Avenida, Zona 1) for Chiquimula; from Chiquimula, buses regularly leave for El Florido, and buses, shuttles, and taxis serve the route between the border and Ruinas de Copán. The trip on a not-so-comfy bus takes about seven to eight hours and costs $7. Shuttles from the capital and Antigua or flights from Guatemala City cost more but are comfortable (☞ Shuttles *in* Smart Travel Tips A to Z).

BY CAR

The Carretera Atlantíca leaves Guatemala City from the north end of town, at 5 Calle in Zona 2. It heads northeast, first through some mountains, later descending into the desert region of Zacapa, and then through the lush Caribbean lowlands to Puerto Barrios. The turnoff for Río Dulce is marked "Tikal." In Río Dulce the turnoff for El Estor and the Castillo de San Felipe is the first street on the left (unmarked), after the bridge. Two miles farther, the road divides: the castle is straight ahead and the right turn leads to El Estor.

Getting Around

BY BOAT

Daily ferry service between Puerto Barrios and Livingston leaves the former at 10:30 AM and 5 PM and the latter at 5 AM and 2 PM. Much quicker and more convenient (but slightly more expensive) launches also connect the two cities, but they don't leave until they are full, which can really delay your plans, especially late in the day from Río Dulce. The ferry is $1 and takes 2 hours, launches are $3 and take 45 minutes. There is no ferry service from Mariscos to the north shore of Lago Izabal.

Police (☎ 948–0120 in Puerto Barrios).

Hospital National (☎ 948–3077 in Puerto Barrios).

There are also medical clinics and pharmacies in Livingston and Río Dulce.

Puerto Barrios is like the capital in terms of urban crime. Don't wander on foot at night, travel in groups; and leave your valuables at home, as robberies are known to happen. For risks associated with international boat trips, *see* Arriving and Departing, *above*.

EL PETÉN AND THE MAYA RUINS

Both an archaeological and a biological wonderland, what is now the jungle department of El Petén was once the heartland of the Maya civilization. For the past millennium, however, since the mysterious abandonment of the area by the Maya and their unaccounted-for disappearance, El Petén has been a sparsely populated backwater, where ancient ruins just seem to crop up from the landscape and nature truly reigns, growing over everything that stands still. Whatever your primary interest—archeology, history, birding, biking—you'll find plenty to do and see in this fascinating region.

Rain-forest travel is easier than ever before with a new paved highway stretching all the way to Tikal from Río Dulce, though four-wheel drives, extensive hiking, and river riding are still required to get to many of the sites, such as El Mirador—but the difficulty doesn't just enhance the adventure, it gives you time to take in the exotic scenery and rare tropical flora and fauna that's with you all the way.

Numbers in the text correspond to numbers in the margin and on the El Petén and the Maya Ruins map.

Flores

★ **㊾** *206 km (133 mi) north of Río Dulce, 61 km (38 mi) northeast of Sayaxché.*

The red-roofed island town of Flores, surrounded by the waters of Lago Petén Itzá, was the last unconquered outpost of Maya civilization in Guatemala, falling to the Spanish in 1697. Today, the pastel-painted provincial capital, connected to the mainland by a bridge, could be called Petén's Antigua, since it has attractive spots to eat and services for travelers and is the center of many nongovernmental organizations (NGOs) working for the preservation of the Mayan Biosphere, an endangered area covering nearly all of northern Petén. Flores is also one of the last remaining vestiges of the Itzá culture, a tribal group with their own language, who built Mexico's monumental Chichén Itzá.

In the 1800s, before it was a cutesy town and departure point for travelers making for the ruins, Flores was called Devil's Island, owing to the prison on top of the hill where a church complex now stands. Since 1994 the building has been home to the **Center of Information on the Nature, Culture, and Craft of Petén** (CINCAP; open Tues.–Sun.), which sponsors a small museum with photographs of the region and information about the local resources, such as *chicle* (chewing-gum base made from tree sap), *xate* (shade palm used in floral decorations), and allspice. A gift shop of local craft specialties sells wood carvings, woven baskets, cornhusk dolls, forest potpourri, postcards, and even locally made peanut butter.

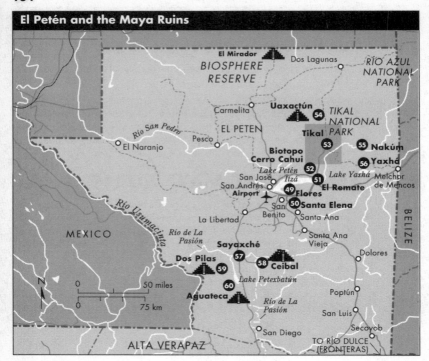

OFF THE ★
BEATEN PATH

NI'TUN – Ni'tun Ecolodge, an offshoot of **Monkey Eco Tours,** is an example of incredibly good taste and clean living. Guatemalan owners Lore Castillo and Bernie Mittelstaedt work hard to provide their guests with the same quality of experience that they strive for in their daily lives. All the buildings on the property are made from stone, sand, guano, leaves, and fallen trees left behind by slash and burn farmers. The social areas, a big open walk-in kitchen downstairs (they are both amazing chefs), and a beautiful airy bar and reading room upstairs, are their proudest work. Understandably, it's hard to resist spending all day listening to their extensive music collection and watching hummingbirds dance around the feeders. Between Bernie's interest in the ancient Maya and Lore's experience working with environmental protection agencies, they have all the know-how to make your stay not only comfortable but educational. Through their expedition company, Monkey Eco Tours, Bernie and Lore specialize in custom-designed, high-quality adventure travel. You can choose from a number of different itineraries from a soft one-day package to the nearby community of San José, the last bastion of Maya Itzá speakers, to the extreme seven-day journey to El Mirador, the Maya site with the highest temples. Everything is included. If you don't have a reservation and are in the Petén, call first, as the lodge is closed when booked for tour groups. ✉ *About 2 km (1 mi) west of San Andres on the shore of Lake Petén Itzá,* ☎ *201–0759,* ⅃⅂⅂ *926–0807 or 978/945–6486 in the U.S., nitun@nitun.com. 4 cabins. Restaurant, travel services. MC, V. Closed when hosting large groups or when guiding trips www.nitun.com.*

Tiny Flores is easy to explore and has plenty of shops, Internet cafés—though they are lacking a bit on the "café" side—and charming architectural details, like narrow streets, thick-walled buildings painted pink, blue, and purple, and plants and flowers hanging over residential and hotel balconies onto the streets. Plan to do banking and gasoline fill-ups in Santa Elena (☞ *below*), the center of local commerce. Take your swimming elsewhere, too, as Flores has no sewage treatment system; swimming close to town is inadvisable.

Dining and Lodging

$ ✕ **El Boqueron.** Conscientious of the needs of vegetarians, El Boqueron owner Don Julio, whose lakeside ranchon is decorated with plants, whips up mostly soy-based vegetarian dishes and a large variety of cold drinks, including carrot juice. ⊠ *Calle 15 de Septiembre and Calle Fraternidad,* ☎ *926–3429. AE, DC, MC, V.*

$ ✕ **Chal Tun Ha.** This little waterfront spot is a quiet alternative to some of the island's more popular restaurants. The building itself is hardly inspiring, though—a cement block on gravel—but its many windows take advantage of the view, and the menu, although small, offers such simple and well-prepared items as grilled chicken and fish or stuffed peppers. On weekend nights Chal Tun Ha turns into a late-night disco. ⊠ *Periferico, at the southwest corner of island,* ☎ *no phone. No credit cards.*

$ ✕ **La Luna.** With its perfect blue walls, homemade paper lamp shades, candlelit tables, Ana Juan prints, and Nick Drake tunes, La Luna inspires the romance of a moon-filled night, although you can just as easily stop in for a daytime snack (they open at noon). Choose from inventive vegetarian and meat dishes, like the unique stuffed squash in white sauce, or just a drink from the bar. Owners Roberta and Sebastian have also recently opened **El Balcon del Cielo**, a rooftop covered terrace off the center square offering drinks and inexpensive snacks. Kick back at sunset to experience the surreal effect of hundreds of blackbirds coming home to roost on the red rooftops of Flores. ⊠ *Calle 30 de Junio,* ☎ *926–3346. No credit cards. Closed Mon.*

$ ✕ **Floating Restaurant Don Quijote.** The curiously charming owner of Don Quijote, Eduardo Frutos, prepares a tasty paella, with a recipe from Valencia. He's proud to announce that travelers have come all the way from Japan bearing pictures of his paella published in a guidebook there. His other, less famous, dishes include lamb, shrimp, and fish. Don Quijote is on a small boat, floating, yet permanently docked, on Flores's southern shore. It's a great place from which to watch the sunset. ⊠ *Two blocks west of the bridge,* ☎ *no phone. No credit cards.*

$ ✕ **Pizzeria Picasso.** If you find yourself returning to Pizzeria Picasso after your first visit, if only in your mind, it won't just be because of the copy of Picasso's *Guernica* on the wall, or because Marie Sharp's hot sauce is on the tables, but because the pizza is made in a huge brick pizza oven and comes out incomparably hot and delicious. A variety of pastas is offered, too. Save room for cheesecake or tiramisu and a cappuccino. ⊠ *Calle 15 de Septiembre, at Calle Fraternidad,* ☎ *926–0673. MC, V.*

$ ✕ **Las Puertas.** On a quiet back street of Flores, Las Puertas (for the
★ restaurant's six screen doors) is a favorite hangout for locals and travelers alike. Owners Christina, an interesting and friendly Chilean expat, and Carlos, a Guatemalan Berkeley-esque radical, pride themselves on serving only fresh, natural foods, and are especially famous for their delicious sandwiches made with homemade bread and mozzarella cheese. For breakfast consider a giant goblet of incredible iced coffee and an omelet. In the afternoon, relax with natural fruit drinks and a variety of board games, when the particularly friendly atmosphere here is felt. And don't forget to stop back at night (they're open until midnight) for a hearty dinner and live music provided by Carlos on guitar and Emilio on bongos. (Ask Christina about her "small paradise," a house she rents by the night during the week just 10 km from El Re-

mate (☞ *below*). ✉ *Calle Central, at Avenida Santa Ana, just down the street from Cafe-Net,* ☎ *926–1061. V. Closed Sun.*

$　✕ **El Tucán.** This lakeside restaurant has a pleasant patio, which serves as a playground for the owner's pet toucans and parrots, but if you opt for the small dining room decorated with highland weavings, you'll have a good view of one of Flores's colorful cobblestone streets. The menu includes a variety of traditional meals, though Mexican cuisine is the specialty. The bread is baked in-house. ✉ *Avenida 15 de Septiembre and Calle Centro America, southeast corner of island,* ☎ *926–0691. MC, V.*

$$　✕▥ **Hotel Sabana.** Not to be confused with the Hotel Santana, the Sabana offers cheap and simple rooms. All the rooms open onto a public porch overlooking the pool area. This is a good choice if you are looking for a few creature comforts like TV and air-conditioning, but are planning on spending most of your time out and about. ✉ *Calle Union and Avenida Libertad,* ☎ FAX *926–3323. 28 rooms. Restaurant, pool. D, MC, V.*

$$　✕▥ **Hotel Santana.** The Hotel Santana offers the best accommodations on the island. All the rooms have TVs and open up onto wide balconies with wicker chairs and a view of the lake. Sitting areas accent the sunny central corridor. ✉ *Calle 30 de Junio, southwest corner of island,* ☎ FAX *926–0662; 926–0491. 32 rooms. Restaurant, air-conditioning, in-room safes, pool. AE, MC, V. hotelsantana@guate.net.*

$　✕▥ **Posada Doña Goya.** For a cheap alternative to the island's more expensive lodgings, try this clean, well-run, and popular budget hotel. You've got to come early in the day to secure a room, even though there's no hot water. The best part of the hotel is the rooftop terrace with hammocks and lounge chairs under a shady *ranchon*. You can also stop by for their famous breakfast fare from 6 AM to 10 AM. ✉ *Calle Union, northwest corner of island,* ☎ *926–3538. 6 rooms, 3 with bath. Fans. AE, DC, MC, V.*

$$　▥ **Casa Azul.** Run by the same owners as the Hotel Petén and Hotel Casona de la Isla, the Casa Azul is the best of the three, having a bit of charm despite its somewhat musty interior. All rooms have a balcony, TV, telephone, and refrigerator. Be sure to have a look at the old photographs in the lobby. ✉ *Northern tip of the island,* ☎ *926–1138. 8 rooms. Air-conditioning. MC, V.*

Nightlife

Las Puertas (☞ *above*) has live music at night. **Chal Tun Ha** (☞ *above*) metamorphoses into a weekend disco. **The Mayan Princess** (Avenida La Reforma and Avenida 14 de Noviembre) café and bar shows nightly movies on a big-screen TV, though the video quality can be poor. **Kayukos** (Calle Union and Avenida 14 de Noviembre) is a bar with a pool table.

Outdoor Activities and Sports

BOATING

Boat trips on Lake Petén Itzá can be arranged through hotels in Flores or by haggling with boat owners who congregate behind the Hotel Santana (☞ *above*). Tours (about $3) often include a stop at Paraiso Escondido, a small mainland park northwest of Flores with a lookout ($1 entrance fee), but expect to pay an additional $3.50 if you want to see the zoo, Lake La Guitara, and lookout point here. **Kayukos** rents canoes.

Santa Elena

🟢　*5 km (¼ mi) south of Flores, connected by a bridge.*

This little out-of-the-way town has nicer hotels than those in Flores, and it has some of the services (banks, gas stations) Flores lacks. Shopping is better left to Flores, however, since the Santa Elena market is crowded, hot, and dirty.

$ ✕ **Doña Amita's Pie.** An avid gardener and Italian cook, Doña Amita, along with her Italian husband, have made a charming indoor-outdoor restaurant hidden on a back street of Santa Elena. With less than one year at their new location, the garden is full of tropical wonders. Sit under the mango, coconut, and almond trees and try one of 15 pasta dishes. And don't forget to have a piece of pie. ✉ *3 blocks east of the bridge, and 1 block north; 1 block from the Catholic church,* ☎ *no phone. No credit cards.*

$$$$ ✕🏨 **Petén Espléndido.** You've returned to the land of hair dryers and telephones in the bathroom at this large, comfortable hotel with all the amenities. Room balconies overlook the pool and the island of Flores. The pool area, with its waterfall and palm trees, is an attractive place to spend an afternoon sunbathing and relaxing. Sit at the shady poolside tables or in the air-conditioned restaurant and enjoy the *especial del día* (daily special) which, for $10, includes soup, bread, main dish, and dessert. A free Actun Can Caves trip is included. The fully equipped convention center has a capacity of 250 people. ✉ *At the foot of the bridge leading to Flores,* ☎ *926–0880,* 🆑 *926–0866. 62 rooms. Restaurant, pool, airport shuttle, convention center. AE, DC, MC, V. hpesplen@guate.net.*

$$$ ✕🏨 **Maya International.** This group of thatched bungalows built over Lake Petén Itzá has lost some of its former grandeur. The lake rose several yards in 1979, flooding the bottom floors of the entire hotel, but the top floors are still in good shape and can be reached via a series of pedestrian causeways. Since the hotel's pool and grounds were flooded, the area between bungalows is now covered with water lilies, on which waterfowl forage for dinner. The rooms are simple, with twin beds and fans, but their private balconies afford some wonderful views, the best ones being in rooms 48 through 54. The hotel's moderately priced restaurant, in a round, thatched building with a wooden floor, is built over the water. The menu, consisting of a set meal and just a few substitutes, changes daily. ✉ *Three blocks east of the Flores bridge,* ☎ *926–1276,* 🆑 *926–0087. 20 bungalows. Restaurant. AE, DC, MC, V.*

$$ ✕🏨 **Casa Elena Hotel.** A newer hotel in this price range in the area, the Casa Elena has an attractive lobby with lots of dark-wood detail and nooks to sit in and an equally pretty restaurant that's airy and has lace curtains. Cheap snacks are available as well as reasonably priced dinner selections, such as fish, chicken, and steak. Bathrooms are tiny and there are no balconies, but the rooms are clean and equipped with TV and telephones. The top floor has a large meeting room overlooking the lake. ✉ *On the road leading to the bridge to Flores,* ☎ *926–2239,* 🆑 *926–0097. 28 rooms. Restaurant, air-conditioning, pool, meeting room. AE, DC, MC, V.*

$$$$ ✕🏨 **Villa Maya.** From your big, bright bungalow along beautiful Lake
★ Petén Itzá, you could conceivably bird-watch from your bed, if you were so inclined. Some 50 species populate the lake region, and a troupe of seven semitrained spider monkeys roams the villa grounds and the 67 acres of rain forest surrounding the lake that are protected by the hotel. The lake and surrounding jungle can be explored by following the trail or renting a rowboat. There is also a small zoo on the grounds. All rooms (4 rooms to a bungalow) have a terrific view of this scenery and are both spacious and tastefully ornamented, with mahogany floors and white walls decorated with colorful weavings and paintings. Vans shuttle you to and from Tikal. ✉ *A short drive north of the paved road, 12 km (7 mi) east of Santa Elena,* ☎ *926–0086; 334–8136 in Guatemala*

City, FAX *334–8134 in Guatemala City. 9 bungalows. Restaurant, pool, horseback riding, boating, travel services. AE, DC, MC, V.*

$$$ 🔲 **Hotel del Patio-Tikal.** Built in traditional Spanish style, this modern hotel has a barrel-tile roof, with porticoes and balconies. Rooms face a large, grassy courtyard and a small patio with chairs and a central fountain. The rooms have red-tile floors. The bathrooms are large, and all the rooms have a ceiling fan, TV, and writing desk; the first-floor rooms have larger windows. The patio restaurant sits under big arches leading into the courtyard, which is a more airy atmosphere than the musty and disheveled bar. ⊠ *2 Calle and 8 Avenida, Santa Elena,* ☎ *926–0104,* FAX *331–5730. 21 rooms. Restaurant, pool, exercise room. AE, DC, MC, V.*

CAVING

There are several caves in the hills behind Santa Elena with interesting stalactite and stalagmite formations, subterranean rivers, and blindfish. The easiest to visit is **Aktun Kan,** just south of town, but it's strongly advised you go with a guide. The bilingual guides of the **Tourist Guide Association of Santa Elena** (St. Elena and San Benito, in the Hotel Tayasal, ☎ 926–3133) lead tours of the lake, all Maya sites, and Aktun Kan. The daily rate is about $40.

El Remate

🗓 *30 km (18½ mi) northeast of Flores. From the main road in Santa Elena, head east then north on CA 13.*

El Remate is a mellow little town on the eastern shore of Lake Petén Itzá known mostly for its tiny and traditional wood-carving industry carried out by families who have dedicated themselves to this craft for generations. El Remate also has a variety of lodging and eateries from the super deluxe to the super strange. Because it's less than one hour from both Tikal and Yaxhá, and with several great exploring options of its own, El Remate is a solid alternative to setting up camp in Flores.

More than 1,500 acres of rain forest and a stretch of lakefront with great hiking trails and swimming options, the **Biotopo Cerro Cahuí** (⊠ West of town, on the dirt road leading to Camino Real, follow the signs, 🏴 $3) is one of the most accessible wildlife reserves in El Petén, protecting a portion of a mountain that extends into the eastern edge of Lake Petén Itzá. Hiking along either of two easy, well-maintained trails will put you in proximity of oscillated turkeys, toucans, parrots, spider monkeys, colorful butterflies, and tepezcuintle. **Tzu'unte,** a 6 km (4 mi) trail, leads to two lookouts with views of nearby lakes. The upper lookout, Mirador Moreletii, is known by locals as Crocodile Hill because it looks like the eye of a half-submerged crocodile from the lake's other side. **Los Ujuxtes,** 4.5 km (3 mi), offers a panoramic view of three lakes. Both hikes begin at the ranger station, where interpretive guides in English are sporadically available.

Dining and Lodging

$$ ✕ **La Estancia Cafetería.** A well-kept local secret, Estancia is low on glitz and high on flavorful fare. Owner Victor Morales's specialty is an exquisite whitefish plate; it's served on a wooden platter with fresh salad, potatoes, and vegetables sautéed in butter. Even though its driveway is filled with cars, La Estancia is easy to miss. Look for the Orange Crush sign and a big ranchon hidden among the trees. ⊠ *On the east side of the CA 13, 2 km (1¼ mi) south of El Remate,* ☎ *no phone. No credit cards.*

$$$$ ✕▥ **Camino Real Tikal.** To experience the natural beauty of Lake
  ★ Petén Itzá and the surrounding jungle without sacrificing certain comforts and amenities, Tikal Camino Real is the finest choice. It's possible to spend days on the hotel grounds alone without exhausting the
possibilities of activities, including kayaking, hiking in the private
biotopo, boating at sunset, swimming in the lake or pool, lounging in
the beach-side hammocks, learning to carve wood, and experiencing
a Maya sauna. Twelve thatched-roof villas set high on the hillside
house all the rooms, each with a porch and view of the sparkling lake.
A fine terrace restaurant serves international and local specialties. Particularly tasty is the sea bass Imix, cooked in a plantain leaf and covered with *salsa pimiento*, a delicate tomato-based sauce. ✉ *On dirt
road to Biotopo Cerro Cahuí, 5 km (3 mi) west of El Remate,* ☎ *926–
0204 or 800/228–3000 in the U.S.,* ℻ *926–0222. caminor@guate.net.
72 rooms. Restaurant, bar, coffee shop, air-conditioning, pool, windsurfing, boating, fishing, shops, exercise room, travel services, airport
shuttle, car rental. AE, DC, MC, V.*

$$$$ ✕▥ **La Mansión del Pajaro Serpiente.** Perched high on the hillside, La
Mansión Hotel has perhaps the prettiest rooms in the Petén. Bed-
rooms have canopy-style double beds covered in bright Guatemalan
spreads and adjoin a sitting room with couch and coffee table. All rooms
are finished in dark tropical wood and are also sunny and airy, with
big windows and perfect views of the lake. Bathrooms are large and
fans pull in lake breezes, so sleeping is comfortable. Up a nearby hill
is a swimming pool, and, farther up, a ranchon has hammocks. The
open-air restaurant serves Maya and international dishes. The best way
to contact the hotel is via fax. ✉ *On the main highway, right side just
before the town when coming from Flores,* ☎ *926–4246,* ℻ *926–1915.
nature@ietravel.com 10 rooms. Restaurant, pool, travel services. No
credit cards.*

$ ✕▥ **La Casa de Don David.** Proprietor and Miami transplant Don David
(original owner of El Gringo Perdido ☞ *below*), along with his wife
Doña Rosa, have been living in the area for over 25 years and are a
great source of travel information and local stories. Just be sure that
while talking to Don David you keep an eye out for his jealous free-
flying pet parrot. Rooms are simple and clean with private cold water
bathrooms. Hammocks are everywhere: on room porches and in the
communal ranchon, which overlooks the tropical fruit garden and the
lake. Perhaps La Casa is most famous for its second-story restaurant,
which has good home cooking with set nightly specials. Have a romantic
dinner in a booth, or eat at the friendship table and make some new
acquaintances. Sack lunches are available for day trips, and Don David
runs boat trips, hiking, and horseback riding and offers free use of several bicycles. To get here from Flores, turn left off the main highway
onto the dirt road leading to the Biotopo and Camino Real. It's 20 meters down on your left. ✉ *On the road to Biotopo Cerro Cahuí. 7 rooms.
Restaurant. No credit cards.*

$–$$ ✕▥ ⚠ **El Gringo Perdido.** With the lake at your doorstep and the for-
est surrounding you, you can pretend you're among the lost ones at
this simple hotel with an adventurous atmosphere. For a few dollars,
you can camp on the grounds or stay in one of the rustic but comfortable
bungalows. The bungalows vary in size, but most have one twin and
one double bed. You'll be asked to share if the place fills up. Each has
its own cold-water bathroom—an outdoor shower has hot water and
an amazing view of the lake. The dining hall has a menu that changes
daily; you can also opt for a twice-daily meal plan. But be warned that
when the owner is away the service declines significantly. ✉ *Just past
Biotopo Cerro Cahui, 3 km (2 mi) west of El Remate,* ☎ *334–0135*

in Guatemala City, akbal@guate.net. 12 bungalows, 40 beds. Restaurant. No credit cards.

Shopping

Whereas other típica here is similar to that found elsewhere in Guatemala, the beautiful **wood carvings** of El Remate are unique to El Petén. More than 70 families in this small town dedicate themselves to this craft, and their wares should not be missed. They are on display on the side of the highway right before the turnoff for the Camino Real hotel on the road to Tikal.

Tikal

★ *35 km (22 mi) north of El Remate, 68 km (42 mi) northeast of Flores.*

The high point of any trip to Guatemala is a visit to Central America's most famous and impressive Maya ruins. Though the forest that surrounds the ruins is today the home of the hummingbird, howler monkey, and grey fox, the area was covered with villages and farms 1,500 years ago, when an estimated 50,000–100,000 Maya people lived here. What remains of that metropolis is an array of well-restored structures, including the tallest pyramid in the Western Hemisphere; some partially excavated ruins; ruins covered over by the jungle; and two museums filled with smaller artifacts that archaeologists have recovered from the jungle and photographs of them at work, with sifters and shovels—all spread over 585 square km (226 square mi). As it is near the center of the forest-covered, protected Tikal National Park, Tikal is ideal for wildlife observation as well as archaeological exploration. Commonly seen critters include spider monkeys, deer, coatimundi, toucans, scarlet macaws, and oscillated turkeys.

Though the area had Maya communities by 600 BC, Tikal's civilization didn't reach its height until around AD 600. One of the first structures built here was a version of the North Acropoli, which dates from 200 BC, and structures were added at an incomprehensibly fast pace, consistent with a population explosion, through AD 100. By AD 100, the Great Plaza had been built, but Tikal was still ruled by the northern city of El Mirador. It wasn't until the arrival of a powerful dynasty around AD 300 that the area arrogated itself to full power. King Great Jaguar Paw sired a lineage that would build Tikal into a city rivaling any of its time. By AD 500, it's estimated that the city covered over 47 square km (18 square mi) and had a population of 90,000.

The great temples that still tower above the jungle were at that time covered with stucco and painted bright colors, and a hierarchy of priests and dynastic rulers used them for elaborate ceremonies meant to please the gods and thus assure prosperity for the city. What makes these structures even more impressive is that the Maya had no beasts of burden, never used the wheel for anything but children's toys, and possessed no metal tools to aid in construction. Of course, as a hierarchical culture they had a slave class, and the land was rich in obsidian, a volcanic glass that could be fashioned into razor-sharp tools.

By the sixth century, Tikal ruled over a large part of the Maya world, probably thanks to a leader called Caan Chac ("Stormy Sky"), who took the throne around AD 426. Under Caan Chac, Tikal became an aggressive military and commercial center that dominated the surrounding centers with a power never before seen in Mesoamerica. The swamps protected the elevated city from attack and allowed the leaders to spot any approaching enemy miles before they reached the city center. Intensive agriculture in the bajos provided food for the huge population. A valuable obsidian trade sprang up from the city's strategic trading position near two rivers, and Tikal formed strong ties with two powerful centers: Kaminal Juyu in the Guatemalan highlands, and Teotihuacán, near present-day Mexico City.

The kingdom-city of Tikal thrived for more than a millennium, trading and warring with city-states both near and far, only to be heavily influenced itself by the civilization of Teotihuacán, which dominated the entire region during the latter half of the Classic Period. But by AD 900, Tikal was in a state of chaos as the entire Maya empire began its mysterious decline and the process of depopulation had begun. Though the site may have been sporadically inhabited for centuries thereafter, the civilization of the Maya throughout the region suffered a rapid decline that remains unaccounted for.

For almost 1,000 years, Tikal remained engulfed by the humid, green tropical mass. The conquistadors must have passed right by the overgrown ruins, mistaking them for tall, rocky hills. The native Peténeros certainly knew of its existence, but no Westerner meddled officially until 1848. The site started to receive archaeological attention in 1877, when Dr. Gustav Bernoulli commissioned locals to remove the carved wooden lintels from across the doorways of Temples I and IV. These items headed to a museum in Basel, Switzerland. In 1881 and 1882, English archaeologist Alfred Percival Maudslay made the first map showing the architectural features of this vast city. As he began to unearth the major temples, he recorded his work in dramatic photographs—you can see copies in Tikal. His work was continued by Teobert Maler, who came in 1895 and 1904. Both Maler and Maudsley have causeways named in their honor. In 1951, the Guatemalan Air Force cleared an airstrip near the ruins to improve access for large-scale archaeological work. Today, Tikal is known to include some 3,000 unique buildings.

As you enter the site, you walk toward the west, and if you keep to the middle trail, you arrive at Tikal's ancient center, with its awe-inspiring temples and intricate acropolises. The pyramid you approach from behind is **Temple I,** or Temple of the Great Jaguar, after the feline represented on one of its carved lintels. It's in what is referred to as the **Gran Plaza,** one of the most beautiful and dramatic plazas in Tikal. Facing Temple I, to the east, is **Temple II,** or Temple of the Masks, dubbed for the decorations on its facade and an exact twin of the Temple of the Great Jaguar. In fact, construction of twin pyramids distinguishes Tikal from other Maya sites of the ancient realm. The Gran Plaza was built around AD 700 by Ak Cacao, one of the wealthiest rulers of his time. His tomb, comparable in magnitude to that of Pa Cal at Palenque, in southern Mexico, was discovered beneath the Temple of the Great Jaguar in the 1960s. The theory is that his queen is buried beneath the Temple of the Masks.

The **North Acropolis,** to the right of Ak Cacao's temple, is a mind-boggling conglomeration of temples built over layers and layers of previous construction. Excavations have revealed that the base of this structure is more than 2,000 years old. Be sure to see the stone mask of the rain god at Temple 33. The **Central Acropolis,** south of the plaza, is an immense series of structures assumed to have been palaces and administrative centers.

If you climb one of the pyramids, you'll see the gray roof combs of other pyramids rising above the green sea of the rain forest's canopy but still trapped within it. Temple V, to the south, and Temple IV, to the west, are both waiting to be restored to some memory of their former grandeur. **Temple IV** is the tallest known structure built by the Maya, and though the climb to the top is difficult and involves some scrambling over roots and rocks, the view is unforgettable. If you can, go at sunrise, when the new light provides fabulous illumination, howler monkeys scream call and response, and toucans fly below.

To the southwest of the plaza lie the **South Acropolis,** which hasn't been reconstructed, and the **Lost World complex,** with its 105-ft-high pyramid, similar to those at Teotihuacán. A few jungle trails, including the marked interpretative **Benil-Ha Trail,** offer a chance to see spider monkeys and toucans. Outside the park, a somewhat overgrown trail halfway down the old airplane runway on the left leads to the remnants of old rubber-tappers' camps and is a good bird-watching spot.

At park headquarters, near the ruins, are the two archaeological museums, three hotels, a tent with típica for sale, and a few small restaurants. Tikal really warrants more than one day. If you want to see wildlife, it's best to stay in the park and get moving before dawn. For a truly stirring experience, come on a full-moon night and stay to view the moonrise (bring a flashlight) after all the tour buses are gone. If you hope to get in a sunrise, sunset, or moonrise from the ruins, it's best to stay inside the park at one of the Tikal hotels. Otherwise the park gates and the guards enforcing business hours may keep you out. ☞ For more information on Tikal, *see* Books *in* Chapter 4. ☏ *No phone.* ✉ *$8; guides about $15 per person.* ☉ *Daily 8–6.*

Dining and Lodging

$$$ ✕☰ **Tikal Inn.** This small hotel set back from the public areas consists
★ of a series of comfortable bungalows around a well-manicured pool area. The rooms are attractive, even modern, and yet have thatched roofs, white stucco walls, and traditional fabrics. There is also a small restaurant for guests, with a menu that changes daily. Rates are reasonable and include breakfast and dinner. ✉ *Tikal,* ☏ *599–6212 for reservations,* ☏ ℻ *594–6944 or 926–0065. 22 rooms. Restaurant, pool, bicycles. No credit cards.*

$$$ ☰ **Jungle Lodge.** The largest hotel in the park has cute duplex cabins (warning: the dividing wall does not meet the ceiling) with porches or a cheaper corridor with a shared bath à la YMCA. The rooms are clean with dated American hotel-like furnishings and are a disappointment given the cabins' attractive exterior and the grounds. The restaurant is best avoided. ✉ *Tikal,* ☏ *477–0570 for reservations,* ℻ *476–0294 in Guatemala City. 46 rooms, 34 with bath. Restaurant, pool. No credit cards.*

Uaxactún

⑤④ *24 km (16 mi) from Tikal via the dirt road between the old museum and the Jungle Lodge.*

Uaxactún (pronounced Wah-SHOCK-tune) has unrestored ruins 4,000 years old, including, if you can imagine, a Maya observatory. Both the ruins and the road here are surrounded by the rain forest, so the trip here can be an ecological endeavor of sorts. The track to Uaxactún is a rock-and-dirt road and kinder during the drier seasons and nearly impassable at other times without a four-wheel-drive vehicle.

OFF THE BEATEN PATH **EL ZOTZ –** A popular eco-tour destination, El Zotz ("the bat" in Q'eqchí) is the site of Maya ruins, a lookout, and a cave from which thousands of bats make a nightly exodus. On a clear day you can see the tallest of the ruins at Tikal from these unexcavated ruins. Troops of hyperactive spider monkeys seem to have claimed this place for themselves, swinging through the treetops and scrambling around each other like children at a game of tag. Unlike those in Tikal, however, these spider monkeys are not

MAYAN CHRONOLOGY

TRADITIONALLY, Western anthropologists have divided Mayan history into three main periods: the Pre-Classic, Classic, and Post-Classic. Although academics question the validity of such a uniform chronology, the traditional labels are still in use.

The **Pre-Classic** (2,000 BC–AD 250) period is characterized by the influence of the Olmec, a civilization centered on the Gulf coast of present-day Mexico. During this period, cities began to grow, especially in the southern highlands of Guatemala and El Salvador.

By the **Late Pre-Classic** (300 BC–AD 250), the Maya had developed an advanced mathematical system, a impressively precise calendar, and one of the world's five original writing systems.

During the **Classic** (250 BC–AD 900) period, Maya artistic, intellectual, and architectural achievements literally reached for the stars. Vast city-states were crisscrossed by a vast number of paved roadways, some of which still exist today. The great cities of Palenque (Mexico), Uaxactún (Guatemala), and Quiriguá (Guatemala), were just a few of the powerful centers that controlled the Classic Maya world. But none matched the majesty and power of Tikal.

The single largest unsolved mystery about the Maya is their rapid decline during the **Terminal Classic** (AD 800–900) period. The current theory is that siege warfare caused rural people to seek shelter in the cities. The growing urban populations drained the agricultural potential of the land around the cities. As crops failed, famine ensued, causing a mass exodus out of the cities and into smaller, sustainable populations.

The Maya of the **Post-Classic Period** (AD 900–1511) were heavily affected by growing powers in central Mexico. Architecture, ceramics, and carvings from this period show considerable outside influence. Although still dramatic, Post-Classic cities such as Mayapán, Chichén Itzá, and Uxmal pale in comparison to their Classic predecessors. By the time the Spanish conquest reached the Yucatán, the Maya were scattered, feuding, and easy to conquer.

used to people and will shake branches and throw twigs and fruit down from the canopy to try to scare you away. During the rainy season the mosquitoes can quite literally drive those who are unprepared insane, so bring your strongest repellent. From El Zotz, a very unmarked trail leads to Templo IV in Tikal. It's best managed with a guide. In Flores, contact **Ecomaya** (☎ 926–1363, FAX 926–3322, ecomaya@guate.net) or **Evolution Adventures** (☎ FAX 926–3337, tours@evolution-adventures.net, www.evolution-adventures.net). For high-end custom-designed trips try **Ni'tun** (☞ Flores, *above*).

Nakúm

⑤⑤ *26 km (16 mi) east of Tikal.*

Nakúm lies deep within the forest, connected to Tikal via jungle trails that are sometimes used for horseback expeditions. You cannot visit during the rainy season, as you'll wallow in mud up to your ankles. Two building complexes and stelae can be viewed.

Yaxhá

⑤⑥ *10 km (6 mi) east of Tikal, 45 km (28 mi) northeast of El Remate, 80 km (50 mi) northeast of Flores; from the paved road at Tikal National Park, take the dirt road heading toward Belize for 1 hr and then another dirt road on the left to the ruins of Nakún and Yaxhá.*

At the ruins of Yaxhá, which overlook a beautiful lake of the same name, two sections of rectangular structures form plazas and streets, probably inhabited between the Pre-Classic and Post-Classic periods. Lake Yaxhá is surrounded by virgin rain forest and is a good bird-watching spot. You can visit the island ruins of Topoxte by boat from El Campamento del Sombrero (contact Juan de la Hoz, ☎ 926–5196), a quiet and restful place to spend the night. The restaurant serves three meals a day and the wooden cabins have screens, double beds, and private bathrooms. There's no electricity in the rooms. During the rainy season only four-wheel-drive vehicle, horseback, or hiking will get you to Yaxhá; the rest of the year the road is passable.

Sayaxché

⑤⑦ *61 km (38 mi) southwest of Flores. Take CA 5 southwest from San Benito (west of Santa Elena) for Sayaxché via La Libertad.*

Down a bumpy dirt road from Flores, this muddy frontier town on the southern bank of the Río de La Pasión is a good base (with spartan services and accommodations) for exploring the southern Petén. This is river-trip country, and the La Pasión and Petexbatún rivers lead to a number of important yet largely unvisited ruins in various stages of excavation.

Dining and Lodging

$$ ✕☷ **La Montaña.** This jungle lodge on the Petexbatún River consists of a series of rustic bungalows built in a clearing hacked out of the rain forest. Rooms have a cement floor, bamboo walls, and private bath. Family-style meals are served in a rustic open-air dining hall. As a guest, you can book a tour of local archaeological sites. ⊠ *For reservations, contact Viajes Turísticos La Montaña, ☎ 928–6114. 8 rooms. Dining room, travel services. No credit cards.*

$ ☷ **Hotel Guayacan.** A really run-down-looking lodge that stands by the south bank of the Río de La Pasión, has decent, clean rooms on the second floor of a motel-like structure, which is surrounded by mud, and equipped with decent beds. The owner can arrange boat trips to Maya ruins. ✉ *South bank of Río la Pasión,* ☎ *928–6111. 25 rooms, 6 rooms with shared bath. Air-conditioning, travel services. No credit cards.*

River Trips

The lowland Río de La Pasión flows into the Usumacinta, which winds for countless miles through the rain forest. Both rivers were important Maya trade routes and thus pass archaeological sites, like the impressive Yaxchilán ruins, down the Usumacinta on the Mexican side of the river. Both are also easily navigated. As a result, they are popular for expeditions, which can last from a day to more than a week. Along the way, you can catch a glimpse of the area's many animal inhabitants, including turtles, crocodiles, and a vast array of birds.

For river trips from Sayaxché, contact **Viajes Don Pedro** (☎ 928–6109) or **Viajes Turísticos La Montaña** (☎ 928–6114). Both have offices by the river. A day trip to one of the ruins costs $30–$60, depending on the number of passengers, but feel free to bargain. Agree on a price before you set out. Several tour companies in the capital also have river trips (☞ Guided Tours *in* El Petén and the Maya Ruins A to Z, *below*).

Ceibal

★ ⑤⑧ *1 hr from Sayaxché by boat on the Río de La Pasión plus a ½-hr climb through the jungle.*

Upriver from Sayaxché is an impressive ruin that served as a Maya tollgate, if you will, for barges plying the river. Though its few and farflung archaeological attractions contain several restored temples, including the only circular one known to date, plazas, and intricately carved stelae. Interestingly, a number of anomalies were found in these monuments, which hint at profound foreign influence, most likely from the Toltecs of central Mexico. Though it can be driven to via a dirt road, which floods during the rainy season, Ceibal is best reached by boat on the Río de La Pasión, followed by a half-hour ascent through the forest.

Lake Petexbatún

2 hrs by boat from Ceibal.

This impressive rain-forest lagoon was the site of a sixth-century kingdom that was likely ruled by a power-hungry prince who fled Tikal and engaged in battles for territory from two twin capitals, Dos Pilas and Aguateca. A three-hour hike from Sayaxché or shorter horseback ride ⑤⑨ west brings you to **Dos Pilas.** Important recent archaeological finds here indicate that continual warfare may have caused an ecological imbalance that led to the collapse of Maya civilization. Most spectacular of the ruins here is a limestone staircase covered with Maya glyphs that recount the battles of the upstart ruler here against his brother at Tikal. Unlike other Maya cities, this one has a defensive wall around it.

⑥⓪ On the southern shore of the lake lies **Aguateca,** a small site, separated by a natural escarpment 200 ft deep, that was likely the final capital after Dos Pilas was subsumed. The stelae and ruins are less excavated, but the trip here is a wonderful river adventure.

The smaller fortress ruins of **Punta de Chimino,** 2½ mi north of Aguateca on Lake Petexbatún, record the last residence of the area's surviving royalty, whose defenders dug several moats into the peninsula thereby making it an island. Now it's the location of a wonderful hotel, the Posada de Matéo, and nothing much else.

Dining and Lodging

$$$ ✕🖬 **Posada de Matéo.** Archaeologists speculate that Punta de Chimino was once the retreat of Maya nobility, and now it can be your retreat, too. Beautiful cabins are scattered along the Punta de Chimino peninsula's edges, each set amid the rain-forest foliage, with a private view of the lake and jungle beyond. Cabins have hardwood floors and modern bathrooms, and half-screen walls keep the jungle near and its insects at bay. Delicious meals using local ingredients like *anacates* (mushrooms) and *loroco* (herbs) in a gratin, for example, are served in an open-air restaurant, and tours of nearby archaeological sites for the hearty or the delicate are included. Transportation (a 1½-hour boat ride) is arranged from Sayaxché. ⊠ *Punta de Chimino,* ☎ *337–0009. mateo@ecotourism-adventure.com. 6 bungalows. Restaurant, travel services. No credit cards.*

El Petén and the Maya Ruins A to Z

Arriving and Departing

BY AIRPLANE

Flights from Guatemala City to Flores/Santa Elena are less than an hour and cost about $60 each way plus a $3 exit tax. Several daily flights leave the capital around 7 AM and return around 4 PM, and tickets can be purchased at any travel agency. **Grupo Taca** (Aviateca, Lacsa, Nica, Taca), ☎ 926–1238; **Racsa,** ☎ 926–1477; and **Tikal Jets,** ☎ 926–0386 or 332–5070. The airport is about a mile outside of Flores. Taxis and shuttles meet every plane and charge about $2 to take you into town.

Air service to the Mexican resort of Cancún is offered by **Aviateca** (☎ 926–0295) and **Aerocaribe** (☎ 926–0923). Flights to the ruins of Pelenque are offered by Aerocaribe. Flights to Belize are offered by Tropic Air. Flight times change frequently. You can call **Business Travel Management** (☎ 360–1363) in Guatemala City for reservations on any of these airlines, in English or Spanish.

BY BUS

Linea Dorada (☎ 926–0070 in Santa Elena; 232–9658 in Guatemala City) has direct bus service between Santa Elena and Guatemala City. The 10-hour trip on an air-conditioned bus with TVs, reclining seats, snacks, pillows, and a bathroom costs $30 or $50 round trip. Buses leave daily at 8 PM from both cities. There are plans for expanded service. Call at least one day ahead for reservations. Local buses are available but stop in every village along the way and can add hours to the trip.

Getting Around

BY BUS

The **San Juan Hotel** (⊠ 2 Calle and 6 Avenida, Santa Elena) is the local bus terminal, with service to the following destinations: Tikal, 6:30 AM and 1 PM (the trip takes two hours); Poptún, 5 and 10 AM, 1 and 3:30 PM; Melchor Menos (border with Belize), 5, 8, and 10 AM and 2 and 4 PM. Local buses are inexpensive but very slow. Local buses serving other destinations like Sayaxché depart from the Santa Elena market.

For Tikal, **San Juan Travel** (⊠ San Juan Hotel, Santa Elena, ☎ 950–0042) runs daily minibus service, with departures at 6, 8, and 10 AM and return trips at 2, 4, and 5 PM.

BY TAXI

Taxis can be hired at the airport to take you just about anywhere in the region, but tours are often cheaper.

Contacts and Resources

CAR RENTALS

If you're not on a tour, the best way to get around El Petén is via four-wheel-drive vehicle. All the major car-rental companies have offices at the airport, and you can call ahead to reserve from **Budget** (☎ 950–0741) or **Koka** (☎ 926–0526). **Hertz** (☎ 950–0204) also rents four-wheel-drive vehicles from an office in the Camino Real Tikal. **San Juan Travel** (✉ San Juan Hotel, Santa Elena, ☎ 926–0042) rents four-wheel-drive vehicles and vans.

EMERGENCIES

Police (☎ 926–1365).

Hospital. Hospital del I.G.S.S. (✉ Santa Elena, ☎ 926–0619). Medical facilities in El Petén are primitive at best. If you're really sick, get on the next plane back to Guatemala City.

Pharmacies. Farmacia Nueva (✉ Avenida Santa Ana, Flores, ☎ 926–1387) and **Farmacia San Carlos** (✉ 4 Calle 1–92, Zona 1, Santa Elena, ☎ 926–0753).

GUIDED TOURS

Adventuras Naturales (✉ 9 Calle 18–17, Zona 14, Guatemala City, ☎ FAX 333–6051 jcruz@tradepoint.org.gt) specializes in eco-tours of the Maya world and bird-watching expeditions. **Expedition Panamundo** (☎ 331–7621) operates out of Guatemala City. **Martsam Travel** (✉ Calle Centroamérica and Avenida 30 de Junio, Flores, ☎ 926–0346, ☎ FAX 926–3225, martsam@guate.net), run by Lileana and Benedicto Grijalva, has many travel and touring options. Guatemala City–based **Maya Expeditions** (☎ 363–4955) has trips down the Sayaxché area rivers and the nearby archaeological sites. The El Petén environmental group **ProPetén** (☎ 926–1370) is planning to offer in-depth adventure trips led by rubber tappers who once worked in the forest.

The following tour companies have trips to El Petén and are based in Antigua: **Inter Quetzal** (☎ 832–5938, martsam@guate.net). **Sin Fronteras** (☎ 832–1226, sinfront@infovia.com.gt). **Vision Travel** (✉ 3 Avenida Norte 3, ☎ 832–3293, vision@guatemalainfor.com ✍).

VISITOR INFORMATION

Arcas (✉ 10 km/6 mi east of Santa Elena, FAX 591–4731) returns illegally captured animals to the wild and is a great resource on the flora and fauna of El Petén.

INGUAT (☎ 926–0669 in the central plaza; 926–0533 at the airport, ◷ 8–noon and 2–4 central plaza; 7–noon and 2–6 at the airport) has two offices in El Petén.

GUATEMALA A TO Z

Arriving and Departing

By Airplane

Guatemala has two international airports: **La Aurora** (☎ 332–6084 to 332–6087), at the edge of Guatemala City, and the smaller **Flores/Santa Elena** (☎ 950–1289), in El Petén, which is a stop for some flights between the capital and Mexico. The main airport is served by the following airlines: **Aerovias** (☎ 332–7470 or 332–5686); **American** (☎ 334–7379); **Aviateca** (☎ 334–7722); **Continental** (☎ 366–9985); **COPA** (☎ 361–1577); **Iberia** (☎ 332–0911); **KLM** (☎ 367–6179); **Mexicana** (☎ 333–6001); **TACA** (☎ 334–0323); **TAPSA** (☎ 331–9180); **Tikal Jets** (☎ 332–5070); **United** (☎ 332–2995).

AIRPORT TRANSFERS

Arrange for your transfers when you make your hotel reservations; many hotels include this in your room rate. A taxi to hotels in Zona Viva costs about $4. The INGUAT desk at the airport can also give you transportation advice.

By Boat

The Río Usumacinta is a "back-door" route connecting Sayaxché, in El Petén, with Benemerito, Mexico. This boat trip requires several days of jungle travel and is best done with a tour group. You'll have to get your passport stamped in Flores. A boat leaves Puerto Barrios for Punta Gorda, Belize, on Tuesday and Friday at 7:30 AM and for Puerto Omoa, Honduras, daily although water-taxi service between Belize and Guatemala is not recommended for the time being (☞ Safety *in* Smart Travel Tips).

By Bus

There is bus service from Guatemala City to both the Mexican and Honduran borders as well as to San Salvador. To La Mesilla, on the Mexican border, **El Condor** (✉ 19 Calle 2–01, Zona 1, Guatemala City, ☎ 232–8504) runs a seven-hour trip, with departures at 4, 8, 10, 1, and 5. **Fortaleza** (✉ 19 Calle 8–70, Zona 1, Guatemala City, ☎ 251–7994) has hourly departures, 1 AM–6 PM, to Tecún Umán, on the Mexican border; the journey takes five hours. For service to El Carmen/Talismán, also on the Mexican border, contact **Galgos** (✉ 7 Avenida 19–44, Zona 1, Guatemala City, ☎ 232–3661). Departures for the five-hour ride are at 5:30 and 10 AM and 1:30 and 5 PM. **Melva International** (✉ 3 Avenida 1–38, Zona 9, Guatemala City, ☎ 331–0874) has service to San Salvador. Eight buses a day run between 4 AM and 6 PM and take five hours. For service to Esquipulas, on the border of Honduras, try **Rutas Orientales** (✉ 19 Calle 8–18, Zona 1, Guatemala City, ☎ 253–7282). Buses run almost hourly from 5 AM to 6 PM and take four hours. For El Florido, take the bus to Chiquimula at 7 or 10 AM or 12:30 PM and change there. On the Caribbean side, **Mundo Maya** ☎ 926–0070, operates from Santa Elena to Belize and to Chetumal Q. Roo, Mexico.

San Juan Travel (✉ San Juan Hotel, Santa Elena, ☎ 926–0042) runs minibus service to Belize City and Chetumal.

By Car

It's possible to enter Guatemala by land from Mexico, Belize, El Salvador, and Honduras. The Interamerican Highway connects the country with Mexico at La Mesilla and with El Salvador at San Cristobal Frontera, and it passes through most major cities. It's also possible to travel to El Salvador via the coastal highway, crossing at Ciudad Pedro de Alvarado, or via CA 8 to Valle Nuevo. Pacific routes to Mexico pass through Tecún Umán and El Carmen/Talismán. To reach Belize, take the highway east from Flores, passing El Cruce before reaching the border town of Melchor de Mencos. There are also two routes into Honduras, through El Florido or Esquipulas: for Copán Ruinas take CA 10 to El Florido. For southern or west points in Honduras take Highway CA 9 east to Río Hondo, where you can take CA 10 south through Esquipulas to Agua Caliente at the border. Note: travelers often get harassed or swindled at Central American borders. Be polite, but watch your belongings carefully. There is no entry tax when you arrive by land, though you may be asked for a bribe. Crossing borders with a rental car can be troublesome; if you need to do so, ask your rental agency for advice.

Getting Around

By Airplane

Domestic carriers fly between the capital and Flores/Santa Elena in El Petén, Puerto Barrios and Río Dulce on the Atlantic coast, and Xela and Huehuetenango in the highlands. **Inter Airlines/BTM** (☎ 360-1360) has schedules and can make travel arrangements for you on any of the local carriers. Or you can make your own arrangements directly through **Aeroquetzal** (☎ 502/334–7689), **Aerovias** (☎ 502/332–7470), or **Tikal Jets** (☎ 502/334–5631).

By Bus

Buses are the most widely used form of public transportation, with service covering almost everyplace that has a road. Buses range from comfortable tour-bus–style vehicles complete with attendants selling snacks, to run-down converted school buses carrying twice as many people as they were built to hold, plus animals. Most interurban buses leave Guatemala City from private terminals scattered around Zona 1 or from the big terminal in Zona 4. Ask at your hotel or call INGUAT (☞ *below*) for information on which bus leaves from which terminal.

If you decide to travel point-to-point without a plan, be sure the bus driver and fare-collector know where you're going, and ask them several times during the trip where you should get off. If you're friendly, and remind them you're there, they are almost always helpful.

By Car

You need only a valid driver's license from your home country to drive legally in Guatemala. Most roads to larger towns and cities are paved; those leading to small towns are generally dirt roads. *Doble-tracción* or four-wheel drive is a necessity in many remote areas, especially at the height of the rainy season. Gas stations can be scarce, so be sure to fill up before heading into rural areas and consider bringing some along with you. Also, don't count on finding repair shops outside the major towns.

Keep eyes peeled for children or animals entering the road. *Alto* means "stop" and *Frene con motor* (brake with motor) means that a steep descent lies ahead. Breaking into cars is common in the capital, so it's best to park in a guarded lot and avoid leaving anything of value in the car. All expensive and most moderate hotels have protected parking areas. *See also* Health and Safety, *below*.

Health and Safety

Guatemalans are friendly and reserved people, who are familiar with violence being directed against them. Since the peace accord was signed in 1996, ending the 36-year armed conflict, most of Guatemala's crime has been fairly petty and common: pickpocketing, muggings, and breaking into cars. In the past, roving groups of bandits have posed a threat, having provoked a number of ugly incidents, including the January 1998 robbery and rape of a group of university students on the Pacific highway. Since that time, there have been no reports of crimes committed by bandits on visitors.

Avoid participating in local rallies; the manner in which protesters are treated is not always peaceful: five Guatemalans were killed protesting a bus fare increase in spring 2000. The increase in adoption of Guatemalan children has provoked the fear for many, particularly rural villagers, that random children will be abducted by foreigners. In April 2000, two visitors suspected of this were killed in a market area of Todos Santos Cuchumatan. Limit your interaction with children to friendly disinterestedness, and be discreet when taking photographs.

Some strategies will help reduce the risks of traveling in an unfamiliar place: take our advice on security problems in specific sections of this chapter. Don't travel after sunset, and avoid hiking on paths known for assaults and robberies, such as some of the volcanoes near Antigua. Hire taxis only from stands at the airport, major hotels, and main intersections. Keep a tight grip on your bags when in crowded areas such as open-air markets, particularly in Chichicastenango. Don't wear flashy jewelry or watches. Keep your passport and the bulk of your cash in a money belt and/or in a hotel security box. Watch out on the roads: one common ploy used by highway robbers is to construct a roadblock, such as logs strewn across the road, and then hide; when the unsuspecting motorist gets out of the car to remove the obstruction, he or she is assaulted. If you come upon an unmanned roadblock, don't stop; turn around.

Both the Agua and the Pacaya volcanoes have been visited by robberies and violence, and though most people who climb them on regular pathways encounter no problems, climbing them without a guide and a guard—except on Saturday, when there's a crowd—is not recommended.

For the latest information on security conditions in the country and advice on the safest routes for traveling to popular sites, contact the **Citizens' Emergency Center** in Washington, DC (☎ 202/647–5225 ✉).

Contacts and Resources

Car Rentals
Avis (✉ 12 Calle 2–73, Zona 9, ☎ 331–2750). **Budget** (✉ Avenida La Reforma 14–90, Zona 9, ☎ 332–5691, www.budget.com.ni, ✉). **Hertz** (✉ 7 Avenida 14–76, Zona 9, ☎ 332–2242, ✉). **National** (✉ 7-69, Zona 9, ☎ 360–3963, ✉).

Most local agencies have branches in at least Guatemala City, Antigua, and Flores. **Ahorrent** (✉ Boulevard Liberación 4–83, Zona 9, ☎ 332–0544 or 332–7515). **Rentalsa** (✉ 12 Calle 2–62, Zona 10, ☎ 332–6911). **Tabarini Rent-A-Car** (✉ 2 Calle A 7–30, Zona 10, ☎ 331–9814, tabarini@centramerica.com, ✉). **Tally** (✉ 7 Avenida 14–60, Zona 1, ☎ 251–4113 or 232–3327, ✉). **Tikal** (✉ 2 Calle 6–56, Zona 10, ☎ 332–4721).

Consulates and Embassies
In Guatemala city: **U.S. Embassy** (✉ Avenida La Reforma 7–01, Zona 10, ☎ 331–1541), **Canadian Embassy** (✉ Edificio Edyma Plaza, 8th Floor, 13 Calle 8–44, Zona 10, ☎ 333–6102), **U.K. Embassy** (✉ Centro Financiero Torre II, 7th Floor, 7 Avenida 5–10, Zona 4, ☎ 332–1601). If you're in Huehuetenango and headed for Mexico, the **Mexican consulate** (✉ 4 Calle and 5 Avenida) is in the Del Cid building.

Guided Tours
Most tour companies based in Guatemala City and Antigua offer trips to destinations all over the country. **Adventuras Naturales** (☎ FAX 333–6051, ✉) specializes in eco-tours of the Maya world and bird-watch-

ing expeditions to Petén and Izabal. **Area Verde Expeditions** (in the U.S.: ☎ 719/583–8929, guatemala@areaverde.com; in Guatemala: ☎ 832–3383 or ☎ 832–6506, mayanbike@guate.net) has unforgettable white-water rafting trips for all levels. **Centro de Reservaciones** (☎ 593–4557) has short excursions to Copán, Río Dulce, and the Quetzal Reserve. **Expedición Panamundo** (☎ 331–7621) has tours of the entire Maya Mundo region (Guatemala, Belize, and Mexico). **Maya Expeditions** (☎ 363–4955, mayaexp@guate.net) is the country's premier white-water rafting outfitter. **Maya Tours** (☎ 331–3575) has adventure and archaeological tours. **Odyssey Ecotours** (☎ FAX 331–0838, odyssey_ecotours@hotmail.com) specializes in nature tours. **Tropical Tours** (☎ 339–3662) concentrates on Alta Verapaz.

In Cobán, **Casa de Acuña** (☎ 951–0482, ✍), run by Sean Acuña, conducts excellent eco-oriented, personalized trips throughout the Sierra de las Minas and El Petén regions.

In Xela, **Quetzaltrekkers** (✉ Casa Argentina, Diagonal 12, 8–67, Zona 1, ☎ 761–2470, quetzaltrekkers@hotmail.com, ✍) runs unforgettable hiking trips and volcano treks.

4 PORTRAITS OF BELIZE AND GUATEMALA

"Central America: A Biological Superpower"
by David Dudenhoefer

"Busing It in Guatemala" by Joanna Kosowsky

Books

Wildlife Glossary

Spanish Vocabulary

CENTRAL AMERICA: A BIOLOGICAL SUPERPOWER

ANANA REPUBLICS and revolutions. Those are the first things that come to mind when most people think about Central America. It's been the business of the news media to familiarize the public with the region's social strife, but never to relate the glory of its ancient ruins, pristine beaches, colorful textiles, and friendly inhabitants. Only recently has a more sophisticated populace begun to associate the inter-American isthmus with its greatest attribute: the tropical outdoors.

Comprising an area slightly larger than Spain but considerably smaller than the state of Texas, the slip of land that connects North and South America claims more species of birds than the United States and Canada combined, and more species of moths and butterflies than the entire continent of Africa. Here are rolling pine forests, rumbling volcanoes, lush cloud forests, serene volcanic lakes, primeval mangrove swamps, stunning palm-lined beaches, sultry lowland rain forests, colorful coral reefs, spectacular cascades, tumultuous rapids, rugged mountain ranges, rare tropical dry forests, scrubby deserts, slow-moving jungle rivers, and stretches of rocky coastline. And because of the region's compactness, all of these landscapes and all of this wildlife occur in convenient proximity.

In geological terms, the inter-American land bridge is a fairly recent phenomenon. Until a few million years ago, the North and South American continents were separated by a canal the likes of which Teddy Roosevelt (father of the Panama Canal) couldn't have conjured up in his wildest dreams. In the area now occupied by Panama, Costa Rica, and southern Nicaragua, the waters of the Pacific and Atlantic oceans flowed freely together. Geologists have named this former canal the Straits of Bolívar, after the Venezuelan revolutionary who wrested much of South America from Spain.

Beneath the Straits of Bolívar and the continents themselves, the incremental movement of tectonic plates slowly pushed North and South America closer. Geologists speculate that as the continents approached one another, a chain of volcanic islands began to bridge the gap. A combination of volcanic activity and plate movement led to the formation of a land bridge, which closed the interoceanic canal and created a terrestrial corridor between the Americas about 3 million years ago.

Because several tectonic plates meet beneath Central America, the isthmus has long been geologically unstable. Earthquakes and volcanic eruptions still disrupt life here on occasion. A curse it may seem, but the fact is that Central America would barely exist were it not for these phenomena. Much of the region's best soil was originally spewed from the volcanoes, and the upward movement of the Caribbean Plate as the Cocos Plate slipped beneath it pushed many parts of the southern isthmus up out of the sea.

The continental connection 3 million years ago had profound biological consequences, since it both separated the marine flora and fauna of the Pacific and Atlantic oceans and connected the American continents. Three million years is a long time by biological standards, and the region's plants and animals have changed considerably since the gap was closed. It's important to understand, however, that Central America's plants and animals are more than just the sum of what passed between the continents; the corridor also acts as a filter, in the sense that many species that couldn't make the journey from one hemisphere to the other ended up settling here. Thus, the rain forests of the eastern and southern portions of Central America comprise the northernmost distribution of southern species like the great green macaw and the poison dart frogs, while the dry forests on the western side of the isthmus define the southern limit for northern species like the Virginia opossum and coyote. To top it all off, the many physical barriers and variety of environments on the isthmus may foster the development of native species.

What all of this means for travelers to Central America is that they might be able to spot a South American spider monkey and a North American raccoon sharing the shade of a rain tree (native to Central America). On a larger scale, it means that the region is home to a disproportionately high percentage of the planet's plant and animal species. Though Central America covers only ½ of 1% of the earth's land area, it houses about 10% of the world's species, so it's no wonder scientists have dubbed it a "biological superpower."

NEARLY ALL OF THESE biological endowments are stored in a virtual mosaic of forests covering the isthmus. Biologists have grouped these into categories—rain, cloud, dry, pine, and mangrove—but because conditions often change within short distances, many forests are considered "transitional," or caught between two categories. Of the major forest types, however, the one that best embodies the complexity of tropical nature is the rain forest.

A pristine rain forest is an impressive sight, with massive trees towering overhead—most of the leaves and branches are more than 100 ft above the ground—and thick vines and lianas hanging from the treetops. Most of the foliage in a virgin rain forest is in the canopy—the uppermost spread of the giant trees' leaves and branches, plus the many plants that live upon them. The branches serve as platforms for a multitude of epiphytes (plants that grow on other plants but don't draw their nutrients from them) such as ferns, orchids, bromeliads, and vines. This is also where most of the forest's animals spend the majority, if not all, of their time.

Because the canopy filters out most sunlight before it can reach the ground, the forest floor is usually a dim and quiet place, with far less undergrowth than you saw in those old Tarzan movies. But many of the plants that do grow look familiar to northern visitors: since the light level of the rain-forest floor resembles that of the average North American living room, your basic house plant thrives here. The exception to the rule of sparse ground vegetation is found wherever an old tree has fallen over, an event that invariably spurs a riot of growth as plants fight over the newfound sunlight.

Up in the canopy, there's not lack of light, but there is a shortage of water. Plants that live up here have learned to cope with the aridity of the canopy environment through such adaptations as thick leaves, which resist evaporation, and spongy roots, which soak up large amounts of water in a short period of time. Both traits are combined in the thousands of species of colorful orchid that grow here; in the case of tank bromeliads, the plant's funnel shape helps it collect a pool of water at the center of its leaves. As tiny oases of the canopy, bromeliads attract plenty of arboreal animals, who drink from, hunt at, or live in the plant's pool. There is even a kind of tree frog whose tadpoles develop in the reservoirs, where they subsist on insects and larvae. While the plant provides vital water for an array of animals, the waste and carcasses of many of these animals in turn provide the plants with nutrients, another necessity in short supply up high.

Unfortunately, the great variety of plant and animal life in the rain-forest canopy is difficult to see from the ground, and most resident animals go to great lengths not to be seen. Still, you can catch distant glimpses of many species, such as the very still forms of sloths—furry figures amid the foliage—or the brilliant regalia of parrots, macaws, and toucans. You can't miss the arboreal acrobatics or chatter of monkeys, who leap from tree to tree, hang from branches, or throw fruit and sticks at intruders below. And hikers may occasionally encounter earthbound creatures like the coatimundi, a narrow-nosed relation of the raccoon, or the agouti, a terrier-size rodent that resembles a giant guinea pig. Other likely possibilities are hummingbirds, the iridescent blue morpho butterfly, and the tiny lizards that stand guard on tree trunks or scurry off into the leaf litter.

An untrained eye can miss the details, so a good nature guide is invaluable. Without one, you can stand in front of 100 different plant species and see only an incomprehensible green mesh. Tropical rain forests are among the richest, most complex, and most productive ecosystems in the world. Scientists haven't even named most of the plant and insect species who live here, and they have thoroughly studied only a small fraction of those they have identified. Though moist tropical forests cover only 7% of the earth's surface, they are believed to contain half the planet's plant and animal species, which means that a small patch of rain forest can hide thousands of different kinds of plants and animals.

Aside from the heat and humidity, the rain-forest ecosystem is characterized by intense predation. While animals spend much of their time trying to find their next meal, both plants and animals spend equal amounts of time trying not to become a meal. Animals tend to accomplish this by hiding or fleeing, but those options aren't available to plants, so they have devised a series of defenses such as thorns, leaf hairs, and other substances that make their leaves less than appetizing. Because of the relative toxicity of much rain-forest foliage, many insects eat only a small portion of any given leaf before moving on to another plant, so as not to ingest a lethal dose of any one poison. The result of this practice is visible in the canopy—almost every leaf is full of little holes. Some insects develop an immunity to one toxin and eat only the plant that contains it—a common strategy of caterpillars, since mobility isn't their strong point.

Popular survival tactics among animals include staying on the move, keeping quiet and alert, and, of course, hiding. Though they're a chore to spot, camouflaged critters are invariably intriguing. Some animals actually advertise: bright colors help them find a mate amid the mesh of green and can also serve as a warning to potential predators. Poison dart frogs are so toxically laced with deadly poisons that South American Indians use them in their darts and arrows. Another scare tactic is mimicry: harmless creatures impersonating venomous ones. One caterpillar has a tail that resembles the head of a snake, and a certain butterfly looks like the head of an owl when it opens its wings.

RAIN FORESTS aren't the only types of tropical forests in Central America. The upper reaches of many mountains and volcanoes are draped with cloud forest, a more luxuriant, precipitous version of the rain forest. Cloud forests are the epitome of lushness—so lush that it can be hard to find the bark on a cloud-forest tree for all the growth on its trunk and branches. Plants grow on plants growing on plants: vines, orchids, ferns, and bromeliads are everywhere, and moss proliferates on the vines and leaves of other epiphytes.

Because cloud forests tend to grow on steep terrain, their trees grow on slightly different levels, which means the canopy forms a less continuous cover than that of a lowland rain forest. Consequently, more pale light reaches the ground and fosters plenty of undergrowth, such as prehistoric-looking tree-ferns and "poor man's umbrellas," which consist of little more than a few giant leaves.

Cloud forests are home to a multitude of animals, ranging from delicate glass frogs, whose undersides are so transparent that you can see many of their internal organs, to the spectacular quetzal, one of the most beautiful birds in the world. The male quetzal has a bright crimson belly and iridescent green back, with two-foot tail feathers that float behind the bird when it flies, ample inspiration for the name the ancient Maya gave it, which means "winged serpent." While the tangle of foliage and almost constant mist can make it hard to get a good look at the cloud forest's wildlife, you'll probably see plenty of other flying objects, including brightly colored butterflies and hummingbirds.

Since the cloud forest is almost constantly enveloped in mist, its canopy doesn't suffer the water shortage that plagues other kinds of forests. In fact, the cloud-forest canopy is practically the wettest part of the woods. The upland portions get few downpours but gain their moisture from a perpetually mobile mist, which moves through the forest and deposits a condensation on the billions of leaves that make up the mosses, orchids, ferns, vines, bromeliads, and other epiphytes. This condensation results in a sort of secondary precipitation, with droplets forming on the epiphytic foliage and falling regularly from the branches to the forest floor. Cloud forests thus function like giant sponges, soaking up the humidity from the clouds and sending it slowly downhill to feed the streams and rivers that many regions and cities depend upon for water. And because some of the precipitation that falls on the cloud forests flows west, it usually feeds streams and rivers that run through arid regions, even at the height of the dry season. For the hiker or camper, the cloud forest means mud, and lots of it. You may not see rain for days, but the ground will always be wet.

The unfortunate fact is that more than two-thirds of Central America's original forests have already been destroyed, and most of those trees have fallen in the last 40 years. It has been estimated that between 3,000 and 3,500 square km (1,158 and 1,351 square mi) of the region's forests were cut every year during the past decade, a rate of deforestation that could leave Central America devoid of pristine forests by the year 2020. Deforestation not only contributes to the demise of the jaguars and quetzals, but has grave consequences for the region's people as well. The forests regulate the flow of rivers by absorbing rains and releasing the water slowly; so deforestation often results in severe soil erosion, which decreases the productive capacity of the land. The destruction of these forests is a loss for the entire world, since their flora and fauna contain unknown substances that could eventually be extracted to cure diseases and serve humankind.

The remaining forests face increasing pressure from a growing and impoverished human population. People hunt within them, cut down their valuable hardwoods, and completely destroy wooded areas in order to establish farms. Forests are cut and burned to make room for banana and coffee plantations, or to create pasture for cattle whose meat is often shipped north. Much of the destruction is the work of small farmers, who fell patches of forest to plant their beans and corn, and after a few years of diminishing harvests, sell their land to cattle ranchers or speculators and move on to cut more forest. The cycle is fueled by persistent poverty and unchecked greed, and though Central American governments have established protected areas and passed laws to limit deforestation, they have not necessarily provided alternatives for the perpetrators.

Conservationists point out that Central American governments don't have the resources to enforce their existing environmental laws, or even to effectively manage their national parks and protected areas. Now that the region is settling into peacetime and rural populations are returning to their lands and a stabler way of life, environmentalists are looking for ways to motivate people to protect the forests. The best way they've found is to show the local population that conservation pays. The campaign to make conservation profitable is twofold. Many local and international groups are concentrating on sustainable agriculture—new, environmentally friendly and often organic farming techniques that allow small farmers to work their land with long-term viability in mind. These efforts are often supported through farming cooperatives, which alleviate some of the risks involved in implementing the new, more fragile techniques. Another strategy is ecotourism—encouraging tourists to visit a country's natural areas, so that the government and rural dwellers in turn gain interest in protecting them—which may ultimately be the most effective way to lure foreign money into conservation.

–David Dudenhoefer

BUSING IT IN GUATEMALA

THE SUN IS RISING in the highlands of Guatemala. Along bumpy back roads, a school bus bounces over rocks and ruts to the whine of *ranchero* drinking music akin to country, declaring the woes of lost loves and long days of working the fields. Outside, villages show the first signs of waking—men carrying machetes walk to their *milpa* or cornfields; girls carrying plastic bowls full of corn dough return from the neighborhood grinder ready to make the day's tortillas; women stoke the cooking fires. Inside the restyled Virginia Public School Bus #121, young students aren't aboard, but a wide range of travelers, from newborns swaddled in hand-woven cloth, toothless grandmas with unflinching stares, cowboy-hat-wearing men in bright patchwork pants and wool skirts, to a European couple reading travel guides.

The driver uses the windshield as a tableau of personal expression: stickers of the Virgin Mary, the Tasmanian Devil, a winking Jesus, the Playboy bunny, and a baby wearing a leather jacket and sunglasses are juxtaposed here, a cast of characters assembled nowhere else, it would seem. Highlighting the driver's more sensitive side is a small menagerie of stuffed animals dangling from the rear-view mirror. As he passes a jalopy on a blind, cliff-side curve, the early morning passengers appear unconcerned. Maybe that's because the sticker above the NO SMOKING sign declares in red glistening letters, *Yo manejo, pero Jesus me guia* (I drive, but Jesus guides me.)

The driver's helper, his *ayudante,* is busy carrying 100-pound bags of beans up the ladder to the bus's rooftop. It's difficult to keep an eye fixed on him: one minute he's squeezing down the aisle selling tickets, the next, he's swinging out the emergency exit used as the back door and climbing along the outside of the speeding bus. He leans out the front door, pointing at the people on the roadside and flipping his hand upward. *"¿Donde?"* Where do you want to go? He jumps off the bus and helps a woman toting a little baby to climb aboard. *"¡Dále!"* he then yells. Then in English, "Put the pedal to the metal!" Young boys look on with admiration as the ayudante runs alongside and jumps aboard just when it seems the bus has picked up too much speed. With his spare moments he pulls up a turned-over bucket and from his perch keeps the driver company by leaning close and telling him any number of fables or rumors or jokes; so animated his face and so attentive is the driver, you wish you could listen in for a while over the din.

The bus roars off leaving a group of colorfully dressed women and their children on the roadside. It is almost noon in a small Guatemalan town on market day. With the children grabbing at their skirts, the women wander off, silently entering a mass of crowded stalls packed with everything from *típica,* traditional clothes, to superglue. They pass by a little girl concentrating on balancing a bowl of hot beef soup in her hands, carrying it to her parents who are busy peddling a dozen different varieties of hot peppers. A little old woman clutches two chickens by the feet and haggles with a man over their price, yanking them up and down in air as she bargains. Behind her, a peddler is enticing some tourists into a sale by showing them an impressive selection of thick wool blankets, even though it's 95°. There are no price tags or cash registers or express aisles; shopping on market day is not an expedient experience—it's a social transaction, in which every purchase requires a discussion or at least a certain amount of feigned indecision.

Being Sunday, the market is filled with churchgoers as well as shoppers. A procession leaves the church and descends into the market led by elderly men wearing black robes, swinging golden globes of incense. One man beats a small drum while another blows into a wooden reed instrument with a ducklike honk. Boys stride ahead and, unconcerned, with long poles, raise the electrical wires to make room for an 18-ft statue of the Virgin Mary to pass. When the procession is gone, the market swings back to its regular affairs and is once again quiet and *tranquilo.* Only a few noises rise above the pitch of hushed talking. Ice-cream vendors ring small bells. A young girl drags a snorting pig along on a leash. Several young boys playing marbles on a dirt patch behind the market argue about the ownership of a shooter. And off in the distance is the ubiquitous cry of ranchero music rising from the radios of the townspeople who peek out of their houses inspired by the passing of strangers and buses.

The sun is setting on the Central American isthmus. The ayudante hoses down the bus while the driver counts the day's take. The peddlers in the market load their wares into woven baskets and boxes and haul them away. The young children drag their feet home for dinner. The bus driver heads off and greets a circle of friends gathered around a domino game at a local drinking house. He orders a round of beers and raises the bottle for a toast, "For a day well done."

–Joanna Kosowsky

BOOKS

Belize

Two histories stand out: *The Making of Modern Belize,* by C. H. Grant, and *A Profile of the New Nation of Belize,* by W. D. Setzekorn. *Jaguar,* by Alan Rabinowitz, an interesting book about the creation of the Cockscomb Basin Wildlife Sanctuary, unfortunately tells you too much about the man and too little about the cat. Aldous Huxley, who wrote *Beyond the Mexique Bay,* is always hard to beat. If you're interested in the Maya, Ronald Wright's *Time Among the Maya* ties past and present together in one perceptive whole. Classic works on the Maya include *The Maya* by Michael Coe, a compendious introduction to the world of the Maya, and *The Rise and Fall of the Maya Civilization,* by one of the grand old men of Maya archaeology, J. Eric S. Thompson. For natural history enthusiasts, three books belong in your suitcase: *A Field Guide to the Birds of Mexico* by E. P. Edwards; *Guide to Corals and Fishes of Florida, the Bahamas and the Caribbean* by I. Greenberg; and *An Introduction to Tropical Rainforests* by T. C. Whitmore.

Guatemala

For travel literature, try Ronald Wright's *Time Among the Maya* or Aldous Huxley's *Beyond the Mexique Bay,* which describes his travels in 1934. Nobel laureate Miguel Angel Asturias is the country's most famous author, and his *Men of Maize* is full of history and cultural insight. Francisco Goldman's *The Long Night of White Chickens* is a lyrical novel that touches on some contemporary social issues. Michael Coe's *The Maya* is an authoritative book on the lost societies of the region's prehistory, as is J. Eric S. Thompson's *The Rise and Fall of the Maya Civilization.* Tour Tikal with a copy of Coe's *Tikal: A Handbook of the Ancient Maya Ruins.* It can often be purchased in the airport, at the area's larger hotels, and sometimes at the park entrance. For a guide to Guatemala's flora and fauna, try John C. Kricher's *A Neotropical Companion.* For historical and political background, try James Painter's *Guatemala: False Hope, False Freedom,* or Jean-Marie Simon's *Guatemala: Eternal Spring, Eternal Tyranny,* which has excellent photographs. Victor Perera's *Unfinished Conquest* is a thorough and fascinating account of Guatemala's guerilla war, while Rigoberta Menchú's memoir, *I, Rigoberta Menchú; An Indian Woman in Guatemala,* opened the world's eyes to the human-rights abuses perpetrated during the country's 36-year "dirty war," and earned the author a Nobel Prize.

WILDLIFE GLOSSARY

AN AMAZING ARRAY OF CREATURES make Belize and Guatemala their home. Many are not terribly hard to see, thanks, in part, to the protection of the country's park and refuge system. Others will elude you completely. A rundown of some of the most common and attention-grabbing mammals, birds, reptiles, amphibians, and even a few insects that you might encounter follows. Common names are given, so you can understand the local wildlife lingo, as are the latest scientific names.

Agouti *Dasyprocta punctata*; *tepezcuintle*): A 20-inch tailless rodent with small ears and a large muzzle, locally known as a gibnut. It's reddish brown on Guatemala's Pacific side, more tawny orange on Belize's Caribbean slope. Sits on haunches to eat large seeds and fruit. Largely nocturnal and highly prized as a regional delicacy, the gibnut is more apt to be seen on an occasional restaurant menu than in the wild. Also known as the royal rat, as it was served to Queen Elizabeth on her last visit to Belize. The gibnut is nearly endangered.

Anteater (*oso hormiguero*): Three species are found here—the giant (*Myrmecophaga tridactyla*), silky (*Cyclopes didactylus*), and collared, or vested (*Tamandua mexicana*); only the latter is commonly seen (and too often as a roadkill). This medium-size anteater (30 inches long with 18-inch tail) is seen lapping up ants and termites with its long sticky tongue; has long sharp claws for ripping into insect nests.

Aracaris (*cusingo*): Slender toucans, with trademark bill, travel in groups of six or more and eat ripe fruit. Collared aracaris (*Pteroglossus*) on Caribbean has chalky upper mandible.

Booby bird (*Sula sula*): This approachable, red-footed bird with a round head became the easy prey of hungry sailors landing at Half Moon Caye, where 4,000 now live in a protected nature reserve.

Caiman (*cocodrilo*): The spectacled caiman (*Caiman crocodilus*) is a small crocodilian (to 7 ft) inhabiting freshwater, subsisting mainly on fish. It's most active at night (has bright red eyeshine) and basks by day.

Distinguished from American crocodile (☞ Crocodile, *below*) by sloping brow and smooth back scales.

Coati (*pizote*; *Nasua narica*): A long-nose relative of the raccoon, with long, ringed tail often held straight up. Lone males or groups of females with young are active during the day, on ground or in trees. Opportunistic and omnivorous, they feed on fruit, invertebrates, and small vertebrates. The occasional solitary male is referred to as a coati mundi.

Crocodile (*lagarto*; *Crocodylus acutus*: Maya word *lamanai* means submerged crocodile. Although often referred to as alligators, you'll find only crocs in this region. The American crocodile can reach 16 ft in length and the *Crocodylus moreleti* or Morelet is a smaller variety (to 8 ft). They seldom attack humans, preferring fish, birds, and the odd, small mammal. The territories of both species overlap in estuaries and brackish coastal waters, but only the American crocodile is able to filter excess salt from its system, and therefore may venture to the more distant cayes. Both species are endangered and protected by international law. Distinguished from the smaller caiman (☞ *above*) by flat head, narrow snout, and spiky scales.

Ctenosaur (*garrobo*; *Ctenosaura similis*): A.k.a. black, or spiny, iguana; its Creole name is wish willy. Large (to 18 inches long with 18-inch tail), tan lizard with four dark bands on body and a tail ringed with rows of sharp, curved spines. Terrestrial and arboreal, it sleeps in burrows or tree hollows. Seen along the coast and cayes. Though mostly vegetarian, it consumes small creatures, and, in turn, may be eaten for dinner. (☞ Iguana, *below*).

Eagle ray (*Aetobatus narinari*): One of the Caribbean's most graceful swimmers. Flat-bodied, like the devil and manta ray, it ranges in size from 6 to 8 ft, with a white underside, and has numerous white spots and circular markings over dark back. Pronounced head with flattened, tapered snout. Long, thin, black tail with one to five venomous spines at base. Swims at depths of 6 to 80 ft. Prefers cruising sandy areas, occasionally stopping to dig for mollusks, upon which it feeds.

Fer-de-Lance (*Bothrops asper*): One of the largest, most common, and most dangerous of all pit vipers. Has a host of names, such as tommygoff in Belize and tomagasse in Guatemala. This aggressive snake may be up to 8 ft in length and has bright yellow on the sides of its head.

Frigatebird (*tijereta del mar*; *Fregata magnificens*): Large, black, soaring bird with slender wings and forked tail; one of the most effortless and agile fliers of the avian world. More common on Pacific coast than Atlantic. Doesn't dive or swim; instead swoops to pluck food from surface.

Frog (*rana*): Some 120 species of frogs exist in Belize and Guatemala; most are nocturnal, except for brightly colored poison dart frogs (*Dendrobates* spp.), whose coloration (either red with blue or green hind legs or charcoal black with fluorescent green markings) warns potential predators of their toxicity. Red-eyed leaf frogs (*Agalychnis* spp.) are among the showiest of nocturnal species. This frog attaches firmly to green leafs with rubbery, neon-orange hands and feet, its eyes bulge out from its metallic green body, which is splashed with white dots and blue patches. Large brown marine toads (*Bufo marinus*) are common at night.

Howler Monkeys (*mono congo*; *Alouatta palliata*): These dark, chunky-bodied monkeys (to 22 inches long and 24-inch tail) with black faces travel in troops of up to 20. Lethargic mammals, they eat leaves, fruits, and flowers. The deep, resounding howls by males serve as communication among and between troops. These monkeys travel only from tree to tree, limiting their presence to dense jungle canopy. They are increasingly difficult to spot in the wild.

Iguana (*iguana*): Largest lizard in Central America; males can grow to 10 ft. They are mostly arboreal and good swimmers. Only young green iguanas (*Iguana iguana*) are bright green; adults are much duller; females dark grayish; males olive (with orangish heads in mating season). All have characteristic round cheek scale and smooth tails. A delicacy among Belizeans who call it bamboo chicken.

Jacana or Northern Jacana (*gallito de agua*; *Jacana spinosa*): These birds are sometimes referred to as "lily trotters" because their long toes allow them to walk on floating vegetation. They eat aquatic organisms and plants and are found at almost any body of water. Expose yellow wing feathers in flight. "Liberated" females lay eggs in several nests tended by multiple males who tend, hatch, and raise chicks.

Jaguar (*tigre*; *Panthera onca*): Largest New World feline (to 6 ft, with 2-ft tail), and the male can weigh up to 255 pounds. This nocturnal, top-of-the-line predator is exceedingly rare. Most common in the Cockscomb Basin Wildlife Sanctuary (☞ Chapter 2).

Kinkajou (*martilla*; *Potos flavus*): A nocturnal, arboreal relative of raccoon with light brown fur (to 20 inches, with 20-inch prehensile tail). Actively and often noisily forages for fruit, insects, and some nectar. Has yellow-green eyeshine. (Its image appears on the Belizean 20-dollar note.)

Leaf-Cutter Ant (*zompopas*; *Atta* spp.): Most commonly noticed neotropical ants, found in all lowland habitats. Columns sometimes extend for several hundred yards from underground nest to plants being harvested; the clipped leaves are fed to cultivated fungus that they eat. Called wee wee ant in Creole.

Macaw (*lapas*): The endangered scarlet macaw (*Ara macao*) is the only species of this bird found in Belize and Guatemala, although a green variety is seen in Costa Rica. Huge, raucous parrots with long tails; immense bills used to rip apart fruits to get to seeds. Nest in hollow trees. Victims of pet trade poachers and deforestation.

Magpie Jay (*urraca*; *Calocitta formosa*): This southern relative of the blue jay, with long tail and distinctive topknot (crest of forwardly curved feathers), is a resident of Guatemala's Pacific slope. Omnivorous, bold, and inquisitive, with amazingly varied vocalizations, these birds travel in noisy groups of four or more.

Manatee (*Tricherus manatus*): An immense and gentle vegetarian mammal often called the sea cow. A type of sirenian, the manatee is said to be the basis of myths and old seamen's references to mermaids. Lives exclusively in water, particularly in shallow and sheltered areas. Scarce today; the Maya hunted the manatee for its flesh, and its image frequently appears in ancient Maya art.

Margay (*caucel*; *Felis wiedii*): Fairly small, spotted nocturnal cat (22 inches long, with 18-inch tail), similar to somewhat larger ocelot (☞ *below*) but with longer tail. It's far more arboreal: mobile ankle joints allow it to climb down trunks head first. Eats small vertebrates.

Morpho (*morfo*): Spectacular, big butterfly. Three species have brilliant-blue wing upper surface, one of which (*Morpho peleides*) is common in moister areas; one has intense ultraviolet upper surface; one is white above and below; and one is brown and white. Adults feed on rotting fallen fruit (never visit flowers).

Motmot (*pajaro bobo*): Handsome bird of forest understory, most with characteristic "racquet-tipped" tails, sits patiently while scanning for large insect prey or small vertebrates. Nests in burrows. Four species are found in Belize and Guatemala.

Ocelot (*manigordo*; *Felis pardalis*): Medium-size spotted cat (33 inches long, with 16-inch tail) with shorter tail than margay (☞ *above*) is active night or day, mostly terrestrial. Feeds on rodents but also eats other vertebrates. Forepaws are rather large in relation to body, hence the Creole name that translates as "fat hand."

Quetzal (*quetzal*): One of the world's most exquisite and elusive birds. Resplendent quetzals (*Pharomachrus mocinno*) were revered as sacred by Mayas. Glittering green plumage and long tail feathers of male quetzals were used in Maya ceremonial costume. No longer in Belize, they can be seen in Guatemala's Quetzal Reserve (☞ Chapter 3) or cloud forests from February to April.

Roseate Spoonbill (*garza rosada*; *Ajaia ajaja*): Pink plumage and spatulate bill set this wader apart from all other wetland birds; feeds by swishing bill back and forth in water while using feet to stir up bottom-dwelling creatures.

Sea Turtle: Sea turtles on the coasts of Belize and Guatemala come in three varieties: green *Chelonia mydas,* hawksbill *Eretmochelys imbricata,* and loggerhead *Staurotypus triporcatus.* All have paddlelike flippers instead of feet and have to surface to breathe.

Spider Monkey (*mono colorado, mono araña*; *Ateles geoffroyi*): Lanky, long-tailed. Live in groups of two to four. Diet consists of ripe fruit, leaves, and flowers. These incredible aerialists swing effortlessly through branches using long arms and legs and prehensile tails. Caribbean and southern Pacific populations are dark reddish brown; northwestern are blond.

Tapir (*danta*; *Tapirus bairdii*): The national animal of Belize is known in Creole as the mountain cow. Something like a small rhinoceros without armor, it has a stout body, short legs, and small eyes. Completely vegetarian; prehensile snout used for harvesting vegetation, and is nocturnal and seldom seen. Lives in forested areas near streams and lakes, where it can often be spotted bathing.

Toucan (*tucán, tucancillo*): Recognizable to all who have ever seen a box of Fruit Loops. Belize and Guatemala have several species, including the aracaris (☞ *above*). Keel-billed (*Ramphastos sulfuratus*) and chestnut-mandibled toucans (*Ramphastos swainsonii*) are the largest (18 inches and 22 inches, respectively), black with bright yellow "bibs" and multihued bills. The much smaller and stouter emerald toucanet (*Aulacorhynchus prasinus*) and yellow-ear toucanet (*Selenidera spectabilis*) are aptly named. All eat fruit, but also some animal matter.

White-Faced Capuchin Monkey (*mono carablanca*; *Cebus capuchinus*): Medium-size omnivorous monkey (to 18 inches, with 20-inch tail) with black fur and pink face surrounded by whitish fur extending to chest. Found singly or in groups of up to 20.

–Elbert Greer

SPANISH VOCABULARY

English	Spanish	Pronunciation

Basics

English	Spanish	Pronunciation
Yes/no	Sí/no	see/no
Please	Por favor	por fah-**vore**
May I?	¿Me permite?	may pair-**mee**-tay
Thank you (very much)	(Muchas) gracias	(**moo**-chas) **grah**-see-as
You're welcome	De nada	day **nah**-dah
Excuse me	Con permiso	con pair-**mee**-so
Pardon me/what did you say?	¿Como?/Mánde?	pair-**doan/mahn**-dey
Could you tell me?	¿Podría decirme?	po-**dree**-ah deh-**seer**-meh
I'm sorry	Lo siento	lo see-**en**-toe
Good morning!	¡Buenos días!	**bway**-nohs **dee**-ahs
Good afternoon!	¡Buenas tardes!	**bway**-nahs **tar**-dess
Good evening!	¡Buenas noches!	**bway**-nahs **no**-chess
Goodbye!	¡Adiós! ¡Hasta luego!	ah-dee-**ohss** **ah**-stah-**lwe**-go
Mr./Mrs.	Señor/Señora	sen-**yor**/sen-**yore**-ah
Miss	Señorita	sen-yo-**ree**-tah
Pleased to meet you	Mucho gusto	**moo**-cho **goose**-to
How are you?	¿Cómo está usted?	**ko**-mo es-**tah** oo-**sted**
Very well, thank you.	Muy bien, gracias.	**moo**-ee bee-**en**, grah-see-as
And you?	¿Y usted?	ee oos-**ted**
Hello (on the telephone)	Bueno	**bwen**-oh

Numbers

1	un, uno	oon, **oo**-no
2	dos	dos
3	tres	trace
4	cuatro	**kwah**-tro
5	cinco	**sink**-oh
6	seis	sace
7	siete	see-**et**-ey
8	ocho	**o**-cho
9	nueve	new-**ev**-ey
10	diez	dee-**es**
11	once	**own**-sey
12	doce	**doe**-sey
13	trece	**tray**-sey
14	catorce	kah-**tor**-sey

15	quince	**keen**-sey
16	dieciséis	dee-es-ee-**sace**
17	diecisiete	dee-**es**-ee-see-**et**-ay
18	dieciocho	dee-**es**-ee-**o**-cho
19	diecinueve	**dee**-**es**-ee-new-**ev**-ay
20	veinte	**vain**-tay
21	veinte y uno/veintiuno	**vain**-te-oo-no
30	treinta	**train**-tah
32	treinta y dos	train-tay-**dose**
40	cuarenta	kwah-**ren**-tah
43	cuarenta y tres	kwah-**ren**-tay-**trace**
50	cincuenta	seen-**kwen**-tah
54	cincuenta y cuatro	seen-**kwen**-tay **kwah**-tro
60	sesenta	sess-**en**-tah
65	sesenta y cinco	sess-**en**-tay **seen**-ko
70	setenta	set-**en**-tah
76	setenta y seis	set-**en**-tay **sace**
80	ochenta	oh-**chen**-tah
87	ochenta y siete	oh-**chen**-tay see-**yet**-ay
90	noventa	no-**ven**-tah
98	noventa y ocho	no-**ven**-tah **o**-cho
100	cien	see-**en**
1,000	mil	meel
2,000	dos mil	dose meel
1,000,000	un millón	oon meel-**yohn**

Useful phrases

Do you speak English?	¿Habla usted inglés?	**ah**-blah oos-**ted** in-**glehs**
I don't speak Spanish	No hablo español	no **ah**-blow es-pahn-**yol**
I don't understand (you)	No entiendo	no en-tee-**en**-doe
I understand (you)	Entiendo	en-tee-**en**-doe
I don't know	No sé	no **say**
I am American/ British	Soy americano(a)/ inglés(a)	soy ah-meh-ree-**kah**-no(ah)/ in-**glace**(ah)
What's your name?	¿Cómo se llama usted?	**koh**-mo say **yah**-mah oos-**ted**
My name is . . .	Me llamo . . .	may **yah**-moh
What time is it?	¿Qué hora es?	keh **o**-rah es
It is one, two, three . . . o'clock.	Es la una; son las dos, tres	es la **oo**-nah/sone lahs dose, trace
Yes, please/ No, thank you	Sí, por favor/ No, gracias	**see** pore fah-**vor**/no **grah**-see-us
How?	¿Cómo?	**koh**-mo
When?	¿Cuándo?	**kwahn**-doe

What?	¿Qué?	keh
What is it?	¿Qué es esto?	keh es **es**-toe
Why?	¿Por qué?	pore **keh**
Who?	¿Quién?	kee-**yen**
Where is . . . ?	¿Dónde está . . . ?	**dohn**-day es-**tah**
Here/there	Aquí/allá	ah-**key**/ah-**yah**
Open/closed	Abierto/cerrado	ah-be-**er**-toe/ ser-**ah**-doe
Left/right	Izquierda/derecha	iss-key-**er**-dah/ dare-**eh**-chah
Straight ahead	Derecho	der-**eh**-choh
Is it near/far?	¿Está cerca/lejos?	es-**tah sair**-kah/ **leh**-hoss
I'd like . . .	Quisiera . . .	kee-see-air-ah
a room	un cuarto/una habitación	oon **kwahr**-toe/ **oo**-nah ah-bee-tah-see-**on**
How much is it?	¿Cuánto cuesta?	**kwahn**-toe **kwes**-tah
It's expensive/ cheap	Está caro/barato	es-**tah kah**-roh/ bah-**rah**-toe
A little/a lot	Un poquito/ mucho . . .	oon poh-**kee**-toe/ **moo**-choh
More/less	Más/menos	mahss/**men**-ohss
Enough/too much/too little	Suficiente/de-masiado/muy poco	soo-fee-see-**en**-tay/ day-mah-see-**ah**-doe/**moo**-ee poh-koh
Telephone	Teléfono	tel-**ef**-oh-no
I am ill/sick	Estoy enfermo(a)	es-**toy** en-**fair**-moh(ah)
Please call a doctor	Por favor llame un médico	pore fa-**vor ya**-may oon **med**-ee-koh
Help!	¡Auxilio! ¡Ayuda!	owk-**see**-lee-oh ah-**yoo**-dah

Dining Out

Ashtray	Un cenicero	oon sen-ee-**seh**-roh
Bill/check	La cuenta	lah **kwen**-tah
Bread	El pan	el pahn
Butter	La mantequilla	lah mahn-tay-**key**-yah
Fork	El tenedor	el ten-eh-**door**
Is the tip included?	¿Está incluida la propina?	es-**tah** in-clue-**ee**-dah lah pro-**pea**-nah
Knife	El cuchillo	el koo-**chee**-yo
Menu	La carta	lah **cart**-ah
Napkin	La servilleta	lah sair-vee-**yet**-uh
Spoon	Una cuchara	**oo**-nah koo-**chah**-rah
Sugar	El azúcar	el ah-**sue**-car
Waiter!/Waitress!	¡Por favor Señor/Señorita!	pore fah-**vor** sen-**yor**/sen-yor-**ee**-tah